ROMAN POTTERY IN THE LOW COUNTRIES

sidestonepress

ROMAN POTTERY IN THE LOW COUNTRIES

Past Research, Current State, Future Directions

edited by
Roderick C.A. Geerts and Philip Bes

PALMA 32

PAPERS ON ARCHAEOLOGY OF THE LEIDEN MUSEUM OF ANTIQUITIES

PALMA: Papers on Archaeology of the Leiden Museum of Antiquities (volume 32)

Published by Sidestone Press, Leiden
www.sidestone.com

Layout & cover design: Sidestone Press
Photographs cover: in the background, a drawing of the excavations at Forum Hadriani, with Caspar Reuvens holding a document (image: National Museum of Antiquities, Leiden); foreground: a jug from the site at Huissen (after Van der Feijst *et al.* 2017, passim). Back: after Van der Feijst *et al.* 2017, passim.

Volume editors: Roderick C.A. Geerts & Philip Bes

ISBN 978-94-6426-288-9 (softcover)
ISBN 978-94-6426-289-6 (hardcover)
ISBN 978-94-6426-290-2 (PDF e-book)

ISSN 2034-550X (print) | ISSN 2590-3012 (online)

DOI 10.59641/2sz49tvu

Contents

Acknowledgements

The moulding and shaping of this volume would have been short and swift if it were not for the efforts and dedication of all contributing authors. We therefore express our deepest appreciation, and truly hope they are as pleased with this as we are. We are also especially grateful to the National Museum of Antiquities, in particular to Lucas Petit and Jasper de Bruin, for their continued support and their offer to welcome this volume to their PALMA series. Eric van den Bandt, Anna Artyushenko, Corné van Woerdekom and Karsten Wentink, at Sidestone Press, receive our gratitude for their guidance during the process of publication. In a broader sense we also wish to thank the board of the Rei Cretariæ Romanæ Fautores, as well as the scientific committee of this congress, for it is the very occasion of this 33rd congress of the RCRF being held in Leiden that prompted the original idea for this volume.

Contributors

Philip Bes
Schwenkgasse 21/10
1120 Vienna
Austria
philipmbes@gmail.com

Jasper de Bruin
National Museum of Antiquities
Rapenburg 28
2311 EW Leiden
The Netherlands
j.debruin@rmo.nl

Xavier Deru
University of Lille
Faculty of Humanities
Department History of Art
and Archaeology
42 Rue Paul Duez
59000 Lille
France
xavier.deru@univ-lille.fr

Roderick C.A. Geerts
ADC ArcheoProjecten
Nijverheidsweg-Noord 114
3812 PN Amersfoort
The Netherlands
r.geerts@archeologie.nl

Bernd Liesen
LVR-Archäologischer Park Xanten
Bahnhofstraße 46-50
46509 Xanten
Germany
bernd.liesen@lvr.de

Annet Nieuwhof
Groningen Institute of Archaeology
Poststraat 6
9712 ER Groningen
The Netherlands
a.nieuwhof@rug.nl

Frederique Reigersman-van Lidth de Jeude
De Romeinse Schaal
Rhijnestein 2
3945 BD Cothen
The Netherlands
aardewerk@romeinseschaal.nl

Ernst Taayke
taaykee@xs4all.nl

Joost J.H. van den Berg
Zeeuws Archeologisch Depot
Het Schuitvlot
Looierssingel 2
4331 NK Middelburg
The Netherlands
jjh.vanden.berg@erfgoedzeeland.nl

Peter W. van den Broeke
Municipality of Nijmegen
Bureau Archeologie en Bodemkwaliteit
P.O. Box 9105
6500 HG Nijmegen
The Netherlands
p.van.den.broeke@nijmegen.nl

Harry van Enckevort
Municipality of Nijmegen
P.O. Box 9105
6500 HG Nijmegen
The Netherlands
h.van.enckevort@nijmegen.nl

References to Typological Works, Abbreviations, and a Note on Language

References to Typological Works

In this volume references are made to the following typological works:

Alzey: Unverzagt 1916
Bonifay: Bonifay 2004
Brouwer: Brouwer 1986
Brunsting: Brunsting 1937
Camulodunum: Hawkes and Hull 1947
Chenet: Chenet 1941
Conspectus (Consp.): Ettlinger *et al.* 1990
Curle: Curle 1911
Dangstetten: Roth-Rubi 2006
Déchelette: Déchelette 1904
Deru: Deru 1996
Dragendorff (Drag.): Dragendorff 1895
Dressel: Dressel 1899
Gauloise: Laubenheimer 1985
Haltern: Loeschcke 1909
Hayes: Hayes 1972
Holwerda: Holwerda 1923 or Holwerda 1941 (specified in individual contributions)
Keay: Keay 1984
Kingsholm: Timby 1985
Ludowici (Lud.): Ludowici 1927
Niederbieber: Oelmann 1914
Nijmegen-Hatert: Haalebos 1990
Oberaden: Loeschcke 1942
Pascual: Pascual Guasch 1977
Pompeii: Panella 1976
Stuart: Stuart 1977b
Von Uslar: Von Uslar 1938
Young: Young 1977

A Note on Language and Chronology

Often, names of places, rivers and areas/regions are written in their native language – for example, Westfalen and not Westphalia. In some cases, however, we opted for the English name, for example Meuse instead of Maas, as this river runs through various countries.

All dates are AD, unless (1) otherwise mentioned; or (2) when confusion could arise (*e.g.* 50 BC-AD 25 – in this example, omitting AD would make it unclear whether 25 concerns BC or AD).

Introduction

Roderick C.A. Geerts and Philip Bes

The volume in your hands has seen the light of day to mark the joyous occasion of the 33rd congress of the Rei Cretariæ Romanæ Fautores being held in Leiden, the Netherlands. And perhaps it was about time: the last time the Fautores visited the Netherlands for an entire congress was back in 1971.

As has become a tradition at Fautores congresses, all participants receive a copy of this volume, which presents a *status quaestionis* of Roman pottery studies in the Low Countries and surrounding regions. For this, the editors, who constitute the organising committee of the congress, have gathered contributions by researchers who are, needless to say, experts in their field. Without their concerted efforts this volume would not have been possible. It is therefore with great delight that we hereby present our communal efforts, with papers on the following four themes: 1: histories of collecting; 2: the social, cultural, and economic meaning of ceramic change; 3: Roman pottery in different cultural and functional contexts; and 4: geographical and chronological dimensions of regional and long-distance exchange.

Before you delve into the papers in this volume, it is worthwhile to summarise the history of Roman pottery studies in the Netherlands[1]. This shows the many excavations and developments that have led to our present state of knowledge and research, and places developments mentioned in the various papers into a historical context.

The first steps into Roman pottery studies began with collectors and their curiosity about and interest in ancient objects; despite their important role, these collectors cannot however be labelled as archaeologists or scholars. During the 16th-18th centuries many Roman-period finds were unearthed and brought together into *cabinets of curiosities* (*e.g.* Chevalier 1709; Halbertsma 2003, 10-11). Description of these finds was rudimentary, and interpretation took place with classical sources and iconography in mind. In rare cases, finds were viewed with a more detailed, local perspective (Smetius and Smetius 1678). As no stratified excavations were conducted during this period, dating now rests on association with other finds, like coins and inscriptions.

The appointment of Caspar Reuvens at Leiden University in 1818 was significant, as he thus became the first professor of archaeology in the world (for a biography see Brongers 2002; Cordfunke *et al.* 2007). The first stratigraphic excavations in the Netherlands took place under his supervision. One of Reuvens' better-known excavations – one of many, in fact – were those of the Roman city of Forum Hadriani in present-day Voorburg-Arentsburg, situated in the province of Zuid-Holland (English:

1 We kindly thank Harry van Enckevort and Rien Polak for making valuable suggestions.

in: R.C.A. Geerts and Ph. Bes (eds) 2024, *Roman Pottery in the Low Countries: Past Research, Current State, Future Directions*. Leiden: Sidestone Press (= *Papers on Archaeology of the Leiden Museum of Antiquities Leiden* 32), pp. 13-18.

South-Holland). These excavations were carried out during several campaigns between 1827 and 1834 and were eventually published in 1923 by the next excavator, Jan Hendrik Holwerda. During the 19th century, pottery studies essentially comprised artefact catalogues, which were usually based on museum collections, or lists of findspots and known sites (Reuvens *et al.* 1845). There was no typological approach to pottery, yet.

This all changed with the large-scale research conducted in Germany into the *Obergermanisch-Raetischer Limes* (ORL, 1894-1937). The sheer quantity of forts that was excavated and artefacts that were found in stratified contexts meant a big leap forward for archaeology. It is therefore not surprising that research into the ORL led to the first overviews of pottery types. One of the best-known is the work by Hans Dragendorff (1894; 1895), who published a paper on terra sigillata which is nowadays still used as a reference work, even if it was not intended as such. Well ahead of his time, Dragendorff even asked his local apothecary to perform a chemical analysis of the components of the sherds and slip (Dragendorff 1895, 19-21). These were the first of many publications that provided typologically organised works resulting from excavated sites (Albrecht 1942; Curle 1911; Dressel 1899; Loeschcke 1909; Oelmann 1914; Ritterling 1913; Unverzagt 1916), museum collections (Steiner 1911; Walters 1908) and specific wares (Déchelette 1904; Oswald and Pryce 1920). Just as Dragendorff (compare Dragendorff 1894 with 1895), in an earlier paper (1879) Dressel published a selection of amphora types that later came to be widely used as a typological 'classic' (1899); in that earlier publication, however, the types were organised and numbered differently. During this formative period, most researchers who worked on pottery could still easily stay in touch with one another, as their correspondence shows (*e.g.* Mees and Schönfelder 2014; Péré-Noguès 2014). Dutch archaeologists used many of these published studies as reference works to typologically classify pottery found at excavations.

In the Netherlands more attention was paid to the comprehensive study of Roman pottery from excavated sites. The most noteworthy excavations were those at Forum Hadriani (Holwerda 1923) and several in Nijmegen (Brunsting 1937; Holwerda 1941; 1944; Vermeulen 1932). A few studies were dedicated to either the integral study of certain pottery groups like Gallo-Belgic ware (Holwerda 1941) or material from one production site such as the Holdeurn (Holwerda 1944). Overviews of complete assemblages nonetheless remained the exception; attention was certainly paid to the dating properties of terra sigillata stamps, decorated vessels, and coins. This is clearly reflected in Dutch (*e.g.* Glasbergen 1944a; 1944b) as well as international publications at the time, as evidenced by the first couple of Fautores Actae (Geerts in prep. a; Zabehlicky-Scheffenegger 2013, 134). The next large studies which were concerned with site complexes and well-dated corpora of pottery in the Netherlands date to the 1960s-1970s: the excavations of fortifications at Nijmegen (Stuart 1963; 1977a) and Zwammerdam (Haalebos 1977) are exemplary of this stage. In addition to the previously mentioned typological studies (mainly Brunsting 1937; Holwerda 1923), those by Stuart (1963; 1977a), Haalebos (1977; 1990) and Bloemers (1978) were works of importance in their own right for the next decades to come, and in fact remain significant until the present day. The main focus of Roman pottery research was Nijmegen, and it was therefore not surprising that in 1971 the 8th Fautores Congress was held there. In the 1990s, following several decades of excavations, the first dissertations on pottery studies saw the light of day, which focused on creating typologies for handmade pottery from both inside and outside the Roman Empire (Taayke 1996; on the Iron Age see also Van Heeringen 1992). Pottery groups other than handmade pottery were certainly not ignored: terra sigillata stamps were discussed in Polak's dissertation (1995; 2000), decorated terra sigillata by Kalee (*e.g.* 1972/1973; 2001) and terra sigillata in the northern Netherlands by Volkers (*e.g.* 2015/2016). Amphorae were studied in detail by Van der Werff (1984; *et al.* 1997), sea salt cylinders by Van den Broeke (1986; 1996) and the ware now known as Low Lands ware by Brouwer (1986). Many of these scholars, whose studies focused on specific pottery groups instead of whole site assemblages, were or are in fact a member of the Fautores and have published in the Actae. Some studies conducted in countries in northwestern Europe had their influence on pottery studies in the Netherlands: overviews of sites and wares (Deru 1996; Vanvinckenroye 1991) but also methodological studies took hold and shaped pottery studies for years to come (Orton *et al.* 1993).

Excavations up to the 1990s were more often research-driven than development-led. This all changed in 1992 with the Valletta Treaty (formally the European Convention on the Protection of the Archaeological Heritage (Revised)) and its ratification in 2007 for Dutch archaeology. From then on, development-led archaeology was a given in the Netherlands, resulting in the emergence of many smaller and larger archaeological companies in order to meet the increasing demand of excavations which took place within the context of this new legislature. This in turn also led to an increase in specialists and their output. These developments also motivated many other European countries to set standards for Roman pottery research in order to improve both the quality of research and the comparability of the output (Barclay *et al.* 2016; Deru *et al.* 1997; Perrin 2011; Van Kerckhove 2018; Geerts *et al.* 2020). The scientific output in the Netherlands is still primarily published in site reports in Dutch; exceptions were a *Festschrift* for Jan Thijssen (Van Enckevort 2009) which included many papers on Roman pottery, and a volume on amphorae (Carreras and Van den Berg 2017a).

Research into kilns and pottery production was also conducted within the Netherlands; the earliest publication is that concerning the Holdeurn mentioned above (Holwerda 1944). Most known kilns from the Roman period were in fact excavated prior to the advent of development-led archaeology (*e.g.* Bloemers and Haalebos 1973; Willems 1977). More recent studies of kilns and pottery production include the study of fabrics and the development and distribution of a workshop's products (Van Kerckhove and Boreel 2014; Van Kerckhove *et al.* 2014; Willems 2005). A recent overview of kilns and their respective products is a publication in the Xantener Berichte series, a copy of which all participants at the congress in Xanten in 2014 received (Liesen 2014).

Besides research output, various initiatives aim for specialists to keep in touch with one another as well as with the international community. One such initiative is the *Dag van het Romeinse Aardewerk* conference ('Day of Roman Pottery'), an annual event that is held in Nijmegen. It was first organised in 1997 and took place for the 25th time in 2024. In 2011, the annual conference of the *Study Group of Roman Pottery* (UK) was held at the University of Amsterdam. The Fautores congress at Xanten (2014) included a one-day excursion to Nijmegen, where a number of presentations were held. And now, after 53 years, the Fautores are back in the Netherlands, this time in Leiden, a congress organised in collaboration with the National Museum of Antiquities and the Faculty of Archaeology of Leiden University.

Over the past few centuries, Roman pottery studies in the Netherlands have changed from being a field of collectors to a group of professional archaeologists: however, the attraction, curiosity and interest into ancient objects remain strong as ever. We strongly feel that this particular attraction, curiosity, and interest very much runs through the joint publication that you are holding, a first *status quaestionis* on Roman pottery studies in the Netherlands. With these collected papers, the editorial board aimed to bring together different types of sites, classes of pottery and scholarly debates, to form a cross-section of pottery research conducted in the Netherlands, in particular in recent years. The papers included in this volume concern the following four themes.

- Histories of Collecting
  Jasper de Bruin describes the role of the National Museum of Antiquities within the fields of Roman archaeology and Roman pottery studies and emphasises the museum's collecting history. The museum also employs various types of research to contextualise its collections and to make these available for other scholars. His paper demonstrates the increased involvement of museums in Roman pottery research.
- The Social, Cultural and Economic Meaning of Ceramic Change
  Three contributions discuss the development of handmade pottery. Peter van den Broeke describes how handmade pottery changed during the early Roman period. Ernst Taayke uses research in the northern Netherlands to describe the developments and influences on handmade pottery outside, but in proximity of, the limes. Annet Nieuwhof uses terra sigillata, produced within the Roman Empire, to reconstruct the ritual meaning it might have had for those living outside the Roman Empire in the northern Netherlands.
- Roman Pottery in Different Cultural and Functional Contexts
  This large section includes four papers on diachronic developments of pottery assemblages from different types of sites. Bernd Liesen compares assemblages from urban sites. Harry van Enckevort discusses the (early) Roman military structures and their specialised pottery production in Nijmegen. Roderick Geerts describes developments in rural settlements. Frederique Reigersman-van Lidth de Jeude presents funerary deposits and their connection to contemporary beliefs and rituals.
- Geographical and Chronological Dimensions of Regional and Long-Distance Exchange
  Two contributions highlight exchange on regional and supraregional levels. Xavier Deru's contribution describes the development of *terra rubra* and *terra nigra*, ceramic categories that were specific to this part of the Roman Empire. Joost van den Berg discusses the development of amphorae circulation on the limes, highlighting (amongst others) the increased importance of regional networks over time.

To conclude this introduction: we wish you a pleasant and informative read.

Fig. 1. Map of the Netherlands with the 12 provinces, some of which are mentioned in this volume (© ADC ArcheoProjecten/ A. Botman).

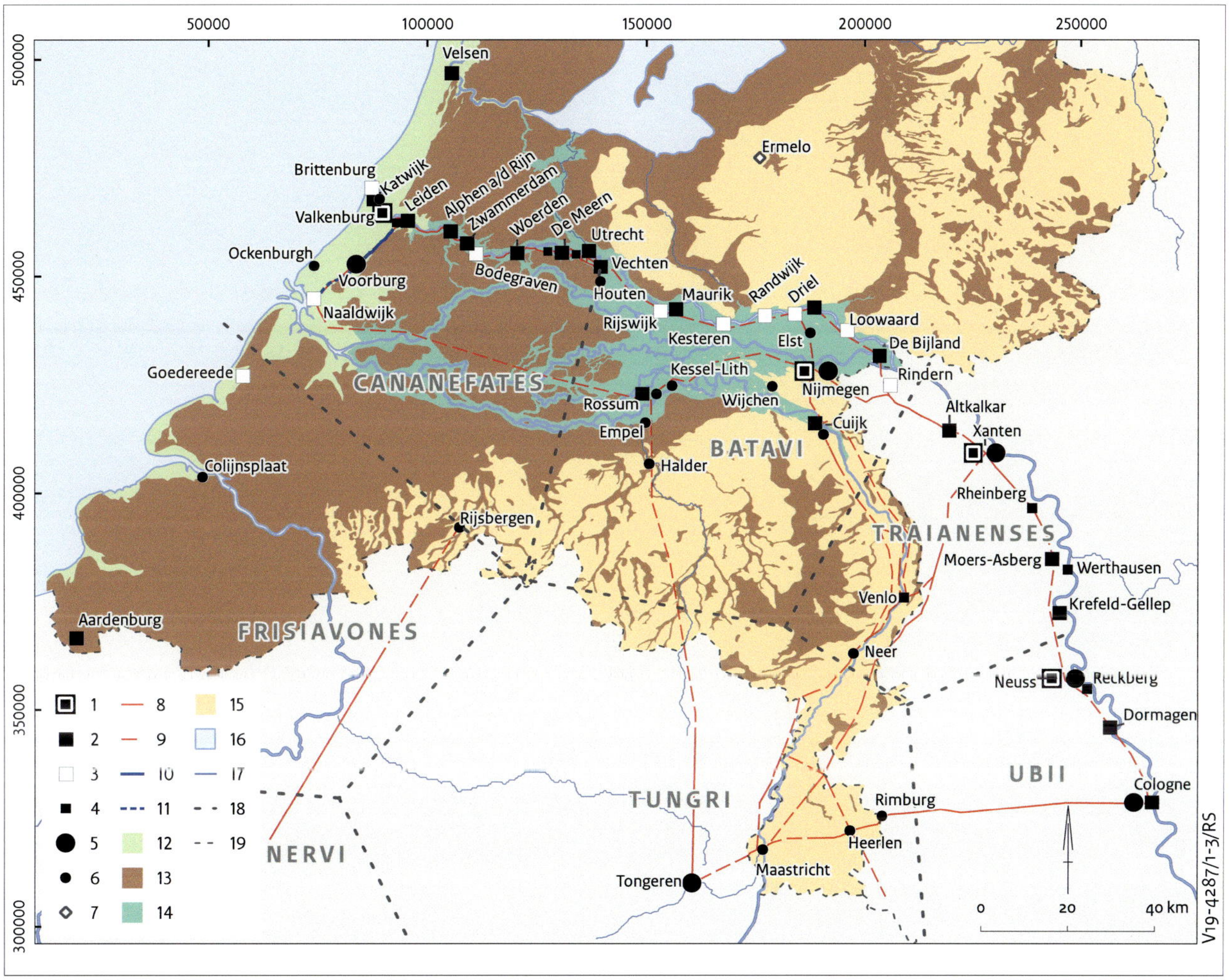

Fig. 2. Map of the province of Germania Inferior; included are the main civilian and military settlements and main geological zones. Legend (adapted): 1. legionary fortress; 2. auxiliary fort; 3. auxiliary fort(?); 4. smaller post; 5. Roman town; 6. *vicus* or regional centre; 7. temporary camp; 8. Roman military road; 9. Roman military road(?); 10. Corbulo canal/*Fossa Corbulonis*; 11. Corbulo canal/*Fossa Corbulonis*(?); 12. habitable coastal landscape; 13. peat bogs; 14. (fossilised) river systems, levees and banks; 15. sandy soils; 16. sea; 17. major rivers; 18. indicative borders of the Roman *civitates*; 19. modern borders (after: Hessing *et al.* 2021, 28, fig. 3, updated by Vestigia © Rijksdienst voor het Cultureel Erfgoed).

PART 1

HISTORIES OF COLLECTING

Roman Pottery and the Dutch National Museum of Antiquities: a Long-Term Relationship

Jasper de Bruin

The relationship between the National Museum of Antiquities and Roman pottery studies in the Low Countries dates back to 1828, when the museum's first director, Caspar Reuvens, had lithographs made of terra sigillata found during the excavations of the Roman city of Forum Hadriani in the Netherlands (Halbertsma 2003, 112-127) (fig. 1). Reuvens saw this material as evidence for Roman activities and as a source of information about Roman life and epigraphy (Brongers 2002, 105-106, 113). Due to Reuvens' untimely death in 1835, the terra sigillata catalogue could not be published. This was all the more unfortunate, because Reuvens' classification of figure and name stamps had the potential to become a standard work. During the years 1867-1870, a large number of finds from the Roman period were collected near Vechten (the Netherlands), the location of the Roman fort Fectio. Finds included large numbers of sherds, and here too, attention was mainly focused on the terra sigillata, which included drawing up lists of the stamps on this pottery (fig. 2).

Attention to Roman pottery within the National Museum of Antiquities was fairly incidental during the 19th century. This changed in 1904 with the appointment of curator Jan Hendrik Holwerda, who started his appointment with a study trip to the excavations of the early Roman fort in Haltern. Here he met Hans Dragendorff, immortalising him in a photo (fig. 3). Both gentlemen shared a preference for research into terra sigillata and due to Holwerda's appointment in Leiden, research into this material was also resumed. For example, rubbings of many terra sigillata sherds were made and a system of card indexes was created, for both figure and name stamps (fig. 4). Holwerda and Dragendorff continued to correspond and Dragendorff regularly gave lectures in Leiden, spending the night at the Holwerda family's home (Verhart 2020, 34-35). In addition to his interest in terra sigillata, he also paid attention to other ceramic finds (Holwerda 1941; 1944; Holwerda and Braat 1946) and specific pottery assemblages, such as a group of pottery from a closed context (waste pit) in the Roman fort on the Kops Plateau in Nijmegen, of which a photo was taken (fig. 5). Holwerda's continuation of Reuvens' excavations in the Roman city of Forum Hadriani led to a publication with a lot of attention to the ceramic finds (Holwerda 1923). Also, a new display of Roman pottery in the museum was created, which provided an overview of all pottery groups and types found in the Netherlands (fig. 6). At this time, the collection of the National Museum of Antiquities

in: R.C.A. Geerts and Ph. Bes (eds) 2024, *Roman Pottery in the Low Countries: Past Research, Current State, Future Directions*. Leiden: Sidestone Press (= *Papers on Archaeology of the Leiden Museum of Antiquities Leiden* 32), pp. 21-28.

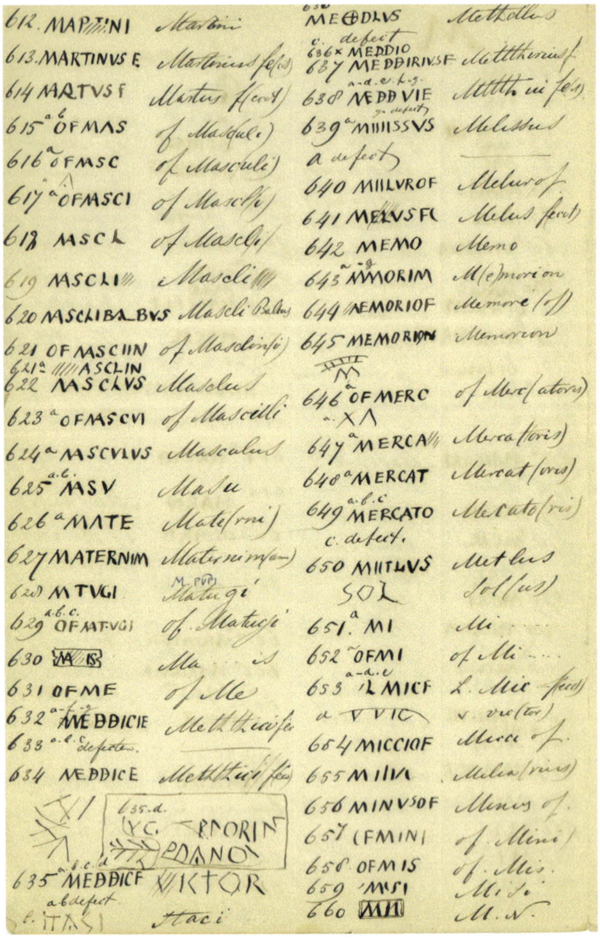

Fig. 1. Lithographs of terra sigillata, found during the excavations of the Roman city of Forum Hadriani, the Netherlands (image: National Museum of Antiquities, Leiden).

Fig. 2. Lists of the stamps on terra sigillata, found between 1867 and 1870 in Vechten, the Netherlands (image: National Museum of Antiquities, Leiden).

was also enriched with several foreign collections of terra sigillata and ceramic mould fragments from Lezoux and Trier (fig. 7). Holwerda also paid attention to the museum's rich collections of Roman pottery from the Mediterranean region (Holwerda 1936).

After the Second World War, the National Museum of Antiquities remained active in the field of research on the Roman period, although the newly established *State Service for Archaeological Research* (*Rijksdienst voor het Oudheidkundig Bodemonderzoek*, or ROB) would soon be responsible for most archaeological field research in the Netherlands. Excavations were carried out in Nijmegen under the supervision of the new curator Hendrik Brunsting, who had obtained his PhD on a study of the pottery from the cemetery of the Roman city of Ulpia Noviomagus (Brunsting 1937). Brunsting uncovered late Roman burials in the bombed city centre of Nijmegen. At the same time, private individuals collected pottery finds in this area and these were purchased by the National Museum of Antiquities (fig. 8). After this, the excavations continued in the fort of the Tenth Legion in Nijmegen. Brunsting left the National Museum of Antiquities in 1967, more or less at the same time as curator Wouter Braat, who had conducted excavations in Roman villae in the Dutch province of Limburg until 1955 (De Bruin in prep.)[1]. After their departure, Piet Stuart took over as curator, who had obtained his PhD in Roman pottery from Nijmegen and whose typology is still widely used in the Netherlands (Stuart 1963). In the years that followed, Stuart taught Roman pottery courses to university students and devoted much attention to this material in the new permanent exhibition in the museum (fig. 9). However, his scientific focus was more on the Latin epigraphy of the altars of Nehalennia, which were found during his curatorship and that were published in 2001 (Stuart and Bogaers 2001). At the same time, a first attempt of the analysis of the numerous pottery finds from Vechten was also started.

An inventory in 1984 showed that more than 5000 stamps on terra sigillata were found in Vechten in the years 1867-1870. This remains one of the largest collections of terra sigillata stamps in the Netherlands. The majority of the stamps, the south Gaulish ones, were

1 The analysis of the excavations of these Roman villae, with attention for finds like Roman pottery, will be published in the foreseeable future.

Fig. 3. Hans Dragendorff, standing on top of a section of one of the Roman ditches in Haltern, photographed by J.H. Holwerda in 1904 (image: National Museum of Antiquities, Leiden).

Fig. 4. Rubbings of terra sigillata fragments, stored in the archive of the National Museum of Antiquities (image: National Museum of Antiquities, Leiden).

Fig. 5. A group of pottery from a closed context (waste pit) found in the Roman fort on the Kops Plateau in Nijmegen, photographed between 1917 and 1920 (image: National Museum of Antiquities, Leiden).

Fig. 6. Display of Roman pottery from the Netherlands in the National Museum of Antiquities in the period 1905-1915 (image: National Museum of Antiquities, Leiden).

Fig. 7. Ceramic mould fragments from Lezoux and Trier, from the collection of the National Museum of Antiquities (image: National Museum of Antiquities, Leiden).

Fig. 8. Late Roman pottery from the city centre of Nijmegen (image: National Museum of Antiquities, Leiden).

analysed and published by Rien Polak (Polak 1995)[2]. The remaining Roman pottery, consisting of many tens of thousands of fragments, was not further examined, but includes several pieces of interest to the Netherlands (fig. 10). In any case, Stuart's work contributed to a more comprehensive insight into the wealth of the collection of Roman pottery in the National Museum of Antiquities. In 1987, Stuart was succeeded by Marijke Brouwer, who at the time was conducting research into Roman pottery in the Dutch province of Zuid-Holland. During her curatorship, a syllabus for identifying Roman pottery was composed, in which the collection of the National Museum of Antiquities played a central role (Blomsma and Brouwer 1989). Brouwer also identified pottery in the museum's collection. After 1997, when the National Museum of Antiquities no longer had a separate curator for the Roman collections in the Netherlands, the Roman pottery collection was only sparsely involved in research, usually carried out by external scholars.

2 The English language edition was sponsored by the Rei Cretariæ Romanæ Fautores and published as the 9th supplement in their series in 2000.

From 2019 onwards, attention to Roman pottery held in the collections of the National Museum of Antiquities has gradually increased again with the instalment of a new curator for the Roman collections in the Netherlands. An important step in the Roman pottery research is the unlocking of several private collections that comprise finds from Vechten that were collected in the 1970s and which were purchased in recent years. For this purpose, a registration process was set up in the period 2021-2023, during which the objects were measured, described, and photographed one by one (fig. 11). Thousands of pottery fragments have now been published in this way in the online collection finder of the National Museum of Antiquities (https://www.rmo.nl/collectie/collectiezoeker/), with a basic description and a photo. Some of these collections are also accessible via the Portable Antiquities of the Netherlands website (https://portable-antiquities.nl/pan/#/public). The advantage of this approach is that researchers, including those abroad, are able to look into the museum's collection down to the level of the individual fragment. The intention is to set up more comparable projects within the museum

Fig. 9. Permanent exhibition in the museum in 1980-1981 of the Netherlands during the Roman period, with a prominent position for Roman pottery (image: National Museum of Antiquities, Leiden).

Fig. 10. A fully preserved jug made from marbled ware, found in Vechten, the Netherlands. Fabric and type are not common in the Netherlands (image: National Museum of Antiquities, Leiden).

in the future, making the Roman pottery from the museum better accessible, and thus easier to study.

But there is more that the museum has to offer concerning the study of Roman pottery in the Low Countries. Many pottery fragments in the collection of the National Museum of Antiquities were found during excavations. Although the registration of these finds was mostly not done on the level of what could be expected today, these objects still have a clear context and therefore a scientific value. A good example is the study of the pottery finds from Heerlen (Coriovallum), that could add information to an excavation that was carried out quite recently (Geerts 2020). Besides the sherds themselves, the scientific library of the museum houses one of the most complete collections of books in the field of Roman pottery studies in the Netherlands and its study rooms are open to scholars on appointment. Finally, the museum became involved in archaeological fieldwork again: during an excavation in Hazerswoude, the Netherlands, a large number of pottery fragments was found at a site with a Roman military character, located along the lower Germanic limes (De Bruin *et al.* 2022, 16-21). Some of this pottery will be analysed within the walls of the museum, marking the re-entry of the National Museum of Antiquities in the study of newly collected pottery assemblages.

All in all, there has been a close relationship between the study of Roman pottery and the National Museum of Antiquities for almost two centuries, albeit with, sometimes, long intermezzos. It is clear that the depots of the National Museum of Antiquities contain large numbers of Roman pottery fragments and that they are worth studying (fig. 12). In order to facilitate this research, the museum has defined the most important aims. Firstly, it is important that these collections are made accessible, so that external scholars can find their way more easily within the often large numbers of sherds. Renewed attention and reappraisal for Roman pottery within the museum is another important aim. This publication, which appears via the PALMA series of the National Museum of Antiquities, is a valuable contribution to these aims. But it does not stop here: within the next two years, new volumes of the PALMA series will appear, focusing on Roman villae in the Dutch province of Limburg and a newly discovered legionary fort in Valkenburg, both including comprehensive studies on Roman pottery.

Fig. 11. Registration of a small part of the terra sigillata from Vechten in the National Museum of Antiquities in the period 2021-2023 (image: National Museum of Antiquities, Leiden).

Fig. 12. Examples of Roman pottery from the collections of the National Museum of Antiquities (image: National Museum of Antiquities, Leiden).

PART 2

THE SOCIAL, CULTURAL AND ECONOMIC MEANING OF CERAMIC CHANGE

From the Iron Age to the Roman Period. Native Pottery in the Batavian Area

Peter W. van den Broeke

Abstract

The decades around the beginning of the Common Era saw rapid developments in the fabric, design, and decoration of handmade pottery in the riverine central part of the Netherlands. In part, these developments can be attributed to the arrival of new groups of settlers. The pottery of the only migrant group known from classical sources, the (Chatto-) Batavians, is remarkably less easily identifiable than that of unattested groups from the north. The immigrants who produced pottery in the 'Frisian' and 'Chaucian' styles seem to have arrived in the central part of this river area via an eastern detour. The many salt containers found in this area are known to have originated along the continental coasts of the North Sea and the English Channel.

Keywords: handmade pottery, Batavi, Chatti, Chauci, Frisii

Introduction

This contribution presents a concise overview of the handmade pottery that was used in the central and eastern parts of the Dutch river area around the beginning of the Common Era (fig. 1). These areas will be collectively referred to as "the river area" below.

In the wake of the turbulent final phase of the Iron Age, beginning with Caesar's acts of revenge around the mid-1st century BC and followed by the arrival of a group of Chatti and standard Roman troops, handmade pottery underwent rapid changes, and new traditions evolved. An important objective of this contribution is to explain these developments. In this context, more than average attention should be paid to an aspect that is often overlooked in publications on handmade pottery in the wider lower Rhine region, namely the organisation of its production. As this ostensibly took place on a domestic level, it may be assumed that the pottery was manufactured by women (Hodder 1981)[1]. This assumption

1 There is indeed some actual evidence of the production of pottery by women in this region in the Iron Age, whereas the manufacture of *briquetage* vessels seems to have been a (largely) male affair in the Roman period (Van den Broeke 2012, 196). The latter is easily conceivable given both the large scale of sea salt production at that time and the low demands placed on the quality of this category of pottery.

in: R.C.A. Geerts and Ph. Bes (eds) 2024, *Roman Pottery in the Low Countries: Past Research, Current State, Future Directions*. Leiden: Sidestone Press (= *Papers on Archaeology of the Leiden Museum of Antiquities Leiden* 32), pp. 31-46.

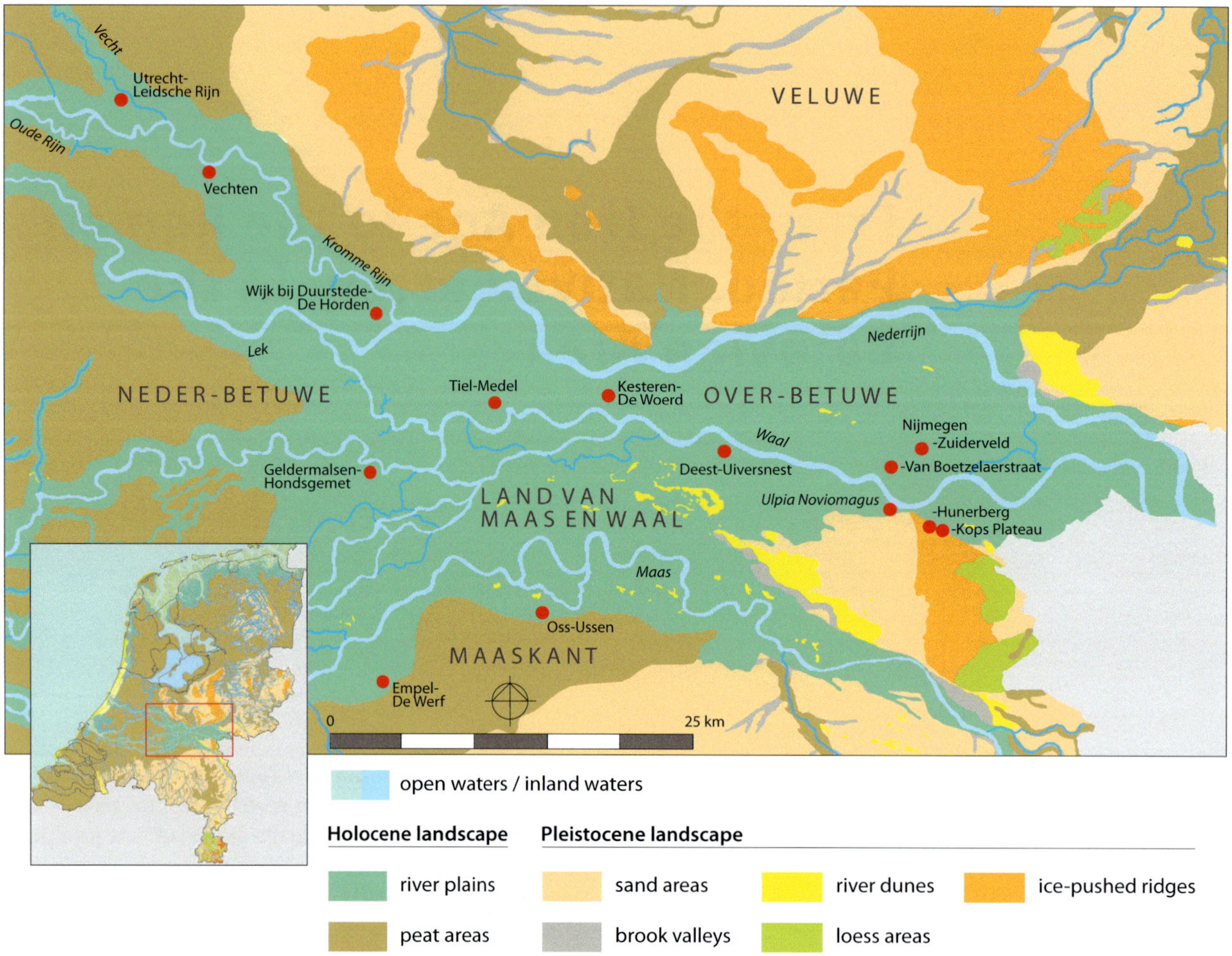

Fig. 1. The eastern and central parts of the river area around 100, showing present-day topographical names and sites mentioned in the text (palaeogeographic map based on Vos et al. 2011; editing by *Rob Mols foto/grafisch*).

should certainly not be ignored when considering a period in which multitudes of men were concentrated in fortifications and women could contribute towards the homogenisation of pottery styles in the case of exogamy in areas inhabited by groups with different cultural backgrounds[2].

Caesar's violent intervention was followed by the arrival of a migrant group known to us from historical sources as the Batavi (Tacitus, *Germania* XXIX; *Historiae* IV.12). This (elite?) group, which had split off from the tribe of the Chatti, is thought to have originated in Hesse. Contrary to what Tacitus describes, archaeological research in the last decades has shown that the area in which the newcomers settled between *c.* 50 and 12 BC was not uninhabited. It would seem that the indigenous population, presumably residual groups of the Caesar-decimated Eburones, merged – imperceptibly to us – with the newcomers from Hesse to form a larger group – the tribe of the Batavians – in the decades around the beginning of the Common Era. Having first been tentatively proposed (Willems 1986, 370-371), this hypothesis has become widely accepted since a study by Roymans (2004).

Views on the size of the occupation area of the Batavians vary substantially (see Vos 2009, 27-29, for an overview). If we base our estimation of the former occupation area of the Eburones on the distribution of coins such as gold coins of Scheers type 31 (Roymans 2020) plus the density of apparent identity markers such as glass La Tène bracelets, then residual groups of Eburones may be assumed to have been living in an area extending northwards to the Rhine, including the Kromme Rijn area (cf. Vos 2009, fig. 5.1; Roymans and Verniers 2010, fig. 2). No rough southern boundary can be identified for the Batavian area. But epigraphic evidence such as the early Roman altar stone

2 Homogenisation will have been promoted in particular if women who had married into a new community produced their pottery groupwise, for example within a family or hamlet, as has been ethnographically documented on many occasions.

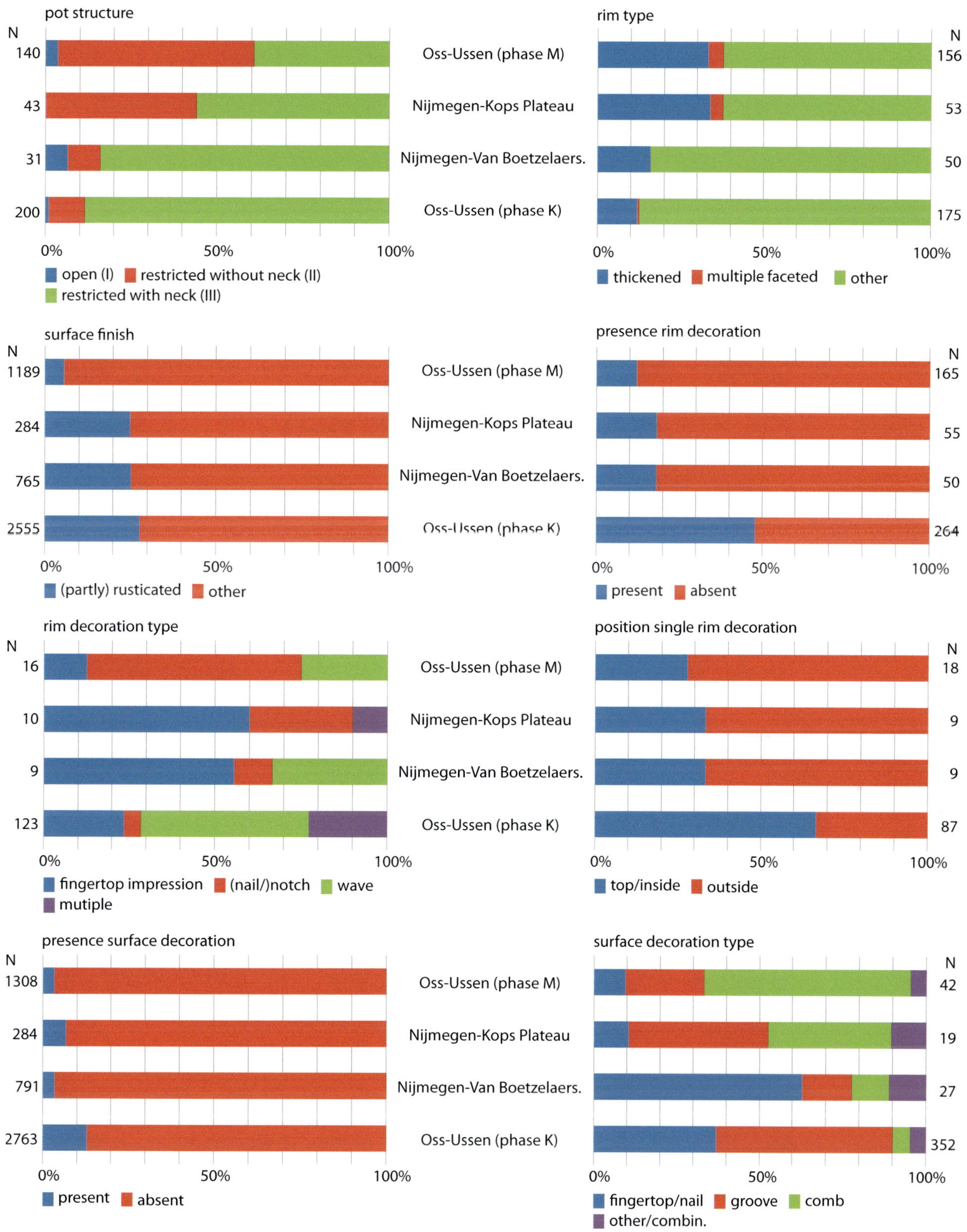

Fig. 2. Some features of regional-style pottery assemblages from the late Iron Age and early Roman period in chronological order (from bottom to top) (drawing: *Rob Mols foto/grafisch*).

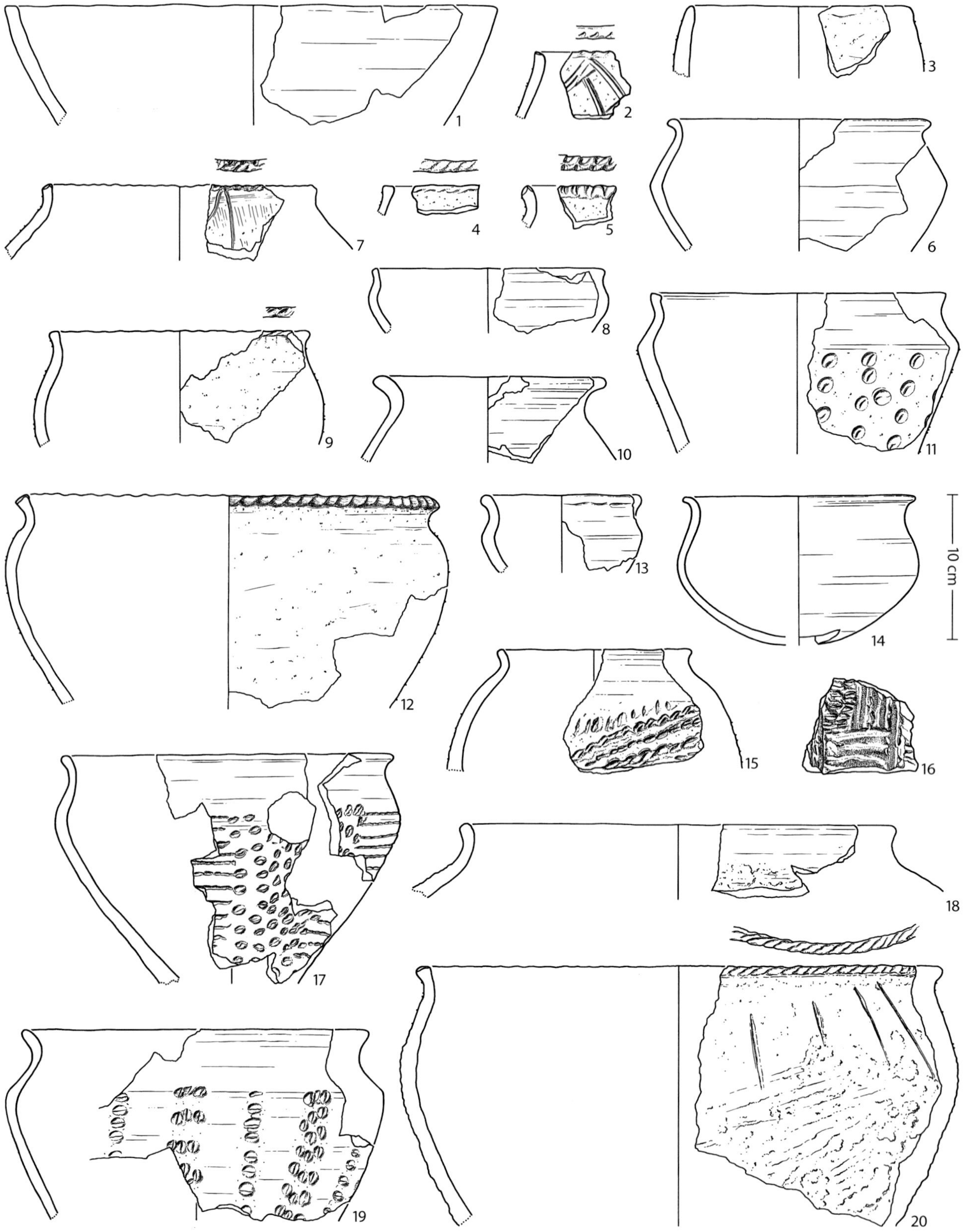

Fig. 3. Handmade pottery from water pit P271 in Oss-Ussen (phase K; 150/125-50/25 BC). Scale 1:4 (after: Van den Broeke 2012).

of Ruimel and references to the Batavian principal deity Hercules Magusanus at the cult site of Empel (Roymans 2004, 64, 242, respectively) make it clear that at least the Maaskant region in the province of Noord-Brabant (English: North-Brabant) also belonged to the area formalised as the *civitas Batavorum* by the Roman authorities.

Figure 2 quantitatively considers the chronologically most sensitive pottery variables from around the beginning of the Common Era for some sites in the river area. They are assemblages that have been classified and described in similar ways, making it methodologically justified to compare them. The following sections cover the characteristics textually. It should be borne in mind that only handmade pottery was made and used in the river area until the arrival of the Romans around 19 BC. No products thrown on a slow potter's wheel are known either.

Characteristics of Late Iron Age Pottery

For a proper understanding of the character of the pottery that was produced in the river area around 100 BC it is best to first look at the coastal provinces of Zuid-Holland and Zeeland. Here, major changes took place in the pottery style groups Santpoort I-II, Broekpolder I-II, and Domburg I-II after around 350/300 BC (Van Heeringen 1988; 1992, 283-288; Van Trierum *et al.* 1988, especially table 3). The Gelderland and Utrecht parts of the river area, and also the northeastern part of Noord-Brabant, were similarly affected by these changes after the mid-3rd century BC, to an extent sufficient to allow us to speak of westernisation, a copying of traits from the western coastal zone. This led to pottery with a completely different appearance in Iron Age phase K (150/125-50/25 BC) (see Van den Broeke 2012, fig. 2.10, for the phasing of the Iron Age in the central and southern Netherlands), a good example being the settlement pottery of Oss-Ussen in the Maaskant region (figs 2-3)[3]:

- The range of vessel types became less varied, with open types (pot structure type I) having become rare by phase K (fig. 3.1). The almost complete disappearance of the previously prominent barrel types led to a very small proportion of neckless restricted types (pot structure type II) in phase K (fig. 3.2-4), whereas the proportion of restricted types with a neck (pot structure type III) was greater than ever (fig. 3.6-15, 17-20)[4]. The latter are mostly characterised by an S-shape, all having a short neck that may be strongly flared. This is also the case with many of the carinated pots (fig. 3.6, 19). Round bases such as that of the bowl shown in Figure 3.14 were highly exceptional and were to remain so into the Roman period. The same holds for base forms other than those with an angular transition to the body and those with an identifiable base disc;
- A steady decline in rusticated pottery (cf. fig. 3.20). The other pots were more often left rough instead of smoothly finished;
- A fairly rapid increase in surface decoration, no longer restricted to the belly but also often above it. After an absolute minimum in the course of the middle Iron Age (1%) the proportion rose to 13% in phase K. The dominant groove decoration was usually superficially applied (fig. 3.2) and often repeated vertically or obliquely on the shoulder (fig. 3.20). Many of the equally popular fingertip and nail impressions reveal labour-intensive patterns such as that known as the *Kalenderberg* pattern (fig. 3.16). Comb decoration is largely absent;
- A sharp increase in rim decoration: 48% of the rims produced in phase K are decorated;
- Differentiation in rim decoration techniques. Notches made with a scoop or knife and wave decorations appeared alongside fingertip impressions. Wave decorations (fig. 3.4, 12, 20) prevailed in phase K. For a short while vessels with several rows of rim decoration were very popular. These rims were decorated using a combination of different techniques (fig. 3.7) or the same technique applied twice, such as two rows of fingertip impressions (fig. 3.5);
- Further differentiation in the position of the rim decoration. The decoration gradually moved to the outside of the rim, instead of only on the top or the inside. In phase K, this was the case in 33% of the vessels with single rim decoration. This trend continued unabated into phase M (early Roman period);
- In addition to the ubiquitous grog, spindly vegetable matter started to be used on a very modest scale to temper the clay for some pots in phase K (Van den Broeke 2012, 141)[5]. The use of clay containing fine sand grains (<1 mm) greatly increased, probably as a result of a more varied, less careful selection of the raw material rather than the addition of fine sand.

3 Phase K was modelled using three more or less closed assemblages (Van den Broeke 2012, 340-341, table 2-16). The pottery assemblage from a water pit shown in Figure 3 yielded a ^{14}C date of 2065±35 BP for thin roundwood (Van den Broeke 2012, 341, cat. no. 31); idem, appendix 4, for an overview of pottery features from the early Iron Age to the middle Roman period.

4 'Neck' is here understood to be a vertical or everted part above the shoulder having a length of basically >1 cm. A neck may consequently coincide with the rim, the top part of a pot with a length of at most 1 cm (cf. Van den Broeke 2012, 39).

5 For the possibility that this could be a southeastern rather than a western trend.

Fig. 4. Handmade pottery from the decades around the beginning of the Common Era. 1-8: Geldermalsen-Hondsgemet; 9-30: Nijmegen-Van Boetzelaerstraat. Scale 1:4 (after: Van Kerckhove 2009; Daniël 2005, respectively).

Another site with a large collection of settlement pottery from around the same time as phase K in Oss-Ussen is Geldermalsen-Hondsgemet, in the western part of the Betuwe region. This site's closer proximity to the west of the Netherlands than Oss-Ussen is also evident from the frequency of the aforementioned pottery characteristics (see also Habermehl 2019, 230)[6]. For example, the practice of manufacturing rusticated vessels had more or less completely ended at Hondsgemet, whereas more than a quarter of the pottery produced at Oss-Ussen still had rusticated walls. Furthermore, rim decoration was almost always applied to the outside, whereas this form of decoration that was to become dominant in phase M at Oss-Ussen was in phase K still being used for only less than half of the vessels (fig. 2).

Geldermalsen-Hondsgemet is also one of the few settlements in the study region where the second half of the 1st century BC seems to be more than minimally represented (fig. 4.1-8) (Van Kerckhove 2009, 151-154, 187)[7]. Important differences with respect to the previously described phase are:

- A decrease in restricted types with a neck (pot structure type III), in favour of neckless restricted types (pot structure type II);
- Less rim decoration, which consists almost exclusively of notches applied to the outside;
- Very little surface decoration, consisting mainly of grooves.

Around this same time the rural settlement Nijmegen-Van Boetzelaerstraat further east in the Betuwe region was inhabited. The range of fibulae found here confirms continuity from the late Iron Age to the Roman period (Heeren and Van der Feijst 2017, 269)[8]. The assemblage shown here (figs 2, 4.9-30) comprises finds from some house features, pits and a well (Daniël 2005; Van den Broeke 2014, table 2, Van Boetzelaerstraat A). The extremely small number of only three fragments of Roman pottery alongside the 793 specimens of regional-style pottery undisputedly shows that this assemblage includes only little handmade pottery dating from the early Roman period.

The pottery of Nijmegen-Van Boetzelaerstraat roughly corresponds to that of Oss-Ussen around the transition from the late Iron Age to the Roman period. However, this is based on only one small assemblage found in a pit dating from the local phase L (50/25 BC-AD 0/25) within this vast settlement area (Van den Broeke 2012, 341 (cat. no. 32), pl. 33, appendix 4). A scarcity of settlement assemblages from the second half of the 1st century BC has also been noted for other parts of the river area and further south (Roymans 2019, figs 11, 13). It is quite possible that this decline is related to events recorded by Caesar in the 50s BC, when the general and his Roman troops took violent revenge on the rebellious Eburones (*De bello Gallico*, VI.5, VIII.2). This also suggests that the end of phase K can be set around 50 BC, and no later. And although the many metal finds tell us that the cult site at Empel was frequently visited in the 1st century BC, no pottery from the period 50 BC-AD 25 has been identified here, unlike pottery from phase K and from the advanced early Roman period (Van den Broeke 2020).

Handmade Pottery from the Augustan Period from Roman Military Camps in Nijmegen

Although assemblages with handmade pottery from Roman military camps in Nijmegen will not be representative of the indigenous range of pottery, they have a qualitative advantage over assemblages from rural settlements: their chronological resolution. This applies to both the Augustan castra on the Hunerberg hill (*c.* 19-15/12 BC) and the somewhat later military camp on the nearby Kops Plateau, whose features from the Augustan period (12 BC-*c.* 15) have been studied (Stoffels 2006; Van den Broeke 2014, respectively; for the castra also see Bogaers and Haalebos 1980). Very little handmade pottery has been published from the nearby early Roman civil settlement *Oppidum Batavorum* (*e.g.* Hendriks 2017). It should be noted that the latest view concerning the arrival of the (Chatto-)Batavi is that it may have roughly coincided with the construction of the castra on the Hunerberg or have taken place some time before (Habermehl *et al.* 2023, 70).

The legionary camp on the Hunerberg yielded a very early, but also remarkably large corpus of native pottery from a Roman military camp: 2859 fragments, amounting to 25% of the total of 11,489 pottery fragments, including those from features containing exclusively Roman ware (Stoffels 2006, 25). A concentration of indigenous pottery has been attributed to the presence of an indigenous woman (wife, worker, or slave) in the centurion's living quarters in one of the barracks, with her own equipment for cooking and/or storage (Stoffels 2006, 76; 2009, 153).

6 For a comparison with this Iron Age phase K, see horizon A, dated 150-70 BC, at Geldermalsen-Hondsgemet (Van Kerckhove 2013). Here, the local pottery phases B and C (150-50 BC at the latest) coincide with phase K (Van Kerckhove 2009, 133-150, 186-188).

7 Local phase D: 50/25 BC-AD 15/25), based on the finds from "erf 19". This assemblage, which was later assigned to horizon C, dated 30/20 BC-AD 14 (Van Kerckhove 2013), contained no Roman pottery, but it did include an Avaucia coin, whose assumed age suggests that all the pottery from this phase was produced in the early Roman period, which began around 19 BC with the construction of the Augustan castra on the Hunerberg in Nijmegen (Kemmers 2006). Also see the contribution by Van Enckevort in this volume.

8 Recorded under the name of Oosterhout-Van Boetzelaerstraat, but the placename Oosterhout is no longer used within the municipality of Nijmegen.

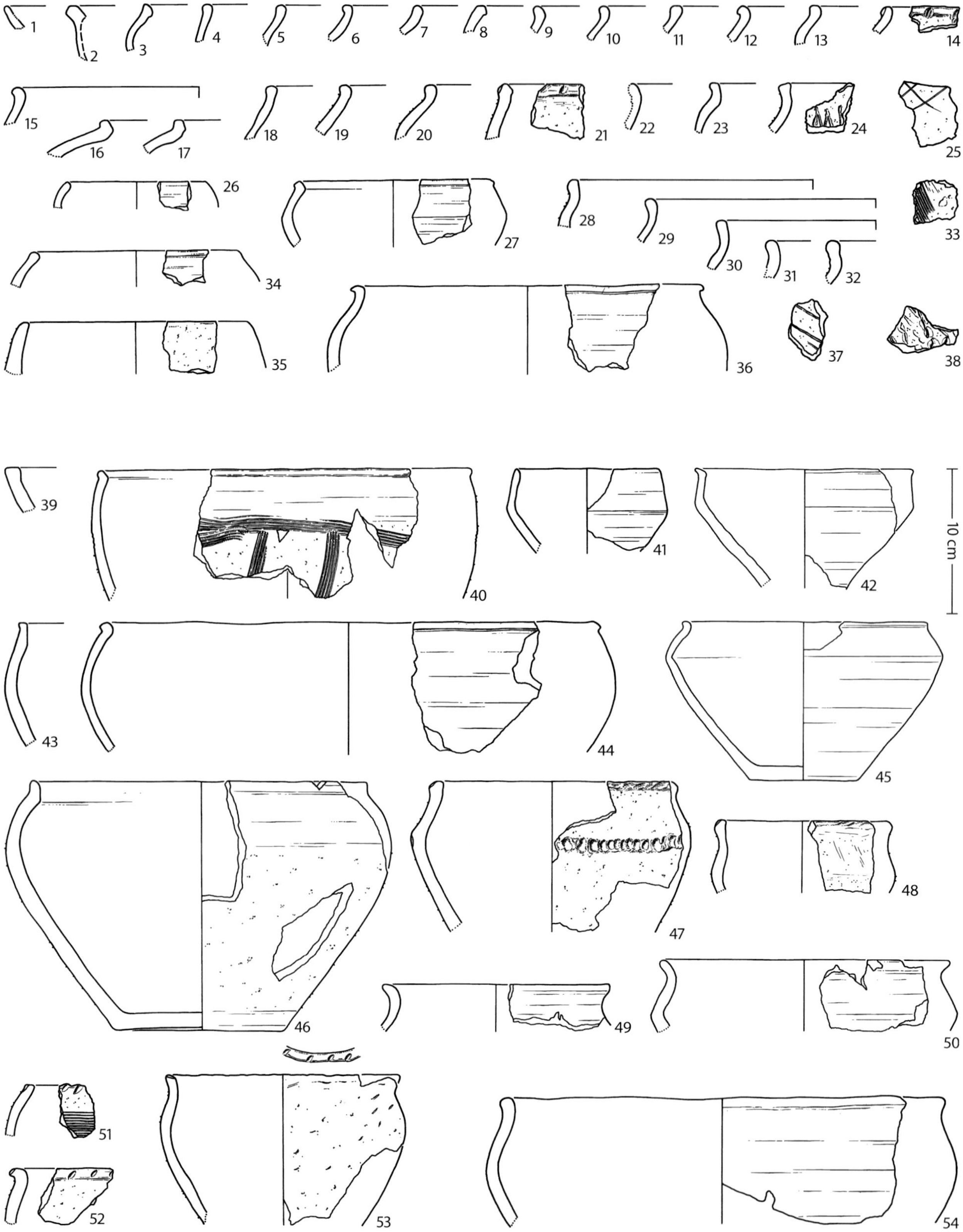

Fig. 5. Handmade pottery from the early Roman period from Oss-Ussen (phase M). 1-38: all rims and a selection of surface decoration from well P256; 39-54: selection from various contexts. Scale 1:4 (after: Van den Broeke 2012).

Nevertheless, the pottery range of this Roman military camp will differ from that of a rural settlement, even though it is known that Roman soldiers had to cook their own meals, and that any indigenous auxiliaries – in this case presumably Batavians – may hence have used their own vessels. Storage jars will have been relatively limited in number here.

The vast majority of the vessels from the Augustan castra are restricted types with necks. About 1 in 7 rims is decorated, with wave patterns prevailing. In the surface decoration, barely applied by this stage, combing comes second after grooves/cannelures[9]. And even though the Geldermalsen-Hondsgemet assemblage contains one unmistakable example of a multiple faceted rim (fig. 4.1), only specimens from the castra can tell us for sure that this rim type was already common in the second decade before the beginning of the Common Era (Stoffels 2006, figs 2.9, 4.8, 4.30, 7.1).

The pottery from the military camp on the Kops Plateau, which was established shortly after the castra had been abandoned, is more or less the same in most respects (fig. 2). Wave decoration on the rim is however conspicuously absent, although the absolute number of sherds with decorated rims is limited, and wave decoration is represented in a younger context (Bogaers and Haalebos 1975, fig. 10.18-19; Van den Broeke 2014, fig. 12.18-19). Also worthy of mention here is an early example of an angular type with a prominently faceted rim that was found in the earliest layers of waste on the slope of the Kops Plateau (Bogaers and Haalebos 1975, fig. 10.3; Van den Broeke 2014, fig. 12.3). However, the proportion of indigenous pottery in the overall range of pottery from the studied Augustan features (9%) is much smaller than that in the castra (Van den Broeke 2014, 32).

Rural Settlements in the Early Roman Period

Until recently, virtually nothing stood in the way of viewing the river area as a whole in characterising the handmade pottery of the early Roman period (19 BC-70). However, the results of research in the past decade now force us to consider the central and eastern parts of this area separately.

Germanisation in the Eastern Part of the River Area

Oss-Ussen can be said to be a rural settlement dating from the early Roman period that is representative of the eastern part of the river area, here interpreted in a broad sense to include the eastern half of the Betuwe region, the adjacent area between the rivers Meuse and Waal and also the Maaskant and its surrounding area. The phase M that was locally distinguished for Oss-Ussen has been dated to 0/25-75 (Van den Broeke 2012). The pottery range of phase M differs markedly from that of phase L, and certainly from that of phase K (fig. 2). The pottery shown in Figure 5.1-38 may be regarded as the earliest assemblage from a closed context – a well exceptionally lined with a Roman wine barrel. The assemblage dates from the first quarter, or possibly also the second quarter of the 1st century[10].

Notable elements of phase M as a whole are:

- Dominance of combing as a surface decoration technique, at least after the beginning of phase M, when this technique was used for more than half of the decorated pottery. The common ornamental pattern is a series of widely spaced comb strokes arranged vertically on the belly, often topped by a single horizontal stroke at the transition to the shoulder (fig. 5.40, 51),
- The predominance of pot structure type II. A reduction in the neck caused the S-shaped vessels that had still prevailed in phase K to evolve partly into convex bowls, many with a flaring or thickened rim (fig. 5.40, 43-44, 46). However, angular pottery is also represented (fig. 5.27, 41-42, 45, 50);
- A large proportion of thickened rims and several rims with multiple faceting (fig. 5.2, 12, 27, 44);
- Rim decoration was still applied in only rare cases, mostly in the form of notches on the outside;
- A larger proportion of the pottery is dark in colour, having been fired in a reducing atmosphere; this is accompanied by a reduction in the average wall thickness.

Most points of this characterisation apply to the eastern part of the river area. However, the proportion of restricted neckless vessels was smaller to the north of the river Waal than in the area to the south of it. And comb decoration was less dominant than further south. A – very early – exception to this is Nijmegen-Zuiderveld (Hendriks 2010, table 12.9).

Developments that took place around the transition from phase K to the early Roman period led to pottery in

9 Figures relating to temper and surface finishing are not taken into account here, because they do not refer to 'sherd families' (specimens), but only to the number of fragments (Stoffels 2006, 30), though some specimens are represented by large numbers of sherds (documentation E. Stoffels).

10 Determination by H. van Enckevort (municipality of Nijmegen) based on 22 fragments of Roman pottery found alongside 373 fragments of handmade indigenous ware (Van den Broeke 2012, 341, cat. no. 33).

the eastern part of the river area that differed markedly from that in the western Netherlands, which it had so closely resembled in phase K. The western influence must have lost much of its impact in the 1st century BC, when the western coastal region seems to have been barely occupied (De Bruin 2017, 190; Van Heeringen 1988; 1992; Van Trierum *et al.* 1988, 39). Within a very short time, the pottery in the eastern part of the river area began to resemble the pottery complex produced to the east of the Rhine known as *Rhein-Weser-germanische Keramik* (RWG), be it *in statu nascendi* (see also Taayke's contribution in this volume). The clearest similarities are the predominance of restricted neckless types – both convex bowls and angular pottery – and the common presence of rims with multiple faceting, a thickening or lip. Counterparts in west Germany are the indigenous pottery found at early Roman military camps and vessels from rural settlements (see *e.g.* Eggenstein 2003, early Roman assemblages in Tafel 7-116). Even pottery from Warburg-Daseburg, more than 200 km east of Oss, shows strong similarities (Günther 1990, figs 65-94).

This change in style affinity suggests a relation to the arrival of the Chatto-Batavians, a suggestion seemingly further strengthened by the striking similarity between the pottery of the early Roman period and the older pottery produced in the immigrants' assumed region of origin, such as that of the Amöneburg hilltop settlement. The relevant finds from this site in northern Hesse date from the first half of the 1st century BC (Weisshaar 1984). Convex neckless bowls and pots dominate the limited pottery range, with combing being the most common surface decoration technique. Nevertheless, it is too premature to label the developments in the pottery of the eastern river area as Batavisation, as the author previously did (Van den Broeke 1987, 111-112). This reluctance is justified by observations such as the continued prevalence of vessels with necks and the limited use of comb decoration in the earliest assemblages from the Roman period, and the high proportion of rusticated pottery. Such a combination of features should not be surprising in a continuously occupied rural settlement such as Nijmegen-Van Boetzelaerstraat. Here, these same features still characterise a large assemblage dating from the mid-1st century (Daniël 2005, pit 5; Van den Broeke 2014, table 2, Van Boetzelaerstraat B). However, the same appears to hold for the pottery from the Augustan castra on the Hunerberg, and certainly that from the Kops Plateau, though we would expect to observe the first Chatto-Batavian influences at the military camps in particular.

For the time being we should therefore cautiously label the developments that took place in this area around the beginning of the Common Era as Germanisation. There are very few objections to considering the eastern river area as a western offshoot of the RWG pottery area. The similarities mainly concern the design of the vessels themselves, and certainly also their rims. The sharp increase in thickened rims and the introduction of multiple faceted rims can be attributed to this Germanisation.

As indicated above, it is still not clear with which pottery tradition the Chatto-Batavians actually entered the river area. The suspected deployment of Batavian troops from Nijmegen makes it conceivable that an RWG-tinted pottery tradition was here introduced in an area otherwise occupied by indigenous (residual) groups with their own regional pottery tradition – perhaps in particular by family members who had been drawn along in the wake of the troops? Such a two-track development could be inferred from the rather early production of RWG-like pottery in the military camps, especially on the Kops Plateau. Worthy of mention in this context is an intriguing rural settlement with various military attributes about 15 km west of the military camps: Deest-Uiversnest (Van Bergen *et al.* 2008). This may have been founded as early as the military camps, given the proportion of five pieces of Arretine terra sigillata out of a total of 17 pieces of terra sigillata in the spatially distinguished find group LA. This assemblage seems to have been closed as early as the first quarter of the 1st century. The proportions of 26% Roman ware and 74% indigenous handmade pottery are unprecedented for such an early rural settlement. It should also be noted that the rim decoration of the handmade pottery consists only of impressions and notches on the outside (Van Bergen *et al.* 2008, fig. 10) and the regionally well-known wave decoration is completely absent, also on the vessels produced later in the 1st century. The decoration was predominantly applied to convex, neckless types. All this is strongly reminiscent of the pottery manufactured east of the Rhine, raising the question whether this may be the handmade pottery of Chatto-Batavians.

Even within a single rural settlement such as Oss-Ussen, a two-track development may have been at issue (Van den Broeke 2012, 144). The very early assemblage shown in Figure 5.1-38 already has a remarkably pronounced RWG touch. However, marriage into this community of a woman from the ostensibly decisive Nijmegen region may have been all it took to generate this micro-differentiation.

The Central Part of the River Area

In order to do justice to the geographical differences in pottery ensembles within the river area, the central part of the Dutch river area will be discussed separately below. This includes the western half of the Betuwe region extending from Tiel and the adjacent part of the province of Utrecht up to the Kromme Rijn area.

This region is characterised by a greater differentiation in the pottery dating from the first decades AD than the eastern river area. Besides sites with pottery with recognisable roots in the traditions of the late Iron Age, such as Geldermalsen-Hondsgemet, there are sites with pottery showing strong northern influences. 'Northern' is in this context understood to comprise the entire zone ranging from the province of Noord-Holland (English: North-Holland) to northwest Germany. Prominent examples of such sites are Tiel-Medel (Van Kerckhove 2019), Utrecht-Leidsche Rijn LR41-42, LR75 and LR84 (Taayke 2009a; 2016; 2017) and Wijk bij Duurstede-De Horden (Taayke 2002). The most recognisable manifestation of the 'Frisian' pottery tradition around the beginning of the Common Era is a convex necked pot with two lugs, many of which show surface decoration in the form of horizontal grooves on the shoulder and contain fine elongated pores produced by the employed vegetal temper (fig. 6.1). Particularly characteristic of the 'Chaucian' tradition is a convex restricted type, neckless or with an extremely short neck, and a specifically faceted rim (*e.g.* fig. 6.12-14, 19). The pottery found at Tiel-Medel also includes a substantial proportion of pottery from the western part of the Netherlands.

Only a few years ago (Van den Broeke 2018), the appearance of a 'Frisian' pottery style and the sharp increase in the use of vegetal temper in this area could be fairly assertively attributed to a repopulation of Zuid-Holland (and Utrecht?) around the beginning of the Common Era, as proposed by Van Heeringen, although the first finds of pottery in Chaucian style from Sportpark Terweide in Utrecht-Leidsche Rijn (Taayke 2009a) already made it clear that the situation was more complicated than previously assumed. These settlers, having arrived here from what is now Noord-Holland, would have been the Cananefates (proposition 5 of Van Heeringen's PhD thesis (1992)). However, extensive study led De Bruin to a more northeasterly area of origin, and to a date of around 40/50 for the earliest, modest influx (De Bruin 2017, 205-207). Even though this late date no longer seems tenable (see Geerts' contribution to this volume), our understanding of the situation can to some extent be updated. The date of the decades around the beginning of the Common Era for the arrival of pottery in the northern – both 'Frisian' and 'Chaucian' – style in the central part of the river area may still be assumed to be correct (see *e.g.* Habermehl *et al.* 2023, table 1; Den Hartog 2017, 120). The same holds for migration, as can in part be inferred from the housebuilding traditions. However, one of the surprising results of the most recent pottery research is that we should not assume that families arrived directly from northern regions. Preliminary publications based on the results of thin-section and XRF analyses and other research state that some of the northern-style pottery was manufactured in west Germany (fig. 6.2, 4), more specifically the Lippe area (Van Kerckhove 2019; Lippe area: Habermehl *et al.* 2023; Van Kerckhove and Boreel in press). This also holds for pottery that is more in line with the RWG style (fig. 6.3, 7-10). Without further investigation it would have been more logical to assume that this pottery had been produced in the eastern part of the river area.

Two factors facilitate an explanation for this outcome: northern auxiliaries joined the Roman army at an early stage already – Frisian auxiliaries are mentioned as early as 12 BC (Cassius Dio, *Historiae Romanae* LV.32), Chaucian auxiliaries a few decades later, *i.e.* 16 (Tacitus, *Annales* I.60, II.17) – and there were several Roman fortifications along the Lippe around the beginning of the Common Era. They were used for only short periods, in some cases no longer than a few years. For example, the Oberaden camp has been found to have been occupied between 11 and 7 BC (Polak and Kooistra 2013).

This information suggests that northern migrants simultaneously arrived in the central part of the river area after a detour. Of relevance in this context are first of all a number of rural settlements with large amounts of northern-style pottery where finds of militaria and specific coin types believed to represent soldiers' pay suggest a link to the Roman army (Den Hartog 2017, 123; Habermehl *et al.* 2023, tables 3-4). Furthermore, a relatively large proportion of northern-style pottery, in particular in comparison with that found at the military camp on the Kops Plateau, came to light in the Vechten/Fectio castellum founded in the late Augustan period (Van den Broeke 2014, 43-45; Stoop-Greijer 2012, especially fig. 115). This further strengthens the hypothesis of a relocation of a military character. We may assume that the soldiers' families settled in the vicinity of the military camps, and that the women manufactured pottery there. A clearer example supporting such an interpretation is the 3rd-century 'Frisian' pottery found at Hadrian's Wall in northern England (Bloemers 1983, fig. 8.6), where Frisian auxiliaries are known to have been stationed. In Housesteads, however, the vessels in question were found not in the fort itself, but in a specific part of the associated *vicus* (Symonds and Mason 2009, 65, 81, 91, 170), suggesting the presence of entire Frisian families rather than just soldiers[11]. Similarly, the few Frisian-style pots known from a military context in Haltern (Bloemers 1973) could represent the 'smoking gun' of

11 Also worthy of mention here is a large pottery assemblage in northern style from the early 2nd century that was found in the middle of the province of Limburg in association with a regionally unknown type of house plan that is well known from the coastal area in the northern Netherlands (Van den Broeke 2018, 81-83). This may have been the pottery of the family of a veteran of the Frisian auxiliaries who had settled in a hamlet of a more regional character.

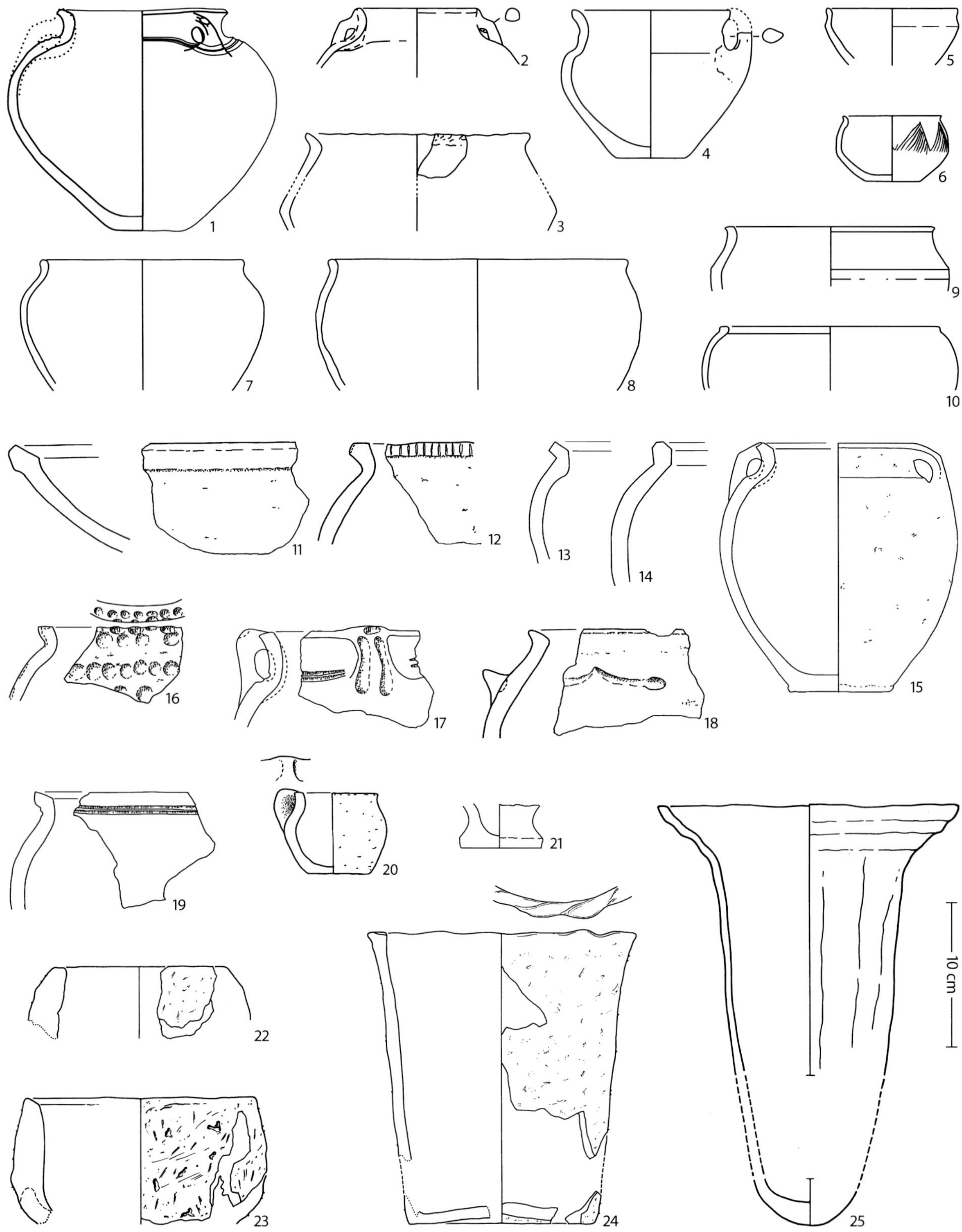

Fig. 6. Handmade pottery dating from the early Roman period found in the central part of the river area (1-21) and sea salt containers from the late Iron Age and the Roman period (22-25). Scale 1:4. 1: Tiel-Passewaaij (after: Heeren 2006); 2-10: Tiel-Medel (after: Habermehl *et al.* 2023); 11-21: Utrecht-Leidsche Rijn (after: Taayke 2009a; 2016); 22-24: Oss-Ussen (after: Van den Broeke 2012): 25: Kesteren-Nedereindsestraat (after: Van den Broeke 1996).

a yet undiscovered rural settlement of northern origin along the Lippe.

An interesting potential effect of a suspected short stay along the Lippe is that a single household in the river area may have contained vessels deriving from three regions made by the same person: a) pottery from the area of origin of the northern migrants that had survived the journey to the Lippe, the short time spent there and the journey to the river area; b) pots traditionally made in the Lippe area and still intact after the journey to the river area; c) pots traditionally made at the new settlement.

This is not to say that the northern style lived on unchanged. Settling in an area with diverse pottery styles that moreover contained an ethnic amalgam will have led to homogenisation of the pottery style, through imitation and possibly also exogamy. This is indeed also evident in the region discussed here (see also Van Kerckhove 2019, 267). The author previously wrote about the pottery from the rural settlement at De Horden in Wijk bij Duurstede studied by Taayke (2002): "The people with a Frisian-like pottery range who settled here around the beginning of the Common Era participated in the ceramic developments known from other parts of the eastern river area at their own pace. Only in the 2nd century did neckless types, including the variants with angular outlines, start to prevail here. In this case we may literally speak of a 'phase difference' in the adoption of pottery elements" (Van den Broeke 2012, 144, translated from Dutch). The term 'Batavisation' could be used for this 'homogenisation' after all, in spite of its (preliminary) rejection above for characterising the developments in pottery observed in the eastern part of the river area after the beginning of the Roman period.

However, this homogenisation in the course of the early Roman period was limited to vessel types and decoration. The average increase in the use of vegetal temper may be regarded as an opposite development. It is no coincidence that this trend is most evident precisely in the central part of the river area, given the observed northern influences. Further east, the proportion of pottery with vegetal temper remained fairly small. In the Nijmegen region and further south it was mostly less than 10%; there, grog remained by far the most popular material for tempering clay.

Other Pottery in the River Area

After the beginning of the Roman period the rural settlements in the entire river area used pottery that had arrived here via the Roman trade and production system, with or without contents (dolia, amphorae, cooking pots, tableware)[12]. In the first decades AD such vessels still constituted a very small proportion of the total amount of pottery, mostly less than 10%, with some exceptions such as Deest-Uiversnest (see above). This proportion steadily increased throughout the early Roman period, but it did vary substantially from one settlement to another. At Kesteren-De Woerd, in the middle of the Betuwe region where occupation can be followed from the beginning of the Common Era until well into the 2nd century, things were very different than in the western part of the Betuwe, where large amounts of Roman ware were used[13]. After the first half of the 1st century, represented by an average of 4% Roman pottery in the features, the proportion did not rise any further than 36% until the first quarter of the 2nd century, and remained stationary at 51% around the middle of the 2nd century (Sier and Koot 2001, 31-34 and appendix 2.2). Even in the rural settlements within the municipality of Nijmegen north of the river Waal the employed amounts of Roman ware were limited. A proportion of 42% (349/833 fragments) can be quoted as an example for a settlement directly opposite Ulpia Noviomagus dating from 50/70-100 (Daniël 2018; Hendriks 2018) In spite of the proximity of the Roman city, where wheelthrown pottery must have been available to the agricultural inhabitants of the land across the Waal, too. Perhaps the occupants of this settlement could not afford the Roman pottery – and its possible contents – due to a lack of means of exchange? Or may we here be observing a desire to preserve traditional values and customs?

Vessels of a completely different character are the – all handmade – containers in which sea salt was supplied from the North Sea coast (Van den Broeke 2012, 155-180). Characteristics of this group are: a) a relatively soft fabric resulting in a chalky or powdery surface; b) a surface colour varying from yellowish white to pale pink and light orange; c) vegetal temper visible in the form of elongated pores. From some point in the 2nd century BC onwards a thick-walled bowl was the dominant type of salt container (fig. 6.22-23). Such bowls were to be found in the rural settlements until the mid-1st century, for example in Nijmegen-Van Boetzelaerstraat (Daniël 2005, fig. 3.14:100/45). This type was succeeded by a more or less cylindrical pot made in the same fabric, almost always crowned with a wavy rim (fig. 6.24; see also Van den Broeke 2014, 52).

In addition to the soft-fired, yellowish salt containers that travelled from the North Sea coast to the interior, sea salt was also supplied from the English Channel

12 This incidentally also included handmade ware, both dolia and various pottery types imported from the south (including 'cork urns').

13 The proposition that handmade pottery was no longer produced in the Betuwe region after 70 (Van Kerckhove 2019, 261) may apply to the western part only. In this respect, the Kromme Rijn area was more similar to the eastern part of the river area (cf. Van Kerckhove 2017, 411).

coast, starting in the Augustan-Tiberian period. This was done in harder, thin-walled pots, mostly orange-red on the outside. These vessels were not of a clearly identifiable type, but a single well-preserved specimen from Kesteren is a round-based, slightly funnel-shaped container (fig. 6.25). Although the distribution pattern initially suggested the territory of the Morini as the area of origin (Van den Broeke 1996), a salt-production site with this pottery was later discovered a little further north, in the territory of the Menapii (Loberge/Looberghe; Donnadieu and Willems 2015, fig. 8; Willems 2014, *e.g.* pl. 2).

Roman-period salt-production sites are only known south of the former Scheldt estuary (Dutch: Oosterschelde), although the coast of Zuid-Holland had certainly also been an important production area until the late Iron Age (Dekoninck 2023)[14]. The aforementioned cylindrical salt containers likewise appear to have been manufactured and filled in the Menapian territory for transport to the interior. Given the substantial proportions of salt containers at several settlements, the salt will have been used for both consumption and preservation of, for example, cheese and meat[15]. A third variant of salt containers produced in the Menapian territory are coarser, orange-red counterparts of the cylindrical containers, but hardly any remains of this type have been found in the river area (Van den Broeke 1996, fig. 6; 2012, fig. 8.3).

Conclusion

From what has been said above it will be clear that the entire river area saw rapid changes in handmade pottery around the beginning of the Common Era. In the central part of this area this development can in part be attributed to the arrival of migrants with a northern background (Frisii, Chauci), though we have no historical evidence to confirm this[16]. Ironically, ceramic evidence for the arrival of the Chatto-Batavians, which is actually documented in historical sources, is less clearly identifiable. It is quite well possible that the greater part of the regionally manufactured pottery was produced by indigenous residual groups of the Eburones. The evolution of an RWG style is not an actual discontinuity in the developments, as can be observed at the rural settlements of Geldermalsen-Hondsgemet and Nijmegen-Van Boetzelaerstraat. It should be noted that angular pottery of a type formally corresponding to Von Uslar 1938, form I (fig. 3.6, 11, 19), was already being produced in phase K, and that this type remained in vogue afterwards (fig. 4.30). At Oss-Ussen, biconical pottery was represented in the single assemblage from phase L (Van den Broeke 2012, pl. 33.5, 11). Furthermore, open dishes and bowls (pot structure type I) were rare from some point in phase K onwards and remained rare for some time into the Roman period, whereas such types were far more common in the trans-Rhenish area (*e.g.* Eggenstein 2003, Roman-period assemblages in Tafel 7-116).

Moreover, the absence of a distinctly identifiable Chatto-Batavian pottery tradition should not be surprising in the case of an assumed arrival of only a male (warrior) elite, not inclined to the manufacture of pottery (cf. Willems 1986, 373). The question whether there are actually any assemblages with Chatto-Batavian pottery in the river area is also motivated by an aspect that has not yet been explicitly discussed above, and that is the material used as temper for the potter's clay. Descriptions of trans-Rhenish pottery from around the beginning of the Common Era suggest that stone grit was often used (Eggenstein 2003, 113; Kyritz 2014, 24 (Kreis Rees)). This was also the case with one of the few published early Roman assemblages from the east of the Netherlands, *i.e.* Aalten-De Heurne (Hulst 1981), where about a quarter of the handmade pottery was tempered with stone grit, mostly quartz, in the first half of the 1st century. Only exceptional finds of pottery tempered with stone grit are on the contrary known from the entire river area, where grog and vegetal temper were the only frequently used materials, with the fine sand observed in the pottery presumably naturally present in the employed clay. The pottery of the remarkable assemblage of Deest also contains grog and sand (Van Bergen *et al.* 2008, 15). Early Roman pottery assemblages from the eastern part of the river area definitely also deserve an archaeometric approach of the kind that Van Kerckhove and colleagues applied to pottery from the central part of this area (see above)[17]. And in view of the results of this research, it is advisable

14 However, some fragments of *briquetage* rods are known from two Roman-period rural settlements: Poeldijk and De Lier (De Bruin 2017, 273). The settlement context suggests refining rather than the production of sea salt.

15 On the other hand, the number of *briquetage* vessel fragments found in the military camp on the Kops Plateau in Nijmegen is so small as to suggest that salt was also supplied in bulk or contained in perishable materials such as leather bags or wooden barrels (Van den Broeke 2014, 53). The Augustan legionary camp on the Hunerberg seems to have yielded an even smaller proportion of *briquetage* vessels (documentation of the author and E. Stoffels), while no pottery of this kind whatsoever is known from the Roman fortifications at Vechten (Stoop-Greijer 2012, 179).

16 Pliny the Elder (*Naturalis Historia* IV.101) mentions Chauci between the Helinium and Flevum, outside the island of the Batavi (and Cananefates). This may be a mistake, but now that the Chaucian component of the pottery in the Leidsche Rijn area has been recognised, it may be considered whether the area between Oude Rijn and Vecht is meant (see fig. 1).

17 Roman-period handmade pottery from Oss-Ussen has also been subjected to thin-section, XRF and XRD analyses and refiring, but the samples in question dated from the middle Roman period, and not the early Roman period (Van den Broeke 2012, 183-186).

to avoid the term, 'origins', in purely macroscopic studies of pottery, and to use the terms 'style' and 'tradition' (*e.g.* regional or northern style/tradition) instead[18].

18 I thank Joep Hendriks and Julie Van Kerckhove for comments on a previous version of this contribution. I am grateful to Bertil van Os, Eef Stoffels, Julie Van Kerckhove and Wijnand van der Sanden for providing illustration and spreadsheet files. Susan Mellor corrected the English text. The final layout of the illustrations was done by *Rob Mols foto/grafisch*.

Meanwhile, in the North… Handmade Pottery beyond the Roman Frontier

Ernst Taayke

Abstract[1]

During the early Roman period three styles of handmade pottery can be distinguished in the north of the Netherlands. Around the start of the Common Era Frisian pottery was dominant in the coastal area, but in the 1st century residents of the salt marshes of the province of Groningen adopted the style of their neighbours in Niedersachsen, the Chauci. The inhabitants of today's eastern Dutch provinces Drenthe, Overijssel and Gelderland, on the other hand, showed a preference for pottery of the Rhine-Weser Germanic culture as defined by Von Uslar. In the next centuries influence from northern Niedersachsen in the form of *Nordseeküstennahe Keramik* steadily grew. After 250 the coastal areas were gradually depopulated, but the tide turned around 400 when new settlers, again with eastern roots, established themselves on some of the former terps, bringing with them Anglo-Saxon pottery. In the meantime, the (Frankish) eastern regions prospered, partly as a side effect of a war economy in which fighting against the Romans and trading with them went hand in hand. Around 500 all earlier pottery styles were swept away, almost as if a ban had been issued on well-finished and decorated pots. In much of what is today the Netherlands the saggy *Hessens-Schortens ware* became the standard, although residents of the coastal areas began to prefer wheelthrown pottery in the form of Merovingian coarse ware.

Introduction

Before the arrival of the Romans only handmade pottery was used in the Netherlands. Production took place locally in small communities, by women – or so we assume. Pottery manufacture appears to have been low status. Preparation of the clay matrix, forms of tempering, shaping, and finishing, decoration, and firing – all these steps were probably based on regional customs and rules. As such, this had a conservative effect, but women often came from elsewhere, bringing slightly different customs with them. Pottery was therefore always changing, but these small changes did not greatly affect the overall result, at least viewed from a distance of twenty centuries. One handful of sherds in a pit may

1 Translation: Gerre van der Kleij.

in: R.C.A. Geerts and Ph. Bes (eds) 2024, *Roman Pottery in the Low Countries: Past Research, Current State, Future Directions*. Leiden: Sidestone Press (= *Papers on Archaeology of the Leiden Museum of Antiquities Leiden* 32), pp. 47-58.

Fig. 1. Distribution of Frisian pottery at the end of the late Iron Age (image: E. Taayke).

not be diagnostic, but studying fragments and pots from hundreds of different findspots in a region will reveal similarities, and recurring combinations of tempering, shapes and decorations may help to loosely define pottery styles that were en vogue for one or two centuries. Apparently, communities were not autonomous islands but stayed connected in a much wider landscape encompassing tens of thousands of square km.

This article looks at handmade pottery produced beyond the Roman limes in what is today the Netherlands, during a period of six centuries from approximately the start of the Common Era to the 6th century, when traditional, geographically limited pottery styles came to an end.

The Beginning of the Common Era/1st Century

Towards the end of the late Iron Age one pottery style in particular stands out in the northern part of the Netherlands, that of the Frisians. Where these people lived, apart from the modern province of Friesland, is not a settled matter, but their pottery can be found from Zuid-Holland and Utrecht to Groningen, and as far east as Niedersachsen in Germany (fig. 1).

Characteristic of pottery in the coastal area in general is a tripartite profile (body/shoulder/neck) and a fabric that is tempered with grit or organic material. What catches the eye in the Frisian style is the appearance of a so-called *streepband* ornament, consisting of two to four grooves made with a serrated, presumably bone object, on the transition from neck to shoulder (fig. 2). This ornament was used between *c.* 200 BC and AD 50. The pottery was well finished and sometimes shows strikingly bright orange or ochre colours.

Most finds come from Friesland, Groningen, and Noord-Holland, but the distribution extends from the German coastal plain to the province of Utrecht and the Betuwe region. Recent research shows that the appearance of stylistically identifiable pottery does not necessarily imply a specific origin and identity of the manufacturers. According to petrographic analysis 'Frisian' *streepband* pottery found near the Dutch town

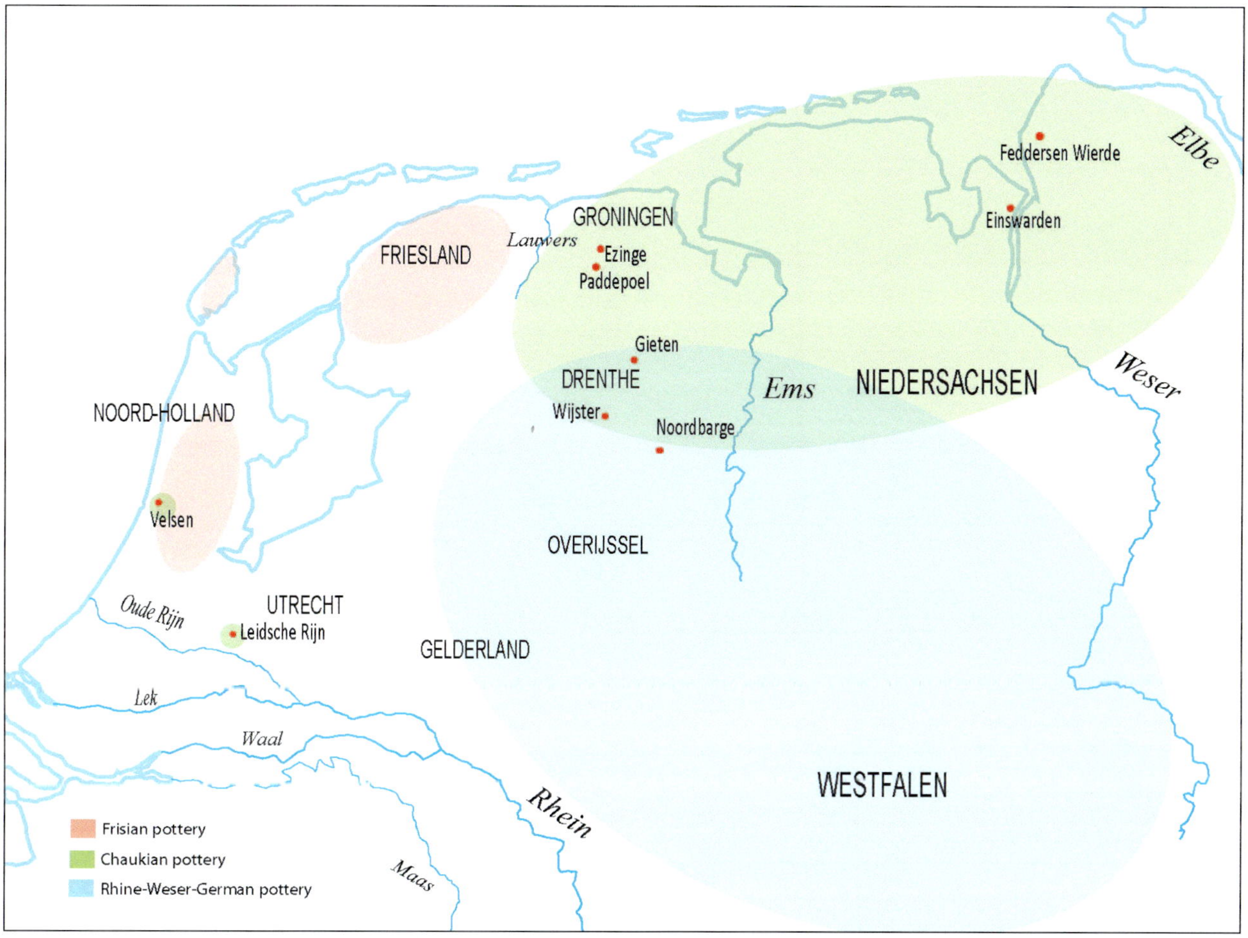

Fig. 3. Pottery groups in the 1st century (image: E. Taayke).

of Tiel in the central river area actually originated in the German Lippe area (Westfalen)[2].

In the year 12 BC the Roman general Drusus sailed with a fleet along the Dutch coast up to the rivers Ems and Weser and besieged the island of Burcana, now vanished, near Juist. A *praesidium*, a type of outpost, was established on the Ems (Amisia), against the Chauci and Amsivarii in particular. The former tribe lived on the coast, roughly between the rivers Ems and Elbe, the latter further inland, near the Ems. Up to sixteen several more expeditions took place, by sea or by land, all intended to control the Weser-Elbe area. But no matter how much effort was invested into this enterprise over the years, involving several legions, the ultimate goal of establishing the Elbe as the northern border of the Roman Empire was never achieved. In 47 all actions were called off.

Fig. 2. Frisian *Streepband* pottery (image: E. Taayke).

2 Information presented by Julie Van Kerckhove at a lecture at the RCE Amersfoort, June 2023. See Habermehl *et al.* in press; also see the contribution by Van den Broeke in this volume.

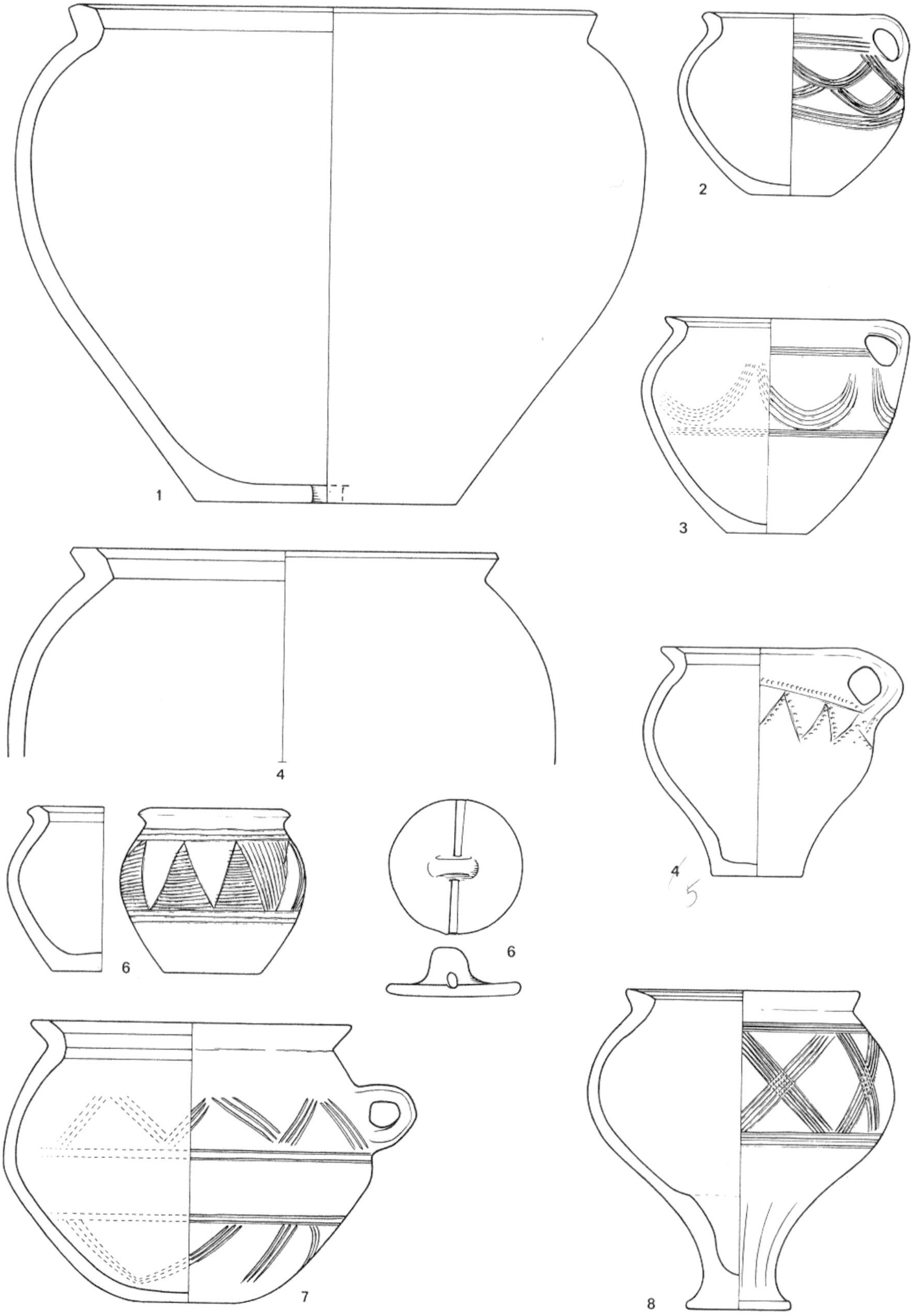

Fig. 4. Chaucian pottery, province of Groningen (after: Van Es 1968).

What the Romans did succeed in, unintentionally, was to present a role model. The appearance of the first Roman ships in 12 BC must have made a crushing impression on the Chauci. How remarkable those men looked, in their glittering attire! They must have looked like Martians, perhaps they even shouted "We come in peace!"[3]. Historically the Chauci are known to have been subjugated twice, in 12 BC and AD 5, but unlike the Frisians they did not become *foederati* and no taxes were imposed on them. They simply lived too far away.

The actions of the Romans awoke something in Chaucian minds, I imagine, which earlier had lain dormant as a vague notion: that perhaps this was an example worth following. Why not start a conquest of their own? Three Chaucian attacks in those early days are documented. Two of these assaults, along the North Sea coast, were described as acts of 'piracy' (in 41 and 47), the third mention involved an attack on territory of the Amsivarii. However, archaeological data show that the Chauci also cast their eyes on their western neighbours who lived in the Groningen salt marsh area (fig. 3). In the first half of the 1st century the Frisian pottery style in this region was replaced by neckless pottery with thick faceted rims, exactly the same type as what was used in the Ems-Weser-Elbe area (Taayke 1996); Schmid (1981) presents a, now slightly dated, overview of 'Chaucian' archaeology, while historical evidence is summed up by Rosenplänter (2010). Particularly conspicuous are the dark polished cups, often decorated with geometric motifs (fig. 4) (see Schmid 1958; 2006)[4]. Most radiocarbon dates from Groningen sites point to the first half of the 1st century.

There are no signs of a violent turnover, and pottery assemblages (*e.g.* at Paddepoel, near the city of Groningen) (Van Es 1968) show that the two styles coexisted for some time. In addition to this stylistic shift, the number of marsh settlements increased considerably and in newly habitable parts of the salt marshes the Chauci style was the only one to be seen. This population increase cannot be explained solely by natural factors, thus suggesting an influx from other regions.

Shortly before or perhaps around the start of the Christian Era, contacts must have existed between the Chauci's core area and what is today the province of Groningen. At Feddersen Wierde, a terp east of the river Weser, hundreds of fragments of Groningen pottery were retrieved of a mixture of pottery types, both the old and the new style (Schmid (2006, 26-27, Tafel 9-11)[5]. Some Groningen pottery was also found in Einswarden, on the west bank of the river Weser (Schmid 1965, 33, fig. 24.3; 2006, 27). These data point to an interaction between the Groningen and Weser-Elbe regions, rather than one-way traffic.

The north of Drenthe offers another example of the contributions of regional pottery research. Three fortifications have been discovered near the villages of Zeijen and Vries. Although their actual function (storage places, outposts, or sanctuaries?) remains uncertain, again a change is observable from distinctly Frisian pottery to Chauci shapes. Waterbolk dated the fortifications to the late Iron Age, but it seems that most of the activity there took place in the first half of the 1st century (Waterbolk 1977; Taayke 1996).

The Chauci, or related peoples, did not stop there. Recently it was established that they may have resided in Noord-Holland as well, particularly the area near the port of Velsen (Flevum) and the area of Assendelver Polders (Het Hain) (Nieuwhof and Diederik 2023). Two decades ago, the present author studied handmade pottery from various excavations in the municipality of Utrecht. Most of it was local pottery from the late Iron Age and the early Roman period, but it came as a great surprise when the excavations at Leidsche Rijn 41-42, along a creek just north of the Rhine, produced hundreds of kilos of pottery closely resembling Groningen or Chaucian wares (Taayke 2009a; 2017). Shortly after that, comparable pottery was found at a nearby site, also within the limes, next to the vicus of castellum De Woerd (Taayke 2009b; 2010a). The relatively sharp dates of Roman pottery and metal objects suggest that these indigenous sites were inhabited between 15/20 and 45/50. Their abandonment roughly coincided with the Roman decision to make the Rhine the definitive border and for that reason to remove native settlements from the immediate border zone.

Rhine-Weser Germanic Pottery

Hesse, in the west of Germany, is considered the area of origin of the Batavians, but its name is also linked to a later exodus of an essentially (to us) nameless people. It was Von Uslar who before the Second World War cast their characteristic pottery types into a powerful archaeological framework, that of the Rhine-Weser Germanic culture (RWG) (Von Uslar 1938). Von Uslar's main types, forms I-VI, still prove useful to describe finds from a large area, in this case from the rivers Rhine and Main to the lower reaches of the Weser (see Nösler 2013 for the Weser estuary).

The style is also prominent in the east of the Netherlands, in the provinces of Overijssel and Gelderland (fig. 3). The pottery produced there around the early 1st century featured rather undefined shapes comprising simple bowls, dishes, and cooking pots with a

3 From the movie Mars attacks! (1996), directed and produced by Tim Burton.

4 The most common decoration is known as *Briefkuvertmuster*.

5 Mentioning 363 *streepband* fragments; in fact, however, the assemblage is a mixture of Groningen Gw4 (some with long necks), neckless Groningen Gw5-like vessels, and V4 (impressions against the rim).

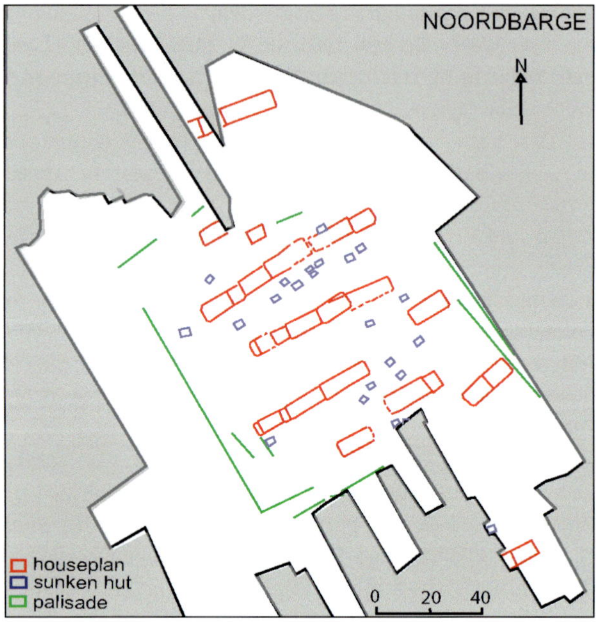

Fig. 5. Noordbarge, 1st-century settlement (after: Harsema 1976; Waterbolk 2009).

rounded profile. Somewhere around the mid-1st century a striking angular shape was added, Von Uslar form I, as was a wall decoration of nail impressions and small polished dimples (*Hammerschlag*).

The site Denekamp-de Borchert (Overijssel) has yielded good specimens of RWG pottery from the 1st and 2nd century (Verniers 2011), but the most striking example of an early RWG settlement comes from the province of Drenthe. At Noordbarge, near Emmen, a large amount of RWG pottery was found near and inside houses with wall trenches and in the infill of numerous sunken huts. The houses appear to have been frequently rebuilt. Both the house type and the sunken huts were new introductions at that time (fig. 5), and the site was surrounded by a palisade, also a new phenomenon (Harsema 1976; Taayke in prep.). The inhabitants evidently came from elsewhere. Re-evaluation of the large-scale excavations at Wijster (also Drenthe) likewise revealed a significant 1st-century RWG component (Van Es 1967; in prep.). A two-period house plan near Gieten yielded northern/Chaucian pottery but the second phase contained mainly RWG pottery (Taayke 2010b).

Coastal Area, 2nd-3rd Century

In the 2nd century, an outside visitor would notice two pottery styles in the salt marsh area (fig. 6). East of the river Lauwers he would see vessels which we today in neutral terms classify as *Nordseeküstennahe Keramik* (NNK) (Von Uslar 1977). These wares consisted of cooking and storage pots with protruding necks, wide-mouthed cups occasionally decorated with a geometric motif, and narrow-mouthed slender vessels with handles on the shoulder. In most instances the finish testifies to the fact that the makers aimed for high quality. In fact, the NNK style was the successor of the 'Chauci' pottery mentioned above, but from the 2nd century onwards that label is no longer very useful[6]. The style was common in Groningen, as before, but now it was also popular in the province of Drenthe.

West of the river Lauwers and a peat marsh zone our outside visitor would enter Frisian territory, which reached all the way down to the point where the river Oude Rijn flowed into the North Sea. In the 2nd and part of the 3rd century, Frisian pottery flourished – in this case, ethnic labelling is apparently not an issue among scholars. It is characterised by wide-mouthed and narrow-mouthed vessels with fairly short protruding necks, and fabrics that are usually tempered with organic material. Larger, wide-mouthed specimens are often decorated with impressions against the rim, and the wavy character of that decoration has led to the name *kartelrand* ware. Cooking pots without rim decoration were often provided with handles. Wall decoration is absent.

Besides daily wares, glossy black pots appeared, often with handles and always undecorated. The most conspicuous shapes are rounded cups, often on a narrow stand. At the base of their development stands a flat-based biconical cup with a glossy black finish, which at the end of the 1st century suddenly appeared both in Groningen and Friesland. This characteristic type appears to have come out of the blue, as it has no connection with indigenous shapes. However, there might be a link with Batavian pottery.

The Frisian style began to display a certain elegance, expressed in rim shapes that resembled those of Roman pottery (Niederbieber 89, Low Lands ware). Some narrow-mouthed pots were extremely slender with drawn-out handles (fig. 7). In Noord-Holland, dark pottery sometimes received a decorative 'mouse-teeth' row on the shoulder, a characteristic also encountered on Frisian pottery found across the North Sea, at Hadrian's Wall (Peters 2003).

As quickly as RWG pottery had reached Drenthe it left again, giving way to the NNK style. In the 2nd and 3rd centuries, RWG pottery was seldom used. Further to the south, however, the situation was totally different. In Overijssel and Gelderland RWG pottery became the norm and remained in use there until the 5th century (Van Es *et al.* 1985; Taayke *et al.* 2012; Taayke 2013). In the 2nd and 3rd century it was often abundantly

6 The Chauci are once mentioned in the 2nd century in connection with a raid on the Belgian coast; after that they presumably merged into/with the Saxons.

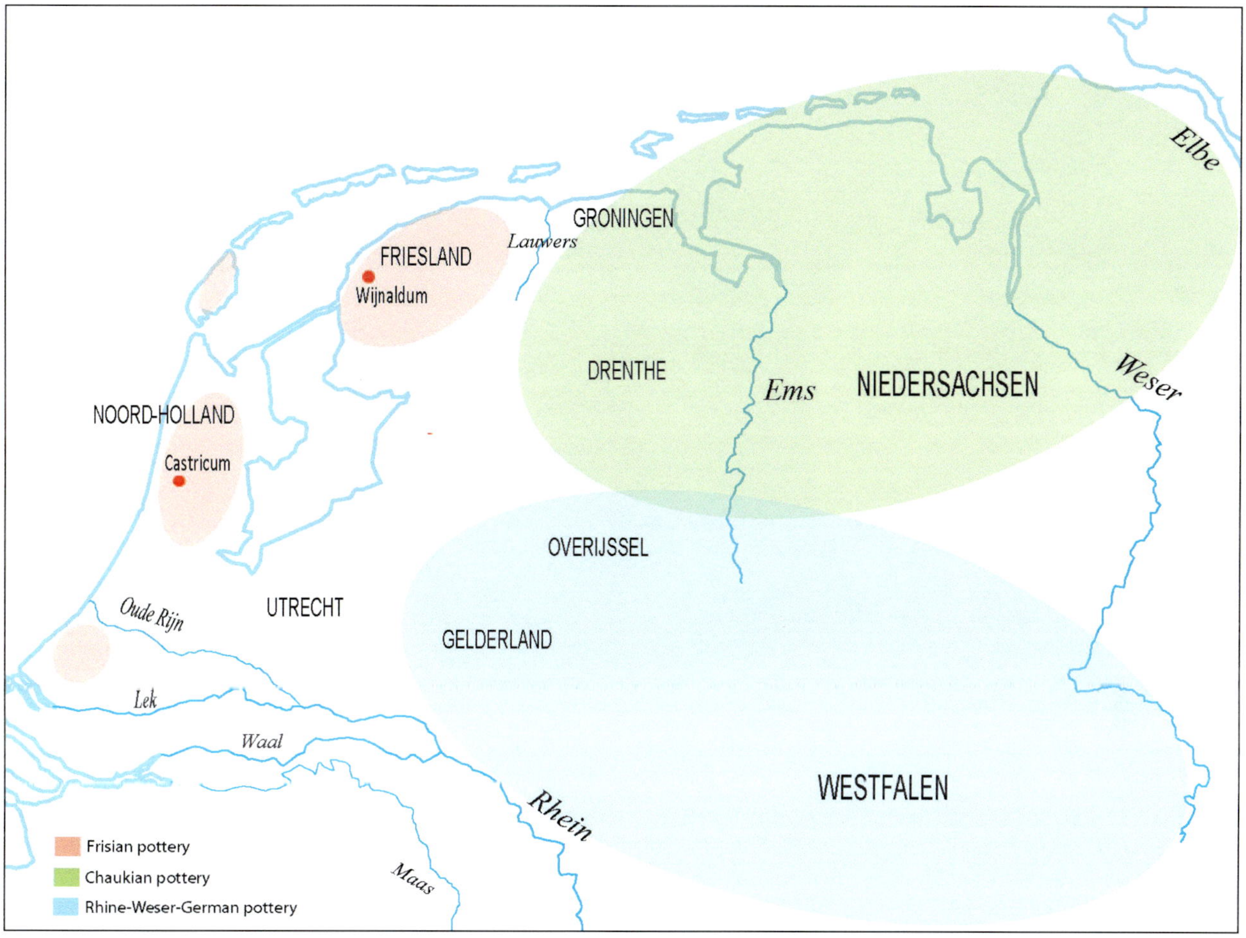

Fig. 6. Pottery styles, 2nd-3rd centuries (image: E. Taayke).

decorated with combinations of impressions and lines. Another striking decoration type was an overall pattern of embossing known as *Warzen*. Handles only occur on narrow-mouthed pots, adopted from the northern repertoire.

The show piece of the RWG style is Von Uslar form II, a cup with a high vertical neck and often on a hollow foot (fig. 8). In Von Uslar's time, the material he studied consisted almost exclusively of burial assemblages, where this type was predominant. Von Uslar dated the type to roughly between 150 and 250, attaching too much importance to finds from the castellum of Niederbieber, which was destroyed around 260. Later settlement studies made clear that the type in fact continued in use up to the 4th century (see *e.g.* Halpaap 1994).

Transition Period (*c.* 250-325)

In the course of the 3rd century the coastal area became gradually depopulated, from west to east. At first the process mainly affected low-lying areas, but social unrest ('piracy' and the first attacks on the limes) probably also played a part. Disintegration eventually followed. In Frisian pottery this is visible in two ways. Up to that point, pottery had been tempered with organic material. Suddenly, however, in the mid-3rd century, grog or coarse shell grit was added to the matrix, and at the same time the finish of the vessels received much less attention. The other aspect was that the Frisian style was sacrificed. The residents of the few terps that remained settled till the start of the 4th century (fig. 9), such as Wijnaldum, now preferred the NNK style of their eastern neighbours: the sturdy RWG vessels with long protruding necks, or wide-mouthed cups, often tempered with stone grit (Taayke 2020a). Interestingly, these handmade products were sometimes accompanied by wheelthrown cups of Low Lands ware quality (cf. Bloemers 1978, especially type III)[7].

7 In their shape, size and firing these cups clearly differ from the *terra nigra* cups that became popular in the eastern Netherlands some decades later.

Fig. 7. Frisian narrow-mouthed pots from the 3rd century (image: E. Taayke).

Fig. 8. Example of a late Von Uslar form II cup. Traces of burning; missing foot. From a 4th-century cemetery at Zweelo (Drenthe) (image: E. Taayke).

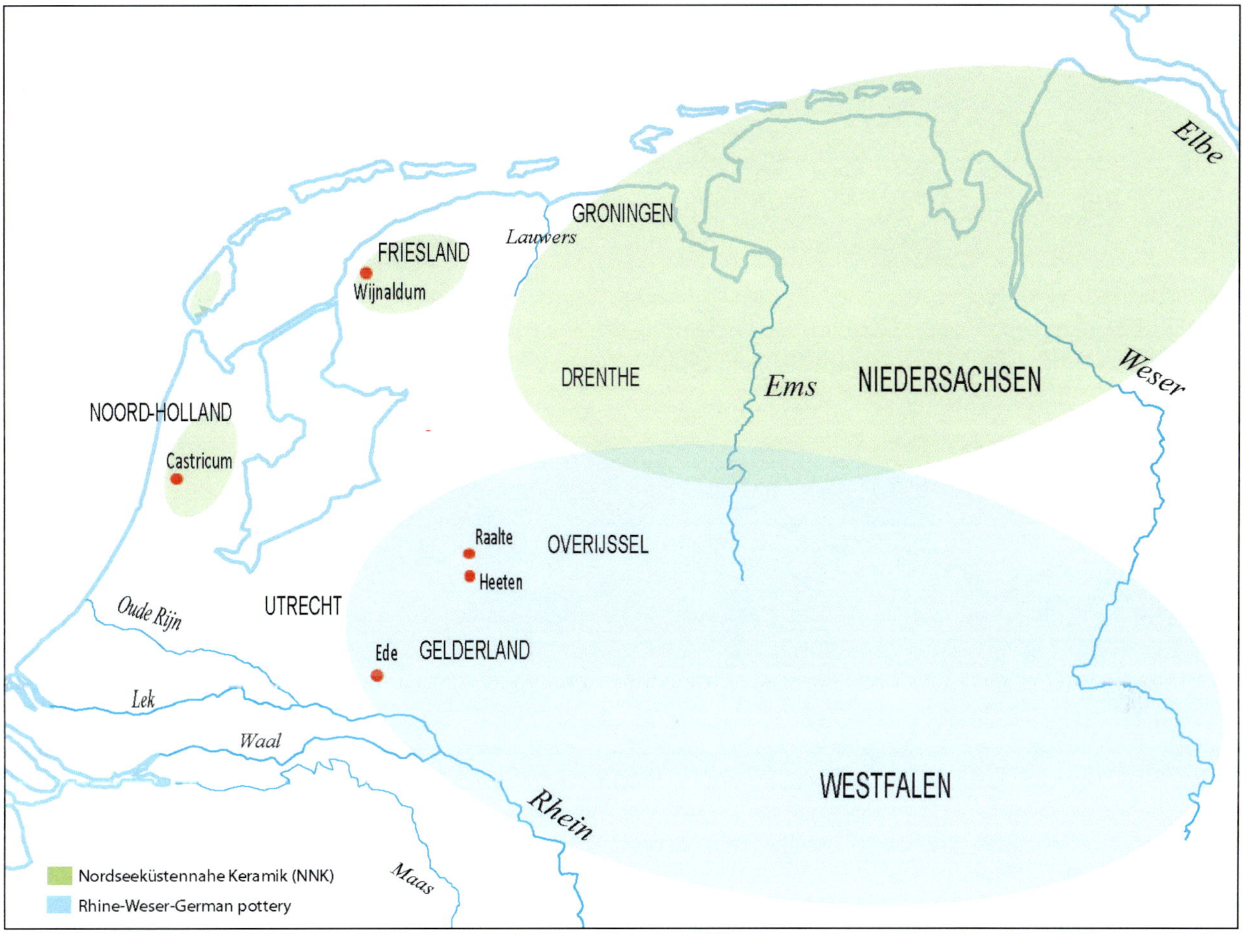

Fig. 9. Pottery styles at the beginning of the 4th century (image: E. Taayke).

Two Worlds/Migration Period (325-500)

By the mid-4th century, the difference between the coast and the Pleistocene areas could not have been greater. The salt marshes were virtually deserted – even a settlement on the Pleistocene island of Texel was abandoned – while at the same time the *Hinterland* was buzzing with activity. A few northern coastal settlements managed to survive, of which Ezinge is the clearest example (Nieuwhof 2013). In Noord-Holland, 4th century pottery has been found at Castricum and Uitgeest-Dorregeest, but it hardly resembles pottery in the north (Nieuwhof and Diederik 2023). Contact between both areas seems to have become sparse.

At the same time, however, many, often large settlements with impressive farmhouses could be found in the sandy east of the Netherlands. Cattle and arable farming were both important there. The 4th century was a time of prosperity; populations benefited from the war economy by fighting the Romans while feeding them at the same time. Franks they were called now, or some of them Saxons. Handmade pottery was carefully shaped and finished (fig. 10). Wheelthrown pottery played a modest part, with the exception of *terra nigra* cups. The same picture can be observed in Drenthe (including Wijster), Overijssel (including Heeten and Raalte) (Van der Velde 2007) and Gelderland (including Bennekom, Ede-Veldhuizen; (Bennekom: Van Es *et al.* 1985; Ede: Taayke *et al.* 2012). On a small scale, Frankish pottery can also be found in Roman territory (see Taayke *et al.* 2003).

Around the mid-4th century pots with long protruding necks were still being produced in the north, but in cooking and storage pots as well as drinking cups there was a growing tendency towards S-shaped profiles. The 4th/5th-century RWG pottery reflected these changes. Angular shapes and bowls made way for tripartite forms with an S-shaped profile. The role of the Von Uslar form II cup was now taken over by *terra nigra* cups (Gellep 273, cf. Pirling 1974). Pottery decoration declined sharply. Line decoration disappeared and many later cooking pots only have impressions against the rim and in a row on the greatest diameter[8].

8 Cf. sites in Overijssel and Gelderland, but also in Westfalen (*e.g.* around Dortmund/Bochum).

Fig. 10. Deposit at Wachtum (province of Drenthe), mid-4th century. The storage pot contained the five smaller vessels (image: H. Faber Bulthuis).

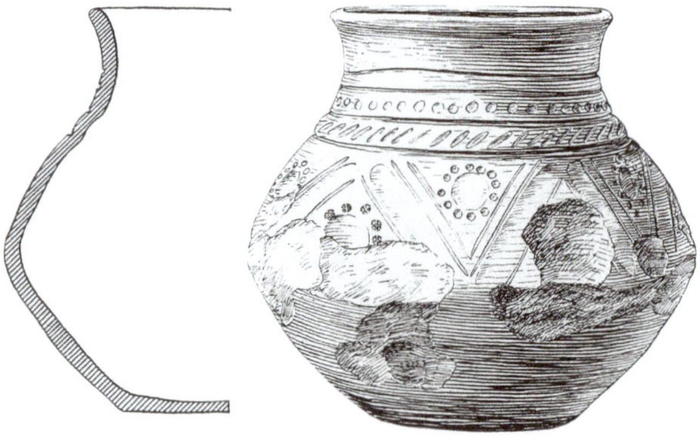

Fig. 11. Anglo-Saxon urn (1856-IV.3), late 4th century, from the cemetery at Midlaren (pencil drawing: J. Ypey).

In the course of the 4th century people in northern Niedersachsen gradually adopted the pottery customs of Jutland and Schleswig-Holstein, as expressed in lavish decorations of horizontal, vertical, and diagonal groove lines and ribs, alternating with small and large impressions. In time, Drenthe was also reached as is manifest in an urnfield (in itself a new tradition) near Midlaren (fig. 11). The new style is called Anglo-Saxon, although the term should not be taken too literally[9]. There are no signs of migration into Drenthe, although individual east-west traffic will certainly have occurred. Anglo-Saxon decorated pottery seems only a minor addition to the 'normal' domestic repertoire of pots and cups. Compared to the second half of the 4th century, the shapes of the 5th-century domestic repertoire did not really change but the finish slowly deteriorated[10]. Further south, in Overijssel and Gelderland, Anglo-Saxon pottery is nearly absent.

The coastal area was resettled in the course of the 5th century (fig. 12), albeit on a modest scale. In this case, immigration is evident. Groups of people ('Angles, Saxons, Jutes') from the Weser-Elbe area settled in England[11], but some apparently preferred the salt marshes of Friesland and Groningen and descended on

9 Angles, situated in Schleswig, played no part in the move to the northern Netherlands.

10 The outside is still smooth, but the inside occasionally shows traces of coarse scraping.

11 This crossing is usually dated to around 450.

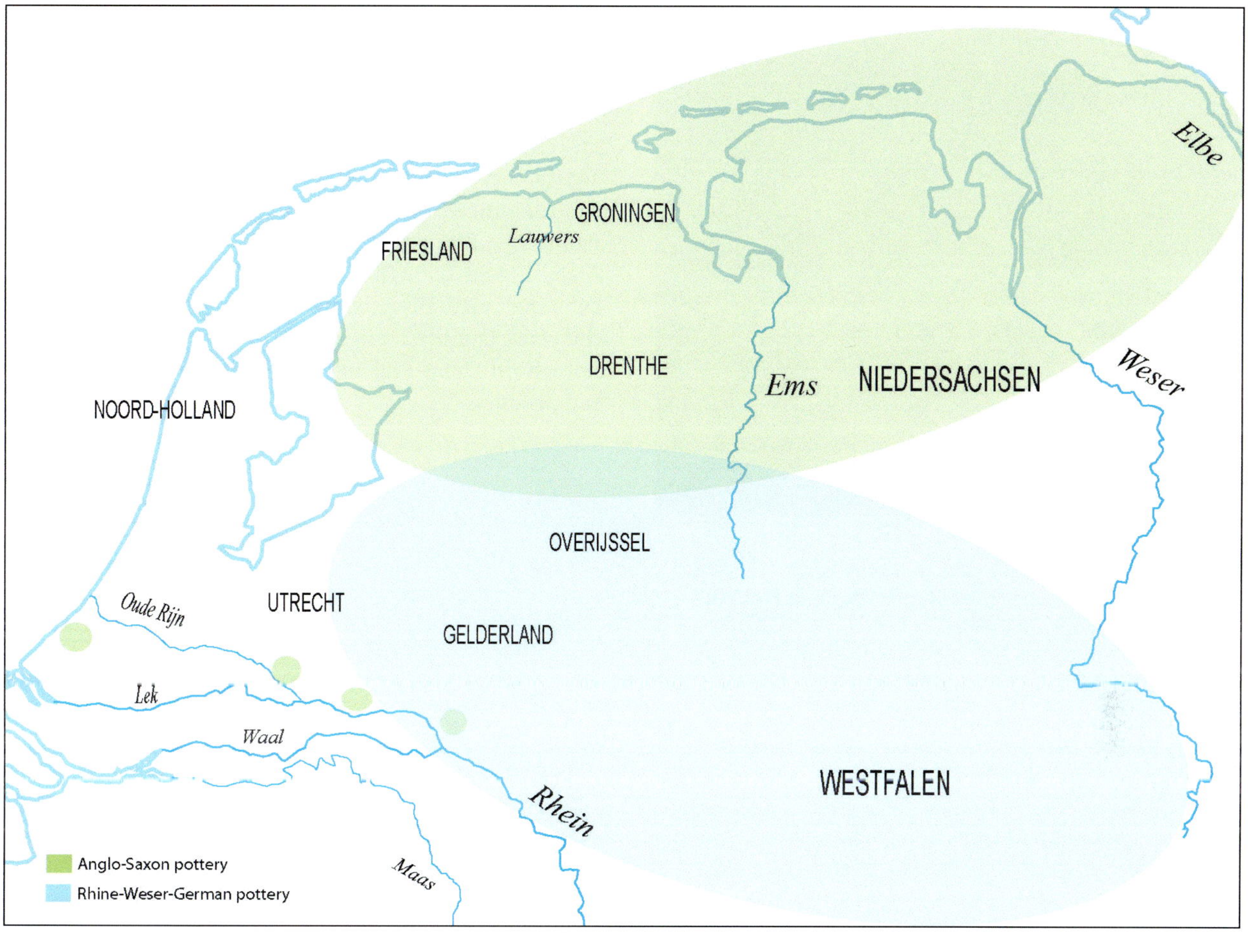

Fig. 12. Pottery groups of the Migration period (image: E. Taayke).

abandoned terps. They, too, largely produced undecorated pottery (Taayke 2020b)[12].

To date, Anglo-Saxon sherds are absent from Noord-Holland although metal finds (hairpins of the Wijster type, for example) do indicate some form of habitation. But the new style would eventually reach Zuid-Holland, albeit at a slightly later stage[13]. Finds from cemeteries near the Rhine[14] indicate that Anglo-Saxon migrants followed this river upstream. Further north, this type of pottery is absent.

The area of origin of migrant pottery found in Roman territory can only be established for 4th-century finds, and even then only broadly. By the 5th century all distinguishing features seem to have disappeared into a melting pot. An example are finds from Gennep, in Limburg, where Saxon and Frankish/RWG features can only be distinguished by applying a large dose of imagination (Schotten 1991; Verhoeven 2003; pers. obs.).

End of an Era

An unbroken pottery tradition had existed since the early Iron Age. Pottery production had been a craft in which pottery-making women, local, regional, and chronological differences notwithstanding, had always more or less consciously acted from a belief in continuity, expressed in shape and decoration as well as function (in multiple senses). Remarkably, some pots from the Migration period are hardly distinguishable from vessels made 40 generations earlier.

Around 500 this tradition was swept away, as if beauty had suddenly been banished, to be replaced by a domestic assemblage of shapeless, unfinished, and undecorated pots (fig. 13). In most cases these vessels are tempered with stone grit, but organic temper is also widespread (Taayke 2023). The type, named after the German

12 A find distribution, with emphasis on decorated pottery, is presented by Knol (1993).

13 Finds from the cemeteries of Rijnsburg and Monster. The Anglo-Saxon pottery dates to the 6th century.

14 Rhenen, Wageningen, Elst-'t Woud and Groessen.

Fig. 13. Sherds of Hessens-Schortens-type ware, and a rim fragment of coarse wheelthrown pottery. Finds from the terp Tritsum (image: E. Taayke).

terps Hessens and Schortens, became prominent in northwestern Germany, the Netherlands and England[15], both in coastal areas and in the Pleistocene *Hinterland*. Regional style groups no longer existed, and therefore an illustrative map is no longer needed. Moreover, the coastal areas from the 6th century onwards showed a pronounced preference for wheelthrown pottery from the Rhineland, especially coarse vessels like Alzey 27 and 32/33 (De Koning 2023). These latter wares remained virtually unknown at a greater distance from the coast and the main rivers, or perhaps people could not afford them and had to make do with their own sad products.

15 Anglo-Saxon decorated pottery persisted in England for quite some time.

A Cherished Material. Terra Sigillata from the Province of Groningen

Annet Nieuwhof

Abstract

This paper presents the results of an inventory of the terra sigillata finds in the province of Groningen, which includes all red or reddish pottery of Roman origin, also Arretine terra sigillata, late Argonne ware, Oxfordshire red/brown-slipped ware, and African Red Slip Ware. A total of 585 fragments were recorded, belonging to a Minimum Number of 458 vessels. Most finds come from terps in the former salt marsh region along the coast. The southern part of the province was overgrown with peat during the Roman period and largely uninhabitable. The distribution of the 585 fragments across the terps is not only representative of their occurrence during the Roman period, but also of the activities of A.E. van Giffen.

Three phases can be distinguished in this material: phase 1, dated between 12 BC and 47 when the northern Netherlands were formally part of the Roman Empire, is represented by only a few fragments. Most terra sigillata finds belong to phase 2, the 2nd and 3rd centuries. Phase 3, the 4th and 5th centuries, is characterised by late Argonne ware and African Red Slip Ware, which is virtually absent elsewhere in the Netherlands. Nearly all the finds from this phase are from Ezinge, one of the few inhabited terps in the northern Netherlands during the 4th century. Approximately 80% of the terra sigillata from phases 1 and 2 shows traces of a particular form of secondary use. This use must be related to a symbolic meaning ascribed to the material, probably because of its colour. This paper discusses the meaning of this secondary use of terra sigillata.

Keywords: terra sigillata; African Red Slip Ware; northern Netherlands; province of Groningen; symbolic use

Introduction

The year 2011 saw the start of a research project that was aimed at the analysis of the finds found during the excavations of the terp of Ezinge (a *terp* is an artificial dwelling mound) in the Dutch province of Groningen, conducted by Albert E. van Giffen

in: R.C.A. Geerts and Ph. Bes (eds) 2024, *Roman Pottery in the Low Countries: Past Research, Current State, Future Directions*. Leiden: Sidestone Press (= *Papers on Archaeology of the Leiden Museum of Antiquities Leiden* 32), pp. 59-74.

between 1923 and 1934[1]. This famous site has become a type site for northwest-European pre-Roman and Roman Iron Age settlements, but the finds and features were never published in full. The analysis focused on the main find categories: animal bones, human remains, metal and stone artefacts, beads, handmade pottery, Roman pottery, especially terra sigillata, and early medieval wheelthrown pottery (all published in Nieuwhof 2014). Terra sigillata and a very small number of other Roman potsherds were analysed by Tineke Volkers, who had been studying terra sigillata in the northern Netherlands since the early 1990s.

When I was collecting the material for the various specialists in the *Northern Archaeological Depot* (*Noordelijk Archeologisch Depot*, or NAD) in Nuis, I already noticed that terra sigillata differed from handmade pottery (which I studied myself) by the fairly small sizes of the sherds, the many traces of processing, and the near absence of complete or restorable vessels. This fitted my emerging ideas about the importance and meaning of fragmentation in rituals and ritualised behaviour in the pre-Roman and Roman Iron Age in this area (Nieuwhof 2015). Tineke Volkers appeared to have noticed the same features; not only were many fragments made into objects such as pendants and playing counters, but many more objects showed traces of processing such as deliberate breakage, cutting, chopping, pecking, abrading, or rounding. Together we published our ideas on the use of terra sigillata in the northern Netherlands, questioning the use of terra sigillata in this area as luxury tableware, instead arguing that it might have been imported into this area in the form of sherds, which were appreciated for the symbolic meaning of the material itself (Nieuwhof and Volkers 2015).

As more evidence was needed, Tineke decided to continue her analysis on the terra sigillata finds from the northern Netherlands, publishing the vast terra sigillata assemblage (2264 fragments) from the province of Friesland (Volkers 2015/2016 (including a contribution on the potters' stamps by Rien Polak); 2017). We both continued working on the subject. For instance, in a second, more extensive paper on the use of terra sigillata in the north, several sites and regions were compared, and the way this material arrived in the northern Netherlands was investigated (Nieuwhof 2020a). Tineke started to analyse the terra sigillata from the province of Groningen in addition to the Ezinge material, but also conducted small studies on other assemblages. In April 2019, for instance, she emailed me enthusiastically that she had also found traces of secondary use on a sherd from a rural settlement in Bemmel, north of the river Waal near Nijmegen, on the Roman side of the limes (Veenstra and Volkers 2020). Her future plans included not only publishing the terra sigillata assemblages from the Dutch provinces of Groningen, Drenthe, and Noord-Holland but also from Niedersachsen in Germany and comparing this material with terra sigillata finds from rural, indigenous settlements on the Roman side of the limes. Unfortunately, her declining health kept her from completing this ambitious research programme. When Tineke passed away in 2022, at the age of 79, her Groningen research was left unfinished. This contribution is dedicated to her memory.

As we had cooperated on this subject for a long time, Tineke had given me her incomplete Groningen database for safekeeping. I have since attempted to complete her inventory and analysis. In this contribution, the results are summarised[2]. In what follows, the history of terra sigillata research in the northern Netherlands will first be discussed, then the constituent parts of the inventory of the terra sigillata in Groningen. Tineke's research questions are leading in the discussion of the inventory: what forms were used and what was the origin of the material? How are they dated and how and when did this material come to the area? And what can we say about primary and secondary use of the terra sigillata?

The History of Terra Sigillata Research in the Northern Netherlands

For a proper understanding of the data, it is necessary to elaborate on the research history of the province of Groningen and the terp region in general. The southern part of the province is a Pleistocene area, that until after the Middle Ages was covered with peat (fig. 1). It was largely uninhabited during the Roman period. The northern part is a former salt marsh area, and until it was diked during the Middle Ages, it was open to the sea and therefore flooded regularly. Nevertheless, it was a quite densely populated and prospering area. Habitation was possible on artificial dwelling mounds or terps (Nieuwhof *et al.* 2019). Around 500 terps were inhabited in Groningen during the Roman period, and many more in the larger salt marsh area of the neighbouring province of Friesland, a total of *c.* 1500 inhabited terp settlements during the Roman period.

1 Acknowledgements: I wish to thank Jelle Schokker (Northern Archaeological Depot, Nuis) and Maaike Modderman (Groninger Museum) for their help with finding the recorded and available terra sigillata from Groningen, Wim Dijkman (Maastricht) for his identification of a specific Argonne specimen, and Rien Polak (Nijmegen) for examining the potters' stamps and identifying the Arretine ware, and for his valuable comments on an earlier version of this paper.
This research project was funded by the Dutch Research Council (NWO), as part of the Odyssee Project.

2 I must emphasise that I am far from an expert on terra sigillata. My work is rather concerned with the landscape and archaeology of the terp region of the northern Netherlands, especially the settlements and habitation history, handmade pottery, burials, and the remains of rituals in this area.

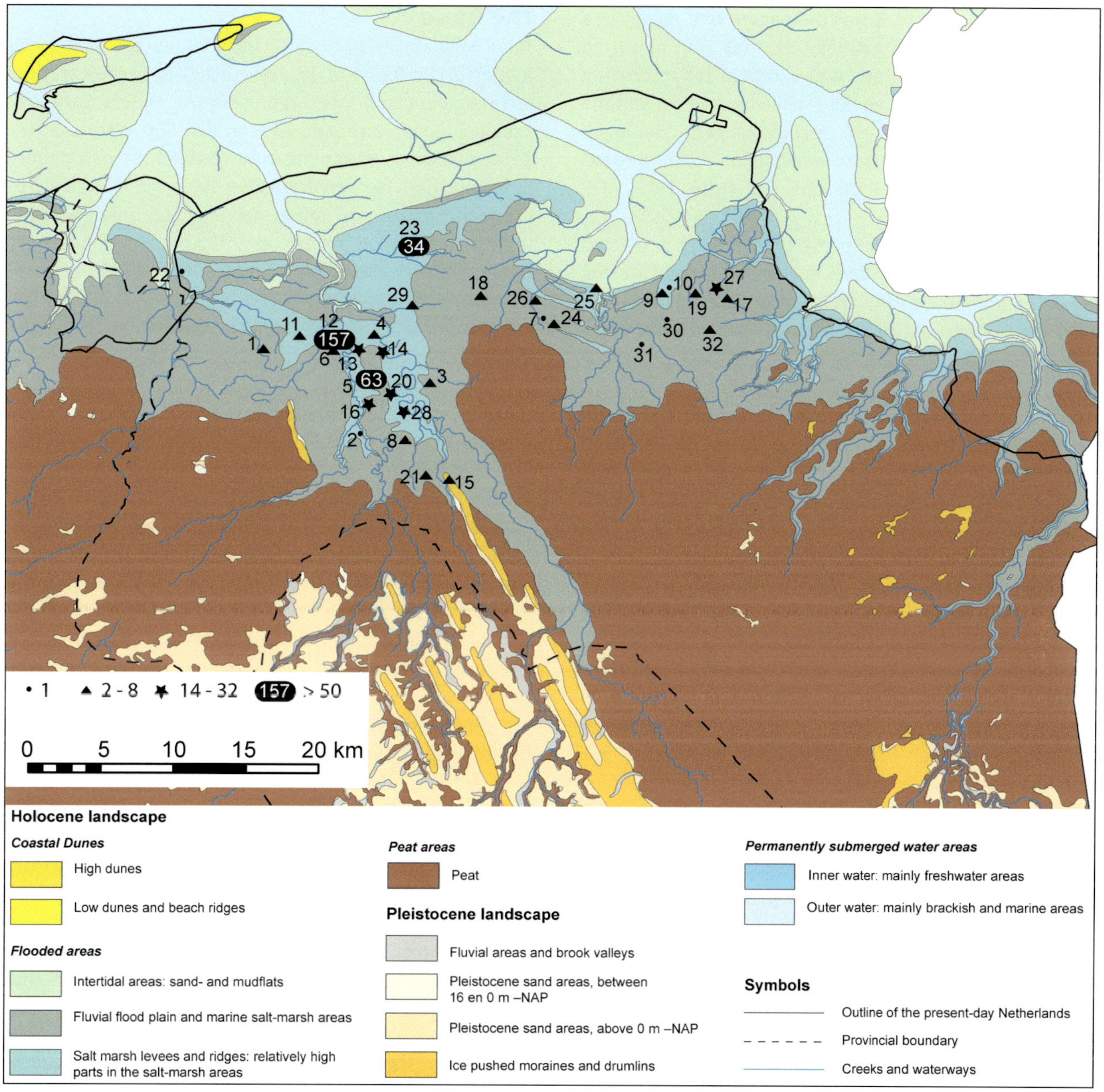

Fig. 1. Palaeogeographic map of the province of Groningen around 100, with sites where terra sigillata was found. Symbols and numbers refer to the Minimum Number of Individual vessels. 1: Aalsum; 2: Aduard; 3: Adorp-Munnikeweg; 4: Antum ("terp north of Garnwerd"): 5: Brillerij; 6: De Bouwerd; 7: De Palen; 8: Dorkwerd; 9: Eenum; 10: Eenumerhoogte; 11: Englum; 12: Ezinge; 13: Feerwerd; 14: Garnwerd; 15: Groningen; 16: Joeswerd; 17: Jukwerd; 18: Onderdendam; 19: Oosterwijtwerd; 20: Oostum; 21: Paddepoel; 22: Panser; 23: Rasquert; 24: Stedum-St. Annahoeve; 25: Westeremden; 26: Westerwijtwerd; 27: Wierhuizen; 28: Wierum; 29: Winsum; 30: Wirdum; 31: Garrelsweer; 32: Tjamsweer (palaeogeographic map: Vos *et al.* 2020 © Rijksdienst voor het Cultureel Erfgoed, Deltares and TNO).

In the 19th century, it was discovered that terps were not natural, but rather artificial mounds, and consisted of highly fertile soil, which was excellent for improving poor soils inland. Between the middle of the 19th and the middle of the 20th century, at least 268 terps in Groningen and 697 in Friesland partly or completely disappeared because of quarrying of the terp soil (Klok 1979, 460; Halbertsma 1944).

This destructive period had a positive side: it created an interest in the many finds that came to light during soil extraction, and in the archaeology of the terp region in general. Finds, including terra sigillata sherds, were collected and thus formed the basis of the later provincial museums. The number of collected terra sigillata sherds grew quickly, also because workers were paid handsomely for even the smallest sherds, at least in Friesland (Boeles 1917, 110). This, perhaps surprisingly, did not lead to deliberate breaking of fragments by the workers; fresh breaks and fitting sherds are very rare (Volkers 1999, 151). In Groningen, find collection was less systematic.

Early terp archaeology used terra sigillata as *index fossils* to date terp layers (Boeles 1951, 146). Terra sigillata was acknowledged as an important material category that not only could be used to date layers and contexts, but also revealed contacts with the Roman Empire; it potentially gave information on the early occupation of the area by the Romans between 12 BC and 47 and on Roman trade with free Germania (Boeles 1911). Boeles' article of 1911, in which he summarised his study of all the terra sigillata finds that were known at the time, can be considered to mark the start of terra sigillata research in the northern Netherlands.

The excavations of the terp of Ezinge brought a significant number of terra sigillata finds to light. At the request of Van Giffen, Kurt Stade of the *Römisch-Germanische Kommission* studied these sherds in the 1930s. His report was never published, partly because of the outbreak of the Second World War, and because Van Giffen never came to publish the excavation results in full. Willem Glasbergen, who was working on the terra sigillata finds from the castellum at Valkenburg during the war years, made an inventory of the terra sigillata from the province of Groningen in this same period, which was published in 1948 in the same volume as the Valkenburg finds (Glasbergen 1944a; 1944b; 1944c).

For a long time, it was not doubted that terra sigillata came to northern coastal regions by trade, and that terra sigillata had been in use here as luxury tableware (*e.g.* Boeles 1917, 113; 1951, 146). First Van Es (1981, 265-266) and later Erdrich (2001a) and Roymans (2017) argued that trade may not have been the only reason why Roman goods came to the area; diplomatic gift exchange also played a role. Moreover, men from the north served as soldiers in the Roman army (Galestin 2009; Erdrich 2001a, 125), and veterans from the Roman army must have taken Roman goods with them when they returned home.

The Dataset

Terra sigillata as used here includes all red pottery of Roman origin found in the area, including early (Arretine) terra sigillata and late Argonne ware, Oxfordshire red/brown-slipped ware, and African Red Slip Ware (ARSW). Terra sigillata is by far the most common Roman pottery in the northern Netherlands; other imported Roman wares are relatively rare. In Ezinge, for instance, only 10 sherds of imported Roman pottery other than terra sigillata were found (Volkers 2014, 147), besides 199 sherds of terra sigillata (table 1).

The majority of terra sigillata finds from Groningen are stored in the NAD in Nuis; some 70 fragments belong to the collection of the *National Museum of Antiquities* (*Rijksmuseum van Oudheden*, or RMO) in Leiden. A small number of terra sigillata finds are part of the collection of the Groninger Museum. The basis of the Groningen inventory is the database left by Volkers, combined with her earlier Ezinge database that was summarised in her paper of 2014, a total of 374 fragments. She began her inventory with the terra sigillata fragments from the RMO. After the description of this material was completed in 2018, she turned to the material from the northern collections, but she could only add a few more records. That is where my work on the inventory began.

The Groningen terra sigillata sherds described by Glasbergen (1944a) were added to the database, as far as they did not belong to the collection of the RMO. Other published finds that were included are the terra sigillata sherds from the excavation at Paddepoel (Van Es 1968), a recent find from the city of Groningen (De Haas 2023) and some sherds that have been identified as Oxfordshire ware (Fulford 1977; Morris 2010). A search in the NAD database yielded several dozen more terra sigillata finds. A very recent addition is a number of terra sigillata sherds that were collected by an amateur archaeologist (the collection *Mensonides*), which in December 2023 was handed over to the NAD. Many of these finds are physically present in the collection of the NAD, others are only paper finds, once recorded but no longer available. They were included in the database to provide as complete a picture of the distribution of terra sigillata as possible. For instance, some sherds described in Stade's report that are not available now and were not included in Volkers' study of 2014 were also added, as were 15 sherds from Ezinge that were recorded in the finds register but have since gone missing. Of the terra sigillata finds from the terp of Oosterwijtwerd that were mentioned by Van Giffen in his doctoral thesis (1913), only one is available in the NAD, but there must have been more. Descriptions of the sherds from all these sources differ, varying from "a terra sigillata sherd", to a full description of form, decoration, production, date, and traces of secondary use. Of the total number of 585 fragments, 505 were analysed to some degree.

Site No.	Location	Number of Fragments	MNI	Found during	Type of Site	Remark
1	Aalsum	2	2	Q	terp	
2	Aduard	1	1	Exc	monastery	
3	Adorp-Munnikeweg	"several"	>1	Exc	terp	Ongoing excavation, MNI still unknown
4	Antum	3	2	Q	terp	Location "terp north of Garnwerd" according to Van Giffen 1913, 163-164, Abb. 14, 20
5	Brillerij	82	63	Q	terp	
6	De Bouwerd	3	3	Exc	terp	
7	De Palen	1	1	Acc	terp	
8	Dorkwerd	2	2	Archaeological observation during Q	terp	
9	Eenum	4	4	Q	terp	
10	Eenumerhoogte	1	1	Q	terp	
11	Englum	2	2	Q + Exc	terp	
12	Ezinge	199	157	Exc	terp	Including 15 sherds that were mentioned in the finds register but are unavailable now
13	Feerwerd	40	24	Q	terp	
14	Garnwerd	34	24	Q	terp	
15	City of Groningen	3	3	Exc		
16	Joeswerd	21	15.5	Q	terp	One sherd possibly of the same vessel as one in Wierum (therefore 15.5)
17	Jukwerd	6	5	Q and archaeological observation during the construction of pipelines	terp	
18	Onderdendam	2	2	Q	terp	
19	Oosterwijtwerd	≥2	1	Archaeological observation during Q	terp	
20	Oostum	48	29.5	Q	terp	One sherd fitting one from Wierum
21	Paddepoel	8	8	Exc	terp	
22	Panser	1	1	Exc	terp	
23	Rasquert	41	34	Q	terp	
24	Stedum-St. Annahoeve	2	2	Survey	terp	
25	Westeremden	4	4	Q	terp	
26	Westerwijtwerd	3	3	Q	terp	
27	Wierhuizen	20	19	Exc	terp	
28	Wierum	31	27	Q	terp	One sherd fitting one from Oostum. One possibly belonging to the same vessel as one in Joeswerd
29	Winsum	2	2	Q?	terp	
30	Wirdum	1	1	Q	terp	
31	Garrelsweer/ Drewerderhof	1	1	Acc	terp	
32	Tjamsweer	5	5	?	terp	
	Province of Groningen	11	8	probably Q		
	Total	585	458			

Table 1. Terra sigillata in the province of Groningen, in numbers of sherds and Minimum Numbers of Individuals (MNI) (=pots) per site. Q: quarrying; Exc: archaeological excavation; Acc: accidental find (table: A. Nieuwhof).

Form	MNI	%
Bowls	171	42.9
Plates and dishes	121	30.3
Cups	35	8.8
Mortaria	29	7.3
Closed forms	14	3.5
Unidentified	29	7.3
Total	399	100

Table 2. Overview of terra sigillata forms found in the province of Groningen. MNI: Minimum Number of Individual vessels that were analysed (table: A. Nieuwhof).

Phase 1: 12 BC-c. 50(100)	
%	Types
0-1%	Consp. 11 (Arretine); Drag. 15/17, 24/25, 29
Phase 2: c. 100-250	
%	Types
0-1%	Drag. 27?, 31 or 18/31, 38, 43, 44, 43/45, 52-54, 54; Lud. Th, Ti', Tl'; Curle 11; inkpot
1-3%	Drag. 18/31, 32, 36; Déchelette 72
3-6%	Drag. 33, 45
13.1%	Drag. 31
36.6%	Drag. 37 (n=147, including 109 mould-decorated)
Phase 3: (3rd)4th-5th centuries	
%	Types
0-1%	Chenet 326, 333b, 345; Hayes 91; Young 51
1-3%	Chenet 320; Hayes 67

Table 3. Overview of terra sigillata types and their relative frequency found in the province of Groningen, per phase. Percentages refer to the *analysed* Minimum Number of Individuals (318 identified and 81 unidentified). See Hayes 1972 and 1980, Young 1977, and the overview by Brulet *et al.* (2010) for typologies otherwise not listed (table: A. Nieuwhof).

Results

Quantities and Fragmentation

The resulting database lists 585 terra sigillata fragments, which is considerably more than the *c.* 400 that were estimated in earlier publications (*e.g.* Volkers 2014, 158). The Minimum Number of Individual vessels (n=458) was calculated by taking fitting sherds together, and all sherds that are so similar in fabric or decoration that they may have belonged to the same individual. Most of the analysed individual vessels are represented by only one sherd (n=350). Only one vessel, a Drag. 45 mortarium from Groningen-Grote Markt (no. 1974-III.4), is complete. A recent find from nearly the same location (De Haas 2023), a cup of type Drag. 24/25 found in a medieval context (no. 2023-673), was more or less cut in half and may only have been damaged when it was accidentally dug up from a 1st-century layer sometime during the Middle Ages. A seemingly complete but restored bowl of type Drag. 37 from the terp of Garnwerd (GM 1942-I.1) consists of eight sherds, making up two-thirds of the bowl (Glasbergen 1944a, 337).

Distribution and Representativeness

The finds come from 30 known locations in the province of Groningen, all settlements (fig. 1 and table 1). Most of these locations are terps. The distribution map (fig. 1) shows that the terps were all located near the former coast of the Waddenzee, or along watercourses leading to the Waddenzee, but it must be noted that it is far from certain that these finds represent the historic presence of terra sigillata in this area during the Roman period. Most of the terra sigillata finds from the terps were found during quarrying and not collected systematically. Some terps yielded many finds (including terra sigillata sherds), others only a handful. This depended on factors such as the enthusiasm and perceptivity of workers and contractors, the part of the terp that was quarried, and the opportunity for workers to sell finds to a museum curator. The role of Van Giffen is especially important in Groningen. From 1908 into the 1930s, he not only conducted excavations, but was also actively visiting the terps that were being quarried and thereby collected finds. The recorded terra sigillata finds not only represent the actual distribution of terra sigillata at the terp settlements in the past, but also Van Giffen's activities (see also Van Giffen 1913).

Forms, Decoration and Provenance

The general form of 399 individual vessels could be established. Most common are bowls, followed by plates and dishes (table 2). Cups and mortaria also regularly occur, though in smaller numbers. Closed forms are rather rare. A type could be identified in 318 cases (table 3). The majority, 36.6%, consists of bowls of form Drag. 37. Plates of form Drag. 31 are also rather common, with 15.1%. Other types occur in much smaller numbers. Of the mortaria, form Drag. 45 is the most numerous, of the closed forms this is Déchelette 72.

Less numerous does not mean less interesting. Conspicuous categories are the later wares: some fragments of Oxfordshire ware (fig. 2; Fulford 1977; Morris 2010), and those belonging to phase 3, the 4th and 5th centuries (see below), with late Argonne Chenet types and several fragments of ARSW. The latter, all from Ezinge, are represented by fragments of types Hayes 67 and 91 (Bonifay types 41 and 48) and a mortarium (ARSW types follow Hayes 1972; Bonifay 2004). The ARSW sherds were first identified by Hans Zeiss, director of the Römisch-Germanische Kommission during the time that Stade was working on the terra sigillata from Ezinge. He had become acquainted with this material on a trip to southern Europe (Volkers 2014, 149). ARSW specialist John Hayes initially regarded them as "freaks" (1972, 422), but was kind enough to come and see this material in person in 2012 and confirmed the identification[3].

A large number of fragments are decorated. Of the fragments of Drag. 37 bowls, 109 are mould-decorated. All Drag. 36 fragments have barbotine decoration. Incised decoration is found on 11 fragments, mostly of form Déchelette 72. Many plates have rouletted concentric circles on the inside. Rouletted decoration was also found on the outside of an early Drag. 37 from the Argonne and on the later Chenet 320 forms. Red stripes were found on the Chenet 345 fragments. Several ARSW fragments have the stamp decoration that is typical of 4th-5th century ARSW (fig. 3).

In 304 cases (MNI), the origin of the fragments could be established (table 4), though not always precisely. There are only 5 potters' stamps that can be deciphered[4]. The majority of the sherds, 39%, was produced somewhere in central or east Gaul, another 16.2% in east Gaul. Of the known kiln sites, Trier is the most important with 10.4%, while Lavoye, Lezoux and Rheinzabern are represented by 6.2%, 5.5% and 5.2% respectively. The provenance of the terra sigillata has been one of the areas of attention of Volkers, since she discovered that there is a difference in the provenance of terra sigillata between Friesland and the rest of the Netherlands including Groningen, at least if we look at the mould-decorated bowls Drag. 37 (Volkers 1991a). Although bowls from Trier are the most common everywhere, also in Friesland, the percentage of Rheinzabern in Friesland is considerably higher than elsewhere. The anomaly was also noted by Erdrich (2001a, 111-117; 2001b, 322-323) and Polak (in Volkers 2015/2016). For the sake of future comparison, the provenance of the Drag. 37 from Groningen is included in table 4. Drag. 37 from Trier is the most common, with 26.2%, followed by Lavoye (13.1%), while Lezoux and Rheinzabern share third place with 9.0%. In Friesland (also in table 4), the percentage of Trier is twice as high, the percentage of Rheinzabern even three times, while the percentage of bowls from the Argonne is smaller in Friesland. These differences remain even if we take into account that the general categories in the Groningen material of central-east Gaulish and east Gaulish are rather large, making the percentages of known production sites here less reliable.

Fig. 2. Three of the 4 Oxfordshire ware sherds found in Groningen (© A. Nieuwhof).

3 The identification as Red Slip Ware from the western Mediterranean was also largely confirmed by Philip Bes (pers. comm.), who noted that some of the sherds are probably not from Tunisia, but from other locations in the western Mediterranean.

4 The names of Borius, a wandering potter (Feerwerd, NAD 1916-VII.12), Iuvenis, probably from Blickweiler/Eschweilerhof (Garnwerd (actually Antum), NAD 1926-VI.85), Saturninus, from Lezoux (Brillerij, NAD 1910-I.269), Sextus and Antiquus, both from Lezoux (both Ezinge, NAD 1968(-1931)-V. 123a and 1932-IV.986), which were published by Glasbergen (1944a, 344-345) and NoTS (Hartley and Dickinson 2008-2012), are certain. Other readings by Glasbergen cannot be confirmed. Since Glasbergen published the 11 stamps then known from Groningen, no new stamps have been found.

Fig. 3. Fragments of ARSW from Ezinge, with the typical decoration of stamps (© A. Nieuwhof).

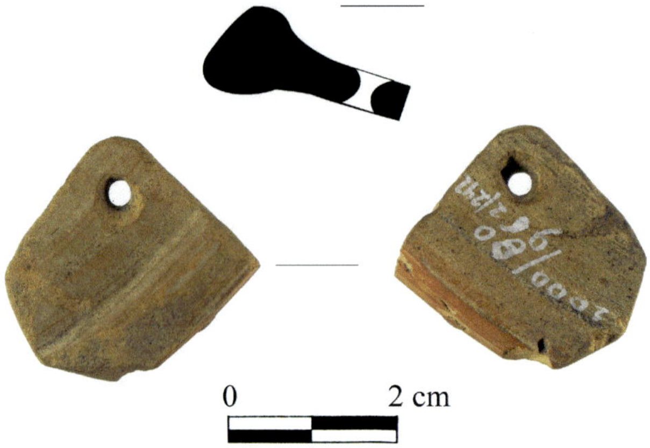

Fig. 4. Pendant made of a rim fragment probably of a plate of form Consp. 11 (Haltern 1b/Service Ia) and dated to the late 1st century BC, from a 1st-century context in the terp of Englum (NAD 2009-V.962) (© A. Nieuwhof).

Phases

Three phases of import can be distinguished in the terra sigillata finds (see tables 3, 5). Phase 1 formally dates from 12 BC to 47, the short period in which the northern Netherlands belonged to the Roman Empire. Only a very small number of sherds belong to this group; two of these are certainly from this period: a small, perforated rim sherd of Arretine terra sigillata (fig. 4; probably form Consp. 11 (Haltern 1b/Service Ia)), which must have been worn as a pendant, and a wall sherd of form Drag. 29. Two others might be from this phase but are probably somewhat later: the large part of a Drag. 24/25 cup mentioned above, and a base sherd of a Drag. 15/17 plate. It only shows that the end of the contacts between the north and the Roman Empire were not as abrupt as the precise end date suggests. In Friesland, a few comparable, relatively late sherds were found, for instance a potter's stamp dated 40-60 (Polak, in Volkers 2015/2016, 305-306).

The evidence for the Roman presence in the north in this early period comes from two sites in particular: Winsum-Bruggeburen in Friesland and Bentumersiel on the Ems. These sites may have functioned as Roman outposts or were residences of local leaders who had good contacts with the Romans. Besides terra sigillata, also a considerable quantity of other kinds of imported Roman pottery were found in these early settlements (much more than from later periods in the north), plus other finds such as coins and other metalwork. Finds from this early period in the north are concentrated in these settlements and very rare elsewhere (Galestin 2001/2002; Ulbert 1977; Volkers 1991b; 2002). As elsewhere in the north (Erdrich 2001a, 93-97; Volkers 2015/2016, 238), there are only a few sherds from the second half of the 1st century: two of form Drag. 27, and three sherds of an early Drag. 37 bowl from La Graufesenque.

The majority of the terra sigillata finds belongs to phase 2, the 2nd and 3rd centuries. The emphasis is on the period between *c.* 125 and 250/260. Probably the latest sherd, from Brillerij (RMO b 1913/11.2p), is from the workshop of Dubitatus in Trier (225-245). As many as 424 fragments, belonging to at least 348 individual pots, belong to this phase. This shows that there were regular contacts with the Roman Empire in this period. The end of this phase not only coincides with the end of the east Gaulish production of terra sigillata (apart from the Argonne), but also with the virtual end of habitation in the northern terp region (Nieuwhof 2011; 2021). Only a few terps, notably Ezinge and probably others such as Garnwerd and Brillerij remained inhabited during the 4th century, although the population diminished. From the beginning of the 5th century, the terp region was repopulated. The material culture of the new inhabitants indicates that they were immigrants from the northeast who came with the Anglo-Saxon migration movement to the west, not only to the northern Netherlands but also to Britain.

Part of the terra sigillata sherds belong to the 4th and 5th centuries, phase 3. Just like elsewhere, there are few fragments from the late 3rd and early 4th centuries, only 4 sherds. Three of these have been identified as Oxfordshire ware, while one belongs to a Chenet 320 bowl dated *c.* 300. A fourth Oxfordshire fragment, belonging to a mortarium, is dated to the 4th century (fig. 2, top). The only available context date concerns a fragment from Ezinge (NAD 1926-VII.214(1)) that was found with a 4th-5th century Argonne sherd and a 2nd-3rd century terra sigillata sherd; although the context is dated to the 5th century, the Oxfordshire sherd may be earlier. Morris (2015, 428)

	All terra sigillata Groningen		Drag. 37 Groningen		Drag. 37 Friesland	
Production site/region	MNI	%	MNI	%	MNI	%
Arezzo/Italy	1	0.3				
South Gaul	2	0.6				
La Graufesenque	2	0.6	1	0.8	4	0.8
Central Gaul	11	3.6	8	6.6	7	1.3
Lezoux	17	5.5	11	9.0	30	5.8
Central-east Gaul	120	39.0	28	23.0		
East Gaul	50	16.2	9	7.4		
Argonne, Lavoye	19	6.2	16	13.1	28	5.4
La Madeleine	6	1.9	5	4.1	2	0.4
Heiligenberg	1	0.3	1	0.8		
Trier	32	10.4	32	26.2	287	55.2
Rheinzabern	16	5.2	11	9.0	159	30.6
Blickweiler/ Eschweilerhof	2	0.6			3	0.6
Argonne (late)	10	3.2				
Tunisia	15	4.9				
Oxfordshire	4	1.3				
Total	308	100	122	100	520	100
Unknown	150		25		107	

Table 4. Places and regions of origin of the terra sigillata from Groningen. The four columns on the right show the provenance of bowls of Drag. 37 in Groningen and in Friesland (after: Volkers 2015/2016, Tabelle 3).

argued that the Romano-British material (there are also some finds of British wares known from Friesland and several from Texel, an island west of Friesland) may have arrived in the 5th century in the northern Netherlands as the personal possessions of individuals who had spent time in Britain. This is in line with the idea that the 5th-century Anglo-Saxon settlers of the terp region stayed in touch with their relatives in Britain, as several other types of finds indicate (Nicolay 2014; Nieuwhof 2021, 62). However, if we examine the fragments themselves, it seems more likely that they actually belong to phase 2: at least three of the finds from Groningen show traces of secondary use; such traces are never found on the 4th-5th century terra sigillata of phase 3 (see below).

The sherds of phase 3 are all dated between *c.* 350 and 420/450. There are two groups. The first consists of 24 fragments belonging to 8 late Argonne vessels, mostly from Ezinge; the second comprises 20 sherds of 15 vessels of late ARSW[5]. These are all from Ezinge. Hayes dated the Ezinge fragments of his form 67 between 390 and 420, those of his form 91 to the 5th century (Volkers 2014, 153-156).

ARSW is rare outside the Mediterranean area. It is virtually unknown in the Netherlands, but there are some finds known from western and northern Gaul and Britain, although most British finds are from around 300 (Bonifay 2020; Bonifay and Pieri 2020, 863; Le Bomin 2020). ARSW is also found in southern Germany (*e.g.* Mackensen 2013; Heimerl 2016). Later ARSW in Britain is mostly found in southwest England (Duggan 2020). Volkers identified some more possible ARSW fragments from the terp region, also in Friesland, but these still need to be confirmed (Volkers 2015). The identification of one of these sherds as ARSW, find no. 50-46 from the terp at Hatsum, was confirmed by Philip Bes. The ARSW finds may have come to Ezinge with veteran mercenaries from the Roman army who acquired them during their service (Volkers 2014; 2015). Even in the late Roman period, men from the north served in the Roman army; Ezinge is also one of the locations where late 4th-century Roman solidi have been found, which are believed to be payments to *foederati* of the Romans (Roymans 2017; Knol 2014, 189-190). The question in that case is why ARSW was not found in other terp settlements where solidi were found. As Ezinge is one of the very few settlements that remained inhabited in the 4th century, the ARSW here may have arrived either at the end of the 4th century, when other settlements were still uninhabited, or in the early 5th century and Volkers was right that ARSW is found in other terps as well, but still not recognised. The finds from phase 3 either belong to still-inhabited settlements in the 4th century such as Ezinge, or to the

5 There is also a rim sherd of a late Roman amphora (NAD 1931-V.563(3)), which according to Volkers (2014) probably came from Nabeul in north Africa, but according to Philip Bes (pers. comm.) rather came from the Iberian Peninsula.

	Total Number of Fragments (n)	MNI	n Volkers	Worked/used	% of Sherds
Phase 1					
20 BC-50 (100)	4	4	3	3	100
Phase 2					
(later 1st)-2nd century	89	78	82	68	82.9
2nd-3rd centuries	302	253	215	169	78.6
3rd century	32	17	25	21	84.0
Total Phase 2	423	348	322	258	80.1
Phase 3					
3rd-4th centuries	4	4	2	2	100
4th century	5	3	5	1	20.0
4th-5th centuries	33	24	31	0	0.0
5th century	3	1	3	0	0.0
Total Phase 3	45	32	41	3	7.3
Total all phases	472	384	366	264	72.1

Table 5. The total number of dated sherds and the Minimum Number of Individuals (MNI) from the province of Groningen per phase. The right three columns show the number and percentages of worked or secondarily used sherds per period, as analysed by Volkers) (table: A. Nieuwhof).

	Analysed by Volkers	%	Analysed by others or not analysed	%	Total
Not recorded	19	5.1	162	76.8	181
No traces of secondary use	91	24.3	3	1.4	94
Traces of secondary use	264	70.6	46	21.8	310
Total	374	100	211	100	585
Including					
Playing counter	15		6		21
Worked triangle	28		6		34
Worked rectangle/square/diamond	30		6		36
Perforated object (bead, pendant, spindle whorl)	8		6		14
Fragment used as a small dish or bowl	2		1		3

Table 6. Number of terra sigillata fragments with traces of working or secondary use. In the second column are sherds analysed by Volkers, in the fourth column sherds that were not analysed or analysed by others, who did not specifically look at traces of use (table: A. Nieuwhof).

new population that settled here during the beginning of the 5th century. This suggests that the ARSW from Ezinge and possibly other terp settlements came via the Atlantic route (see Duggan 2020) from Britain, but, although there is quite some evidence of contacts between the North Sea coastal regions in this period, as noted above, southwest Britain, where the ARSW is found, does not seem to be one of the areas that participated in the exchange network that connected the North Sea regions. It is therefore more likely that the ARSW from Ezinge came over land from the south.

The date of production is not necessarily the same as the date of use or import. When studying the terra sigillata finds from the Frisian terp of Wijnaldum, which was excavated between 1991 and 1993, Volkers found that only nine out of 61 2nd-3rd century terra sigillata fragments came from contemporaneous, that is 2nd-3rd century contexts, while the majority was either from undated or from early medieval contexts (Volkers 1999). This suggested to her that most of this material may have been imported only in the early Middle Ages, although she did notice that terps of early medieval date had no terra sigillata at all (Volkers 1999, 154). Her cautious conclusion was that the period of import of terra sigillata in the terp region needed further investigation. Some of the Groningen terps indeed provide an opportunity to learn more about the import of terra sigillata. The excavation

Fig. 5. Terra sigillata pendants, at least one spindle whorl, and a large disc made from a foot ring, of which the use is unknown. Numbers preceded by "b" belong to the collection of the RMO, the others belong to the NAD (© A. Nieuwhof; T. Volkers).

of the terp of Englum in 2000 showed that the earliest terra sigillata sherd in Groningen (fig. 4) came from a pit with 1st-century pottery (Nieuwhof 2015, 311). The Ezinge excavations provide more information on contexts and dates. Ezinge is one of the few terps, besides Wijnaldum, that was excavated and documented in such a way that finds can be linked to contexts, which are dated on the basis of the stratigraphy in combination with the dating of the handmade pottery (Nieuwhof 2020b).

In Ezinge, a significant proportion of the terra sigillata fragments was found in contemporaneous contexts: 37.2% of 2nd-3rd century terra sigillata in phase 2 contexts, and 31.4% of 4th-5th century terra sigillata in phase 3 contexts (Nieuwhof 2020a, table 1). Within these contexts, fragments do often come from slightly later contexts than the production date, for instance 2nd-century sherds in 3rd-century contexts – in other words, these fragments are residual. Nevertheless, quite a number of sherds are found in later contexts; 24.8% of the phase 2 sherds, for instance, are found in phase 3 contexts. This might be explained in two ways: the first is that sherds were dug up from earlier layers at the time of occupation, a quite common phenomenon in terps. That may have been the case for some sherds, but it is certainly not the only explanation. The other is that terra sigillata had a symbolic meaning; this made it treasured material that was passed down to following generations. In the discussion (see below), examples will serve as evidence for this latter assumption. In any case, there is no reason to assume that terra sigillata was only imported during the early Middle Ages, at least in Ezinge.

Primary and Secondary Use

One of the most interesting features of the terra sigillata in the north is the presence of traces of secondary use. Such traces were found earlier in the Ezinge terra sigillata assemblage (72% of the analysed phase 2 fragments: Volkers 2014, 157) and in the terra sigillata from Friesland (77%: Volkers 2015/2016, 240). Quite a few sherds are worked into objects such as pendants, spindle whorls or playing counters. These sherds not only show traces of deliberate cutting, rounding, and smoothing, but also of wear caused by later handling and other uses. The surface layer along the fractures is often worn, there may be notches and incisions on the fractured edge, straight cuts, or impact marks that suggest the help of a tool to break sherds[6]. However, similar traces are often also found on sherds that were not made into clear objects. If compared to terra sigillata from sites south of the limes such as Forum Hadriani or Nijmegen, the sherds from the northern Netherlands are on average considerably smaller than those in the Roman settlements, where traces of secondary use, though not entirely absent, are rather rare (Volkers 2015/2016, 241; Geerts 2023).

The analysis of the Groningen inventory showed that not only the Ezinge terra sigillata, but also many other terra sigillata fragments show traces of secondary use. Besides objects such as pendants and playing counters,

6 An experiment with handmade pottery showed that iron awls were sometimes deliberately used to break pots (Nieuwhof 2015, 168-170). Similar traces are sometimes found on terra sigillata.

Fig. 6. Round and roundish playing counters and a variety of other shapes, all deliberately made and with traces of wear (© A. Nieuwhof; T. Volkers).

there are also many other intentionally shaped sherds, such as more or less triangular, rectangular, and trapezoidal fragments with traces of wear along the fractures (figs 5-6). Among the terra sigillata examined by Volkers (table 6), 70.6% of the fragments shows traces of secondary use. If the three phases are distinguished, it becomes clear that none of the 4th-5th century fragments show such traces (one of the fragments is conspicuously square but does not have a worn surface or traces of smoothing, see fig. 3), against 80.1% of the 2nd-3rd century sherds (table 5). In the terra sigillata examined by researchers who did not consistently pay attention to secondary use, traces were found on 20.6% of the sherds (table 6). These usually concern easily identifiable secondary objects such as playing counters and perforated sherds.

Discussion

In this discussion, the focus will be on the use of terra sigillata in the northern coastal region, in particular Groningen. It is clear that secondary use of terra sigillata was very common in this area. Wat does this say about the meaning of terra sigillata for the inhabitants? Did they value terra sigillata as tableware or rather as a material with a symbolic meaning? And how were the fragments used after they were created?

Symbolic Meaning

We have already argued elsewhere that it was the symbolic meaning of terra sigillata as a material that made it so popular in the north (Nieuwhof 2015, 146-147; 2020a; Nieuwhof and Volkers 2015). What that meaning was is most likely related to its colour, which distinguished it from other wares. Shininess may have been another attractive characteristic of this ware, but it should be noted that indigenous vessels are sometimes highly polished too. The colour is what really sets it apart. While playing counters and spindle whorls are sometimes made of handmade sherds, and there may be traces of deliberate breaking and secondarily perforated bases on handmade pottery from ritual contexts (Nieuwhof 2015, 168-171), ceramic pendants, most likely amulets, were only made of terra sigillata. The decoration and quality do not play a role in secondary use; undecorated sherds and even mortaria were also used (see figs 2, 6), and decorations, if they occur, are often cut through. The warm orange-red colour may have given this material an intrinsic meaning that was associated with life, warmth, protection, and good luck. It was therefore used to make amulets, and terra sigillata sherds, with or without traces of secondary use, were sometimes deposited in ritual deposits, possibly to make them more effective when good luck and protection were needed (Nieuwhof 2015, 220-211; 2020a, 103). Terra sigillata may have come to the northern coastal area in the form of sherds, with veterans from the Roman army who knew that these were appreciated at home, as diplomatic gifts in the form of complete vessels or fragments, or as payment for local products, comparable to the trade of beads by early Modern European colonial traders (for a full discussion, see Nieuwhof 2020a, 104-106).

The northern Netherlands are not the only region where terra sigillata with traces of secondary use are found. In particular, terra sigillata finds from Scotland show very similar traces (Campbell 2011; 2012). Many fragments there are abraded in a way that suggests they may have been used as colourants, as abrasives or polishers in metalworking activities, or for medicinal purposes. But here too, its first meaning was probably symbolic, and terra sigillata also played a role in ritual deposition practices in Scotland (Campbell 2011, 224-227, 338-342). The fragments from the Groningen terra sigillata assemblage often have worn surfaces along the breaks, but these are not what may be expected if the sherds were used for polishing or to make powder. Frequent handling and adaptation of the objects because of an ascribed symbolic meaning seems to be the best explanation of the finds and the traces of use that were attested.

The symbolic use of terra sigillata in the northern Netherlands and in Scotland fits with what we know of the use of material culture of a dominant colonial power in indigenous contexts. There are many examples from the more recent past that show that a foreign material culture is never immediately fully adopted (Van Dongen 1995); only elements may be adopted, and often only for symbolic or ceremonial purposes. This also seems to be the case in the northern Netherlands. Although there were many contacts between the indigenous societies of the north and the Roman Empire, only terra sigillata and copper-alloy statuettes, which were also found in conspicuously large numbers in the northern coastal area (Veen 2018), were adopted. Both are categories with a symbolic meaning, and they were probably used in ways that were not intended or foreseen by the producers.

Use

Whether the terra sigillata crockery was used as tableware in the north is far from certain. The one complete mortarium is an exception. There are only a few examples of terra sigillata vessels of which several sherds are preserved. These may have been used as complete vessels for a while. In most cases, part of these sherds was worked and used after the vessel broke. A good example is a Drag. 37 bowl from Oostum, of which 7 sherds have been preserved; two are round playing discs, a third is a small square rim sherd with smooth breaks (Glasbergen 1944a, fig. 67.4; Nieuwhof 2020a, fig. 7). There are also several fitting sherds that were worked and used independently of each other. It shows that broken terra sigillata was certainly not discarded as waste, and that the secondary use of terra sigillata may well have been the most important use.

The protective, evil-averting (apotropaic) and good luck-bringing properties that may have been ascribed to terra sigillata made it an excellent material for making pendants (probably amulets) and playing counters. It is also found in ritual deposits associated with houses, as we know from the excavations in Ezinge (see Nieuwhof 2020a, tables 2-3)[7]. An example is a 3rd-century house with a deposit of 6 playing counters made from the same vessel (see fig. 6, top left) outside the southwest corner, and an assemblage of four different sherds, three of which show traces of secondary use, outside the northwest corner (Nieuwhof 2020b, level H, find nos 957-958). Another is an

7 For the use of the term ritual (rather than intentional, structured, *etc.*) deposit, see Nieuwhof 2015, 111-112.

Fig. 7. Two sides of two fitting base sherds of a plate. The fragments were found in Oostum (1971-X.61(4)) and Wierum (1966-VIII.1(5)), terps that are less than 2 km apart (© A. Nieuwhof).

assemblage (find no. 405) consisting of a 2nd/3rd-century Drag. 31 plate fragment, a small, square sherd of a 4th/5th-century ARSW plate (fig. 4), and a horned cattle skull, together found in a 5th-century well (see Nieuwhof 2020b, 158)[8]. In the fill of a sunken hut from the 5th century, a complete handmade miniature pot was combined with 10 lead rings (probably loom weights), a bone needle, a two-pointed bone pin beater, a 2nd/3rd-century worked terra sigillata sherd and 5 ARSW sherds belonging to 3 vessels (Nieuwhof 2020b)[9].

These few examples show that terra sigillata from the 2nd/3rd century is often deposited long after it was produced, and that it is often combined with 4th-/5th-century terra sigillata. It is not likely that the earlier sherds in these deposits were all accidentally dug up and reused. These deposits rather suggest that the earlier material was kept for a long time within families and was passed down as heirlooms for generations before finally being deposited. Terra sigillata was still valued in the early Middle Ages, as several deposits in early medieval contexts in Ezinge testify. Already Van Giffen (1913, 36-37) described in his dissertation that he had found a small terra sigillata pendant in a medieval globular pot. This proved to him that the terp residents appreciated these fragments, which their ancestors must have acquired. It is likely that families or households had collections of heirlooms, memorabilia, and other meaningful objects, even including bones of family members, to be kept and passed on, or deposited at special occasions (Nieuwhof 2015, 227, 292).

Terra sigillata also played a role in maintaining social relations. Terra sigillata is not unique in this respect, handmade pottery was also used in fragmentation-and-enchainment practices, a term introduced by Chapman (2000). This (still hypothetical) practice entails deliberate breaking of crockery, and distributing the fragments among people, for instance the participants of an event, symbolically connecting them. The fragments thus created became memorabilia, which were kept within families and reminded them of people and events (Nieuwhof 2015, 292). For modern researchers, terra sigillata has the advantage over handmade pottery that it is more conspicuous, and that it occurs in much smaller numbers. This makes it possible to recognise and combine fragments that belong together. In Ezinge, for instance, fitting sherds were found in contexts that belonged to different households. This may indicate that sherds were exchanged by people within the settlement. But they could also be exchanged over larger distances. The most striking are two rather unassuming, small, but fitting base fragments, found in two different terps: Wierum and Oostum, settlements that are less than 2 km apart (fig. 7)[10]. Not fitting but possibly belonging to the same Drag. 37 bowl are 2 sherds from the terps of Joeswerd and Wierum, *c.* 2 km apart (Glasbergen 1944a, Wierum 10 and Joeswerd 8, fig. 68, nos 19, 25). The terra sigillata from phase 3 was no longer worked, but it was apparently still valued, as it is also frequently found in ritual deposits.

8 The location of this well in the settlement is uncertain as it was not noted in a field drawing. The most likely candidate is well 27.

9 Sunken hut 41, levels I and J, find nos 1077, 1079, 1079a.

10 The fragments were acquired in Wierum in 1914 and Oostum in 1916, as is noted on the sherds, but numbered only much later: Oostum 1971-X.61(4) and Wierum 1966-VIII.1(5).

Nevertheless, the lack of traces of secondary use may indicate that terra sigillata gradually came to be adopted as it was intended in this period, namely as tableware.

Conclusion

The majority of 1st-3rd century terra sigillata in the northern Netherlands, including Groningen, was either imported as sherds, or as complete vessels that were broken at some point after they arrived. The fragments were made into other items, stored, and sometimes handled, before finally being deposited. Many fragments, 80%, show traces of working and wear. It is likely that terra sigillata was not primarily valued as tableware, but as a raw material with a symbolic meaning. The use of fragments as pendants, possibly amulets, and terra sigillata deposits in and near houses, suggests that this meaning was associated with protection and good luck. Terra sigillata from the 4th-5th century still occurs in ritual deposits, and was apparently valued, but does not show traces of handling or working.

Volkers found in Wijnaldum that many middle Roman terra sigillata fragments were found in early medieval contexts and deduced that most terra sigillata fragments were probably only imported during the early Middle Ages. The Groningen assemblage does not confirm this hypothesis. Where the dates of contexts are available, as is especially the case in Ezinge and (in one case) Englum, it is clear that most terra sigillata sherds are found in contemporaneous contexts: 1st-century sherds in 1st-century contexts, 2nd-3rd century sherds in 2nd-3rd century contexts, and 4th-5th century sherds in 5th-century contexts. Earlier sherds in later contexts may sometimes have been dug up unintentionally from earlier layers, but this is not the best explanation of the frequent associations of middle and late Roman terra sigillata sherds, or the occurrence of middle Roman period terra sigillata in later ritual deposits. It is more likely that sherds were kept and passed on for generations as heirlooms, even for hundreds of years, until they were finally deposited.

Terra sigillata thus had two lives and two consecutive biographies. The first biography starts with production and ends with destruction or repurposing; the study of this first life includes themes such as potters' stamps, typologies, transport routes and provenance, trade, and traces of use as tableware or in food preparation. The second biography begins with the fragments that were created when a vessel broke; this second life may be revealed by examining traces of wear and working, object shape, fitting sherds, also in wider areas, associations with other objects, contexts, and context dates.

The fragments were passed on and exchanged, broken further, worked, handled, played with, worn as pendants, and stored, until they were finally deposited. It shows that members of indigenous societies outside the Roman Empire were selective in their choice of materials from Roman material culture. In the northern Netherlands, they preferred terra sigillata and also copper-alloy statuettes. The secondary use of terra sigillata fragments shows that they had their own ideas about the usability of these Roman goods. In more recent societies that have been confronted with European colonial powers, the symbolic use of selected elements of a foreign material culture came first, way before its practical use as intended by its producers. In the northern Netherlands, that stage was reached no earlier than the 4th/5th century, as the absence of traces of secondary use on late Argonne ware and ARSW may indicate.

PART 3

ROMAN POTTERY IN DIFFERENT CULTURAL AND FUNCTIONAL CONTEXTS

Ceramics in the Urban Sphere: the Social Strata of their Users

Bernd Liesen

Abstract

This overview on the consumption of pottery in urban sites in the province of Germania Inferior gives insights into supply chains. Significant differences between the Colonia Ulpia Traiana and the Colonia Claudia Ara Agrippinensium do not concern products imported from the Mediterranean and from central and eastern Gaul, but pottery groups from the North Sea coast, northern Gaul, and Germania Superior. It is not possible to obtain a reliable comparison between the coloniae and the large settlements in the north of the province (Arentsburg, Nijmegen), and comparisons between contexts from these sites do not give evidence of different social strata within the population. Significant differences can always be explained by the infrastructural connection.

Keywords: Roman, Germania Inferior, urban, pottery

Introduction

This paper provides an overview on the consumption of pottery in urban sites in the province of Germania Inferior, with a view to gaining an insight into the supply chains and the social strata of consumers. Besides the coloniae at Cologne and Xanten, the municipia of Atuatuca Tungrorum/Tongeren, Forum Hadriani/Voorburg-Arentsburg and Ulpia Noviomagus/Nijmegen are taken into consideration (fig. 1).

Sites

The urban centres of Germania Inferior are the Colonia Claudia Ara Agrippinensium/ Cologne (CCAA) and the Colonia Ulpia Traiana/Xanten (CUT). CCAA was promoted to a colonia around 50. It was the capital of the province and, from 260 to 275, of the Gallic Empire. After the reform of Diocletian in 285, it was the capital of Germania II. The estimated number of inhabitants was about 30,000 (Nissen 1895, 165). The city finally fell to the Franks in 459. Close to the city was the naval base of the *classis Germanica*. The CCAA was connected to the neighbouring regions via the Rhine, the road along the Rhine and other roads to northern Gaul (Andrikopoulou and Jenter 2018). The economy of the region around the CCAA can be described as a villa-landscape (Rind 2015). In the

in: R.C.A. Geerts and Ph. Bes (eds) 2024, *Roman Pottery in the Low Countries: Past Research, Current State, Future Directions*. Leiden: Sidestone Press (= *Papers on Archaeology of the Leiden Museum of Antiquities Leiden* 32), pp. 77-86.

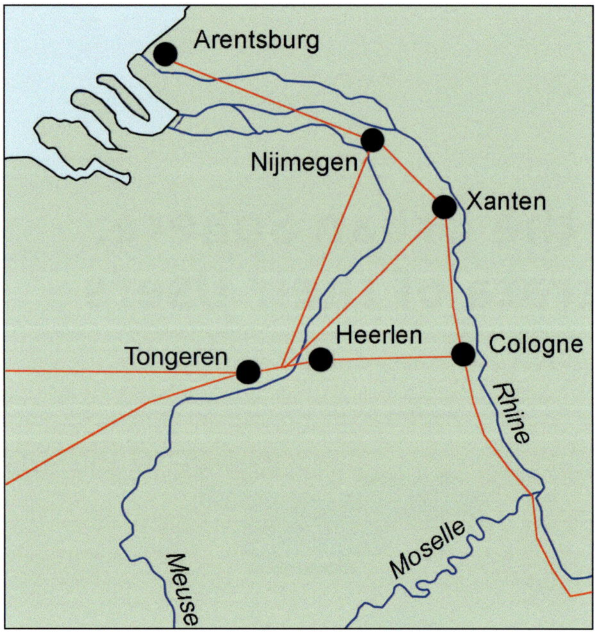

Fig. 1. Urban centres in Germania Inferior (© B. Liesen, LVR-Archäologischer Park Xanten/LVR-RömerMuseum).

suburbia there were large pottery workshops, producing a wide range of pottery. During the 2nd century, the city exported large quantities of pottery to the neighbouring regions and beyond and the city gained some economic power (Jaschke and Schmitz 2018).

The CUT was founded around 98. It was close to the legionary fortress of Vetera II, where since around 120 the Legio XXX was garrisoned. The CUT was inhabited by around 10,000 people (Weiß-König 2008, 525). In the later 3rd century, the city was reduced from 40 to 9 insulae (Rudnick 2024). Around 370 it was abandoned (cf. Komnick 2015, 587-588). The CUT was connected via the river Rhine, the road beside it, and roads to Tongeren, Heerlen, Cologne and to the sites along the limes (Andrikopoulou and Jenter 2018; Selke 2022). In the hinterland there were some small vici and villae (Brüggler 2018). So far, there are no large pottery workshops known in the CUT. All in all, the economy of the CUT was presumably not export-oriented. It is likely that products of local workshops were mainly consumed by the citizens of the CUT and by members of the military units in the vicinity (Liesen 2008; Reuter 2008).

Data

In comparison to the extensive excavations throughout the CCAA, there is, concerning the pottery, a significant lack of published data of statistical value. Even extensive excavation reports comprise just a selection of finds. In most cases no attempt was made to analyse the pottery in its social or economic setting. However, a number of cemeteries, a large number of pottery workshops and some sites in the vicinity of the CCAA have been well published. Furthermore, there are many valuable publications on different groups of pottery. As a result, one can glean much information regarding existing trade connections. There are, however, limited sources containing information on wealth or on other aspects of economic or social development.

At Xanten, we have rich quantitative data concerning contexts of the 2nd to 3rd centuries, giving a sufficient dataset to gain an insight into local production and consumption. In addition, a number of extensive studies regarding specific groups of pottery exist.

Pottery Consumption in Cologne/Colonia Claudia Ara Agrippinensium and Xanten/ Colonia Ulpia Traiana

Fine Wares

As at all sites in Germania Inferior, in Cologne La Graufesenque was predominant with regard to the terra sigillata market (cf. Berthold *et al.* 2017, 207-221). From the late 1st century onwards, a number of central and east Gaulish workshops started to export plain and decorated ware. In the 2nd century Blickweiler, La Madeleine, Chémery-Faulquemont, the Saturninus/Satto group and Trier predominate (Liesen 2002; 2007). Central Gaulish workshops, Sinzig and Rheinzabern did not achieve a strong position in the market (Liesen 2007). There is some evidence that in the 3rd century Trier produced the largest quantity of decorated vessels, whilst Rheinzabern played a comparatively minor role (Liesen 2002). Regarding decorated ware, Trier lost its position at the end of the 3rd century, and from the early 4th to the 5th century the Argonne workshops supplied the market with roulette decorated bowls (Bakker 2015). African Red Slip Ware reached the capital of the province in just small quantities (Höpken 2021).

Colour coated ware (fig. 2), another important group of fine wares, was produced in large quantities, in particular during the 2nd century in the workshops at the Rudolfplatz (Höpken 2005, 66-85). It was exported all over the province (Oenbrink 1998, 142-150). Thus, most of the colour coated ware in later 1st and in 2nd century contexts in the CCAA comes from local pottery workshops (Berthold *et al.* 2017, 223). In the later 2nd century beakers, probably from the Argonne workshops (Oelmann Technik B), appear (Liesen 2004a, 469). In the 3rd century, there was only a small production of colour coated ware at the Rudolfplatz (Höpken and Liesen 2005), whereas vessels made in Trier (*Trierer Schwarzfirnisware*) replaced the local products (cf. Höpken and Liesen 2009, 462). As a result of the loss of

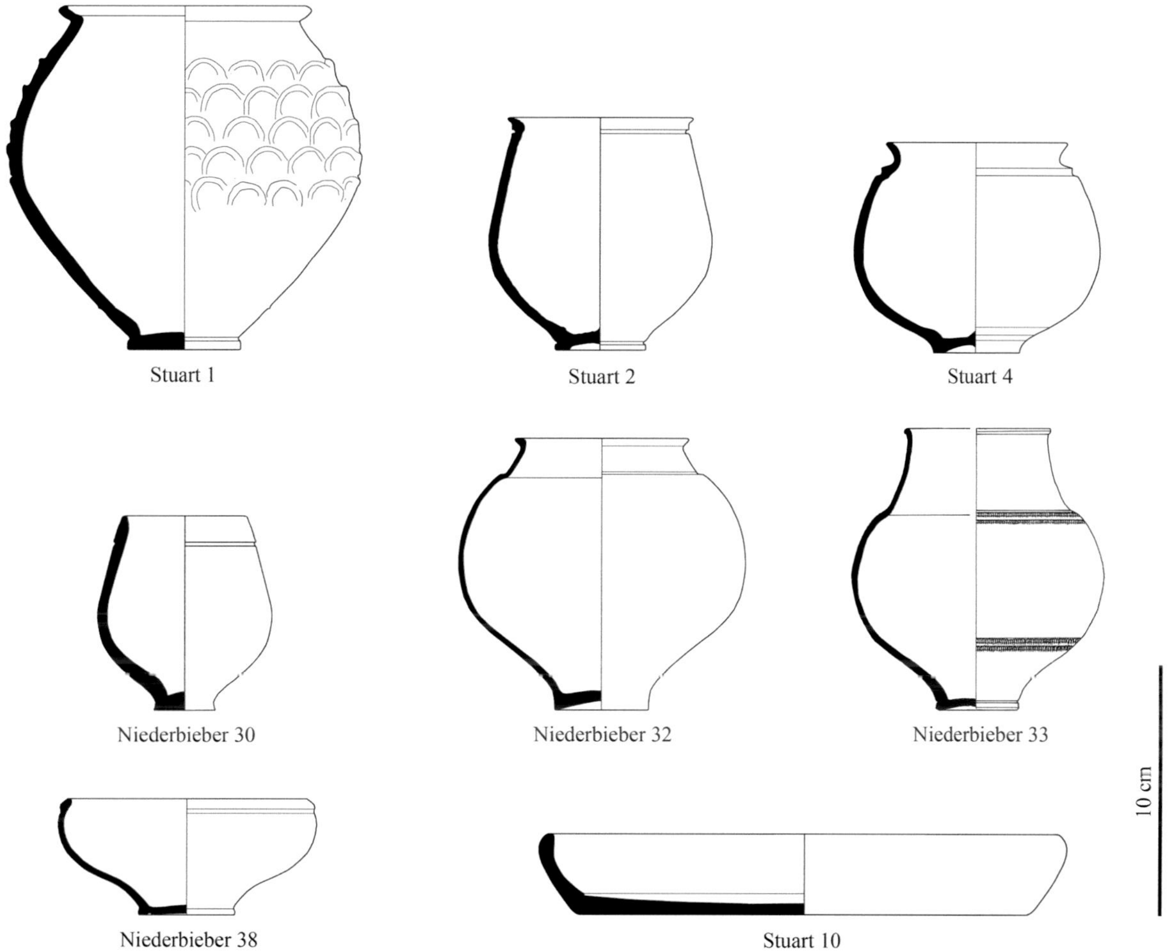

Fig. 2. Colour coated ware: vessel types (edited after: Willmitzer 2023, type pls 4-5).

their economic base, some potters evidently moved from Cologne into the hinterland. From then on, they may have shipped their products via the rivers Scheldt and Meuse. The products from Trier were available until the first half of the 4th century. In late Roman contexts marbled ware, possibly from Karden, is represented in the city by a number of vessels (Liesen 2004b, 475). Just one Rhône valley ware vessel was found (Audin and Binsfeld 1964). Late Roman *terra nigra* bowls are not very common throughout the city. Their origin is unknown, probably they were produced in Rhenish workshops (Frank 2023). At Xanten, in the 2nd century, terra sigillata from Trier, central Gaul and La Madeleine is predominant (Franke 2022, 20; Willmitzer 2023, 59-68). In the 3rd century Trier gained a stronger position in the market than Rheinzabern (Willmitzer 2023, 66-67). From the early 4th century until the final stage of the settlement around 370 the Argonne workshops supplied the city with roulette decorated bowls, but this group has been largely unpublished (cf. Otten and Ristow 2007, 556-557). In the 2nd century, colour coated ware is predominantly represented by products from Cologne, which were replaced in the 3rd century by products from Trier (Willmitzer 2023, 79-86). At Xanten, 3rd to 4th century marbled ware is rare (Daszkiewicz *et al.* 2024). Occasionally, Rhône valley ware found its way to Xanten (Thüry 2017).

Cooking Wares

From the 1st century onwards, a large production of burnished (fig. 3) ware and coarse (figs 4-5) ware was established in the CCAA (Höpken 2005). One can assume that a large amount of these wares found in the CCAA are of local origin. Both groups were produced until the 4th century (Schäfer *et al.* 2023), and burnished ware with painted decoration and small copies of Mid Roman Amphora 1 produced in Cologne were distributed in Germania II (Liesen 1999a; 2001).

In the late 2nd century, cooking vessels from Eifel workshops, such as Soller (Haupt 1984) or the group of Urmitz ware, along with related products from Koblenz, Andernach and Bonn (Friedrich 2023; Henrich 2023),

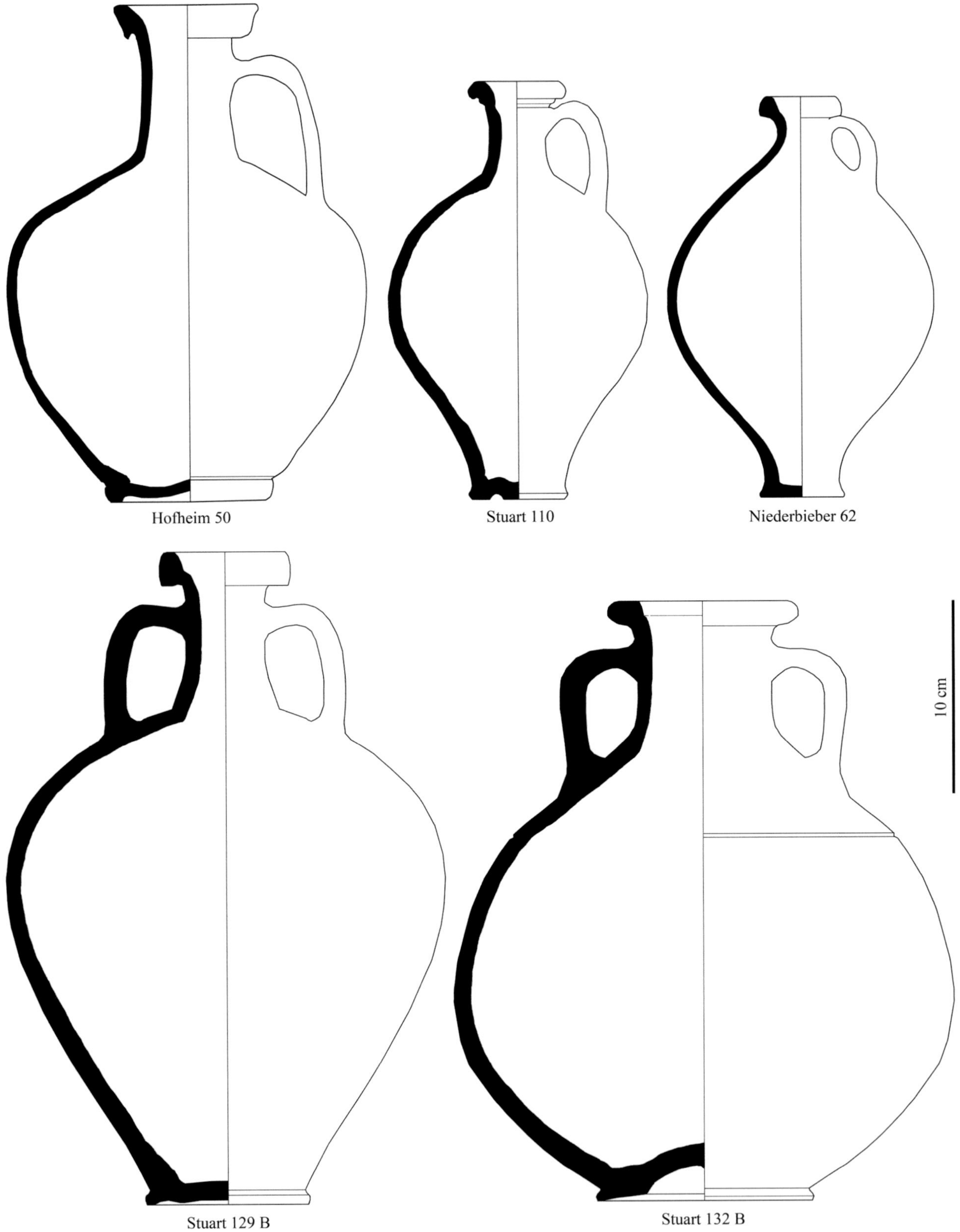

Fig. 3. Burnished ware: vessel types (edited after: Willmitzer 2023, type pls 11-12).

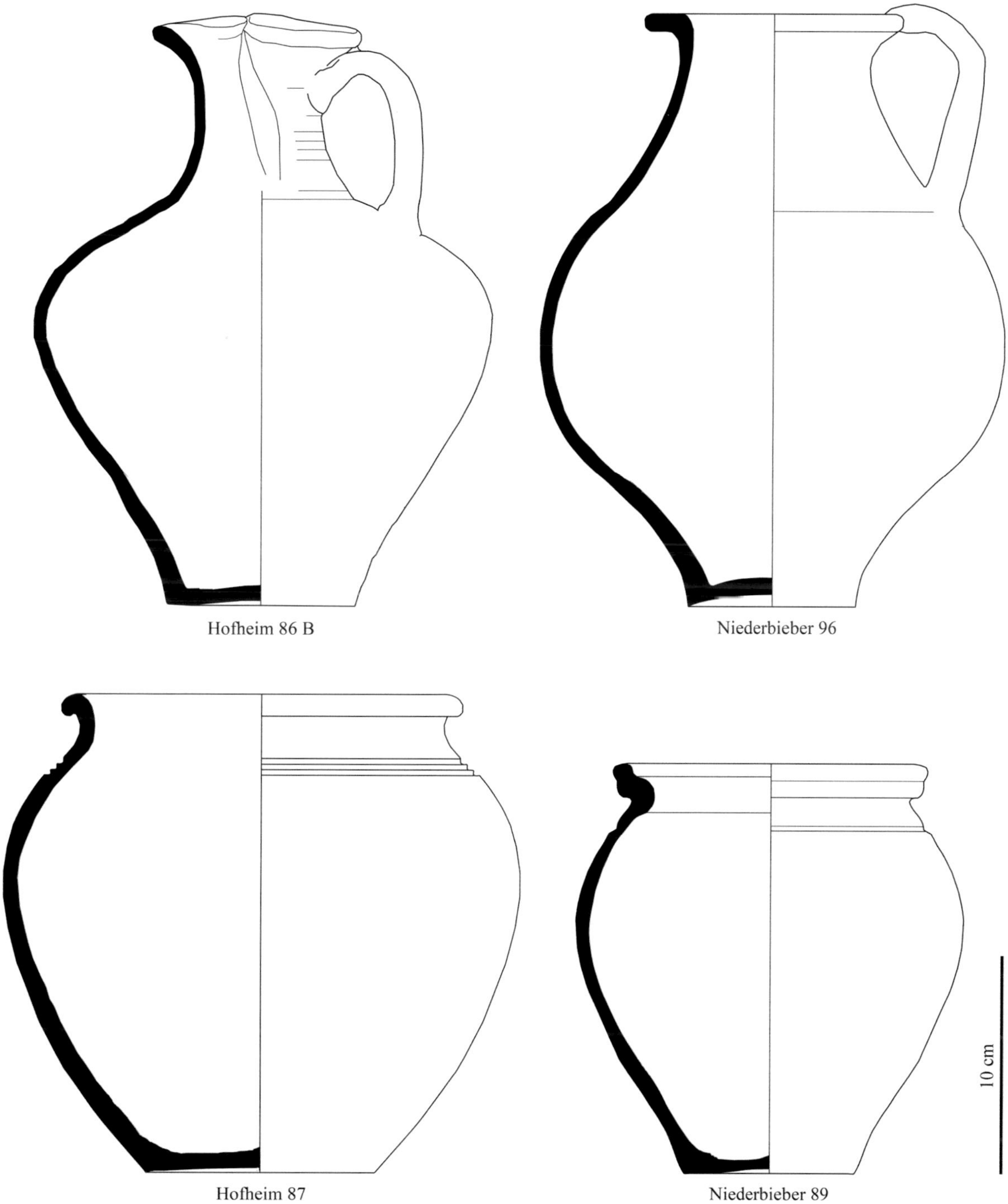

Fig. 4. Coarse ware: vessel types (edited after: Willmitzer 2023, type pls 17, 20-21).

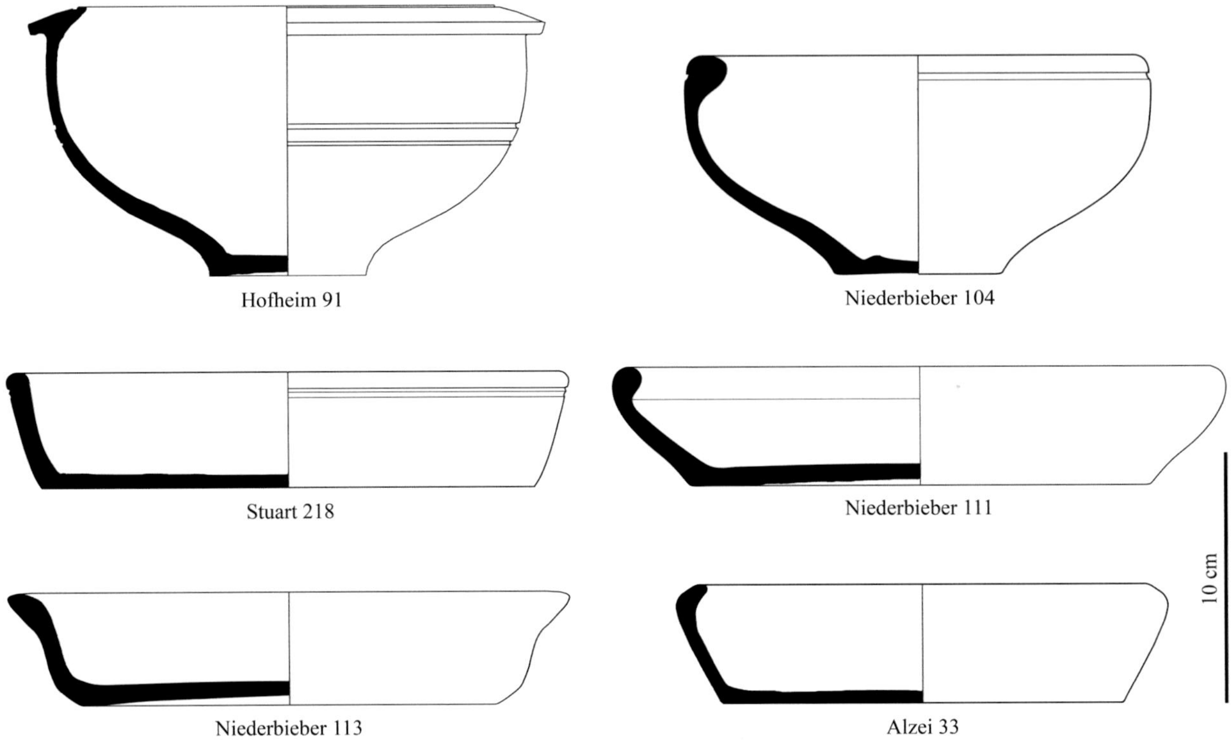

Fig. 5. Coarse ware: vessel types (edited after: Willmitzer 2023, type pls 20-23).

came onto the market. Coarse ware from Mayen was predominant in the 4th and 5th centuries (Grunwald 2023, 441-453). In the later 2nd century, mortaria from the Eifel region became common (Haupt 1984). A number of stamped vessels indicate imports from northern Gaul (Bavay region), but their quantity is small (Pfahl 2018).

So far, there is no evidence for a large-scale production of burnished ware and coarse ware in Xanten during the 2nd and 3rd centuries. Some small workshops within the CUT are known (Hinz 1963) and a presumably small quantity of vessels may have had their origin in the pottery workshops in the vicus (Heimberg and Rüger 1972) and in the large tile factory of the Legio XXX at the Halenboom (cf. Otte 2023 for legionary pottery from these workshops). Baking dishes produced there are not well represented in contexts of the CUT (Sieler 2014).

According to macroscopic analyses, in the later 2nd century imports from Eifel workshops, such as Soller and the production sites of Urmitz ware, and related wares gained a strong position on the local market (Willmitzer 2023, 108-125). In the 4th century, the fortified town was supplied by production sites at Mayen with cooking pots, bowls, and dishes (Liesen 2023). Stamped mortaria produced in Soller and probably other workshops in the Eifel region were imported in some quantity (Pfahl 2018) (fig. 6).

Amphorae and Other Wares used for Storage and Transport

CCAA: according to Höpken there was a local production of 2nd century types of Gaulish-style flat based amphorae (Höpken 2005, 145, pls 125.33-101, 158.40-019, 159.40-020). In 4th century workshops copies of Mid Roman Amphora 1 were amongst the type range (Höpken 2005, pl. 181.42-105, 42-106). Dolia (fig. 6) were produced in large quantities in Cologne (Höpken 2005, 144-145) and its hinterland (Aeissen and Höpken 2010). Obviously, there is no evidence for any long-distance trade involving these vessels.

In the later 1st and the 2nd century, olive oil was shipped in Spanish Dressel 20 amphorae (Mayer 2016); other types, such as Africana I from Tunisia, are poorly represented (Ehmig 2007, 218). Augst 21 and Haltern 70 amphorae were used to import olives from Spain and southern Gaul (Ehmig 2007, 218-219; Höpken 2019), the latter were also used to transport *defrutum*, fish sauce, and wine. Garum was shipped in Dressel 7-11 and Dressel 9 similis amphorae manufactured in the Iberian Peninsula and in workshops situated in the Rhone valley and southern Gaul (Ehmig 2009, 396-398). In the early stage of the CCAA, wine came from the eastern Mediterranean, Italy, Spain, and southern Gaul (Ehmig 2007, 219). Wine amphorae from southern Gaul and Spanish olive oil amphorae are predominant in

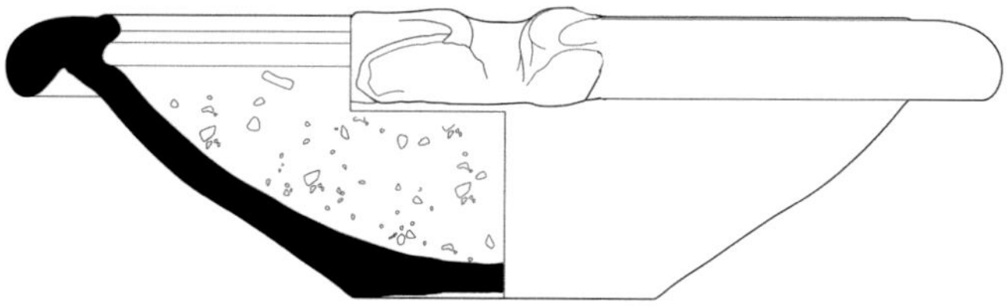

Hofheim 80

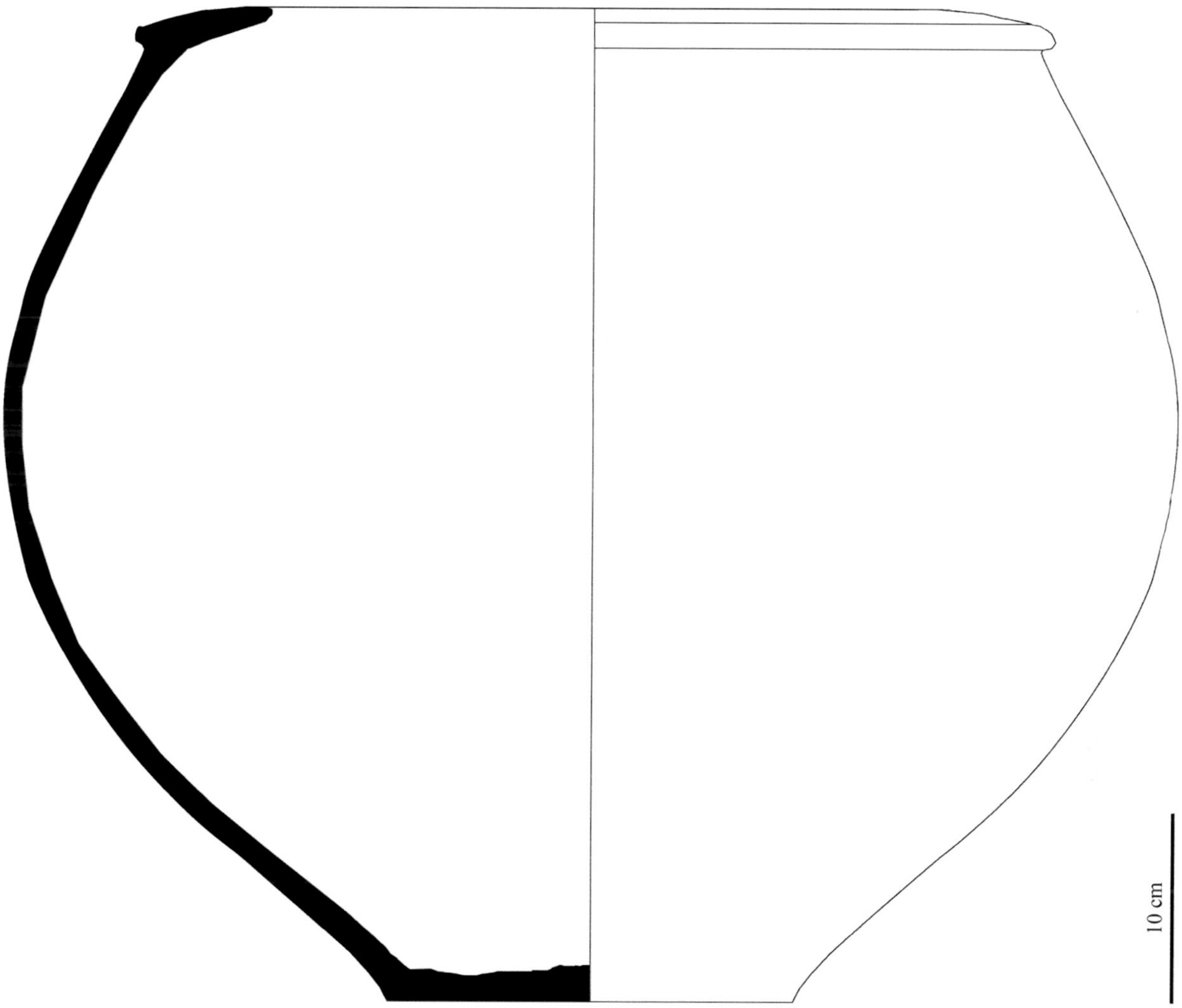

Hofheim 78

Fig. 6. Mortaria and dolia: vessel types (edited after: Willmitzer 2023, type pl. 24).

the 2nd century (unpublished data). Only small quantities of 3rd to 5th century amphorae have come to light. The type range consists of Spanish Dressel 23, a Mid Roman Amphora 1 from Sicily or northern Africa (Päffgen 1992, pl. 23.II.1.1), as well as north African Africana II, Keay IB and Dressel 30 (Liesen 2004a, 473; 2004b, 757-758). Late Roman Amphora 3 (unpublished) and Augst 53 from the eastern Mediterranean (Liesen 2004a, 474) are also worthy of mention. It is likely that some Kapitän 2 (Liesen 2004a, 474) came from the Aegean, but there is no archaeological evidence for workshops. Low Lands ware 1 containers Arentsburg 140-142 (Liesen 2004a, 471) are found in very small numbers (fig. 7).

In Xanten, 2nd and 3rd century Spanish olive oil amphorae Dressel 20 (Remesal Rodríguez 2018) and wine containers Gauloise 4 from Gallia Narbonensis make up the majority of transport containers from the Mediterranean (Marimon Ribas and Calzada Baños 2018).

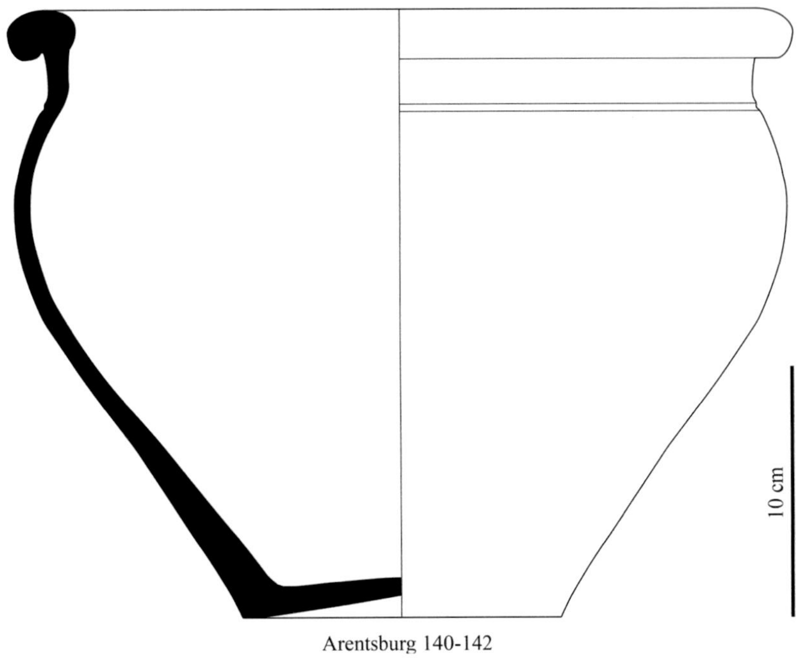

Fig. 7. Low Lands ware 1 bowl (edited after: Willmitzer 2023, type pl. 16).

Possibly, still in the 2nd century, Dressel 2-4 variants from Egypt were imported in very small quantities (Martin-Arroyo Sánchez 2018, 72). Scheldt valley amphorae from northern Gaul are also represented in some quantity (Schmitz 2014), as well as amphorae Niederbieber 75, possibly from northern Gaul (Schmitz 2006, 161). Their contents are unknown. Copies of Dressel 20 from Germania Superior, possibly used for shipping beer, are rare (Carreras Monfort *et al.* 2018, 145-147). A very small quantity of 3rd and 4th century amphorae also came to light. The type range consists of Dressel 23, Kapitän 2, Africana IIC, Reynolds AM 14 (Revilla Calvo 2018, 173; Liesen 2019, 331) and small specimens probably of Late Roman Amphora 3 (unpublished).

Some other types of containers are worthy of mention: Low Lands ware 1 containers (Arentsburg 140-142), possibly used for shipping mussels or oysters from the North Sea, are found in some quantity (Liesen 2016) (fig. 7), whereas salt containers in *briquetage* are rare (Willmitzer 2023, 130). In the 2nd century, handmade pottery from the Menapian region was imported (Jung 2014).

Terracotta Figurines, Masks and Lamps

In Cologne, mouldmade terracotta figurines and masks formed one of the most significant and widely distributed groups of pottery produced in the workshops at the Rudolfplatz (Lange 1994; Rose 2006). Unsurprisingly, the vast majority of the 2nd century terracotta figurines and masks found in the CCAA proper are of local origin. The production of discus lamps and factory lamps (Firmalampen) is attested for some workshops in the 1st and 2nd centuries (Höpken 2005, 148-150; Cahn 2009, 284-303). Small Firmalampen, macroscopically ascribed to the Rudolfplatz workshops, were exported, and predominantly used as grave goods in the CCAA and all over the province (cf. Pirling and Siepen 2006, 404-407). So far, it is certain that amongst the finds from the CCAA there are products from abroad, which may, according to macroscopic analyses, have been imported from Italy, Trier or perhaps from other, none localised workshops (cf. Ihde 2018, 146).

At Xanten, some moulds indicate a small-scale production of terracotta figurines and Firmalampen in the 2nd century (Hinz 1963, 396-401), but certainly the vast majority of terracotta figurines, masks and Firmalampen were imported from Cologne and Trier (Liesen 1999b, 12; Rose 2023; Rudnick 2023; Willmitzer 2023, 51-53).

Discussion

As far as the products imported from the Mediterranean and from central and eastern Gaul are concerned, differences between Xanten and Cologne are only apparent with regard to the chronological development of the two cities. Significant differences relate to pottery groups from the North Sea coast, northern Gaul, and Germania Superior. As the sources of the groups which were shipped via the Scheldt and Meuse – Scheldt valley amphorae, Low Lands ware 1 and handmade Menapian ware – were closer to Xanten, they are much better represented in the CUT than upstream on the Rhine in the CCAA. On the other hand, copies of Dressel 20 from Germania Superior are recorded at Cologne in some quantity, whereas they are not frequent at Xanten.

Due to the lack of data, it is not possible to obtain a reliable comparison between the coloniae and the large settlements in the north of the province, not only regarding the pottery itself as a trading good, nor as a container for foodstuffs or other goods. Archaeological excavations have yielded large datasets for Voorburg-Arentsburg, whereas data from 2nd and 3rd century contexts at Nijmegen are scarce, except for terra sigillata.

Pottery production of the 2nd and 3rd centuries is attested at Nijmegen, but only a small number of kilns has been exhaustively published (Hendriks 2014; Weiß-König 2023). Thus, due to the lack of published data from 2nd and 3rd century contexts, even taking into consideration the extensively examined workshop on the Maasplein, so far there is no sufficient information on the consumption of the locally produced pottery in comparison with imports. At Arentsburg there is, apart from some dolia, no significant evidence for the use of local products (Van Kerckhove 2014, 371).

Looking at decorated terra sigillata as an imported fine ware, at Arentsburg there is a clear predominance of vessels made in east Gaulish workshops (Van der Linden 2023, 494, fig. 22.5). Data from Nijmegen (Van Diepen and Niemeijer 2011, 172, fig. 8; Hendriks *et al.* 2023, 96-99), Xanten and Cologne match this quite well. Regarding the 2nd century workshops, there is evidence that in Cologne, Xanten, and Nijmegen central Gaulish terra sigillata achieved a somewhat higher proportion than in Arentsburg. However, in Tongeren, central Gaulish ware is much more frequent than in all settlements along the Rhine (Van der Linden 2023, 494, fig. 22.5).

The majority of the colour coated ware found at Arentsburg seems to have been imported from Cologne and other Rhenish workshops, until the workshops at Trier pushed them out of the market from the late 2nd century onwards (Van Kerckhove 2014, 333-340). In the 3rd century, the high quality black-slipped ware from Trier was predominant.

Further characteristic features of the consumption at Arentsburg are, in comparison to Xanten and Cologne, the large quantities of Low Lands ware (Van Kerckhove 2014, 350-358) and close to 14% of small- and medium-sized transport containers (Van Kerckhove 2014, 345-347). Pottery from Britain, present in small quantities at Arentsburg, is completely absent in Xanten and Cologne – the only vessel from Britannia found at some distance from the coastal area was in a burial at Krefeld-Gellep and should be interpreted as a personal belonging (Pirling and Siepen 2006, 184). The bulk of burnished and coarse wares at Arentsburg was imported from workshops in the Rhineland, the Moselle valley, and the Neuwied Basin. The amphora type range consists mainly of Dressel 20, as well as Gauloise 4 and typologically identical regionally produced vessels (Van Kerckhove 2014, 350-358).

As in Xanten and Cologne, certain rare and/or extraordinary vessels, such as Rhone valley ware, are attested at Nijmegen (Spickermann 2018, 605, fig. 6). It seems however likely that those were either personal belongings of individuals or occasional imports. They do not reflect a permanent demand of an urban elite.

Due to a lack of data, even for the most significant pottery groups, comparisons between the contexts, each with its own chronology and size, do not provide any evidence for different social strata within the coloniae. Significant differences between certain groups of pottery at different sites with an urban settlement structure can always be explained by the infrastructural connections (roads, rivers) of those sites in relation to the production regions. Regarding the pottery, sites such as Cologne, Xanten and Arentsburg were (re)distribution points for smaller settlements and military camps in the vicinity. Concerning the amphorae, this means that in the larger cities many foodstuffs could have been packed into smaller containers and then transported to their final destination. Presumably, the data from contexts associated with the various coloniae are not suitable to reconstruct the consumption habits correctly.

The wealthy military (CUT) or administrative (CCAA) elites were so small that any traces of their consumption of exclusive products are not reflected in the spectrum of finds. It is interesting to note that – apart from Dressel 23 – it was just the amphorae from distant production areas (eastern Mediterranean, north Africa) that continued to reach the Rhine limes even during the late phase of Roman occupation. This suggests that it was precisely these products which were luxury goods and still imported on demand by a small wealthy elite, while the goods that were affordable for non-elite consumers which had previously been imported in large quantities were replaced by regional products.

Acknowledgements

I am deeply indebted to C. Bridger (Xanten) for his valuable support.

Augustan Military Pottery Assemblages on the Hunerberg in Nijmegen

Harry van Enckevort

Abstract

For more than 100 years, excavations have been carried out on the Hunerberg in the eastern part of Nijmegen. In the course of this research, a great deal of pottery from the Augustan period has been collected. It shows that the soldiers in the (second) Augustan fortress (19-16 BC) used little arretina and relatively many beakers of fine ware. The large (amphorae, dolia) and small vessels (pots, bowls) suggest that some of their food (and other products) was brought from afar, but also that much food was brought in handmade pottery from the Batavian region. The contents of some pits from the years 10-20 contain much less fine ware, although the same amount of arretina, but more Gallo-Belgic wares (beakers, plates). The quantity of large vessels is broadly similar, and the proportion of handmade pottery does not seem to have decreased.

Keywords: Nijmegen-Hunerberg, Augustan pottery

Introduction

The remains of two Augustan fortresses have been found on the Hunerberg in the eastern part of Nijmegen. Of the oldest, little is known beyond the reconstructed outline of a ditch (fig. 1.1). It was probably only in use for a short time in or just before 19 BC (Van Enckevort 2021, 191-192). The existence of the youngest and best-known Augustan fortress was postulated as early as 1916 (Holwerda 1917, 11-16, especially the map on 12); half a century later, Hendrik Brunsting (1969) was able to determine its size (42 ha), on the basis of additional excavations (fig. 1.2). Jules Bogaers and Jan Kees Haalebos excavated some parts of the fortress in 1973-1977 (Bogaers and Haalebos 1977; 1980) and 1987-1997 (Haalebos 1995). Haalebos incorporated the results of the excavations into a detailed map and concluded that the fortress could have been occupied by at least 15,000 soldiers, belonging to two legions and several auxiliary units (Haalebos 1991; 1995, 9-26; 1998, 8-18; 2000, 13; 2006, 350-352. See also Willems and Van Enckevort 2009, 31-35).

in: R.C.A. Geerts and Ph. Bes (eds) 2024, *Roman Pottery in the Low Countries: Past Research, Current State, Future Directions*. Leiden: Sidestone Press (= *Papers on Archaeology of the Leiden Museum of Antiquities Leiden* 32), pp. 87-96.

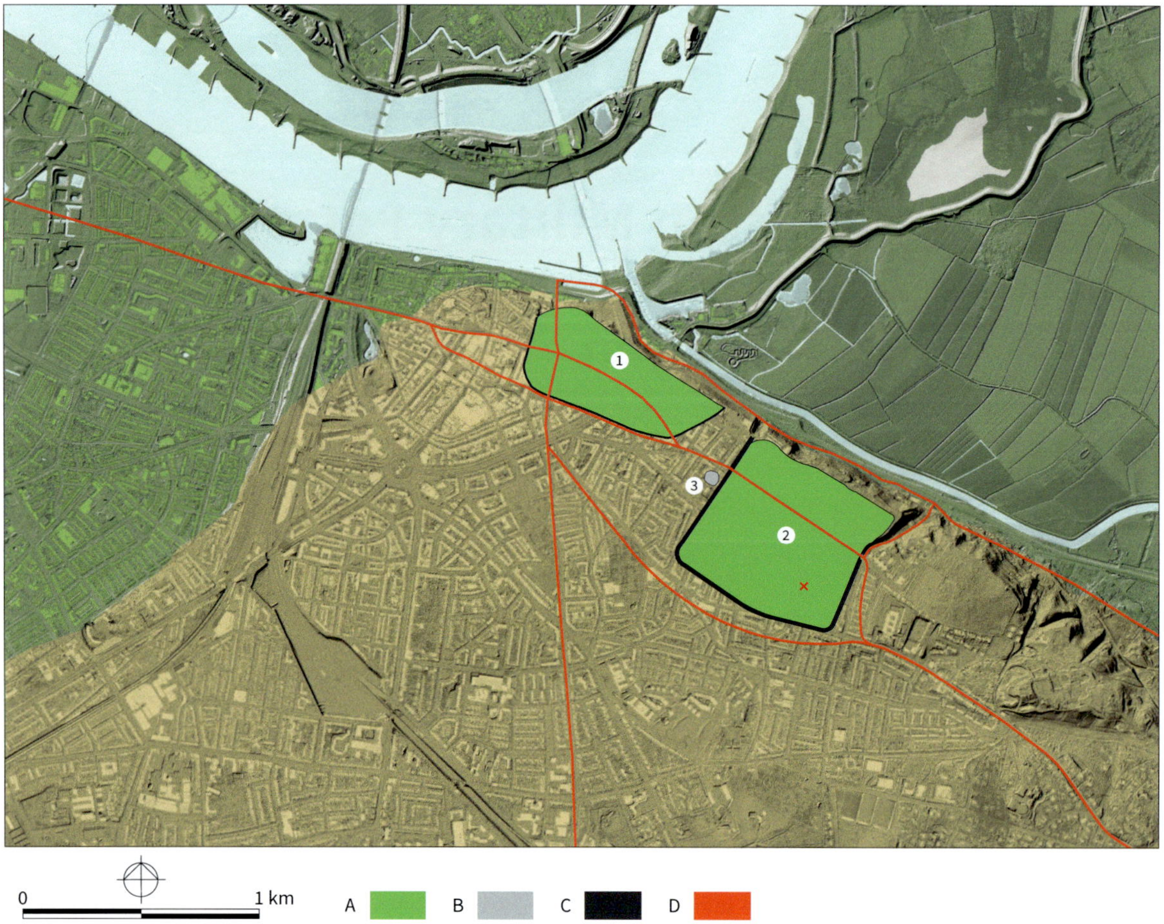

Fig. 1. Overview of Nijmegen 19-16 BC. The brown shaded area covers the ice-pushed ridge and the outwash plain (*sandr*) of Pleistocene origin above the 10 m contour line. The red cross marks the location of the pottery kiln. A: military settlement; B: cemetery; C: ditch; D: road; 1-2: fortresses; 3: military cemeteries (© Bureau Archeologie, Municipality of Nijmegen/R. Mols and L. Scheffer).

Category	Fragments	Function				
		Tableware	Small Container	Large Container	Flagons	Kitchenware
Arretina	2.0	2.0	-	-	-	-
Fine ware	16.6	16.6	-	-	-	-
Gallo-Belgic ware	5.6	5.6	-	-	-	-
Pompeian red ware	0.1	-	-	-	-	0.1
Smooth ware	20.2	-	*	-	20.2	-
Amphorae	11.1	-	-	11.1	-	-
Dolia	0.8	-	-	0.8	-	-
Mortaria	0.7	-	-	-	-	0.7
Coarse ware	19.0	-	19.0	-	-	-
Cork ware	2.1	-	2.1	-	-	-
Handmade pottery	21.8	-	21.8	-	-	-
total %	100.0	24.2	42.9	11.9	20.2	0.8

Table 1. Overview of the pottery (2892 fragments) from the years 19-16 BC from the second fortress (after: Niemeijer 2017, 10-12, table 1); * only a few fragments.

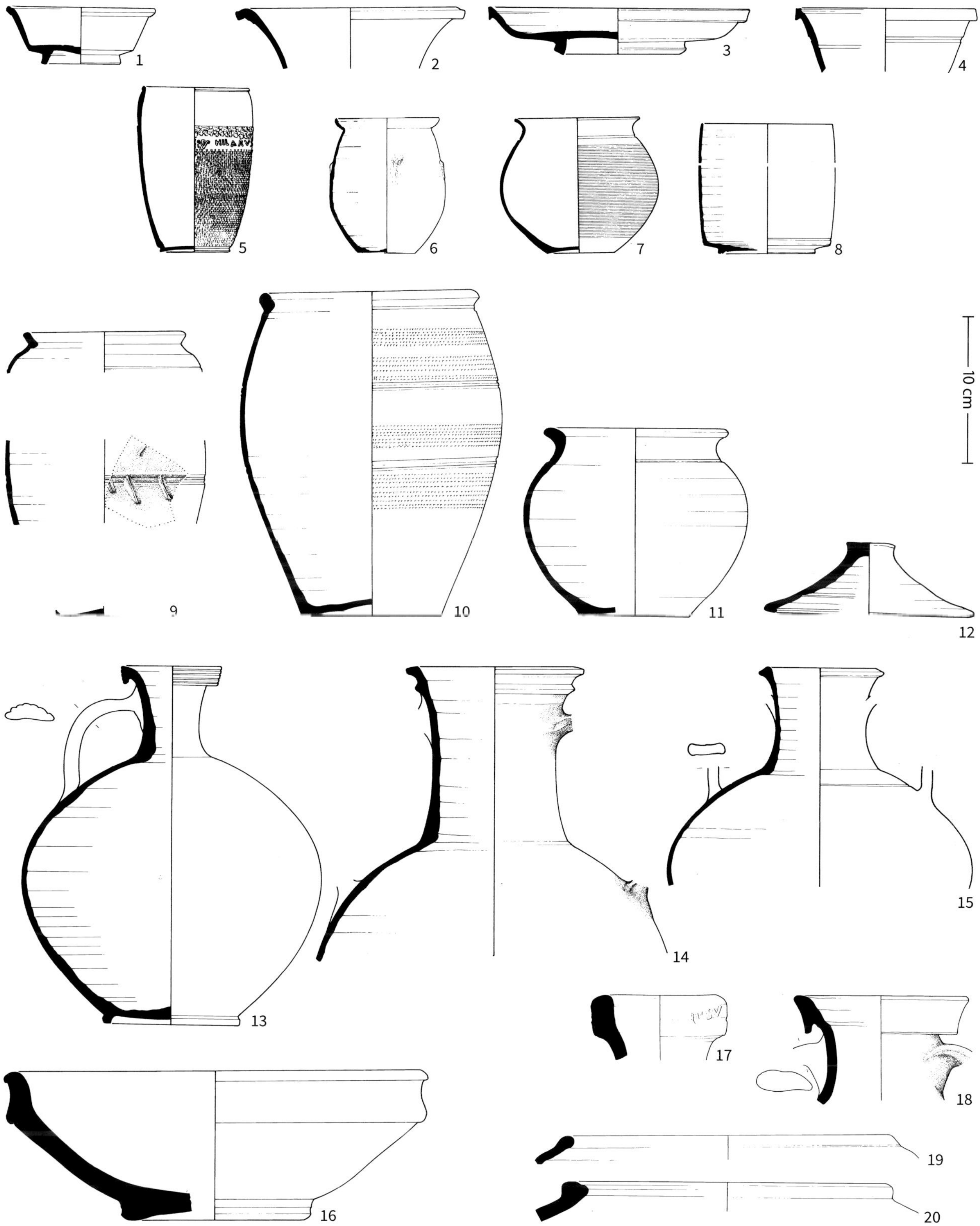

Fig. 2. Selection of the pottery from the western part of the youngest Augustan fortress. 1-4: arretina; 2-8: fine ware; 9-10: Gallo-Belgic ware; 11-12: coarse ware; 13-15: smooth ware; 16: mortarium; 17-18: amphorae; 19-20: dolia. Scale 1:4 (after: Niemeijer 2017, 13-19, figs 4-9).

Fleur Kemmers concluded that the fortress must have been built in 19/18 BC, based on the coin series she studied. She links its construction to Agrippa's second governorship of Gaul and the simultaneous military build-up in the north of the province, especially along the Rhine, in preparation for the campaigns in Germania. Coins from northern Italy of the Divos Julius type suggest that the legions stationed at Nijmegen may have been raised in this region. Several Celtic coins from regions along the route from northern Italy to Nijmegen, via the valleys of the rivers Rhône, Saône, Moselle and Meuse, seem to support this assumption. The end of the Augustan fortress seems to be linked to the *Clades Lolliana* in 16 BC, when Roman troops under Marcus Lollius were ambushed by Germanic tribes (Suetonius, *De vita Caesarum – Augustus* XXIII; Tacitus, *Annales* I.10, III.48). It is not clear whether the units stationed in Nijmegen at the time were actually involved in this event (Kemmers 2005a, 49-57; 2005b, 988; 2007, 189-197; 2008, 67-68, 170).

Ryan Niemeijer has published some of the Augustan features in more detail, especially the western part of the two ditches (Niemeijer 2013), and the buildings in this part of the fortress (Niemeijer 2016; 2018. See also Haalebos 2002; Niemeijer 2015). Excavations in the eastern part of the fortress provided additional evidence for the ditches as well as for several interval towers (Heirbaut and Van Enckevort 2009, 15-20, 27-28, 98-106). It seems that the two ditches were not used at the same time. The outer ditch was open for much longer than the inner one, probably until the Flavian period (Heirbaut *et al.* 2009. See also Bloemers 1979a; 2016, 7, figs 3.8, 4, and 35-40; Polak 2014, 19). Why this was the case, is unknown. Outside the rampart and the two ditches, evidence of a fourth defensive zone was found, including *stimuli* and probably also *cippi* or *lilia* (Heirbaut and Van Enckevort 2009, 101-104)[1].

Since the 1987-1997 excavations, lamps (Zandstra and Moust 2014), mortaria (Kloosterman 2014b), pottery in general (Niemeijer 2014; 2017), and an Augustan pottery assemblage (Haalebos and Willems 1999a, 77; 1999b, 247-248) have been published. Large quantities of regionally produced handmade pottery used for transporting food show that the army was heavily dependent on (Batavian) supplies from the area (Stoffels 2006). At the same time, the many amphora fragments show that the army was also supplied through the military trade network extending into the Mediterranean regions (González Cesteros 2014, 241-253; Van den Berg *et al.* 2017).

1 Julius Caesar mentioned in his account of the siege of Alesia (*De bello Gallico* VII.73) rows of holes with sharpened sticks (*cippi*), short stakes with iron hooks (*stimuli*) and camouflaged trap-pits with sharpened stakes (*lilia*).

Pottery from the Western Part of the Augustan Fortress

In 2017, Niemeijer published an overview of the pottery from the years 19-16 BC found in the western part of the Augustan fortress during the 1987-1997 excavations. The second column in Table 1 lists the sherds found in a selected number of features (which included a small percentage of younger finds). Almost a quarter has been attributed to tablewares, of which only a small proportion is counted as arretina. 95% of the arretina (bowls, plates, and platters) came from Italy (Arezzo), only 5% came from Lyon. Early forms belonging to the 'Pre-Service' and 'Service Ia' are well represented (Consp. 7, 8 (fig. 2.1), 10, 11, 13 (fig. 2.2)), although later forms such as Consp. 12 (fig. 2.3) and 14 (fig. 2.4) have also been found. The later forms (Service II) are missing (Niemeijer 2014, 9-15; 2017, 9, 12. See also Haalebos 1991, 102-106). Among the fine wares, the fabrics indicate an origin in the Rhône valley, the Rhine region and possibly Nijmegen. ACO beakers are the most common (fig. 2.5), followed by beakers Oberaden 31/Dangstetten D2 beakers (fig. 2.6), beakers with or without horizontal grooves Oberaden 30/Dangstetten D3 (figs 2.7, 5.2), and beakers Oberaden 39/Dangstetten D.5.3 (fig. 2.8). The so-called *Soldatenbecher* Oberaden 20/Dangstetten D4 is missing, suggesting that it came into use several years later (Haalebos 1991, 106; Niemeijer 2014, 19-29; 2017, 12-16). The oldest forms of the Gallo-Belgic wares also appear in this pottery assemblage. These were probably produced in the western part of the *civitas Treverorum*. Best represented are several variants of the beakers Deru P23/Holwerda 1 (fig. 2.9)[2] and Deru P13/Holwerda 3 (fig. 2.10) in an oxidised fabric, although a relatively large number of fragments of beakers Deru P13/Holwerda 3 in *terra nigra* were also found (Niemeijer 2017, 15-16).

Coarse ware pots with an outwardly curved rim conform Stuart 201 (fig. 2.11) and lids (fig. 2.12) are well represented in a large number of different fabrics. Some of these have vertical polished stripes on the surface and can be classified as a Holwerda 2 type. The pots also include handmade examples of so-called cork ware Holwerda 94/Haltern 91 (figs 4.3, 5.15; Niemeijer 2017, 16-17). These *Haltener Kochtöpfe* were in widespread use until around 100, as evidenced by the many sherds found in the Nijmegen fortifications on the Hunerberg and the Kops Plateau, as well as in Xanten (Mittag 1999). Because of the presence of calcium carbonate (CaCO3, calcite) as a tempering material, the origin of these pots has been sought in the Condroz and/or the Entre-Sambre-Meuse region in Belgium (Lepot and Vilvorder 2015; Venant 2016). The use of calcium carbonate would have had a preservative effect on the contents (Tuijn 1998), which is why Lepot and

2 All references to Holwerda types in this contribution concern Holwerda 1941.

	Region	Type	Content	MaxNI
Iberian Peninsula	Baetican mainland	Oberaden 83	olive oil	2
		globular	olive oil	8
		Haltern 70	*sapa*, *defrutum* or olives conserved in those products	1
		cylindrical	olive oil	4
	Marismas	Dressel 7-11	fish sauce	2
	Baetican coast	Dressel 7	fish sauce	4
		Dressel 7-11 (fig. 2.18)	fish sauce	15
		Dressel 12	fish sauce	1
	Tarraconensis	Pascual 1	wine	4
Italy	Etruria	Dressel 1B	wine	1
	Adriatic	Lamboglia 2/Dressel 6A (fig. 2.17) (cf. Lindhagen 2009; Carre *et al.* 2014)	wine	4
Aegean	Kos (Asia Minor)	Dressel 2-5	wine	7
	Rhodes (Asia Minor)	Camulodunum 184	wine	6
	Knidos	Pompeii 38	wine	1
Gaul	Lyon	unknown	wine	1
	Languedoc/Marseille	unknown	wine	1
total N				62

Table 2. The amphorae from the western part of the youngest Augustan fortress (after: Van den Berg *et al.* 2017).

Vilvorders (2015, 240) suggestion is not surprising. They suggest that preserved meat was transported in such pots over long distances from the Condroz to the consumers. This assumption is supported by a pot found on the nearby Kops Plateau containing the bones of 28 preserved song thrushes' briskets (Lauwerier 1993).

Three-quarters of the flagons are made of an orange fabric, only a quarter is white. Flagon Stuart 103/ Oberaden 43 (fig. 2.13) is the best represented. In addition, flagons Stuart 133/Oberaden 52 (fig. 2.14), Stuart 131/ Oberaden 48-49 (fig. 2.15) and the so-called 'honey pots' Stuart 146 were also common (Niemeijer 2017, 17). The fact that most of the flagons in the Augustan period were made of an orange, slightly sandy fabric is also evident from the finds from the neighbouring Kops Plateau. This is also confirmed by Roth-Rubi's research on flagons of this period, in which she also examined smooth ware from military centres on the banks of the rivers Rhine and Lippe (Roth-Rubi 1979). The amphora sherds give a good picture of the contacts between Nijmegen and other parts of the Roman Empire between 20 and 10 BC. They also show that in this early period the soldiers in the fortress were supplied with olive oil, fish sauce and wine (table 2).

Rare are the Oberaden 21 plates in Pompeian red ware (Niemeijer 2017, 17), which were used to bake or heat food in an oven. On a larger scale, sherds of mortaria with vertical rim Haltern 59 (fig. 5.10) produced in Lyon and nearby Saint-Romain-en-Gal have been found (Kloosterman 2014b, 199, 201, 203-205). In addition, several fragments of large handmade dolia Stuart 147 with a wheelthrown rim with a black coating (fig. 5.11) have been found. Whether these early dolia came from the löss area between Tienen in Belgium and Cologne in Germany (Borgers 2023, 628) will have to be determined by future research. Furthermore, several sherds of dolia with a small twisted *Wulstrand* were found (fig. 2.19-20), which can be specifically dated to this early period.

From Table 1 (columns 3-7), some conclusions can be deduced about the function of the pottery. Among the tableware, the low proportion of terra sigillata is striking; the tableware is strongly dominated by the fine ware beakers. It can also be concluded that more than half of the pottery comes from small and large containers used for transporting food, wine, fish sauce, olive oil or other goods. The small wheelthrown vessels (cf. figs 2.11, 3.1-6, 5.12-14) are often called cooking pots. Yet, as the fabrics of such pots are often unsuitable for cooking, they are more likely to be containers in which food or other goods were transported (cf. Van Enckevort 2000, 134-135; Collins *et al.* 2009, 193). If the contents were food, some of such pots and their contents were heated in an oven or on a charcoal fire and, when empty, thrown on the rubbish heap, just like modern cans. Other pots were only used for their contents and

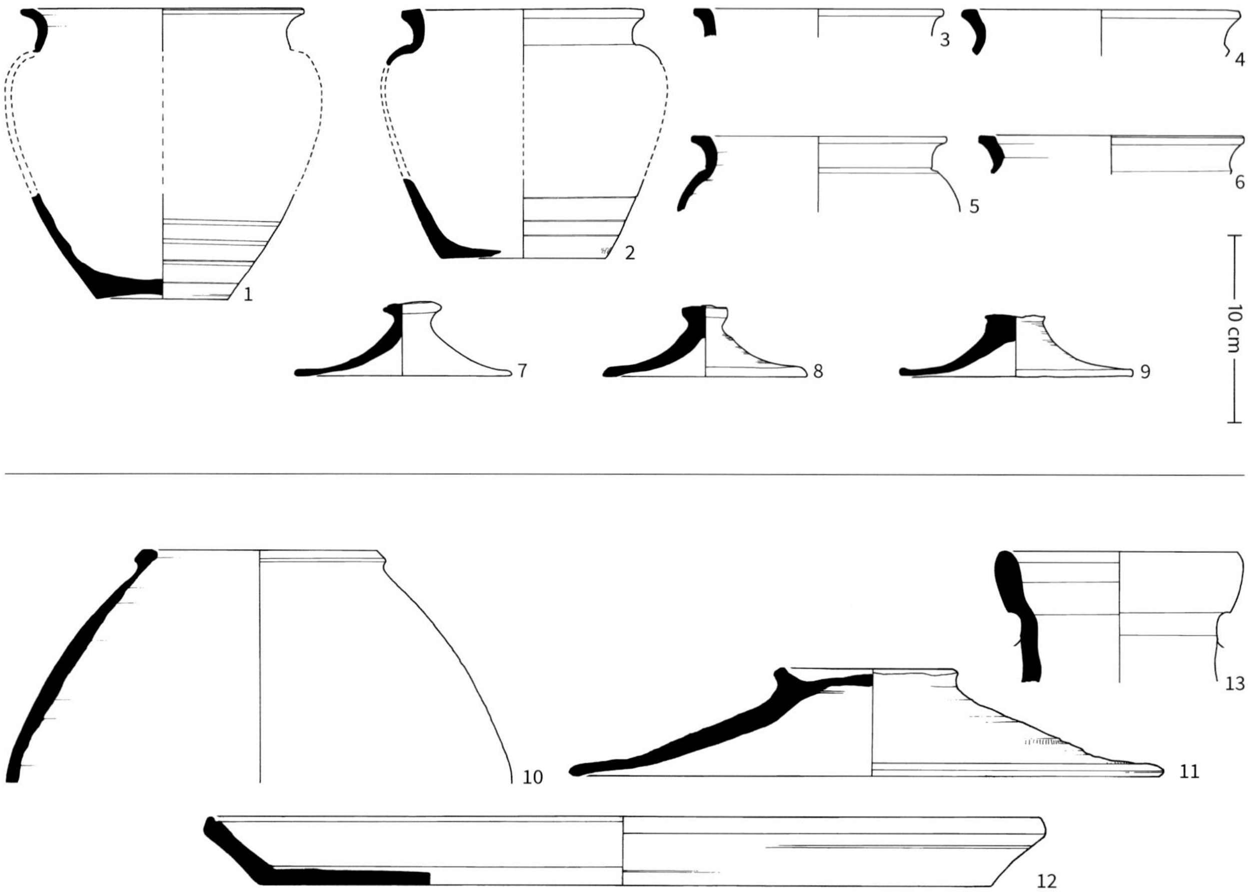

Fig. 3. Pottery from the potter's kiln. Scale 1:4 (© Bureau Archeologie, Municipality of Nijmegen/M. Verhoeven).

then thrown away. Food was cooked in large metal cauldrons or smaller metal pots. The large number of sherds of small handmade pots shows that the soldiers in the fortress obtained a lot of food from the rural Batavian settlements around Nijmegen (Stoffels 2006; Van den Broeke this volume).

An Augustan Potter's Kiln

There is evidence that *immunes* with special skills produced pottery in the fortress, using a kiln in the southeastern part of the fortress (fig. 1). The remains of this kiln were discovered in March-April 2003 during the renovation of a sewer (Heirbaut and Van Enckevort 2009, 43-45). It was a 280 cm wide and a 120 cm deep pit, which was identified as a stoke-hole. At the bottom there was a 15 cm thick layer containing a lot of charcoal, fragments of fired clay and pottery sherds. The pieces of fired clay came from the dome of the kiln, which was about 1 m in diameter, and from the grate. Some of the pieces contained fragments of pots used to reinforce the construction of the dome and to absorb thermal shocks. These pieces are probably the remains of an up-draught kiln. In the space underneath the dome, above the grate, the potter stacked the dried pottery to be fired. Archaeological research and experimental studies have shown that the upper part of the kiln was partially broken off after firing and cooling in order to remove the fired products (Bryant 1973).

In addition to the kiln fragments, the layer contained a number of sherds of locally produced pottery. Some of these sherds were heavily burnt and greyish white to yellow in colour. The main product appears to have been an S-shaped pot with a flattened rim (fig. 3.1-6). The shape is very similar to the coarse ware pots of type Stuart 201 (Stuart 1977b, pl. 19), but the fabric is clearly much finer than the usual Rhenish fabric for this time. The lid fragments appear to belong to the pots. Two of the lids have a knob-shaped finished handle (figs 3.7-8). Such lids are rarely, if ever, found in a Roman context in Nijmegen. The third lid has the wide handle (fig. 3.9), which is more characteristic of lids from the Roman period in the lower Rhine area (Stuart 1977b, pl. 23.400-401). In addition to these sherds, there are a number of sherds which were not produced in the kiln. These include several fragments of a late 'Celtic barrel-shaped' pot made in *terra nigra* (fig. 3.10, cf. Metzler 1995, 372, fig. 197.A.4.1-3 and 390-392), and

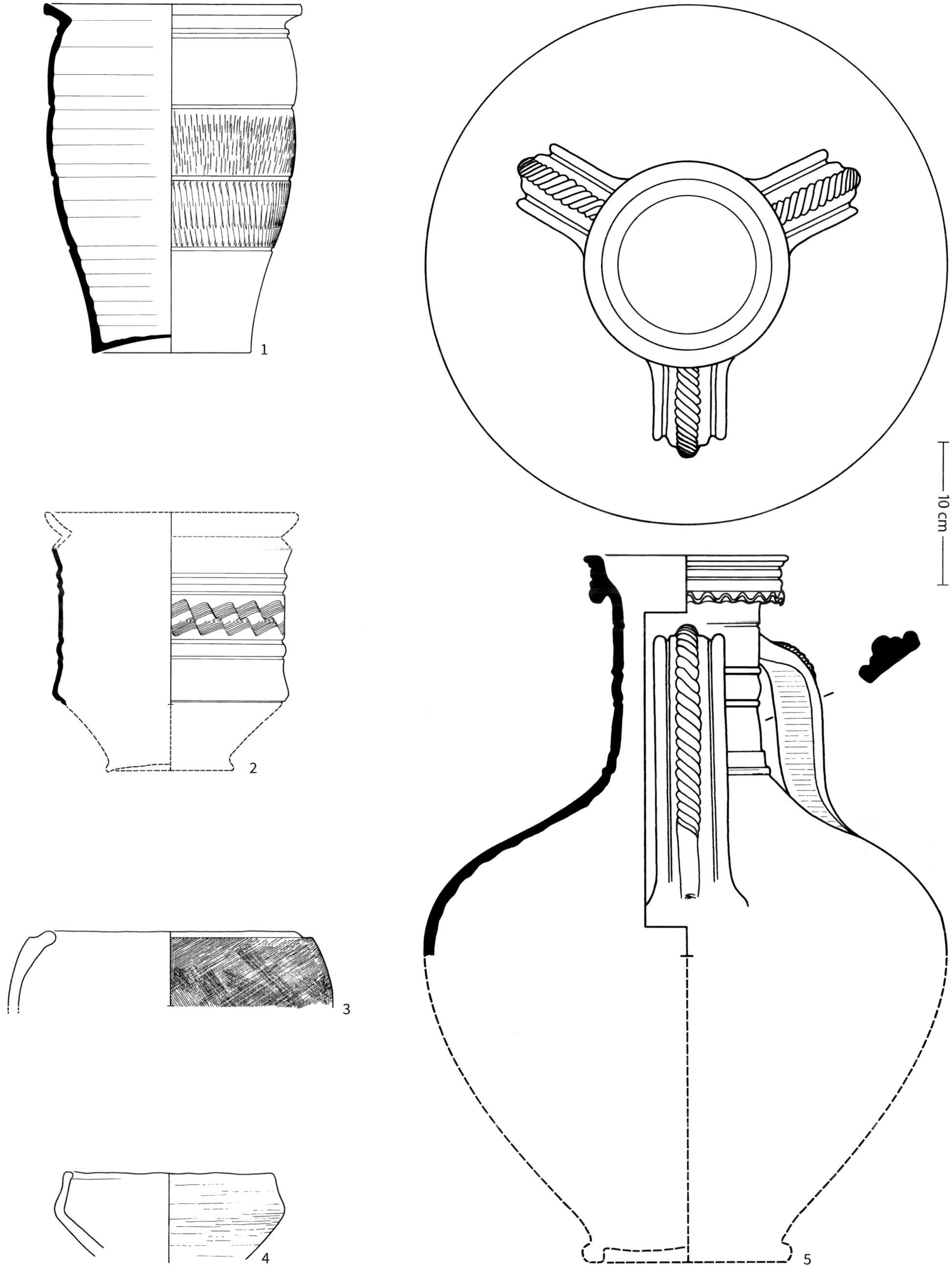

Fig. 4. Pottery from a pit on the east side of the Hunerberg. Scale 1:4 (© Bureau Archeologie, Municipality of Nijmegen/ A. Simons).

of a lid with the remains of a few bands of rouletting (*federend Blättchen*) at the top, as used on a larger scale in the southeastern part of Gaul in the period before the beginning of the Common Era, and whose fine fabric is similar to that of the barrel-shaped pot, but in an oxidised red-orange fabric (fig. 3.11, cf. Bats 1993, 361; Pyl 1993, 306). Sherds of a coarse ware plate of an unknown type in an orange fabric with a gully in the rim (fig. 3.12) and some burnt sherds of an olive oil amphora Oberaden 83 were also found (fig. 3.13). No parallels of the first three types (fig. 3.10-12) are known from Nijmegen, so it can be assumed that this pottery was brought to Nijmegen by the potters from southern regions on their journey.

Encampments dated between 10 and 20

In 1991, Jan Kees Haalebos published an article in which he noted that the eastern side of the (youngest) Augustan fortress was dominated by late Augustan/early Tiberian arretina from Service II (Haalebos 1991, 106, fig. 7 and 197). At the time, he had no explanation for these finds. It has since become clear that they were probably left by soldiers who had set up an encampment in the eastern part of the abandoned fortress. The remains of more than ten such encampments are now known to have been set up between the command post on the Kops Plateau (Van Enckevort 2021, 193-194) and the Batavian capital *Oppidum Batavorum* (Willems and Van Enckevort 2009, 138-139). Although good dating is lacking in several cases, these camps are thought to have been built in the late Augustan/early Tiberian period. The encampment near the Keizer Trajanusplein is the one that is best studied (Willems 1990, 21-22; Van Enckevort 2011, 34, fig. 11C and 64-68; Bloemers 2016, 40-52). Finds from the ditch show that it only existed for a short time, probably between 10-20 (Bloemers 1979b; 2016, 50; Willems 1990, 21-22). For most of the other fortified encampments, only sections of the ditches have been recorded; little is known about the internal structures and dating of finds. Only in one encampment on the Kops Plateau, one without a ditch, traces of the layout of a stable complex have been found (Van Enckevort and Zee 1996, 40). The military units quartered in these encampments were probably part of the army commanded by Germanicus for his campaigns across the Rhine between 14 and 16 (Van Enckevort 2021, 187, 194-196). The next two sections present pottery from three pits dating from this period.

A Pit with a *Lagena* with Red Slip

The pottery from the excavations in the eastern part of the abandoned youngest Augustan fortress has hardly been studied beyond the arretina mentioned above. Only the inventory of a pit with sherds of a special type of *lagena* covered with red slip (colour coated) has been studied (fig. 4.5; De Clercq and Van Enckevort 2004). The twisted roll on the three flat handles of this *lagena* matches a handle with red slip from Aalter, Belgium (De Clercq and Van Enckevort 2004, 435, fig. 1). The fabric of both is fine, granular, grey-yellow to brown-yellow (with a grey core in the thickest parts) with black and white inclusions and a few mica flakes. These handles are similar to a handle from Camulodunum (Hawkes and Hull 1947, fig. 3.166c). The undercut rim and the reeded collar of the Nijmegen *lagena* resembles Camulodunum types 161-167 and similar forms from Verulanium (Stead and Rigby 1989, 142, fig. 57. Gl7, GL12). This type of handle appears to be strictly limited to this form and remains a relatively rare feature at a time when flagons and *lagenae* with simple flattened handles are largely dominant.

Among the *lagenae* with reeded collars from Camulodunum and Verulanium two fabrics can be distinguished. Fabric 1, the "standard fabric", is fine, granular, reddish brown (often with a grey core) with rounded red, black and white inclusions, and some mica. The slip is white. Rigby and Freestone (1986) identified the region of origin as central Gaul (Morvan). Although not yet studied, sherds of such *lagenae* (in two different fabrics) have also been found on the nearby Kops Plateau. The other fabric with the red slip has not yet been attributed, but it seems plausible that it was also made in (central?) Gaul. It seems that this kind of *lagenae* is found in Britannia in a few 'pre-conquest' sites and early sites in Gaul (De Clercq and Van Enckevort 2004). In the same context fragments of two *terra rubra* beakers (fig. 4.1-2) of types Deru P13/Holwerda 3 and Deru P29/Holwerda 9 (orange fabric) were found together with sherds from a cork ware pot (fig. 4.3) and a handmade bowl (fig. 4.4).

Two Pits with Beakers, Amphorae, and a Lot of Handmade Pottery

Outside the *porta principalis sinistra* of the abandoned youngest Augustan fortress, pits were found along the *via principalis*. No other features of this period were found in the immediate vicinity. The pits were probably filled with the refuse of a small military unit that had camped (in tents?) on the site (Hendriks and Van Enckevort in prep.). A small quantity of arretina was found in these pits, including a sherd of a conical cup Consp. 22 (fig. 5.1). Fine wares are hardly represented, only a fragment of a beaker with horizontal grooves Oberaden 30/Dangstetten D3 (fig. 5.2). Gallo-Belgic wares are well represented, including two *terra rubra* beakers Deru P29/Holwerda 9 in an orange fabric (fig. 5.3), characteristic of this period in Nijmegen. A rim fragment (of a bowl?) has the same fabric (fig. 5.4). In addition, a large number of sherds of at least three *terra rubra* beakers Deru P13/Holwerda 3 in a brown fabric, a similarly shaped beaker in *terra nigra* (fig. 5.5),

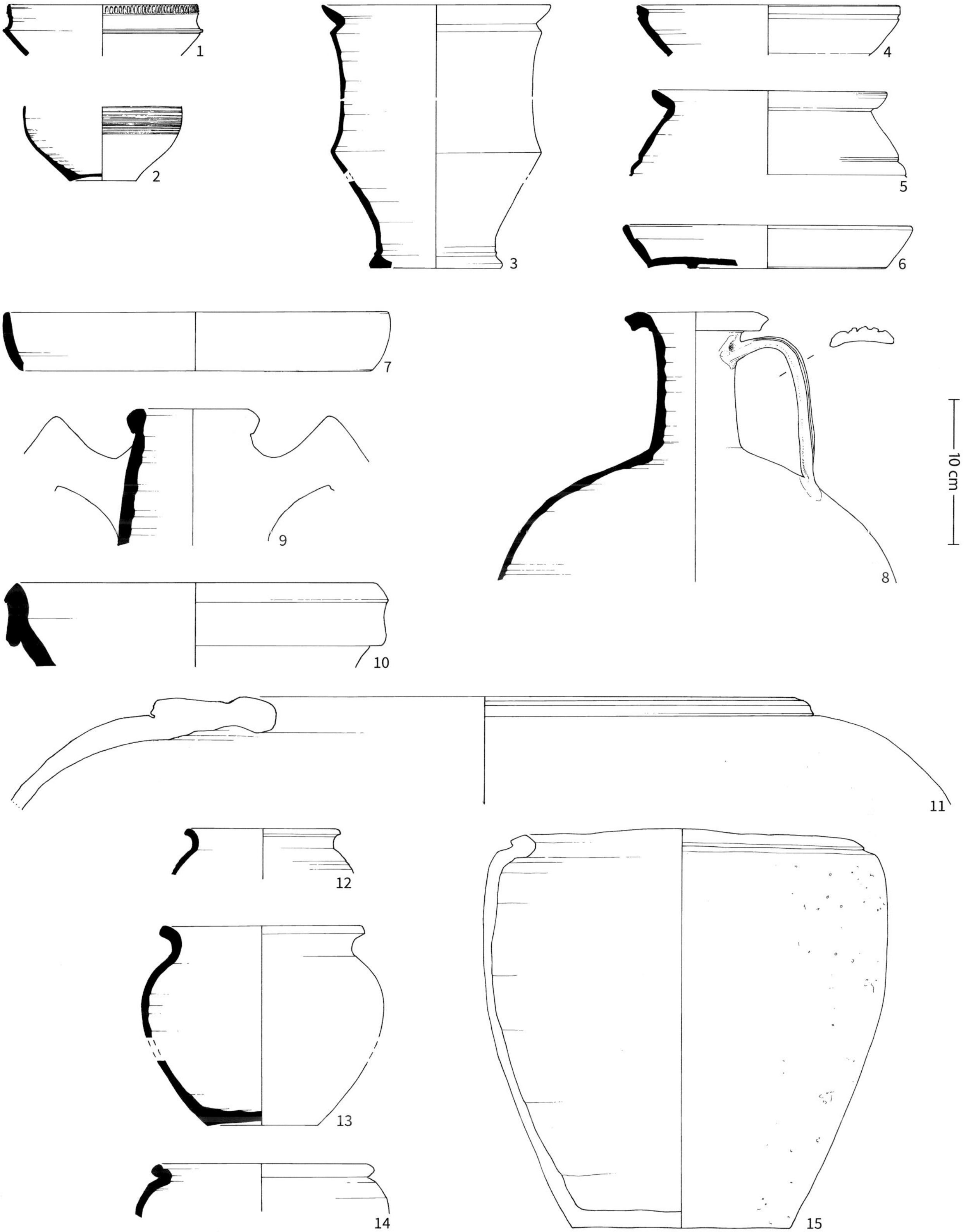

Fig. 5. Wheelthrown and handmade pottery from two pits on the west side of the Hunerberg. Scale 1:4 (© Bureau Archeologie, Municipality of Nijmegen/M. Verhoeven).

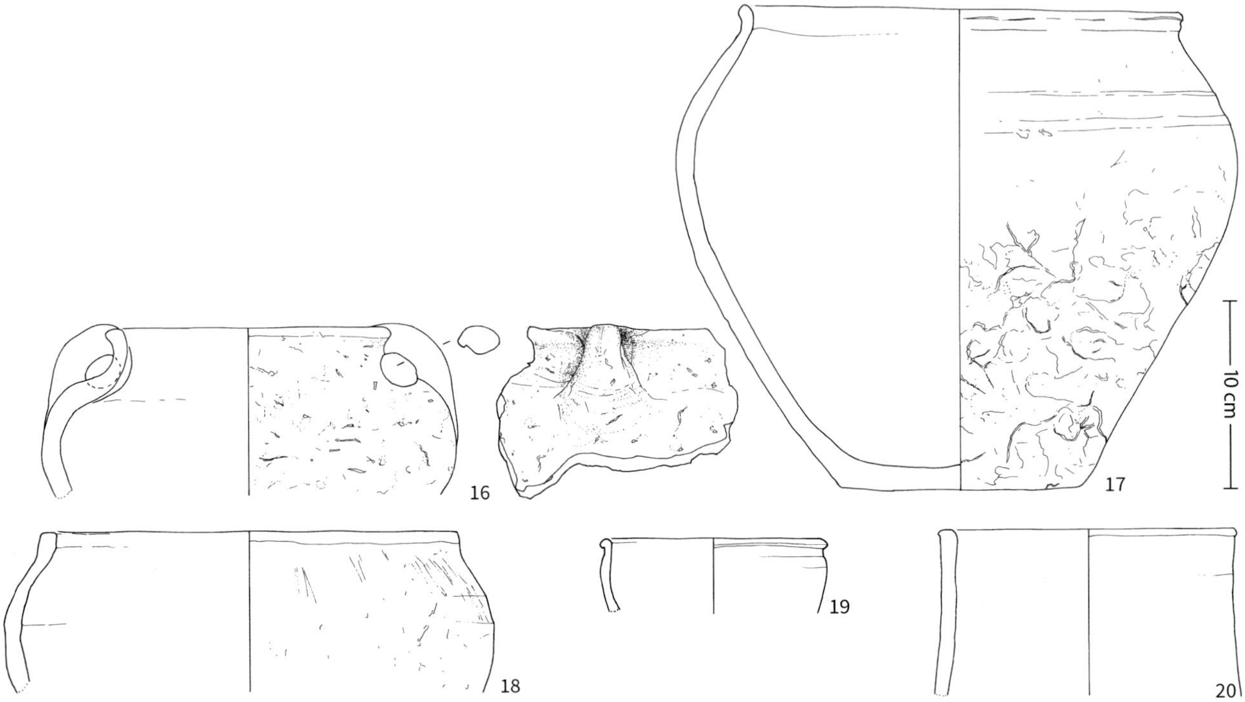

Fig. 6. Handmade pottery from two pits on the west side of the Hunerberg. Scale 1:4 (© Bureau Archeologie, Municipality of Nijmegen/M. Verhoeven).

and several plates in the same fabric, including one Deru A38/Holwerda 79 (fig. 5.6) and one Deru A41/Holwerda 81 (fig. 5.7), were found.

Of the smooth ware only fragments of two flagons Stuart 103 (fine-sandy, orange fabric) and one flagon Haltern 45 (fig. 5.8) in a different oxidised fabric could be identified and distinguished among sherds from several flagons in an oxidising white or brown fabric. Four different amphorae are represented by sherds in both pits: Dressel 7-11 (Spain), Haltern 70, Oberaden 83 (>4) and Camulodunum 184 (fig. 5.9). Two fragments of a mortarium Haltern 59 from the Rhône valley were also found (fig. 5.10). The pits also contained several rim fragments of a dolium Stuart 147 (fig. 5.11) and wall fragments of at least ten other specimens. The smaller vessels are well represented and in different fabrics. These include several sherds of a wheelthrown pot, Stuart 201, in cork ware (fig. 5.12). Such pots are also known from the Kops Plateau (author's own observation). Apart from a large rim fragment of another coarse ware pot Stuart 201 (fig. 5.13), few other sherds of such pots have been found. Rather rare in Nijmegen are handmade pots with a moulded rim, which can be attributed to the "Céramique grossière micacée" type Besançon/Camulodunum 262 (fig. 5.14; Tyers 2001; Barbier and Luginbühl 2021, 84-85). Several sherds of such pots have also been identified on the Kops Plateau. Fragments of some handmade cork ware pots Holwerda 94 (fig. 5.15) have also been found.

Much of the content of both pits consists of handmade pottery. This includes the rim fragment of a two-eared pot (fig. 6.16), which may originate from the Frisian area in the north of the Netherlands and northwest Germany. A small rim fragment is from a thin-walled, slightly funnel-shaped salt vessel from the English Channel coast, in particular from the civitates of the Morini and Menapii (Van den Broeke 1996; this volume, especially fig. 6.25). This makes it one of the oldest dated examples of this type of salt vessel. The remaining sherds are from handmade pots and bowls (fig. 6.17-20), which were produced on a large scale in the Batavian settlements near Nijmegen in the early Roman period (personal communication Peter van den Broeke).

Conclusion

The legionary soldiers stationed on the Hunerberg in Nijmegen between 19 and 16 BC obtained most of their eating and drinking utensils from southern regions. They also produced a limited amount of drinking cups, pots, and lids, as evidenced by the debris near a pottery kiln found within the fortress. Most of the food and drink needed was also brought in ceramic vessels (amphorae, dolia, pots) from far away, although the sherds of handmade pottery found indicate that relatively many pots containing food were also brought in from the surrounding Batavian region. Several decades later, during the years of Germanicus' campaign across the Rhine, this picture had changed little.

Pottery from Rural Settlements in the *Civitas Cananefatium*

Roderick C.A. Geerts

Abstract

This paper assesses changes in the pottery assemblages of rural settlements of the *civitas Cananefatium*. To do so, securely dated assemblages of six representative sites are highlighted. These assemblages show changes throughout the Roman period. The changes can be summarised as an increase in the diversity of (functional) pottery groups and vessel forms. These developments are clear when comparing the oldest assemblages, comprising mainly cooking and storage vessels, with the youngest, comprising, amongst others, amphorae, beakers, bowls, cooking pots, dolia, jugs, mortaria, pitchers, plates, and storage vessels. The periods during which the pottery assemblages changed can partly be associated with general developments in the *civitas*, for instance those related to the accessibility of the *civitas* or an increase in trade. Furthermore, the paper shows the potential of previously studied sites with regard to refining the dating of the foundation and abandonment of the rural settlements.

Keywords: civitas Cananefatium, pottery assemblage

Introduction

This paper will focus on the analysis and changing character of pottery assemblages from rural settlements in the *civitas Cananefatium* during the Roman period. This *civitas* corresponded to what nowadays is the Dutch province of Zuid-Holland. Most of this region consisted of a large peat area and habitation was located on the clayey soils outside this peat area. Waterways played a significant role in the infrastructure and choice of location of the settlements. This *civitas* was characterised by a lack of pottery production, so all pottery was imported, which had its impact on the composition and development of the pottery assemblages.

Brief Description of the *Civitas*

Before going into the developments of the pottery assemblages, the *civitas* and its main features will be shortly introduced. The *civitas* was situated on the Roman border, the limes. To the north the river Rhine was used as a natural border, along which many

in: R.C.A. Geerts and Ph. Bes (eds) 2024, *Roman Pottery in the Low Countries: Past Research, Current State, Future Directions*. Leiden: Sidestone Press (= *Papers on Archaeology of the Leiden Museum of Antiquities Leiden* 32), pp. 97-108.

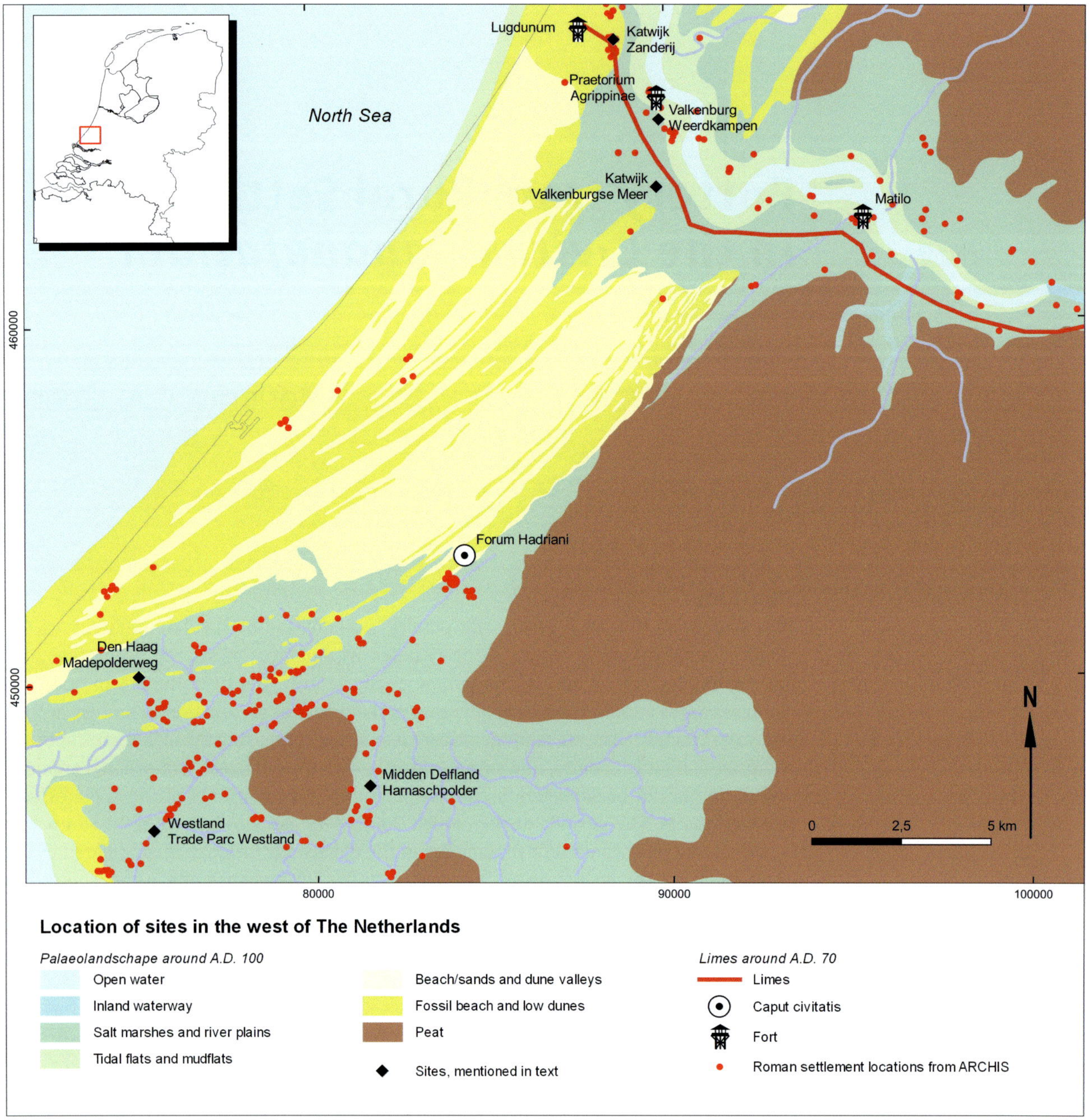

Fig. 1. Map with the discussed sites plotted on a paleogeographic map of the Netherlands around 100 (© ADC ArcheoProjecten/ A. Botman, palaeogeographic map: Vos *et al.* 2020 © Rijksdienst van het Cultureel Erfgoed, Deltares and TNO).

military installations, like forts and watchtowers, were constructed (for an overview see Hessing *et al.* 2021). Those installations continued along the coast and constituted a coastal defence line that stretched to northern France (Dhaeze 2011; 2019). Initially the influence of this military infrastructure and the urban centre of Forum Hadriani on the pottery assemblages of the rural settlements seems to have been limited (as noted before, see De Bruin 2008). Nonetheless, the location of the *civitas* on the limes had its influence on daily life: recruitment for the army (Roymans 1996, 23-24; 2004, 222-223), surplus production for the military installations and the urban centre (Van Dinter 2017), systems of land allotment that were laid out (Van Londen 2006), and through infrastructural works the *civitas* also played a role in trade networks (*e.g.* Van de Zande 2023).

Despite the fact that a large part of the *civitas* comprised clayey soil, these clays were not exploited

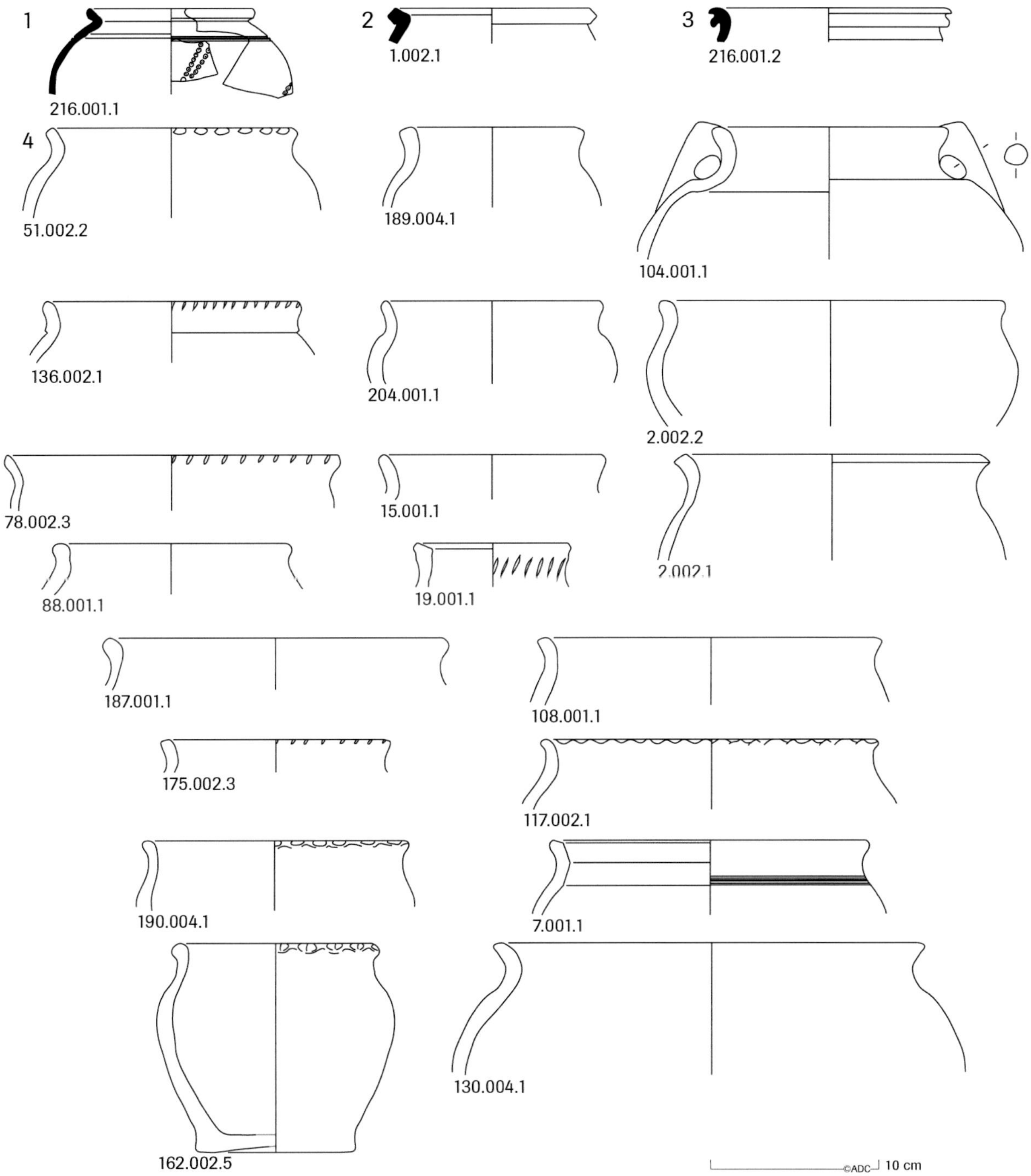

Fig. 2. Selection of pottery from the rural settlement at Valkenburgse Meer. 1: *terra nigra* pot Deru P23.1 with barbotine decoration; 2: coarse ware pot Vanvinckenroye type 471, 489 or 602; 3: Rhineland granular grey pot Hofheim 89; 4: handmade vessels of Bloemers types IA, IB and IV (after: Geerts 2024c, fig. 5.5-8 combined © ADC ArcheoProjecten).

for the ceramic industry except on a household level. Potters seemed to have preferred the (tertiary) clays further to the east and south (see the contribution by Van Enckevort in this volume). As such, the *civitas* imported all ceramics, except the regional handmade ware in Frisian style (see Taayke this volume).

Selected Pottery Assemblages

In order to describe the changes in pottery assemblages in rural areas throughout the Roman period, selected sites and assemblages are highlighted below. These assemblages are representative of the developments in the whole *civitas* (described in more detail in Geerts 2024a). The overview below is not the first attempt at a diachronic typological analysis of the assemblages in the *civitas* (De Bruin 2008; Geerts 2021a). Differences are most notable in the percentages of different pottery groups present and in a greater variety of pottery types. In general, all ceramic assemblages from rural settlements present similar patterns, as comparisons between rural settlements as well as comparisons with other site types show (*e.g.* De Bruin 2008; Geerts 2012; 2021b). New research into the end of the Roman period has demonstrated that activities in the *civitas* still took place in the early 4th century (De Bruin 2017, 277-282; 2019, 239). This showed that when pottery assemblages of rural settlements are reassessed early 4th-century activities are now recognised at most rural settlements based on certain pottery types being attested (Geerts and Reigersman-van Lidth de Jeude 2019). Thus, a thorough and comprehensive reassessment of more rural settlements is needed. The same holds true for the early Roman period. Whereas settlements are thought to have started around 50 (Bakx 2013, 299; De Bruin 2017, 197), new research has shown there is evidence for substantial habitation already in 39-40 (Geerts 2024b), which means starting dates of rural settlements also need to be subjected to further research. These and other avenues of future research will be highlighted after the pottery assemblages are presented. In total, six assemblages will be highlighted, each of which spanning a period of around 50 years.

Pre-Flavian Period

At Valkenburgse Meer, a site with a small, single farmstead was located (Geerts 2024c) along a natural stream that flowed from the forts at Valkenburg to those at Leiden. At the site 1840 fragments of pottery were found, comprising 20 wheelthrown sherds and 1820 handmade sherds. In the early Roman period handmade pottery was still ubiquitous, although wheelthrown ware did trickle in. The technological and typological similarities of handmade pottery throughout the Roman period makes secure dating a challenge, however, both this site and the material from the legionary fort at Valkenburg (Geerts 2024a) show some trends/characteristics associated with early Roman handmade assemblages.

The handmade pottery in the *civitas* has Frisian characteristics like vessel form and temper (Taayke this volume). Defining characteristics for the site at Valkenburgse Meer are the high amount (82%) of grog-tempered pots; from the Flavian period onwards, organic temper became more common and grog temper is only found in a small percentage of the pottery. Furthermore, the amount of decorated pottery is higher: decoration slowly disappeared during the Roman period, while it was common during the (late) Iron Age (Van Heeringen 1992, 201-204). The handmade vessels on site are characterised by their vessel form and size, as Bloemers organised his typology (1978) primarily by size, including rim diameter, followed by differences in vessels' S-shaped profile. Vessels of Bloemers type I are small, while Bloemers type IV pots are larger vessels (fig. 2). Both occur in similar quantities on site, the smaller vessels being slightly more common (23 specimens of type I and 15 of type IV).

The wheelthrown pottery comprises many body sherds. Only three vessels could be assigned to a type (fig. 2). These are, first, a *terra nigra* pot Deru P23.1 (Deru 1996) with barbotine decoration that can be dated to the period 40-70. Second, of a similar date is the Rhineland granular grey pot (Anderson 1981, 103; Willems 2005, 92) Hofheim 89 (Ritterling 1913). The final vessel is a pot that can be a Vanvinckenroye type 471, 489 or 602 (Vanvinckenroye 1991), which are also common in the mid-1st century. Even though their number is small, all wheelthrown pottery supports a pre-Flavian date for this site.

Flavian Period

At Katwijk-Zanderij a settlement has been excavated that was in use during 40-190 (Van der Velde 2008, 386). The settlement comprises a few farmsteads which were in use at the same time, and their development could be traced well throughout the use period of the site. Its proximity to the limes made the researchers suggest that the site could not have been founded without approval of the Roman military (Van der Velde 2008, 383). Because of the clear Flavian component at the site, it is included here; Flavian material is found on many sites, but its signature is less clear because of later use of these sites.

The pottery assemblage at Katwijk-Zanderij comprises 46% handmade pottery and 54% wheelthrown pottery. Not all handmade sherds were studied in detail, however, all wheelthrown material was. It has been noted that the amount of decorated handmade pottery

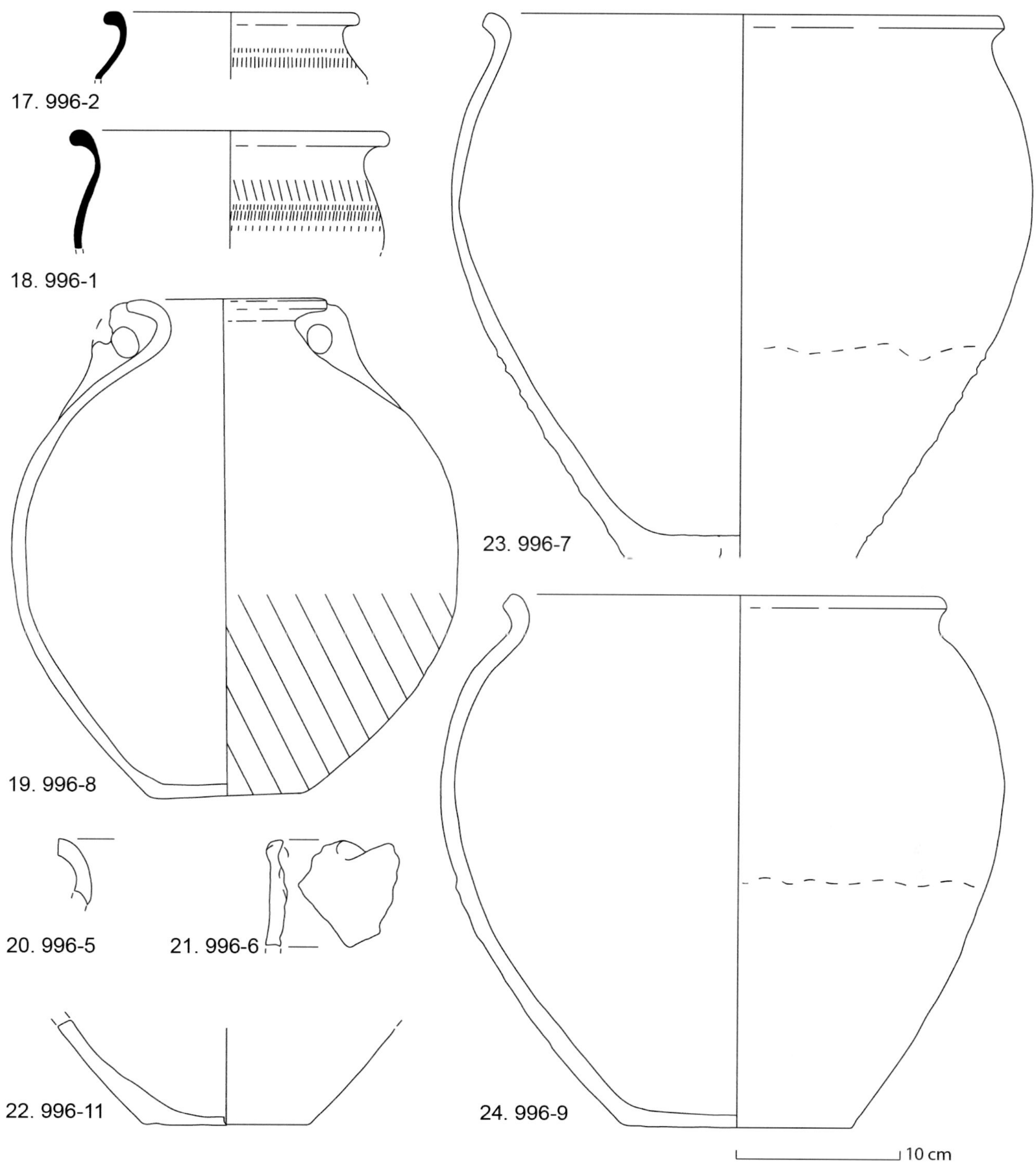

Fig. 3. Selection of pottery from the rural settlement at Midden-Delfland: two Holwerda 131 bowls and handmade pottery (after: Geerts in prep. b, fig. 5.17-20 combined © Archeologie Delft).

was relatively low, and decoration was mostly limited to the rims of vessels.

What makes this site interesting is the introduction of wheelthrown pottery. The assemblage contains much south and central Gaulish terra sigillata, *terra nigra* and cork urns. These decorated terra sigillata vessels indicate a date in the Flavian period and early 2nd century. *Terra nigra* and cork urn vessels, like Deru P23, also suggest a date in the Flavian period or early 2nd century. The colour coated vessels comprise beakers Stuart 1 with scale decoration, a combination dated to the Flavian period. Low Lands ware appeared during this period, though distinctive types that would dominate younger assemblages are not all present. Holwerda[1] 131 bowls with rouletted decoration are mainly found, while undecorated bowls Holwerda 133-136 and large vessels Holwerda 140-142 are found albeit in low numbers; the latter two were more common during the 2nd and 3rd centuries (see the contexts below). Coarse ware vessels comprise pots Stuart 201 and 202. An interesting component are the Stuart 204 beakers dating to the second half of the 1st century. The amphorae comprise Spanish olive oil amphorae Dressel 20 and south Gaulish wine amphorae Gauloise 4. Dolia are present in low numbers while mortaria in slightly higher numbers (respectively 1% and 2%).

Trajanic-Hadrianic Period

In the Harnaschpolder in Midden-Delfland multiple Roman-period settlements have been excavated. The settlement at site MD22-08 comprises several farmsteads within a land allotment system that covered most of the region. One of the farmsteads is of particular interest because of the dendrochronological date, which allow to date the construction of the building to 133 (Bakx in prep.).

The aforementioned farmstead, house 3, is oriented east-west and flanked by two ditches on each side. What makes the pottery assemblage interesting are the composition of the assemblage, the relatively complete vessels, and the dendrochronological date. The sherds from the postholes from the house itself are low in number, handmade and do not give any secure dating. All the material from the four ditches, however, is what makes this house particularly interesting.

The assemblage is dominated by handmade pottery (85%) which comprises Bloemers types I, II, III and IV. In contrast to the assemblage at Valkenburgse Meer, Bloemers type IV, large pots, dominate the assemblage with 25 specimens. Bloemers type I pots are represented by 10 specimens, while Bloemers type II, huge vessels, and Bloemers type III, closed pots, are represented by 3 specimens each. Many of these vessels are largely complete (fig. 3). The wheelthrown pottery comprises a terra sigillata fragment of a Drag. 37R bowl, a colour coated beaker in technique b, a Brunsting type 37 mortarium, a Stuart type 147 dolium, Low Lands ware vessels Holwerda types 115, 131 and 140-142, coarse ware bowl Niederbieber type 104, pitcher Niederbieber type 96 and a Niederbieber type 89 pot. These types show a clear 2nd-century signature; indeed, many were not yet in production during the 1st century, whereas some were still produced well into the 3rd century.

Most of the material was found in the outer ditches which shows that the ditches closest to the house were kept clean on purpose. Furthermore, the concentration of material in the eastern part of these outer ditches indicates that most material was dumped from the side of the house where the farmyard was located.

Antonine Period

At the Madepolderweg in Den Haag (in the province of Zuid-Holland) a Roman-period settlement was excavated, which dates to the 1st and 2nd century (Vossen and Geerts 2022). This settlement comprised up to three farmsteads, wells, and land allotment ditches. Judging from the sharp decline of finds and features outside these ditches they clearly marked the edge of the settlement, a pattern that is observed at multiple sites in the region.

In order to discuss pottery assemblages from the Antonine period three of the land allotment ditches will be discussed (ditches GR2, G1 and G2); these individual ditches nonetheless contained low amounts of pottery (Geerts 2022). The pottery found in ditch GR2 comprises 106 sherds of which 71 were handmade. Wheelthrown pottery that provides a secure dating are the terra sigillata Drag. 31 plates, oxidised Low Lands ware, coarse ware pots Niederbieber type 89 and a colour coated beaker Stuart type 2 in technique b (fig. 4). In ditch G1 handmade pottery dominates as well with 94 out of 131 sherds. Again, the wheelthrown pottery provides the better datable material, comprising a coarse ware pitcher Niederbieber type 96, smooth walled jug Stuart type 110B, colour coated beaker fragments and Scheldt valley amphorae (fig. 4). Ditch G2 is again similar regarding the number of handmade sherds attested: 18 out of 36 fragments. The wheelthrown pottery comprises fragments of a Gauloise 4 amphora, dolia, oxidised Low Lands ware, coarse ware bowls Niederbieber type 104, a coarse ware pot Niederbieber type 89 and large pots in Low Lands ware of type Holwerda 140-142 (fig. 4).

What these ditches have in common is the relatively high amount of handmade pottery. To some extent, as these ditches are presumed to have been dug in the first half of the 2nd century, this material shows they were in use for a longer period. The wheelthrown vessels clearly show which types were prevalent during the 2nd century.

1 All references to Holwerda types in this contribution concern Holwerda 1923.

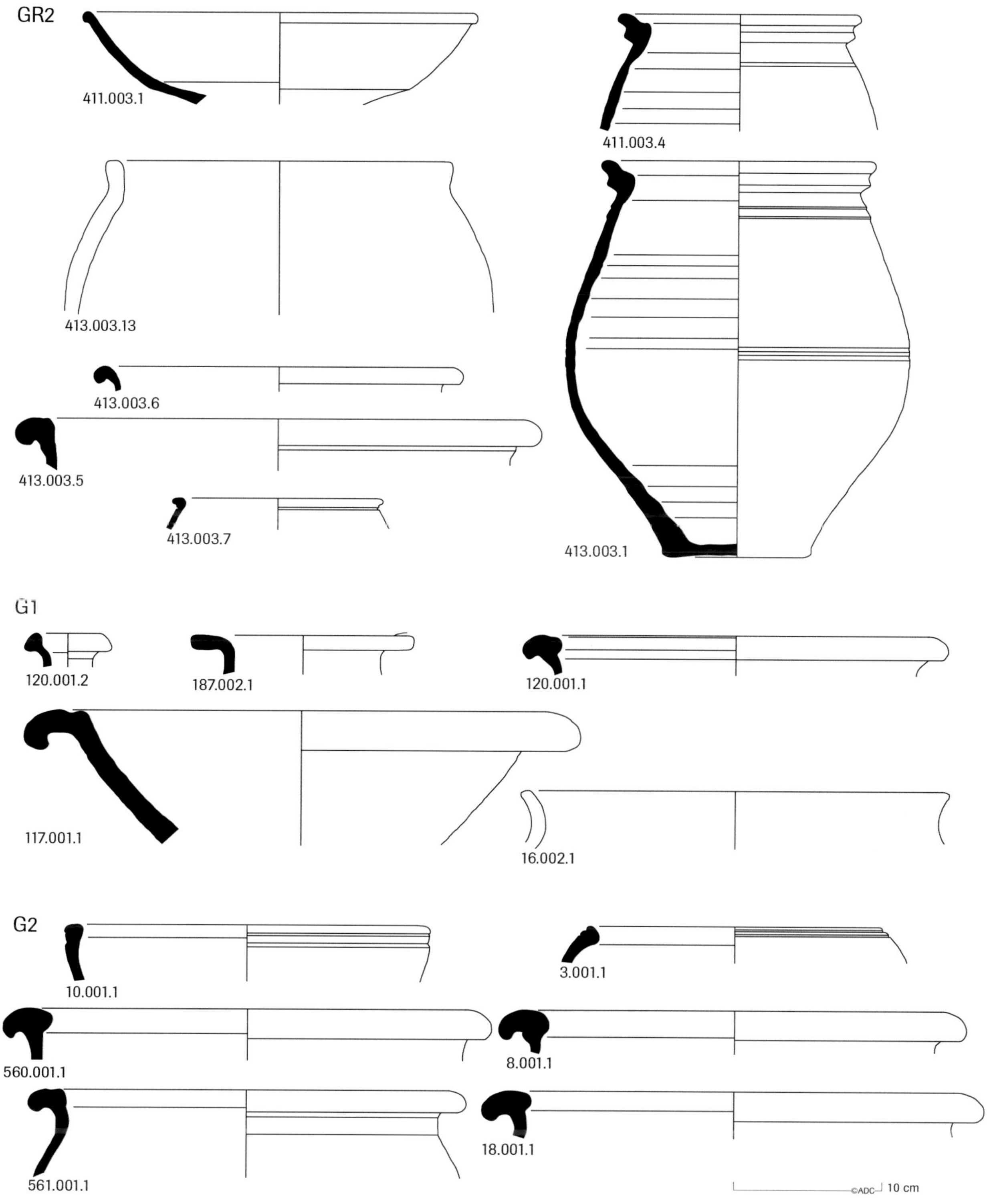

Fig. 4. Selection of pottery from the rural settlement at Den Haag-Madepolderweg: from top to bottom, ditch GR2, G1 and G2 (after: Geerts 2022, fig. 5.45-47 combined © ADC ArcheoProjecten).

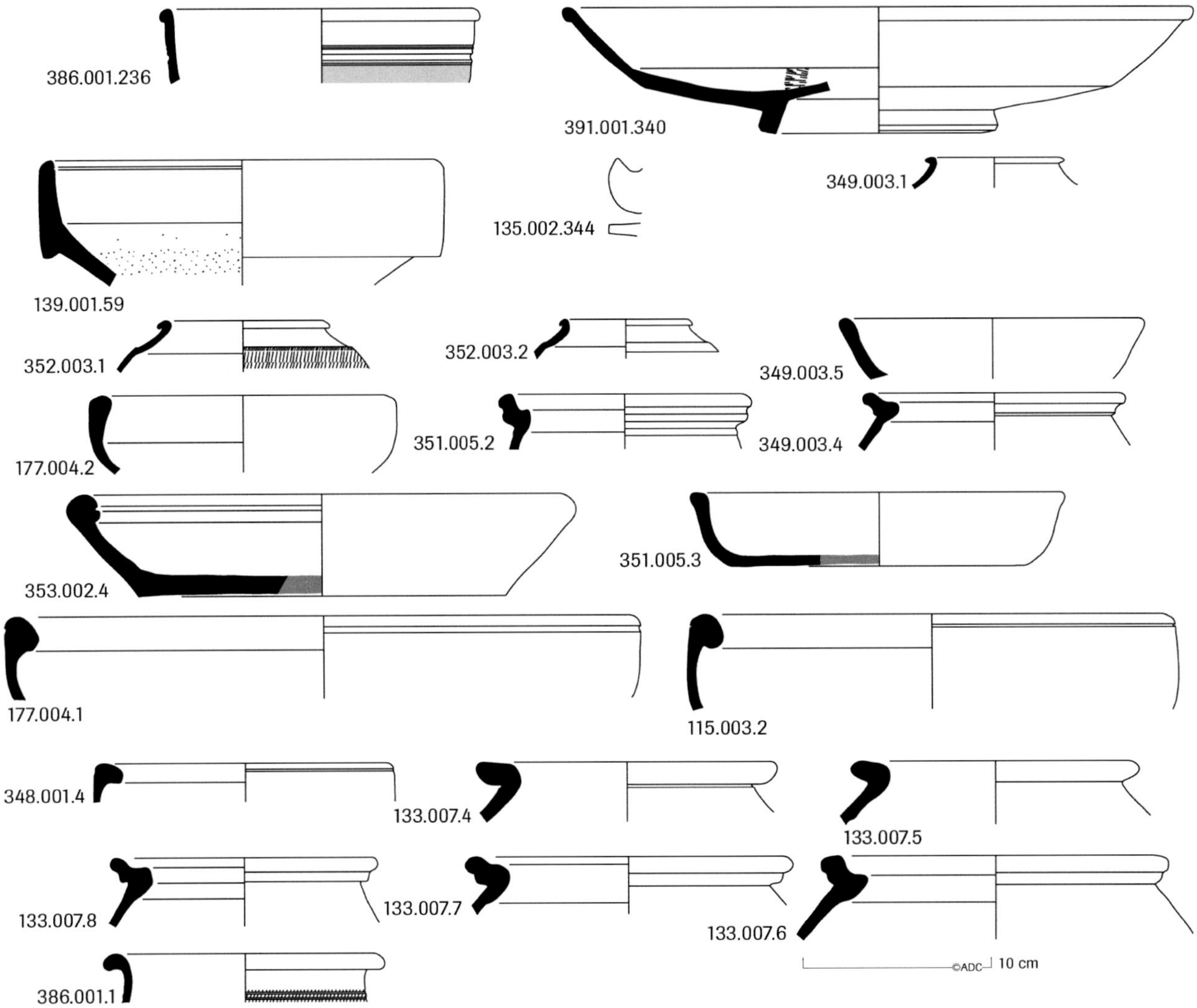

Fig. 5. Selection of pottery from the rural settlement at Trade Parc Westland Mars from the floor of house S1 (after: Geerts 2019a, fig. 5.42 © ADC ArcheoProjecten).

Severan Period

The settlement at Trade Parc Westland Mars was characterised by large-scale peat extraction during the Roman period (Van der Feijst 2019), which resulted in a lowering of the terrain by 1 m by the middle of the 2nd century. These activities removed most evidence of habitation datable to the 1st and 2nd century. During the 3rd century several low podia (*terps*) were made of clay on which houses were constructed. These houses were well preserved, with *in situ* wooden foundations and floor levels, and organic finds, like the bones of a porpoise. Dendrochronology allowed to date the felling of two of the wooden posts from house S1 to the autumn/winter of 131-132 and one post from house S5 to the autumn/winter of 216-217. For the purposes of this paper only house S1 will be discussed (for the others, see Geerts 2019a; 2021c).

All 1087 MNI (Minimal Number of Individuals, fig. 5) found in house S1 derive from five distinct contexts: the construction phase; the floor level; the abandonment layers; and the dwelling mound layers to the north and south of the house. These make a detailed dating of the construction and abandonment of the house possible.

The sherds that provide the best *terminus post quem* for the construction of the podium and therefore the construction of the house are fragments of terra sigillata mortaria and coarse wares from the region of Urmitz (Germany). Both can be dated from the late 2nd century onwards. This is a clear discrepancy with the dendrochronological dates of 131-132 and suggests that the wood was reused. Sherds datable to the second half of the 3rd century were present in the layer that covered the house. Terra sigillata comprises a Drag. 18/31R

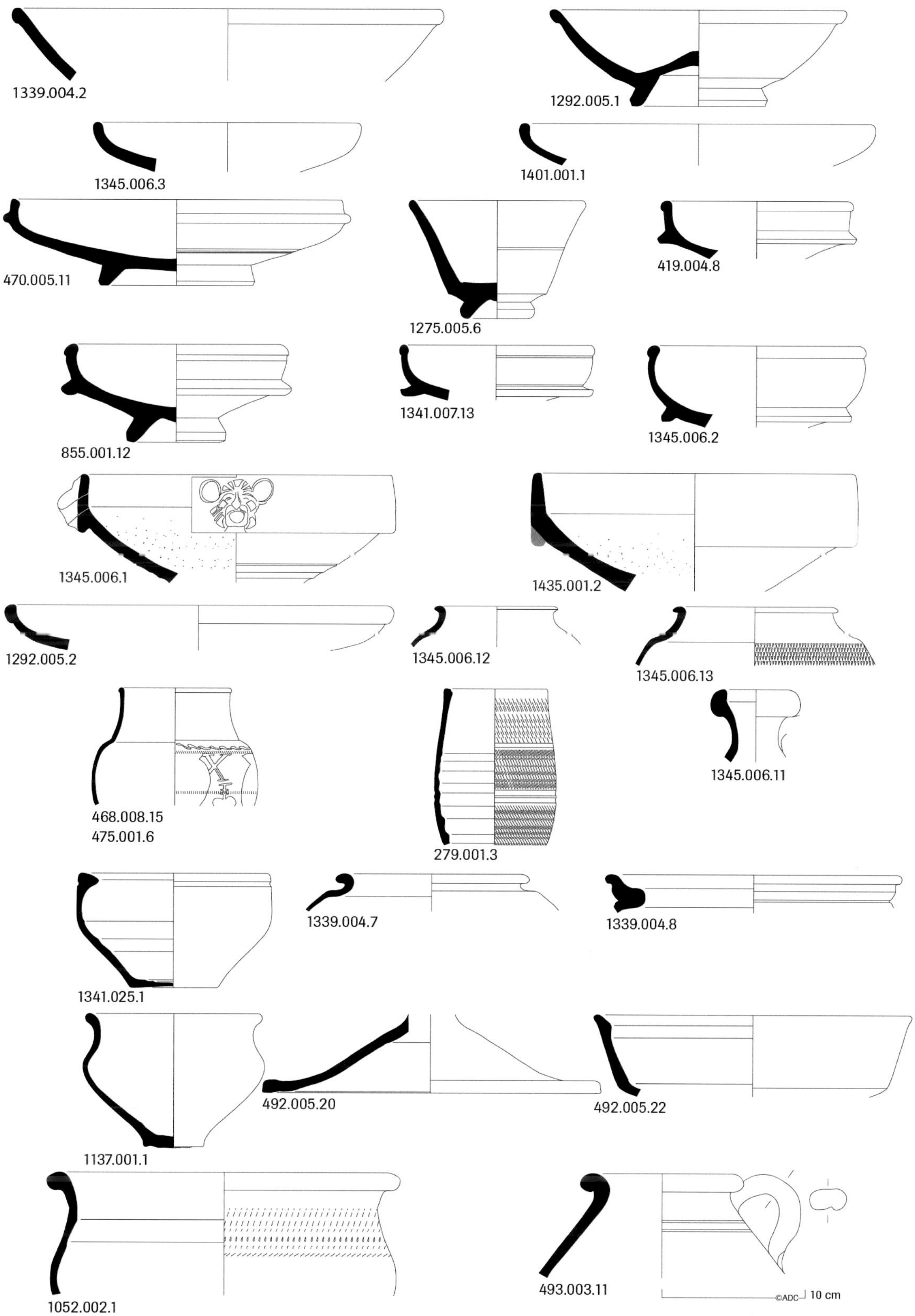

Fig. 6. Selection of pottery from the rural settlement at Valkenburg-Weerdkampen (after: Geerts 2021a, fig. 10.132 © ADC ArcheoProjecten).

dish, 2 Drag. 31R dishes, 3 Drag. 37 decorated bowls, the handle of a Drag. 39 plate, and 2 Drag. 45 mortaria. Other tableware consists of 5 Niederbieber type 32 colour coated beakers in techniques b and c, fragments of high gloss ware from Trier, and a smooth walled Stuart type 110B flagon. The coarse ware consists of 3 Low Lands ware bowls Holwerda type 133-136, 8 Low Lands ware large pots of Holwerda type 140-142, 1 large pot Holwerda type 142, 4 Niederbieber type 104 bowls (3 from the Urmitz region), 1 Niederbieber type 112 plate from the Urmitz region, 2 Niederbieber type 113 plates (1 from the Urmitz region), 7 Niederbieber type 89 pots (3 from the Urmitz region), and 2 Niederbieber type 201B pots from the Urmitz region. This assemblage differs from the other contexts within the house because of the presence of colour coated beakers, high gloss ware and coarse ware plates, which are all datable to the 3rd century. Furthermore, the larger proportion of pottery from the Urmitz region suggests a later date, as this production centre increased its export output during the 3rd century (Friedrich 2012; Kiessel 2010).

The pottery assemblage shows that the podium and house were constructed in the beginning of the 3rd century. During the course of the 3rd century the house seems to have been abandoned, the layer covering its remains suggesting that this occurred sometime during the second half of the 3rd century.

Late 3rd-Early 4th Century

At Valkenburg-Weerdkampen a settlement has been excavated, which comprised several farmsteads on plots of land along the road that led from the fort at Valkenburg to Leiden (Loopik and Vos 2021). This land allotment system was of importance for the dating of the settlement, as it had two clear phases. The construction phase of the second ditch, which was dug after the first was filled up, could be dated to after 270.

This ditch system contained 3442 sherds of many vessels that were dumped in the ditch (fig. 6). These sherds comprise almost half of the total number of sherds found across the entire site. The sherds have been analysed (Geerts 2021a) and what follows is a summary of the composition of the assemblage. In total 498 rim fragments were found, and one-third of the assemblage comprises tableware. The tableware is dominated by terra sigillata and smooth walled ware. A selection of types present allows the following list to be drawn up: 36 terra sigillata mortaria of type Drag. 45, 42 sherds of decorated bowls Drag. 37, 13 Drag. 32 plates, 24 colour coated beakers Niederbieber type 32, 5 high gloss beakers Niederbieber type 33 among which are several motto beakers, 4 smooth walled jugs Stuart type 111 and 7 of type Niederbieber type 67. Two-thirds of the assemblage consists of coarse ware, half of which is Low Lands ware. The most common types are 56 coarse ware pots Niederbieber type 89, 1 plate Niederbieber type 110, 11 plates Niederbieber type 111, 13 plates Niederbieber type 112 and 1 plate Niederbieber type 113 (Heeren (2016) showed that these types were more common during this period). Amongst the Low Lands ware in total 11 plates of the types Brouwer 13.1, 13.2, 13.5 and 13.6, 33 bowls Holwerda type 133-136 and 91 large pots Holwerda type 140-142 are attested. The amphorae comprise mainly Scheldt valley amphorae, some Spanish olive oil amphorae, and sherds of a few others.

The high gloss motto beakers are most important for the dating of the land allotment system. Based on their decorative motives they were not produced before 270, therefore, their presence in the oldest fill of the second ditch means this was not dug long before 270. All the pottery in this land allotment system can thus be dated to the late 3rd and early 4th century.

The assemblage comprises many pots and sherds. Some of the near-complete vessels are indicative of the usage of these ditches as a garbage dump. However, these vessels are found in all fills of the ditches, signalling that these did not only end up in the ditches upon abandonment of the settlement. A low amount of burned and weathered sherds shows the farmyards were kept clean and material did not lay around on the walking surface for a long time. The few sherds datable to the 1st century show that some older features were dug up during the digging of the ditch.

Patterns

In the previous sections six sites and assemblages have been discussed that are representative of their respective period. Several patterns emerge from the discussion of these assemblages. During the 1st century rural sites relied heavily on their own household production of pottery; all handmade vessels are indicative of this. The low amount of wheelthrown pottery shows that this was introduced in the *civitas* but arrived at rural settlements only in restricted quantities. During the Flavian period more and more vessels found their way to the rural settlements. Imitations of wheelthrown and glass vessels in local handmade fabrics show that local potters of these rural settlements were influenced by these newly introduced vessels (Geerts 2013; 2014; 2019b). During the 2nd century the *civitas* underwent changes on many levels. Forum Hadriani was given market rights under Emperor Hadrian, infrastructural works were carried out (*e.g.* roads were built) and the land allotment system was expanded (for the latest developments see Van Londen 2006, 183-186). These developments made within the *civitas* improved accessibility and as a result the amount of imported goods increased. This is reflected in the pottery assemblages as handmade pottery gradually disappeared after the mid-2nd century. During the 3rd century it is clear that handmade pottery had disappeared entirely and only wheelthrown vessels were used. During the entire Roman period pottery assemblages from rural settlements remained different from those attested on other types of sites, even though during the 3rd century pottery assemblages resemble those from military and urban sites more closely. Differences are to be found in the diversity of vessel shapes and activities taking place on each type of site, which dictated the types of vessels used.

Conclusion

In summary, the development of pottery assemblages from rural settlements shows gradual changes. This is chronologically reflected in changes that took place within the *civitas*. Those changes influenced the pottery assemblages for instance by improving accessibility to pottery from outside the *civitas*. The pottery shows an increase in the diversity of (functional) pottery groups and vessel forms on site, developments that likely reflect changing habits and/or eating patterns as that is what pottery mainly was used for. Within these changing assemblages there are moments where the changes or dating thereof are yet unclear, particularly during the beginning and end of the Roman period. Newly excavated sites suggest occupation of rural settlements might have started well before the middle of the 1st century. Also, a reassessment of 3rd-century pottery types suggests that sites were most likely still inhabited in the early 4th century. In order for both patterns to be confirmed a critical reassessment of excavated and published sites is needed as well as attention to these phenomena in future research.

Developments in Funerary Pottery between Rhine and Meuse (1st-3rd Century)

W. Frederique Reigersman-van Lidth de Jeude

Abstract

The pottery that was placed in Roman graves more or less reflects the developments in pottery production. Multiple changes presented themselves from the 1st to the 3rd century. This not only concerned developments in pottery production but also new customs in burial rituals. The excavations and analyses of dozens of cemeteries in the Dutch river area picture the similarities and differences in funerary rituals, but above all show how the perceptions of the community changed. In order to understand the changes in burial gifts one has to be aware of the developments in production and daily use of pottery to begin with. Both pottery production and burial gifts will be discussed. Two moments of major changes will be dealt with and an explanation will be offered.

Keywords: funerary pottery, Roman cemeteries, grave goods, Dutch river area, chronological developments

Introduction

The research of large cemeteries in the municipality of Nijmegen in the 20th century offered a great opportunity to study grave goods. Pottery turned out to be the most common and informative gift for the deceased that has survived in the soil. The first well excavated and published Roman cemetery in the Netherlands was the one at Nijmegen-Hees (Brunsting 1937). This publication became an important standard work, not just for cemeteries, but first and foremost for the study and typology of Roman pottery in general. Stuart was next to provide the Dutch archaeological world with a thorough study by publishing the Roman pottery found at both the military site and several cemeteries at Nijmegen (Stuart 1963). Both publications and typologies are still in use in the Netherlands and neighbouring countries. The last important work in this light is by Haalebos and concerns the cemetery of Nijmegen-Hatert (Haalebos 1990). Haalebos tightened up dating issues by considering not just the pottery but complete burial assemblages including all categories of finds.

in: R.C.A. Geerts and Ph. Bes (eds) 2024, *Roman Pottery in the Low Countries: Past Research, Current State, Future Directions*. Leiden: Sidestone Press (= *Papers on Archaeology of the Leiden Museum of Antiquities Leiden* 32), pp. 109-120.

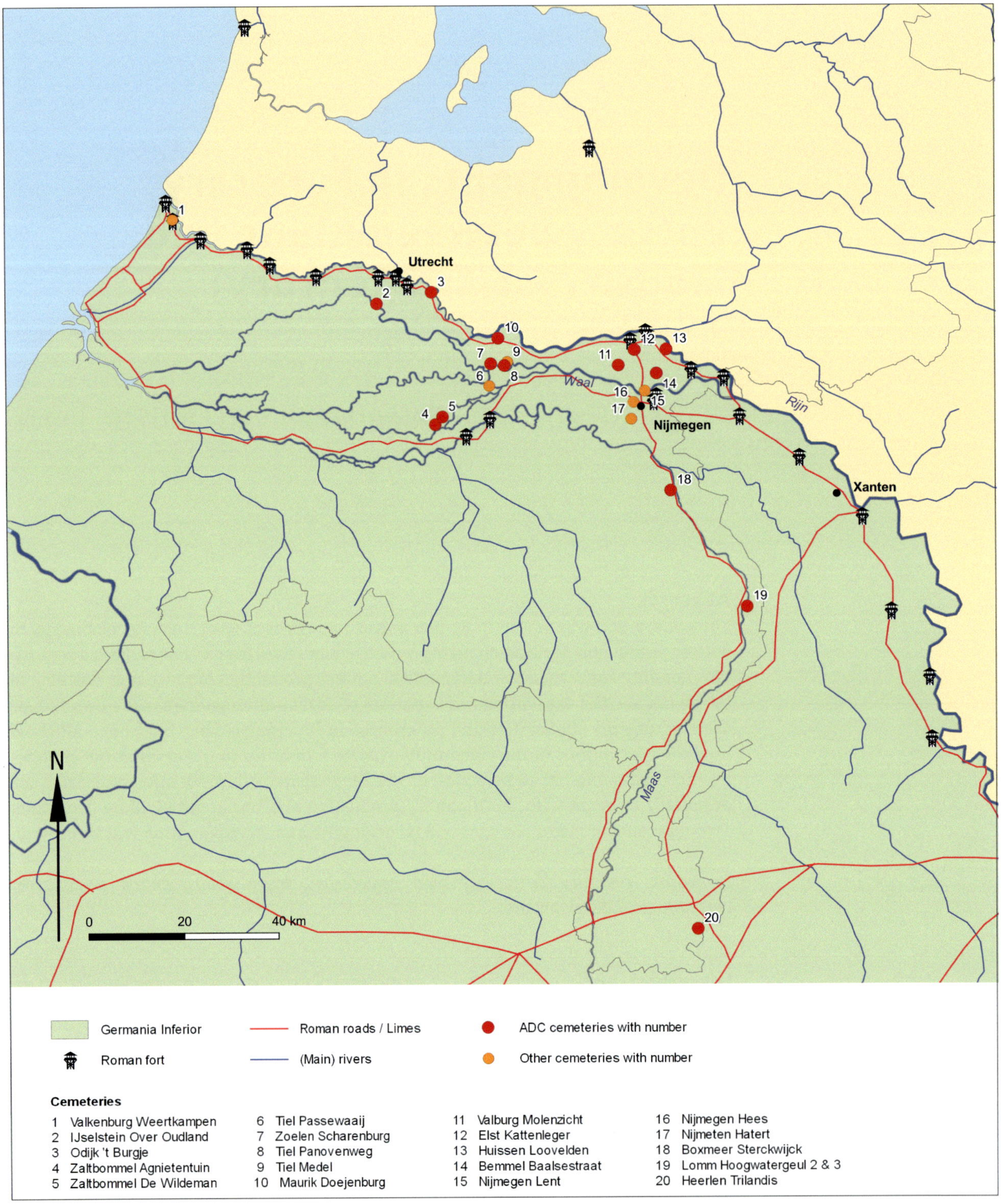

Fig. 1. Map with selection of Roman cemeteries in Germania Inferior (© ADC ArcheoProjecten).

Following the Treaty of Valletta in 1992 rescue or development-led archaeology became the norm. As a result, archaeological research in the Netherlands has developed significantly over the past 30 years. This proved to be a great opportunity for science-based pottery studies, partly conducted in a commercial setting. The study of recently excavated cemeteries also focuses on the questions of rituals, gender, age, and social diversity.

This article will focus on differences in ceramic burial gifts from different points of view. Incidentally, it is worth bearing in mind that first and foremost general trends are discussed here. Each community maintained local customs, so different emphases can be observed in each cemetery. Some of these differences will also be discussed below. This article can be considered a digest of the various published pottery studies by the author, including the article published in the 2016 Fautores Acta, and in the upcoming proceedings of the 2022 Limes Congress (Reigersman-van Lidth de Jeude 2016; in press), supplemented by thoughts on the development of funerary rituals and its relationship to pottery production in particular. The results of excavations in Nijmegen and Tiel by others are also incorporated.

The most important question to be dealt with is: how can chronological developments in the combinations of grave goods in the 1st, 2nd and 3rd century be explained and what role did pottery production play? The latter aspect appears to have been strongly influenced by contacts with Roman culture and rites, and this paper will investigate if that is the only explanation. But before discussing these matters some of the limiting factors in the investigation will be outlined.

The data presented in this article are derived from the individual pottery studies of a number of the excavated cemeteries. There is not yet a database with the data of all analyses of (ceramic) grave goods aggregated. Trends and patterns in the rituals have nonetheless become clear for each cemetery and many similarities but also differences have emerged.

Limiting Factors during Research

The investigation of cemeteries is somewhat hampered by several alterations of the sites over the past 2000 years or so. Some of the problems will be discussed here briefly. The graves and burials that we come across nowadays are the ones that were not very visible in the field. Most of the visible graves, such as burial mounds and those with a more monumental character, were looted at some point. Sometimes the ransacking left the graves completely empty. Only the sarcophagus or traces of the wooden coffin remained. In other cases, the graves were disrupted by farming, building and other uses of an area in more recent times.

Another reason for a limited excavation of a cemetery can be the impossibility of excavating the entire cemetery. This is a consequence of rescue archaeology: archaeological research is usually restricted to the part of the archaeological site that will be developed and therefore needs to be rescued. This means that most archaeological sites in the Netherlands can only be partially excavated.

Some of the graves appeared to be empty, not because they were robbed but because the buried person seemingly did not receive any gifts from his or her relatives. We are, however, not certain whether they did not actually receive any gifts or that the gifts simply disappeared over the centuries, being made of degradable, organic materials such as cloth, leather, wood, wicker, *etc.* It is assumed, though, that the human remains were often gathered from the funeral pyre and subsequently interred in a burial pit in some kind of organic container like a bag or a piece of cloth or leather (Van der Feijst and Geerts 2021, 11).

And last but not least: the study of merely ceramic grave goods paints a one-sided picture of rituals of the Roman era. After all, metal objects such as iron (shoe) nails and bronze fibulae, but also knives, scissors, small utensils, and coins, are also often found in graves. Occasionally, metal objects are even the only grave goods. Less frequent, but still fairly common grave goods are glass beads and vessels, bone artefacts like spindles and distaffs, and animal bones. The animal bones can be interpreted as a meal for the afterlife and probably not as the remains of a meal for the mourning relatives. Degradable goods such as the above mentioned as well as herbs and food are only very rarely found, but also played a part in the rituals[1].

Cemeteries

Most of the recent excavations of Roman cemeteries took place in the Dutch eastern river area, the area chosen as a case study for this paper because of the many examples of well excavated and published cemeteries. The Dutch eastern river area is the region in the Netherlands in which the three large rivers Rhine, Waal and Meuse converge (fig. 1). The limes, with its string of forts and vici, followed the south bank of the Rhine. In the hinterland, in the fertile region between the rivers Rhine and Waal, an important branch of the Rhine, many larger and smaller rural settlements, farms and a few villae rusticae emerged and flourished. Likewise, a number of similar settlements existed between Waal and Meuse. Figure 1 shows the main rivers in the Netherlands and the location of a selection of the cemeteries excavated. Van der Feijst and Geerts (2021, 10-23) recently provided a concise overview of the six most

1 The article by Van den Broeke *et al.* 2021 deals with a rare white lead dispenser for cosmetic use made from the stem of a plant found in a cemetery north of Nijmegen at Waalsprong.

No.	Site	Start Date	End Date	n Graves	Reference
E16	Nijmegen-Hunerberg	19 BC	70	16	Van Enckevort 2011
12	Elst-Park Lingezegen 'Kattenleger'	5 BC/AD 25	200/250	26	Verniers *et al.* 2018
17	Nijmegen-Hatert	10	260	226	Haalebos 1990
19a	Lomm 2	0/25	160	7	Gerrets and De Leeuwe 2011
10	Maurik	0/50	200	30	Veldman 2012
8	Tiel-Panovenweg	0/50	200	44	Kenemans and Vossen 2023
18	Boxmeer-Sterckwijck	0/50	225/250	93	Blom and Van de Velde 2015
13	Huissen-Loovelden	25/50	325/350	105	Van der Feijst *et al.* 2017
19b	Lomm 3	25	100	12	Gerrets and Williams 2011
9a	Tiel 'Medel' Hazenkamp	25/75	230/250	49	Habermehl *et al.* 2019
6	Tiel-Passewaaij	40	270	380	Aarts and Heeren 2011
5	Zaltbommel-De Wildeman	50	200/225	86	Veldman and Blom 2010
11	Valburg-Molenzicht	50	250/300	37	Van der Feijst and Veldman 2018
9b	Tiel 'Medel' De Reth	50/70	270	39	Habermehl *et al.* 2019
3	Odijk-'t Burgje	50/70	550/600	51	Van der Feijst and Loopik 2020
16	Nijmegen-Hees	70	250/270	42	Brunsting 1937
1a	Valkenburg-Marktveld	70	300	115	Loopik and Vos 2021
15	Nijmegen-Lent	100	250	100	Van den Broeke *et al.* 2021
13	Bemmel-Baalsestraat	100	300	50	Van der Feijst *et al.* in press
7	Zoelen-Scharenburg	100	250/275	34	Veldman 2011
1b	Valkenburg-Weerdkampen	100/125	225	16	Loopik and Vos 2021
2	IJsselstein	125	200	6	Verniers 2012
20	Heerlen-Trilandis	125	250/275	9	Weekers-Hendrikx 2018
4	Zaltbommel-Agnietentuin	150	250	6	Van Benthem 2020

Table 1. Overview of the cemeteries included in this study, highlighted are the number of graves, and start and end date of each site (table: F. Reigersman-van Lidth de Jeude).

interesting cemeteries (indicated with orange dots in fig. 1) in the eastern river area. These six cemeteries represent the variety in rural funerary rituals in the Dutch eastern river area because of their size, wealth, and duration.

The cemeteries found in rural areas, such as Zaltbommel, Zoelen and Tiel, served a small settlement or several neighbouring farmhouses. The inhabitants cremated and buried men, women and children in central cemeteries close to their homes. Recent excavations at several locations also brought to light cemeteries that served the inhabitants of villages nearby the limes or the city of Ulpia Noviomagus (Nijmegen). The cemeteries of Boxmeer and Lomm are strictly speaking not situated in the river area, but their developments form a valuable addition.

In table 1 the basic data of the cemeteries included in this article are given in a more or less chronological order; the numbers correspond with the map (fig. 1). The data often reflect only part of the cemetery. The number of graves is therefore only an indication of the number of people that once were buried on the sites[2]. The dating of the cemeteries in this table is based on the data retrieved during the excavations. Further research might be able to complete the data. However, after analysing the grave goods, consisting mainly of pottery and metal objects, it became clear that most cemeteries were first put to use in the first half or third quarter of the 1st century. This therefore happened more or less simultaneously before Roman influence became common or Roman material culture became standard (see below). The cemeteries remained in use throughout the Flavian period and the 2nd century. A number of cemeteries were still in use at the beginning of the 3rd century, while only a few persisted into the second half of the 3rd century. Graves that could be dated in the 4th or 5th century are rare. Cemeteries dating from the late Roman period onwards

2 The cemeteries southwards along the Meuse near Lomm and Heerlen have shown a somewhat different tradition and consisted of a small number of graves.

Fig. 2. Special pottery and personalised gifts. a: sieve-pot, Zaltbommel-De Wildeman CR34; b-d: imitations of a glass bowl and a bronze washing set, Huissen-Loovelden GR71. Graffiti. e: Zaltbommel-De Wildeman CR39; f: Huissen-Loovelden CR26 (© ADC ArcheoProjecten).

(*e.g.* Rhenen and Wijchen) are not included in this study (Wagner and Ypey 2011; Heeren and Hazenberg 2010).

South of the river Meuse many cemeteries were found as well, sometimes dating from the Iron Age into Roman times. The cemetery of Boxmeer-Sterckwijck fits in this tradition. In the coastal area large cemeteries seem to be absent, despite the increased density of settlements and population growth in the second half of the 2nd and the 3rd century. These regions are however not part of this study.

Ceramic Grave Goods

In most graves in rural cemeteries at least one gift was found. Often this would be some kind of pot or a fibula. During the early Roman period, when people did not have so much wheelthrown pottery at their disposal, the deceased were mostly accompanied by handmade pots, bronze fibulae, and occasionally glass beads, or a combination of these objects. When wheelthrown pottery became a more common consumer good, the dead were buried with more fashionable grave goods like *terra nigra*, terra sigillata or colour coated vessels and jugs.

The pottery found in the graves does not differ very much from the pottery that can be found within the settlements, although there is a difference in the proportion in which forms occur. Most objects found in the graves were objects for general, everyday use like jars, beakers, plates, and jugs. The pottery could thus serve both a domestic and a ritual function. People chose tablewares like terra sigillata plates and cups, and colour coated plates and beakers to accompany the deceased, but also kitchen wares like coarse ware plates were common burial gifts. Pots used for cooking or storage were less common grave goods.

Although the pottery vessels found in the graves were fairly common household goods, certain kinds of common vessel forms did not have this double function. Large storage vessels like dolia and Mediterranean amphorae for wine or olive oil are mostly absent in graves, although they were in use in every household. The smaller regional flat-based amphorae seem to have had a different status than the large ones in this respect, but not until the second half of the 2nd century did they appear regularly in graves. Other fairly seldom types in graves are decorated terra sigillata bowls and terra sigillata mortaria. Coarse ware mortaria are equally rare. Occasionally, mortaria appear in graves, but can be considered exceptional (Krekovič 2016, 514-517). In some cemeteries mortaria appear less seldom than others, especially after 150[3].

Some of the grave goods may have been personal belongings or may have had a special meaning to the deceased person in life. The rare pot with a narrow opening and small holes in the top and plates with graffiti may be interpreted as such (fig. 2a, e-f). The same goes for the very rare, high-quality imitations of bronze and glass vessels (fig. 2b-d) found at the cemetery of Huissen-Loovelden that can be interpreted as a washing set (see below, Reigersman-van Lidth de Jeude 2017, 94-96). Another possibility for the interpretation of personalised pottery gifts is that relatives, neighbours, *etc.* honoured the deceased with the gifts they deemed appropriate for the occasion.

Chronological Changes

It is not surprising that the ceramic grave goods to some extent followed the developments of pottery production and the influx of new pottery types into daily life. This means that the graves can be dated satisfactorily when the combination of vessels in a grave is thoroughly studied. This development, however, appears to be not the only one when we study the vessels that accompanied the dead. The chronological changes, visualised in Figure 4 (see below), seem to represent not only the developments in pottery production, but also changes in funerary rites. The chronological developments will be discussed in three phases: 1st century pre-Flavian, Flavian until the mid-2nd century, and the second half of the 2nd and 3rd century.

1st Century, pre-Flavian

At the beginning of the 1st century the indigenous people in the river area gave one or more pots (and brooches) to their deceased. These were the same pots they used in daily life: handmade pots they had made themselves. Following the Roman occupation of the region newly introduced wheelthrown pottery began to appear in graves. At first this would happen only occasionally and only for those who had direct contact with the occupiers. The people that took part in, or had intensive contacts with Roman civilisation, such as veterans, local leaders and perhaps merchants and their families, would be accompanied by 'luxurious' wheelthrown pottery, glass objects and/or military equipment. The imported Roman pottery in these graves would consist of vessels that had no parallels in the indigenous pottery range, like the jug found in Elst-Park Lingezegen 'Kattenleger' CR13 (figs 3 and 4, second from above). Most graves in the first half of the 1st century, however, were provided with the traditional handmade pottery.

Roman wheelthrown pottery is present in almost every grave, sometimes combined with handmade pots, in the civilian cemetery of the Batavian capital *Oppidum Batavorum* at Nijmegen-Hunerberg (east of no. 16 on fig. 1) and in the rural cemetery of Nijmegen-Hatert from the

3 In Flavian times at Nijmegen-Hatert mortaria were added quite often; see Haalebos 1990, 171.

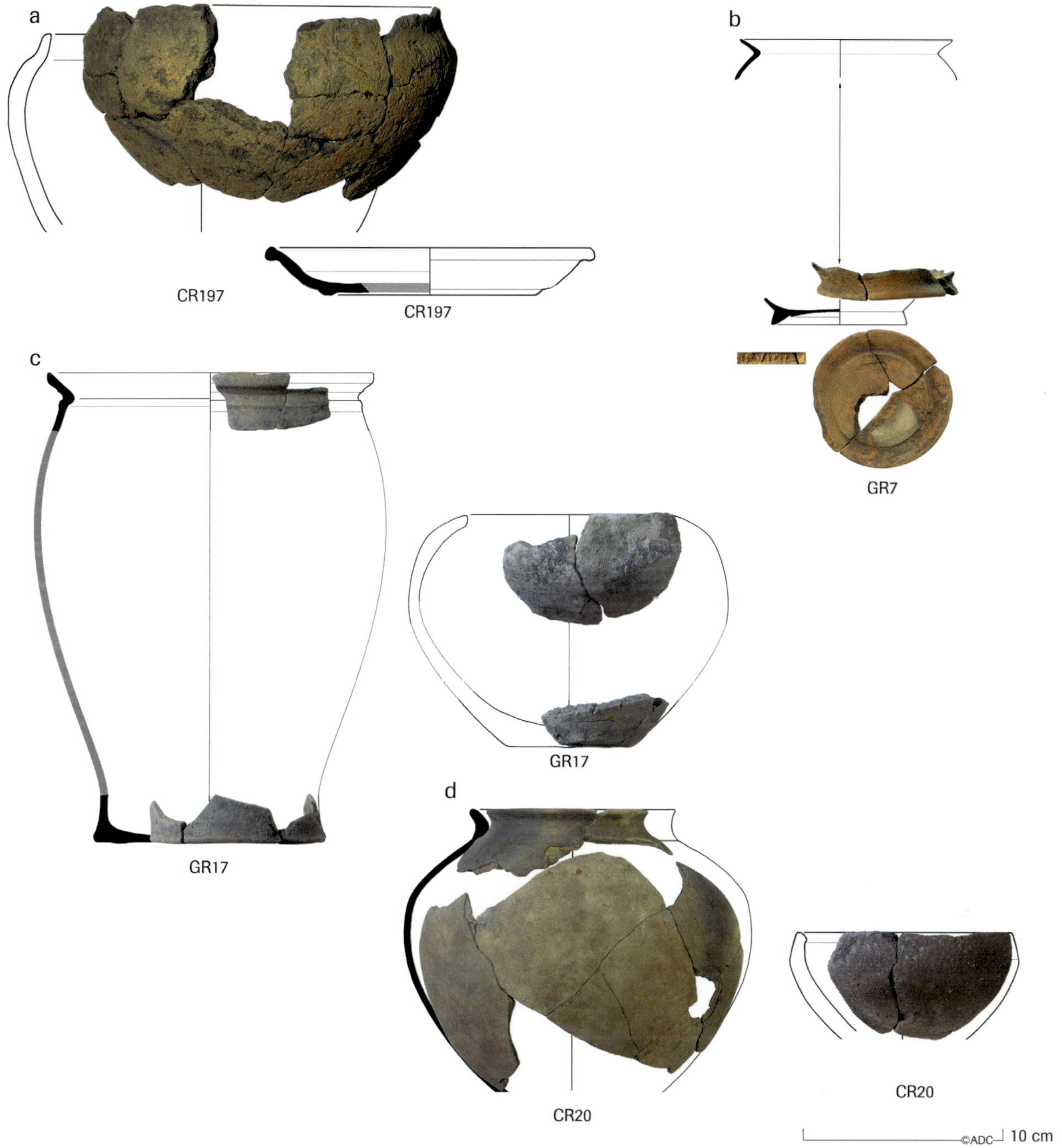

Fig. 3. Early wheelthrown pottery in rural cemeteries. a: Elst-Park Lingezegen 'Kattenleger' graf 7 (after: Verniers *et al.* 2018, 234 © ADC ArcheoProjecten); b: Boxmeer-Sterckwijck CR197 (after: Blom and Van de Velde 2015, 376 © ADC ArcheoProjecten); c: Tiel-Panovenweg CR17 (after: Kenemans and Vossen 2023, 463 © ADC ArcheoProjecten); d: Tiel-Panovenweg CR20 (after: Kenemans and Vossen 2023, 469 © ADC ArcheoProjecten).

time the burial grounds were put into use (table 1; Van Enckevort 2011, 15-30; Haalebos 1990, 29-40). This can be explained because of the better accessibility of the new Roman objects on the periphery of the Roman camp. People from the rural settlements along the Meuse also had access to the new Roman goods at an earlier stage than the people in the rural settlements in the river area because the Roman occupation spread from the south along the Meuse to Nijmegen during the last two decades of the 1st century BC (Hiddink 1999).

Wheelthrown pottery gradually became available to more people, and grave goods changed from mere indigenous handmade pots to wheelthrown pots of Roman design, or a combination of both. This gradual change in grave goods can be observed by the middle of the 1st century. Graves with a combination of indigenous handmade pottery and wheelthrown types, like beakers, plates, and jugs, thus began to occur, provided there was some contact with Roman culture.

It is noteworthy that in most rural cemeteries one or two early 1st-century graves contained wheelthrown pottery, whilst the majority of the early graves contained handmade pots. It seems that in most rural settlements some people had already been in contact with Roman culture at an early stage (fig. 3). It is nonetheless not until the middle of the 1st century or the Flavian period that the majority of the graves were provided with wheelthrown pottery. This new pottery therefore gradually became a more common phenomenon as a grave good. In this light it should be noted that in the rural settlements and cemeteries of Lomm 2 and Lomm 3 along the Meuse, Roman goods became a commonplace a few decades earlier than in most rural settlements in the eastern river area.

In graves with only wheelthrown pottery, it is striking that people were inclined to give an equivalent of their handmade pots in this phase. *Terra nigra* urns (mostly wheelthrown variants of vessels in Celtic tradition; see Deru 1996, 201-208), colour coated beakers (white fabric covered with orange or black paint), or small coarse ware jars were the first vessel forms to appear in the graves of ordinary people. The so-called beakers are often the same size as the pots, which is rather large for a drinking vessel. Whether or not they were actually meant to drink from will not be discussed in this article.

The *terra nigra* urns are often terribly damaged and were shattered into hardly recognisable small pieces by the fire. The beakers and other vessels from graves that are dated slightly later are less damaged. This raises the question whether there was a difference in the cremation ritual for some time, or whether this is a result of the kind of fabric. In other words: did *terra nigra* naturally disintegrate more easily than other pottery or did it shatter so much due to differences – temporary or local – in cremation rituals?

Flavian Time to Mid-2nd Century

In the Flavian period, Roman culture became more widespread and typical Roman pottery more readily available for rural communities in the river area. Wheelthrown pottery was now more widely embraced,

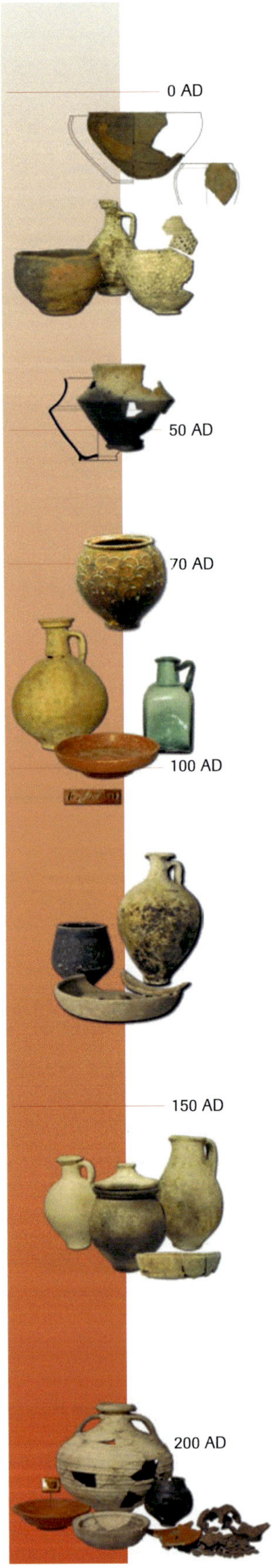

Fig. 4. Chronological development of pottery in graves. From top to bottom: Boxmeer-Sterckwijck CR97; Elst-Park Lingezegen 'Kattenleger' CR13; Lomm 3 CR8; Huissen-Loovelden grave 70; Elst-Park Lingezegen 'Kattenleger' CR6; Zaltbommel-De Wildeman INH2; Elst-Park Lingezegen 'Kattenleger' CR3, 2-6; Zoelen-Scharenburg CR6 (© ADC ArcheoProjecten).

Fig. 5. Greater variety in pottery after 150. a: Zoelen-Scharenburg CR9 (after: Veldman 2011, 274); b: Boxmeer-Sterckwijck CR25 (after: Blom and Van de Velde 2015, 314 © ADC ArcheoProjecten); c: Zoelen-Scharenburg INH6 (after: Veldman 2011, 321 © ADC ArcheoProjecten).

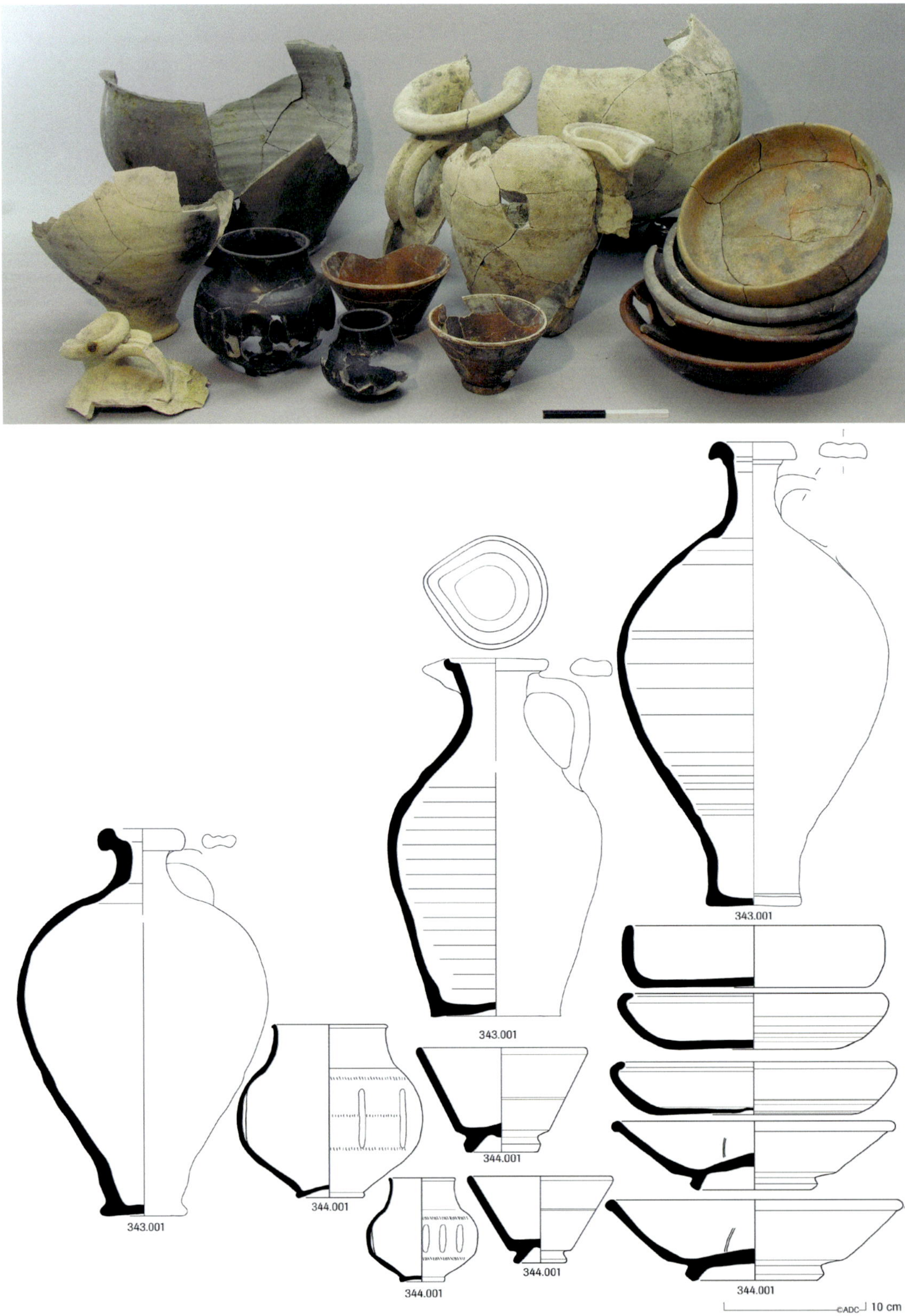

Fig. 6. Greater variety in pottery after 150. Zaltbommel-Agnietentuin CR2 (after: Van Benthem 2020, afb. 9.7 © ADC ArcheoProjecten).

whereas handmade pottery decreased in importance, and gradually disappeared from the villages and farmhouses. Simultaneously it lost its popularity in funerary rites.

In keeping with ancient tradition, at least one jar-like vessel was interred in most graves. The above-mentioned colour coated beakers became more and more popular grave goods, whilst the popularity of *terra nigra* urns and coarse ware pots gradually decreased. Combinations of a beaker with a plate or jug also became more usual. In richer graves a large set of many luxury goods such as several terra sigillata plates and cups, beakers, metal objects, glass bowls, and jars can be found. In the cemeteries of Huissen-Loovelden and Bemmel-Baalsestraat there are several examples of this kind of exuberance (Van der Feijst and Geerts 2021, 13-15). In these graves some of the gifts are undamaged and look unused, as if they were newly purchased for the occasion (Reigersman-van Lidth de Jeude 2017, 89).

From this time onward, grave goods seem to have reached a level of standardisation, meaning that the variation in ceramic grave goods became more limited. This is especially the case in the first half of the 2nd century, when gifts mostly consisted of a beaker, a plate, and a jug (a similar practice is observed in Belgium, see Hanut and Henrotay 2014, 50). This combination of standardised grave goods can represent different aspects of the funeral rites. The vessels can be interpreted as a banquet set but also as a washing set, and both interpretations can be valid (Van der Feijst *et al.* 2017, 87, 89-99). However, the interpretation that the set of vessels were part of a ritual meal either for the deceased in the afterlife or for the mourning relatives is the most common interpretation. In some cases, the beaker or plate was replaced by a cup or small bowl. Incomplete sets, with one or two of the shapes missing, also occur (Reigersman-van Lidth de Jeude 2016, 410-411). Metal finds became a little less common.

Among the most popular grave goods were terra sigillata plates and cups. Coarse ware plates were also often deposited. Colour coated beakers were equally popular in the graves. In the 2nd century, colour coated plates also appeared as well as the first small coarse ware bowls. Although the fabric can differ, these vessels were more or less of the same shape and functionality, at least as a grave good. This does not necessarily mean that terra sigillata, colour coated, and coarse ware plates had the same function in daily life, nor is it obvious that terra sigillata cups and small coarse ware bowls did.

The types of plates and beakers found in the graves were mostly in use in the settlements as well. The jugs placed in the graves followed the prevailing types in the same way the plates and beakers did. Less common types of plates, beakers and jugs in settlements were equally less common in graves.

Mid-2nd to 3rd Century

After the mid-2nd century, between 150-175, another change can be observed in the ceramic gifts. Perhaps the most striking change is that not only cremation, but also inhumation began to be practised from the middle of the 2nd century onward. In the 3rd century inhumation became more popular and this prevailed in late Roman times. Also, in ceramic gifts a change is visible. Although the standard combination (with its accepted variations) of a beaker, plate, and jug was still in use, this became less predominant. It seems that conventions surrounding the ritual were somehow loosened. More ordinary (and less expensive?) vessels became part of the ritual as well. Cooking jars and storage pots appeared in the graves and sometimes were even used as a container for the cremated remains. Large, flat-based amphorae and coarse ware pitchers were added or replaced the jugs (figs 5-6). Coarse ware mortaria now appeared in most cemeteries. Metal objects gained in popularity again. Bone objects like spindles or distaffs were also new gifts that became more common, especially in women's graves. This change in the execution of the funerary ritual remained prevalent throughout the 3rd century.

Changes in the performance of the ritual seem obvious, but the pottery in the graves still followed the development of pottery production. Here also some significant changes took place. From the middle of the 2nd century several new techniques evolved, with a tendency towards more robust and durable fabrics. The most prominent changes in pottery will be briefly discussed.

Colour coated beakers now also appeared in a red fabric and towards the end of the century this fabric had superseded the former white fabric. The red fabric now even reached a kind of perfection, acquiring a hard firing with a shiny metallic coating, the so-called high gloss ware ("Qualitätsware" (Oelmann 1914) or "céramique métallescente" (Brulet *et al.* 1999); see figs 5c, 6).

Another change in technique can be observed regarding the production of smooth-walled jugs. Type Stuart 111 that came into production around 170 (Haalebos 1990, 160-161) was formed in one piece, and did not, like previous types, have a neck that was attached separately. Simultaneous with the appearance of this jug type was the increase in coarse ware pitchers of diverse design, like those Oelmann described based on finds from Niederbieber (Oelmann 1914, 74-75, types 96-98). In the 3rd century the proportion of smooth-walled jugs decreased in favour of these pitchers. The coarse ware found in Kastell Niederbieber was manufactured in production centres in the region of Urmitz and Neuwieder Becken, with fabrics that were harder fired and look less porous.

The last important change to be mentioned here is the appearance of terra sigillata mortaria at the expense of coarse ware mortaria. This may, or may not, have had to do with a different attitude towards coarse ware mortaria that had been in use ever since the Romans set foot in the region. Terra sigillata mortaria probably followed the development of coarse ware types (see for example Vanvinckenroye 1991, types 347-353). At first the flange was positioned more horizontally (cf. Curle 21). Later, the rims were more vertically shaped and hung loose from the bowl (Drag. 43) and became part of the bowl (Drag. 45). The decorative spouts in the shape of the head of a lion, bat or monkey were, of course, reserved for terra sigillata mortaria.

Reflections

The analysed grave goods from the cemeteries show both similarities and differences in terms of the execution of the burial ritual. However, each community had its own characteristics and customs and therefore different preferences in the rituals can be distinguished in each cemetery, either in choice of vessels, wealth or gender and age.

One of the similarities is that some of the grave goods were part of the cremation ritual and placed near or even on top of the funeral pyre. Consequently, the pottery shows signs of burning and vessels can be completely shattered. In Zaltbommel, Zoelen, Tiel and Boxmeer the number of unrecognisably burnt and fragmented vessels is much larger than in Huissen and Bemmel. In addition, the degree of burning also varies between the different cemeteries. In every cemetery, there are graves that contain only burnt gifts, only unburnt gifts, or a combination of both. In some cemeteries, there is a higher percentage of unburnt gifts.

Graves without any gifts occur as well. In the cemeteries of rural settlements in the hinterland this was a more common phenomenon than in cemeteries on the periphery of the Roman city of Ulpia Noviomagus. This seems in contradiction with the large amount of grave goods in other graves of the same date in the same cemetery, but is it? Was it accepted to bury a person without any grave goods or is there a pattern in graves without grave goods? It may be related to the gender or age of the deceased, for example, but this requires further investigation. In that light, but also in general, the possibility that perishable materials were also part of the ritual should be seriously considered.

The above-described chronological developments can be recognised everywhere in the eastern river area and along the Meuse (*e.g.* Haalebos 1990, 193-196; Aarts and Heeren 2011, kaartbijlage 3; Reigersman-van Lidth de Jeude in press). What reason can be given for the major changes in the Flavian period and the late Antonine period? Changes in the Roman Empire in the Flavian era, such as the foundation of the city of Ulpia Noviomagus with all its activity, brought Roman culture within reach of the indigenous population. When people got used to Roman culture, they not only used the new pottery, but also incorporated Roman customs into their own. Eventually they adopted the new rituals entirely.

After the middle of the 2nd century there was no apparent change in cultural influence from elsewhere. Nevertheless, there were some substantial alterations both in funeral rites and pottery production. Should they be considered as just another stage of development or could there also be another explanation? What was the trigger, or were there more triggers? Without any indication or evidence of a change in philosophy of life or other social development it is not possible to give a satisfying answer to these highly intriguing questions.

To conclude: after the rather general analysis of the ceramic grave goods using the individual cemeteries as a starting point, several developments and trends were observed, and a number of conclusions presented here. To answer the new questions that were put forward in this article, a broader investigation is required, combining all the data. A large all-encompassing study may reveal anomalies in the patterns per cemetery. Then, hopefully, the Roman burial ritual in general and the developments outlined here in particular can be explained.

PART 4

GEOGRAPHICAL AND CHRONOLOGICAL DIMENSIONS OF REGIONAL AND LONG-DISTANCE EXCHANGE

Gallo-Belgic Ware from Xanten to the Sea

Xavier Deru

Abstract

Thanks to the pioneering work of Holwerda, the region extending from Xanten to the sea, largely located in the Netherlands, has been recognised as a significant consumer of Gallo-Belgic ware (*terra nigra* and *terra rubra*) during the 1st century. Recent quantification, however, reveals that this pottery was less prevalent than in the province of Belgica and even in a substantial part of Germania Inferior.

Workshops producing these vessels were scarce in the region, making imports particularly noteworthy. Some of these imports originated from the Rhineland, notably Xanten, and took advantage of river transport. The production of Gallo-Belgic ware is still not well documented in northern France. However, the fabric, stamps, and a limited number of workshops suggest that this region supplied the Netherlands in the second half of the 1st century. Since the Augustan period, the Champagne area had been exporting Gallo-Belgic ware to regions including Belgica, Germania, and Britannia. Similar to terra sigillata, *terra rubra* and *terra nigra* represented a Roman brand, albeit one already transformed by Gaulish craftsmen.

Keywords: terra nigra, terra rubra, Gallo-Belgic ware, Germania Inferior, Holwerda

Introduction

In the Low Countries, particularly in the regions surrounding the major rivers (Meuse, Waal, Rhine), from the late 1st century BC to the early 2nd century, habitation was diverse. It ranged from native rural settlements to the first urban sites and Roman military forts, each associated with cemeteries. Different communities had varying consumption patterns and differential access to regional markets, including Gallo-Belgic ware.

Gallo-Belgic ware is a broad category of pottery established in the late 19th century by German archaeologists based on ethnic ideology. This flawed and ambiguous classification, still followed by some, grouped together pottery produced using different techniques and for different purposes (tableware, cooking ware, and storage) spanning the 1st century BC to the 4th century. In 1996 the author (Deru 1996), proposed narrowing this group down to table vessels generally dating from the 1st century whilst retaining

in: R.C.A. Geerts and Ph. Bes (eds) 2024, *Roman Pottery in the Low Countries: Past Research, Current State, Future Directions*. Leiden: Sidestone Press (= *Papers on Archaeology of the Leiden Museum of Antiquities Leiden* 32), pp. 123-132.

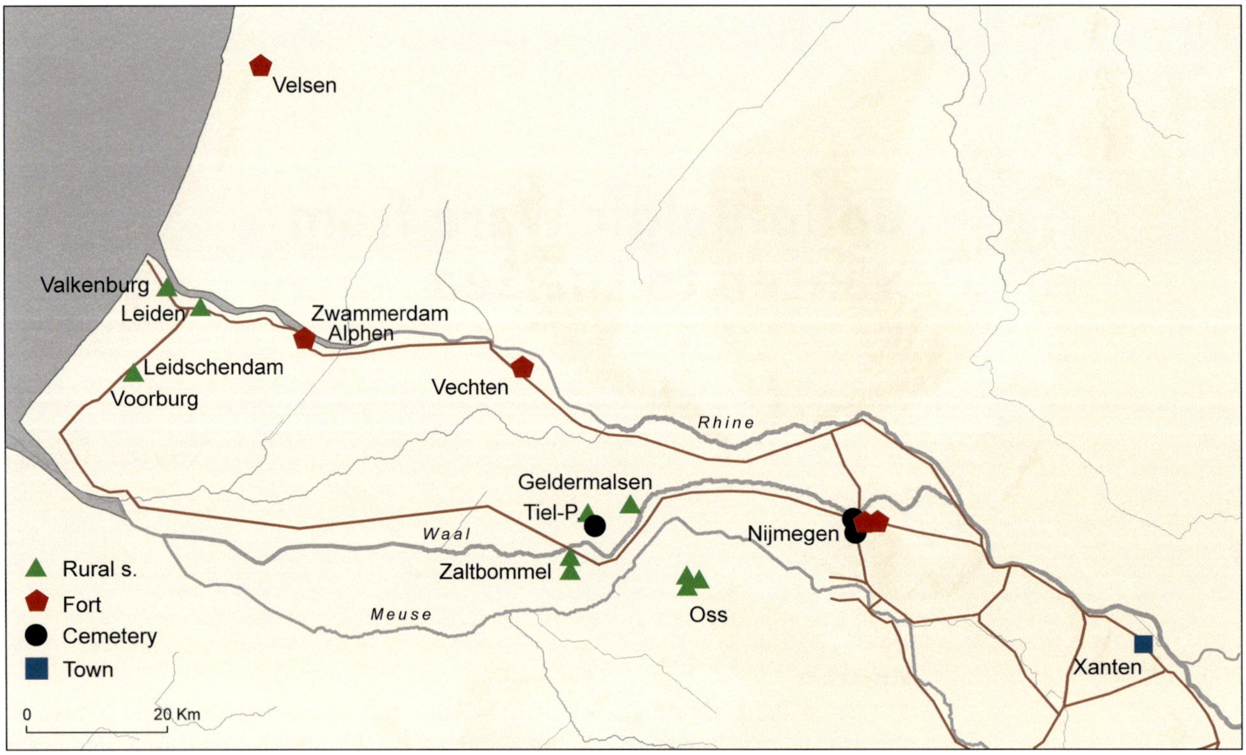

Fig. 1. The Dutch river area. Roman sites cited in this paper (© ABG).

the various techniques within a single typology. It is more efficient to consider that Gallo-Belgic wares consist of two types: *terra rubra* and *terra nigra*, each with sub-techniques (*e.g.* glossed, slipped, smoked, *etc.*, known as TR2, TR1, TR3, *etc.*). They share common forms (see www.onicer.org). Dishes, cups, bowls, beakers, and bottles make up the repertoire of *terra rubra* and *terra nigra* wares.

Gallo-Belgic wares (*terra rubra* and *terra nigra*) provide evidence of shifts in pottery production and consumption in northern Gaul, a process that was also taking place in central and southern Gaul before the Roman conquest. This phenomenon was complex and involved craftsmen, merchants, and investors. It is certain that the Rheims and Marne-Vesle areas were at the heart of this change, but numerous workshops emerged during the 1st century with different objectives.

The Gallo-Belgic Ware in the Netherlands

In 1941, Holwerda published a seminal book on Gallo-Belgic ware (Holwerda 1941), which continued the work of German scholars. He proposed a new typology which is still used in the Netherlands. From an international perspective, this publication made it seem like the region was a producer and, certainly, a major consumer of Gallo-Belgic tableware. The dynamism and quality of Dutch archaeology supported this initial impression.

Rural Settlements

The Dutch river region is characterised by non-villa landscapes where pottery mainly consisted of handmade wares. Quantifications are typically not provided by phase but by site. However, quantified information on *terra rubra* and *terra nigra* dates to the 1st century. The proportion of *terra rubra* and *terra nigra* ranges from 1% to 6% in 4 different settlements in Oss (Wesselingh 2000), 5 settlements in Zaltbommel (Veldman and Blom 2010), and sites in Geldermalsen-Hondsgemet (only 1% *terra rubra* and *terra nigra*, phase 3; Van Renswoude and Van Kerckhove 2009, 158-179), Tiel-Passewaaij (Heeren 2009), as well as in Leiden, Valkenburg, and Leidschendam (Van der Velde 2008) (fig. 1). To get a more accurate overview of the representation of *terra rubra* and *terra nigra*, we need to examine the more romanised sites north of the *civitas Tungrorum* (Hiddink 2013; 2014; Van der Velde *et al.* 2009).

Forts

The fortification of the frontier is well-documented in the region, which started during the Augustan period in Nijmegen, being particularly significant at the Kops Plateau and Ubbergen. Other forts along the Rhine underwent transformations after the Batavian Revolt (69/70). Soldiers had access to both regional and extraregional markets and had different eating habits than the native population. In Nijmegen, *terra rubra* and *terra nigra* were uncommon

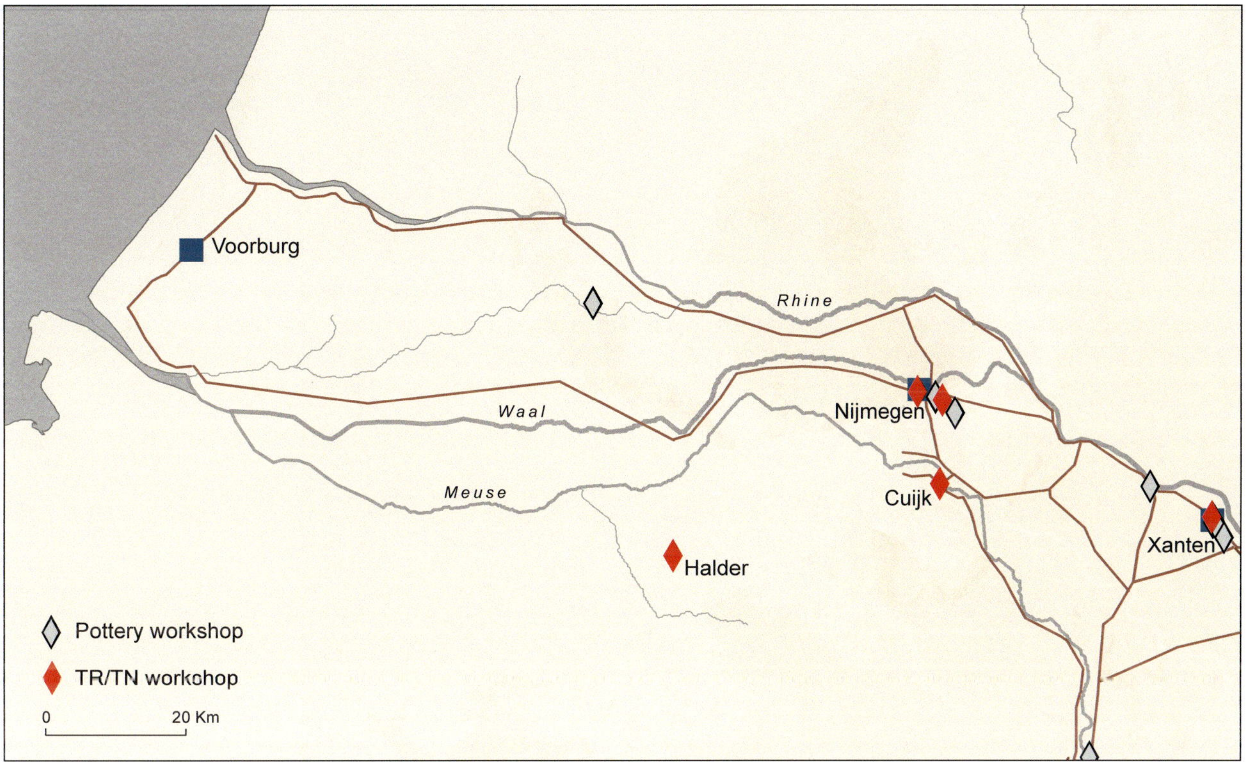

Fig. 2. The Dutch river area. The pottery workshops (© ABG).

during the initial phase (Niemeijer 2013) but later constituted 7% at the Kops Plateau and the Hunerberg legionary camp. A similar proportion was calculated at Vechten (Zandstra and Polak 2012), while it was lower at Zwammerdam (4%; Haalebos 1977), Velsen (Bosman 1997; 2022) and Alphen aan den Rijn (Polak *et al.* 2004). Unlike rural farmers, soldiers preferred high-quality vessels (such as terra sigillata and colour coated wares), and Gallo-Belgic ware was not their first choice.

Cemeteries

The pottery found in burials was heavily influenced by (regional?) funerary practices. In the region, some pottery was burnt with the deceased, whilst other pots, often drinking vessels and flagons, were deposited with bones and ashes in the grave. Handmade pottery remained important in the region, but the proportion of *terra rubra* and *terra nigra* was higher compared to other sites (Tiel-Passewaaij, phase 3.1: Heeren 2009, 105; Nijmegen-Hatert: Haalebos 1990; Deru 1996, 402-406). In the 1st century, Gallo-Belgic ware, given its range of functions (dishes, bowls, beakers, and bottles), could account for up to half of the pottery. By the end of the 1st century, other high-quality pottery such as terra sigillata and colour coated ware replaced *terra rubra* and *terra nigra*.

While Holwerda's work emphasised Gallo-Belgic ware, it was not particularly important in the region. In contrast, in Belgica, during the middle of the 1st century, both in towns and the countryside, Gallo-Belgic ware constituted 50% of the pottery (Corsiez 2019; Deru 2014; Mathelart *et al.* 2018), and in cemeteries, it accounted for 80% (Dananai 2019; Loridant and Deru 2009).

Supply

Low Countries and Germania Inferior

In the region, only a few workshops producing *terra rubra* and *terra nigra* have been excavated (fig. 2). These workshops are mostly located in agglomerations, with one exception in a fort. Two workshops have been attested in Nijmegen, two in Xanten, one in Cuijk, and one in Halder. Kiln 1, found at the Kops Plateau, produced thin-walled ware, jugs, and *terra rubra* beakers (TR P7/8), primarily for the fort's garrison (Stoffels 2014). The other workshop in Nijmegen (Maasplein) exhibited a diverse range of vessels (flagons, coarse wares, *terra nigra*) and fabrics (Hendriks 2014). *Terra nigra* dishes (A21), bowls (B23, B27, B30), and perhaps beakers were produced there. The spectrum of *terra nigra* production is quite late, and the site does not offer a representative sample of Nijmegen's corpus. In Cuijk, only one form is known, imitating terra sigillata bowl Drag. 29 (TN B19), with characteristic compass-drawn decoration

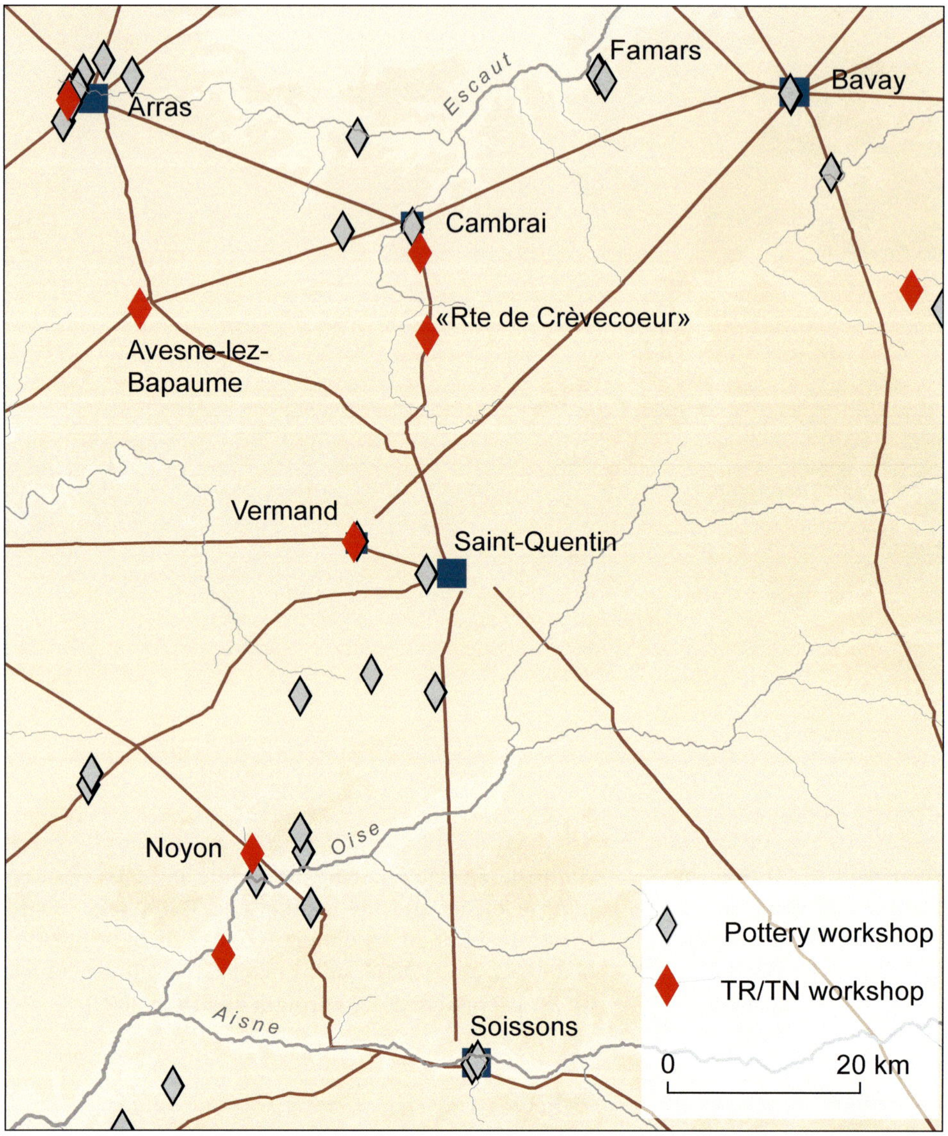

Fig. 3. Northern France. The pottery workshops (© ABG).

(Niemeijer and Thijssen 2014). The fabric is very fine. Halder (Willems 1977; Borgers *et al.* 2017) is best known for the production of stamped mortaria, but bowls (B22) and beakers (P11) are also evidenced. These workshops supplied goods to the local market, with evidence of a broader distribution found in Xanten, where production was located outside the walls of the colonia before its foundation. Xanten produced colour coated ware, lamps, flagons, cooking ware, and Gallo-Belgic ware (Liesen 1994; Boelicke 1995; Lauinger 2014). The production of *terra rubra* is uncertain, but *terra nigra* comprised dishes (A42; Holwerda 81), cups (C13?; Holwerda 82/83), bowls (B1/Holwerda 86; B16/17?; B21?/Holwerda 55c), beakers (P1?/Holwerda 17/18; P54/Holwerda 26; P58-64/ Holwerda 28/29) and bottles (BT1-3/Holwerda 25). Dishes and cups had stamps, and without fabric descriptions at consumer sites, epigraphy remains the best indicator of distribution. Fabric analyses have only been conducted in recent years, making it challenging to create distribution maps for local or regional *terra rubra* and *terra nigra*. However, some forms are specific to the region. Dishes and cups are rare in local workshops, but TN A24-26 (Holwerda 89), found in the river area, originated from the Rhineland. The same applies to pots P58-64 (Holwerda 28/29) with barbotine decoration. Fishbone stamps are also unique to this region. On the other hand, TR/TN P10-12 (Holwerda 13/14/15/19) and the earlier P13 (Holwerda 3) probably came from the Tongeren region (Veldman and Geerts 2014; Brulet 1983).

Imports from Hauts-de-France

Hauts-de-France is a newly defined administrative region that corresponds to the western part of Gallia Belgica. Workshops producing Gallo-Belgic ware were scattered

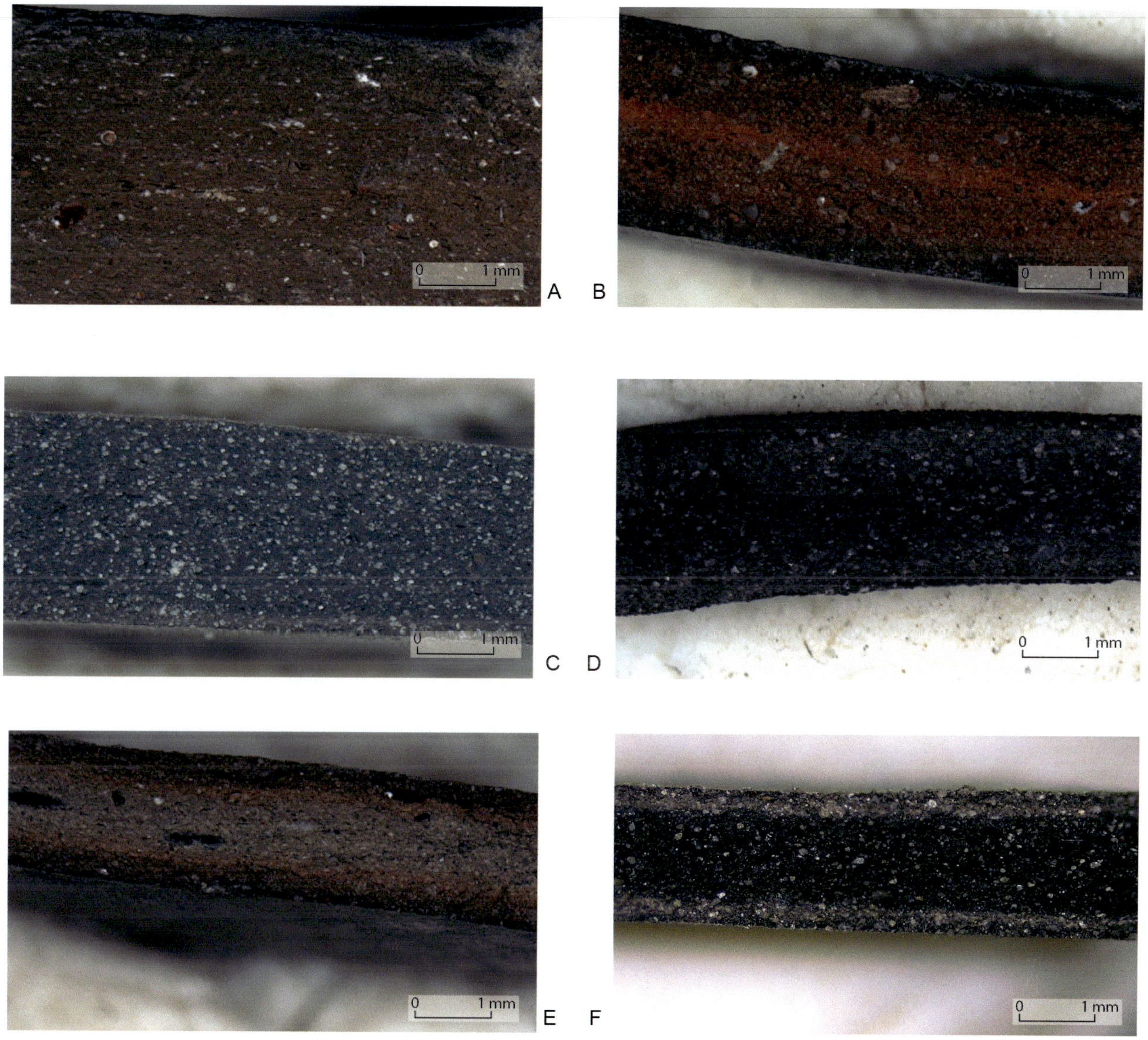

Fig. 4. *Terra nigra* fabrics from northern France. A: soapy/SAVO; B: Noyon; C: Avesne; D: Cambrai; E: Vermand; F: Rues-des-Vignes (© X. Deru).

throughout the region, except for the Somme valley due to the absence of clay there (Deru and Fronteau 2010). Most of these workshops did not export to the Low Countries, and the fabrics and stamped beakers from this region found in the Dutch river area cannot be attributed to specific workshops.

'Savonneuse/Soapy' Fabric

S.J. De Laet (University of Ghent) excavated a cemetery in Blicquy and identified a fabric known as "céramique à pâtes savonneuses" (SAVO). This fabric is exceptionally fine, with minimal quartz inclusions and foraminifera (Deru and Vachard 2002). Several workshops may have exploited this clay, but only one is known with certainty, in the small town of Famars (Nord) (Borgers *et al.* 2020; Willems 2023, 352-391), and perhaps in Bavay (Willems 2023, 215-261), although the facts and hypotheses are challenging to disentangle (fig. 3). In the river area, *terra nigra*, mica-dusted ware, and flagons are known in the SAVO fabric, and the distribution map suggests transportation via the Sambre-Meuse rivers, similar to mortaria (Deru 2021), despite Famars being located near the river Scheldt.

Stamped Terra Nigra Beakers

Recently, three workshops have been identified as producers of *terra nigra* beakers with stamps under the bottom: Cambrai, Route de Crèvecoeur (Herbin *et al.*

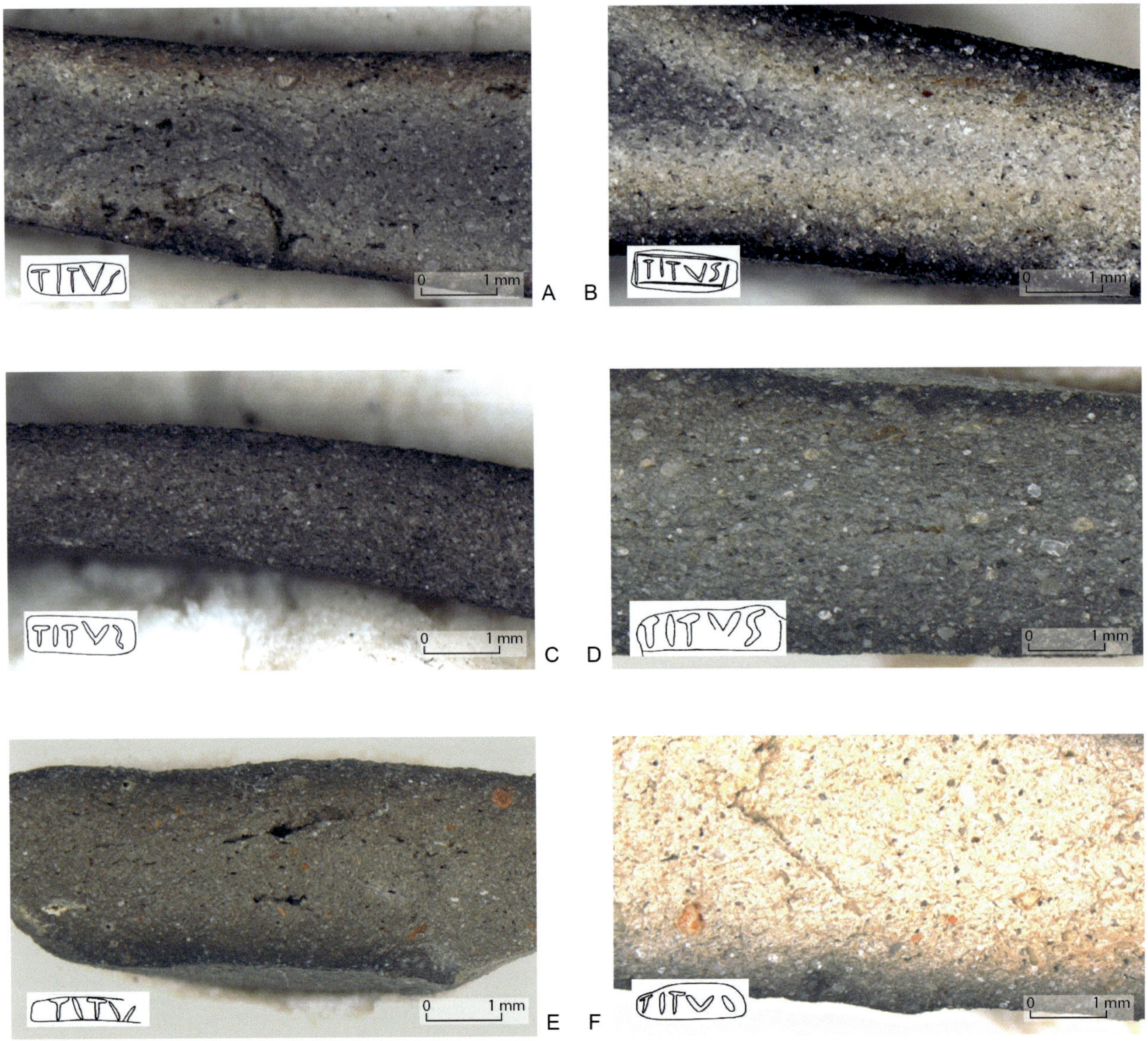

Fig. 5. Stamps of TITVS and the relevant fabric. A, C, E and F: found in Bavay; B and C: found in Nijmegen (© X. Deru).

2019), Les-Rues-des-Vignes (Deru 2022), and Vermand (Hosdez *et al.* 2019). They are located in an area extending from Cambrai to Noyon (France). Two other sites (Noyon (Ben Redjeb 1992) and Avesnes-lès-Bapaume (Maniez and Afonso-Lopes 2019) produced similar beakers but unstamped (figs 3-4). They were active during the second half of the 1st century. In these workshops, production was diverse, but the *terra nigra* pots (TN P46-48, P54-56; Holwerda 26-27) were of high quality, featuring thin walls and smooth, black surfaces. The fabrics are similar, with small quartz inclusions, but not very distinctive. Some stamps are illiterate, while others bear names such as Camari, Dimio, Iaucilio, Vererius, or Uxpuro (Rues-des-Vignes). On the bottom of pots of the same form, quality, and fabric, names of other potters like Belliaxus, Eburus, Cimio, Lucanus, *etc.*, are found. Bavay has a few examples of each, as does Museum Kam (Nijmegen), but having a rich collection does not necessarily establish it as a production centre (*contra* Willems 2023, 223). These beakers are found across a wide region, including northern France, Belgium, and the Netherlands, although few of them have been discovered (fig. 5). Titus, for example, utilised various stamps and worked in different places. We could also be dealing here with different potters named Titus (fig. 6).

However, these various fabrics and stamps are found both in the north of France and in the Netherlands. Although the actual workshops of these potters are unknown, I suspect they operated in the Cambrai and Vermand regions. The distribution map of Rues-des-

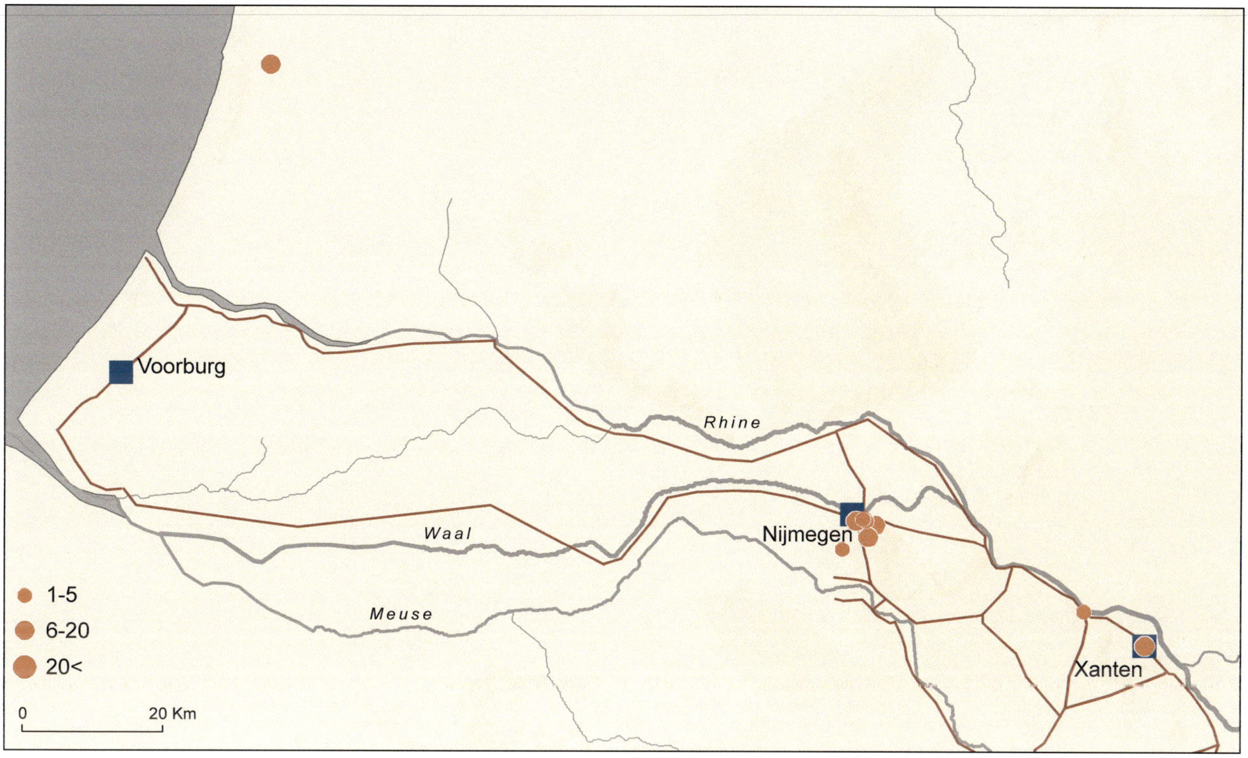

Fig. 6. The Dutch river area. *Terra nigra* stamped imports from northern France (© ABG).

Vignes products suggests that Britain received supplies via Boulogne-sur-Mer, and the east was served by the Boulogne-Cologne road, but distribution further north was unexpected (Deru 2022). Like Famars, Cambrai is situated on the Scheldt, but distribution via the road or the rivers Sambre-Meuse seems more likely.

Imports from the Champagne

The significant role of Gallo-Belgic workshops in the Champagne has been highlighted by V. Rigby since the 1970s but was ignored in France for a long time. The Champagne, specifically the Marne-Vesle district, exported products to Britain during a transitional period, from the reign of Augustus to Claudius. In Belgium, this production was termed "à pâte gris clair" thanks to the pioneering work of S.J. De Laet, although its origin remained unknown for some time. In the 1990s, the author published information about several workshops (Biegert *et al.* 2004/2005, with older references), some of which had been excavated earlier, and research on this topic has continued. The SFECAG Congress in Rheims has contributed updated publications (Mathelart *et al.* 2018; Huart and Mathelart 2018) (fig. 7). In the Netherlands, Gallo-Belgic ware from the Champagne is well-recognised by specialists. Fabric, forms, and stamps are used to identify these products. Jugs and mica-dusted ware might also have been supplied through these same trade networks. Cooking wares, however, were intended for the local market. Imitations of Italian Sigillata were specific to the Champagne in northern Gaul but existed elsewhere in central or southern Gaul. The ease of production and stacking made dishes and cups suitable for trade over long distances, but beakers were not transported in large quantities for an extended period. Some forms were not exported at all, such as *terra nigra* bottles or bowls, as they were produced everywhere. The map shows the number of stamps from twenty potters (fig. 8). Imports from the Champagne, like those from the north of France, have been found in towns, forts, and cemeteries, however, they are more numerous and date earlier, starting from the end of the 1st century BC.

Conclusion

From an external perspective, the Netherlands appeared to be a significant consumer of Gallo-Belgic ware, largely due to Holwerda's book and recent publications. However, the reality is more nuanced. While rural communities did not acquire or where unable to afford the wheelthrown regional pottery during the 1st century, soldiers and urban residents could access these products. The Champagne imports were known, but it is crucial to delve deeper into the trade relations between northern France and the regions around the major rivers. For this

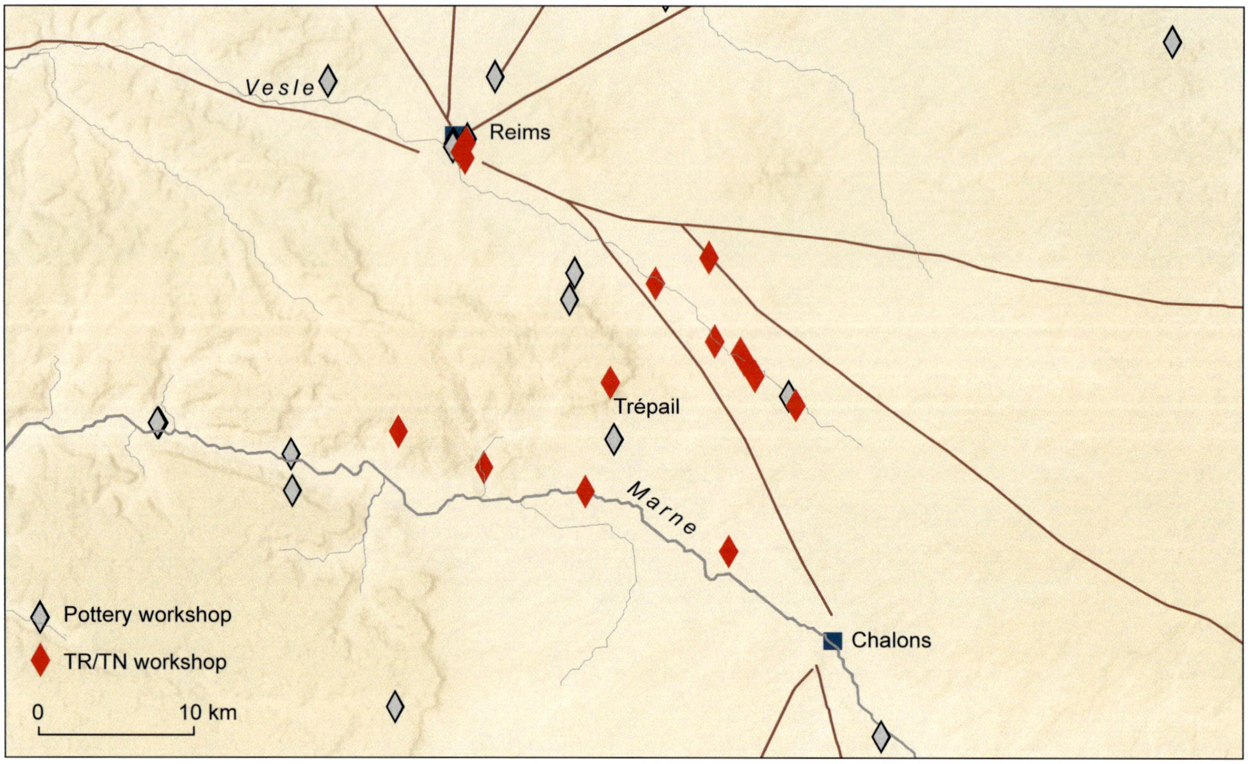

Fig. 7. The Champagne. The pottery workshops (© ABG).

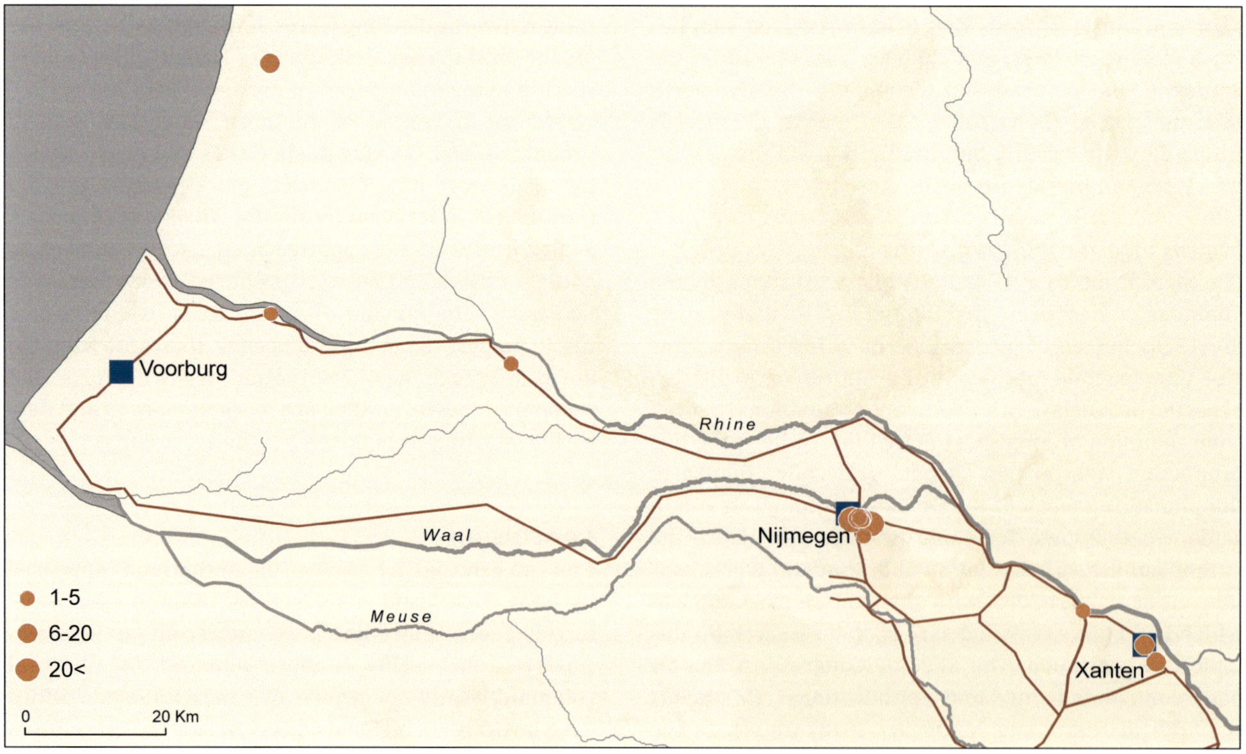

Fig. 8. The Dutch river area. *Terra rubra/terra nigra* stamped imports from the Champagne (© ABG).

it is necessary to study and publish the fabrics present within the *terra rubra* and *terra nigra* corpus on sites, as this will increase our knowledge on the distribution of wares from the various production centres.

Acknowledgements

H. van Enckevort, R. Polak, B. Liesen, V. Pilard, V. Deloffre (†) to have allowed me drawing stamps and taking samples.

Roman Amphorae on the Limes

Joost J.H. van den Berg

Abstract

This paper outlines the diachronic import of Mediterranean as well as the manufacture and circulation of local/regional amphorae in the Roman Netherlands, particularly the Rhineland. It presents amphora evidence from selected sites to address questions concerning supply mechanisms, the role of the military, and the relation between imported and 'regional' foodstuffs, all as part of a 'way of life'. It shows that significant import during the early stages of Roman occupation gradually, though not exclusively, had to make way for amphora manufacture at various places in the Low Countries and adjacent areas. These developments not only concerned the actual vessels but also their contents, such as fish-based products and alcoholic beverages being now produced in the (continental) northwestern part of the Empire. Small quantities of wine but above all olive oil continued to be imported, however, the latter particularly from southern Spain though also here related products could have been produced regionally.

Keywords: Mediterranean amphorae, regional amphorae, Roman Rhineland, Roman long-distance and interregional trade and transport

Introduction

Sites on the Dutch part of the Roman limes provide some intriguing insights into the import of products in amphorae from the Mediterranean. On the one side, this is a story of military supply and transport, providing a region of the Empire with Mediterranean goods that could not be produced locally, such as wine, fish sauce and olive oil. And on the other side, it is a story of a region that slowly developed its own alternative products, often transported in regional amphorae.

The study of the interactions between military supply, commercial activities, and the development of a more localised economy in relation to amphorae is very much ongoing. Particularly, identifying regional amphorae and understanding their chronology is still somewhat of a challenge and identifying which exact content goes with which fabric/type is now neigh impossible. The aim of this contribution is to provide a more generalised overview of the current state of research for the Dutch part of the limes, from the first occupation by Roman troops at Nijmegen-Hunerberg (*c.* 19 BC) until the late 3rd century[1].

1 The following paper is in large part a summarised and somewhat updated version of the conclusion in Carreras and Van den Berg 2017a. More extensive references can be found there.

in: R.C.A. Geerts and Ph. Bes (eds) 2024, *Roman Pottery in the Low Countries: Past Research, Current State, Future Directions*. Leiden: Sidestone Press (= *Papers on Archaeology of the Leiden Museum of Antiquities Leiden* 32), pp. 133-148.

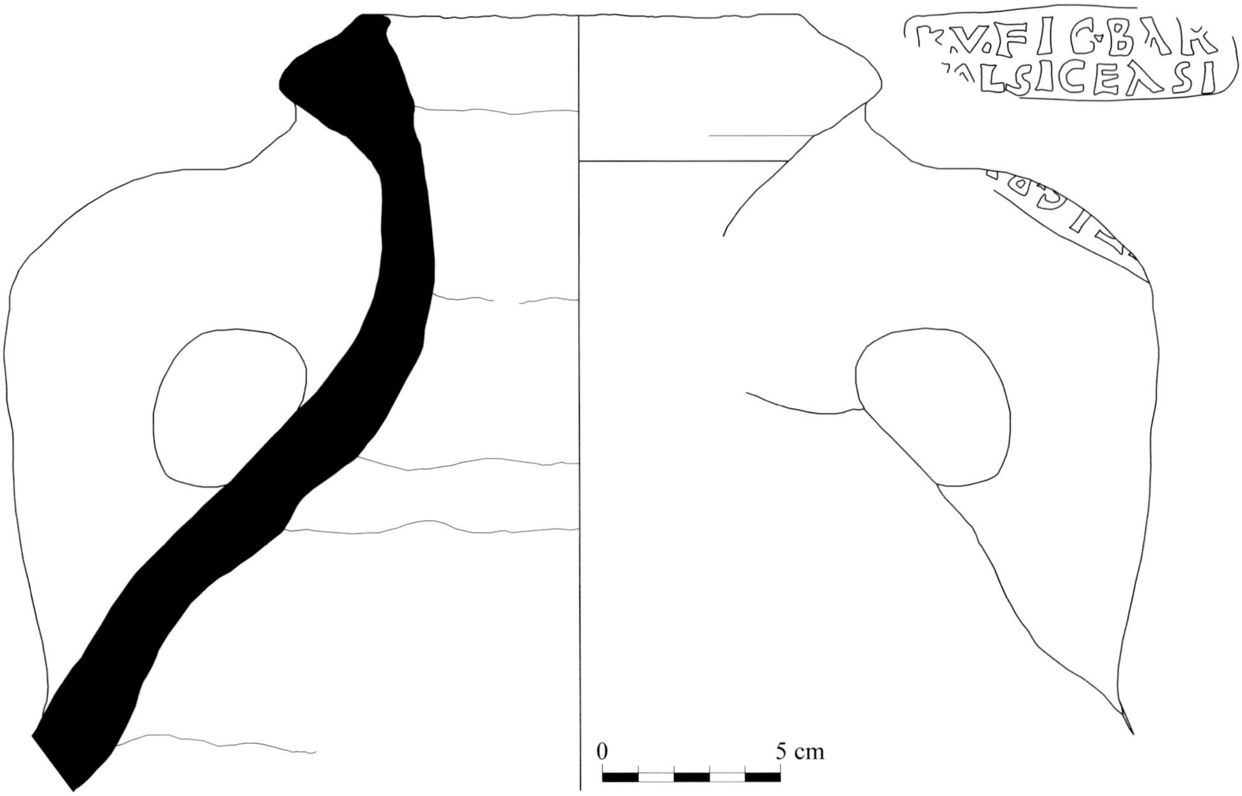

Fig. 1. A comparatively late Dressel 20 from the castellum at Vechten.

The goal here is to outline the trends, rather than to detail every identified typology or specify every find site, in the full understanding that such a generalised approach does not allow the space to detail every argument of the discussion.

Mediterranean Amphorae

The Import of Olive Oil

From the Augustan period onwards, olive oil was imported en masse from the mainland of Baetica to the German limes. In fact, Baetican olive oil represented one of the most regularly imported goods throughout the three centuries of Roman occupation. In this period the Romans certainly seemed disproportionately motivated to make sure every part of their Empire received olive oil. The consumption of olive oil on Roman sites in the Netherlands already started with the arrival of the first legions on the Hunerberg in Nijmegen. In the early Augustan period, it concerned type Oberaden 83, in the mid-Augustan period Haltern 71 and from the Tiberian period onwards Dressel 20. On early Roman sites, ranging from rural settlements to cities and castella, Baetican olive oil amphorae are nearly always present (fig. 1).

With the full integration of Germania Inferior as a province into the Roman Empire the presence of Dressel 20 amphorae became even more widespread. This comparatively peaceful period, with very little conflict and a functional infrastructure (both by sea/rivers and road), allowed for an enormous import of oil. For sites on the Dutch part of the limes this period of prosperity in terms of olive oil import seemed to continue at least until the beginning of the 3rd century. Dressel 20s of the (post-)Severan period are seemingly less common. An almost complete example from the 220s or 230s was found on the Druten 1 river barge (van den Berg 2015) (fig. 2), showing that at least in this case, Dressel 20 amphorae travelled as by-cargo on river ships.

Baetica was without doubt the primary source for the import of olive oil. Other important regions like south Italy, north Africa and Istria are rarely represented. North African amphorae have also been found at Nijmegen, but no type yet that is associated with olive oil (Van den Berg 2017a). There is, however, a Dressel 6B from Istria that was found on the Kops Plateau (Van den Berg 2012) (fig. 3). The type is not known from any other site in the Netherlands but has been found at Burginatium and Xanten (Van den Berg 2012, 224).

The Import of Fish Sauce

Amphorae containing fish sauce were primarily imported from the coast of southern Spain and southern Gaul (including Lyon). The import of Mediterranean fish sauce mostly concerned the 1st century and was far less common in the 2nd and 3rd centuries.

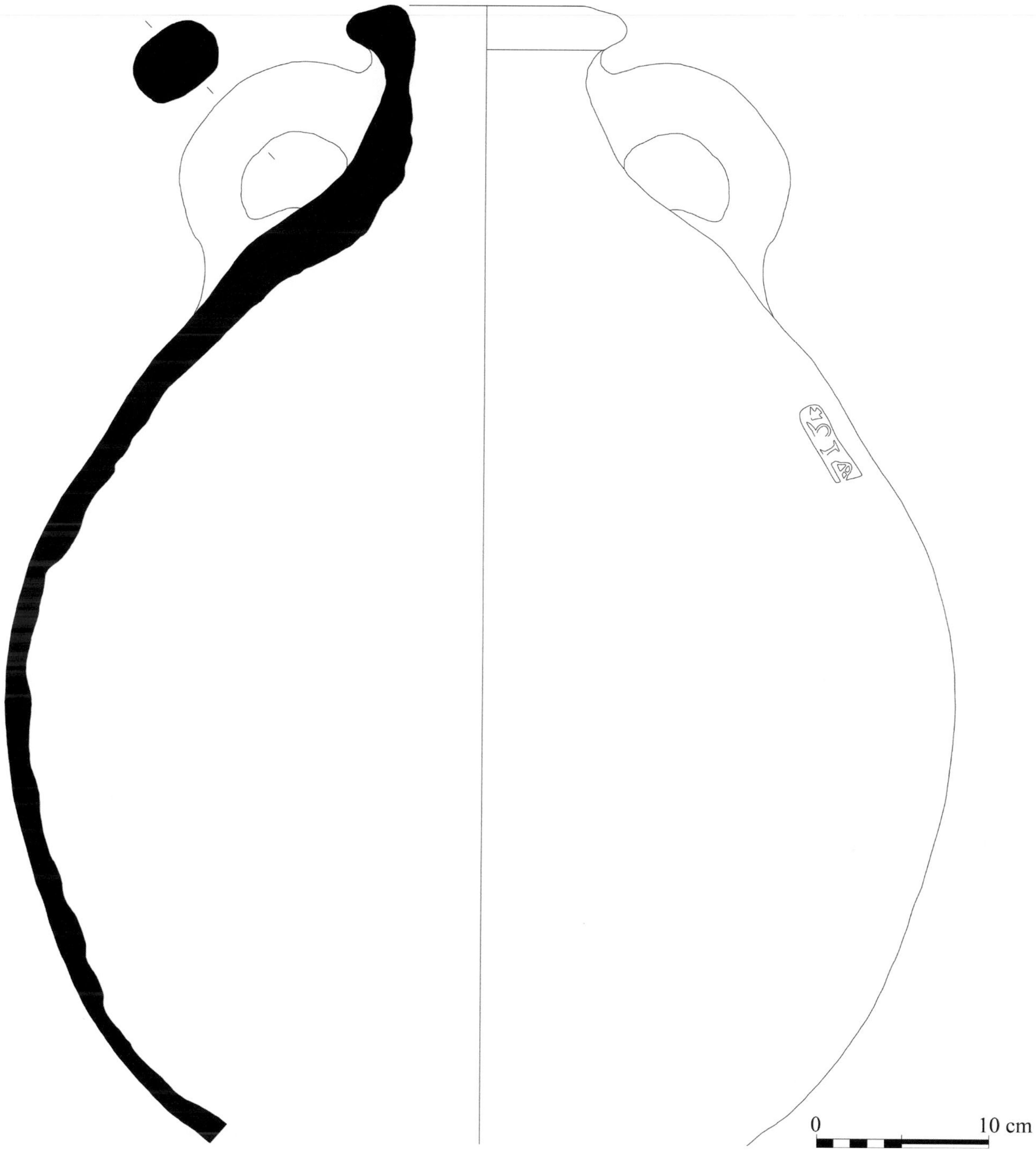

Fig. 2. The Dressel 20 amphora from the Druten 1 river barge.

The import of south Spanish fish sauce was at its height at the beginning of the Roman occupation. At the early and mid-Augustan camps, they made up a significant proportion of the total amount of amphorae (fig. 4), though this percentage decreased the longer a camp was in active use. Of course, during the Augustan period already part of the fish sauce came from southern Gaul (Dressel 9 similis) and Lyon (Lyon 3), perhaps even carrying transhipped Baetican fish sauce as well. However, the competition of fish sauce amphorae from Gaul does not explain why there was a decline in fish sauce imports after the Augustan period. This being said, in the pre-Flavian period fish sauce amphorae from both south Spain and Gaul remained an important part of the amphora spectrum on Dutch sites.

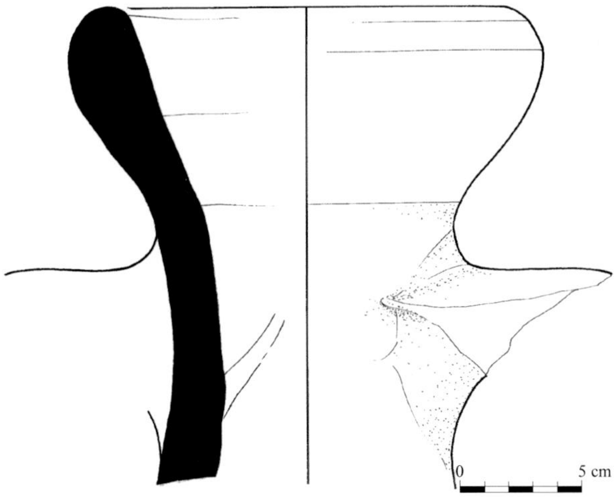

Fig. 3. An Istrian Dressel 6B from Nijmegen-Kops Plateau (drawing: R. Reijnen © Radboud Universiteit).

Amphorae from Africa that possibly contained fish sauce are present at the early camps such as Nijmegen and Neuss. So far, the typology of these early African imports remained somewhat of a mystery, with only non-diagnostic fragments being found. The recent discovery of a rim from Heerlen sheds light on this case because it seems to be a very late iteration of Dressel 18 (fig. 5). At Nijmegen and Vechten examples of type Vindonissa 592 are also present in Flavian contexts (Van den Berg 2017a).

By the Flavian period fish sauce amphorae became less common. Variants of the Beltrán II occurred in small numbers. There may have been further import from Lusitania in the coastal region of the Netherlands in the form of Dressel 14A, of which an example was found in the vicus of castellum Matilo at Leiden-Roomburg (Polak 2009, 16, fig. 1.6). By the second half of the 2nd century fish sauce amphorae seem to have disappeared entirely from sites in the Roman lower Rhineland, perhaps in part because it was replaced by local fish products. Some 3rd-century fish sauce amphorae have been documented at Vechten, such

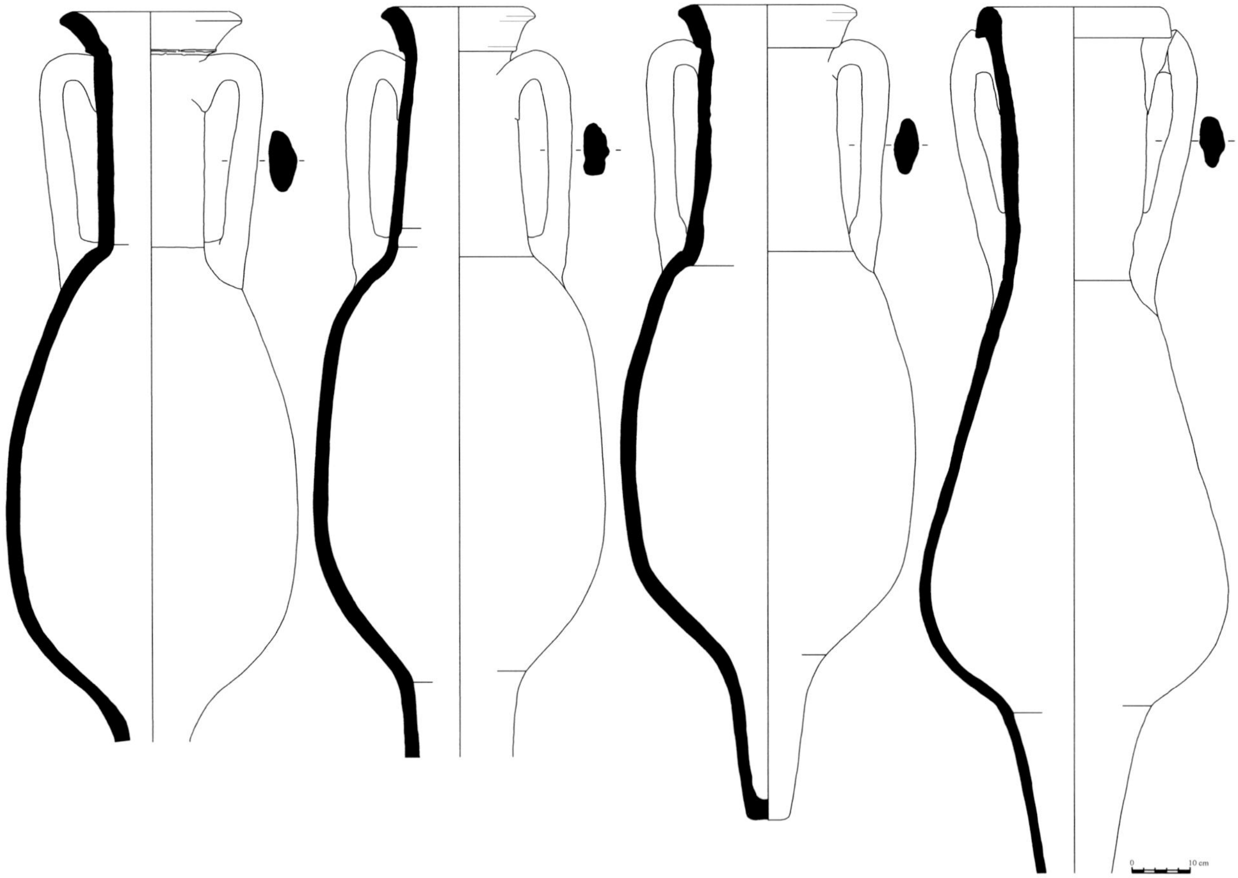

Fig. 4. Three archaeologically complete examples of Dressel 7-11 (left) and a complete Augst 30 (right) found at Vechten.

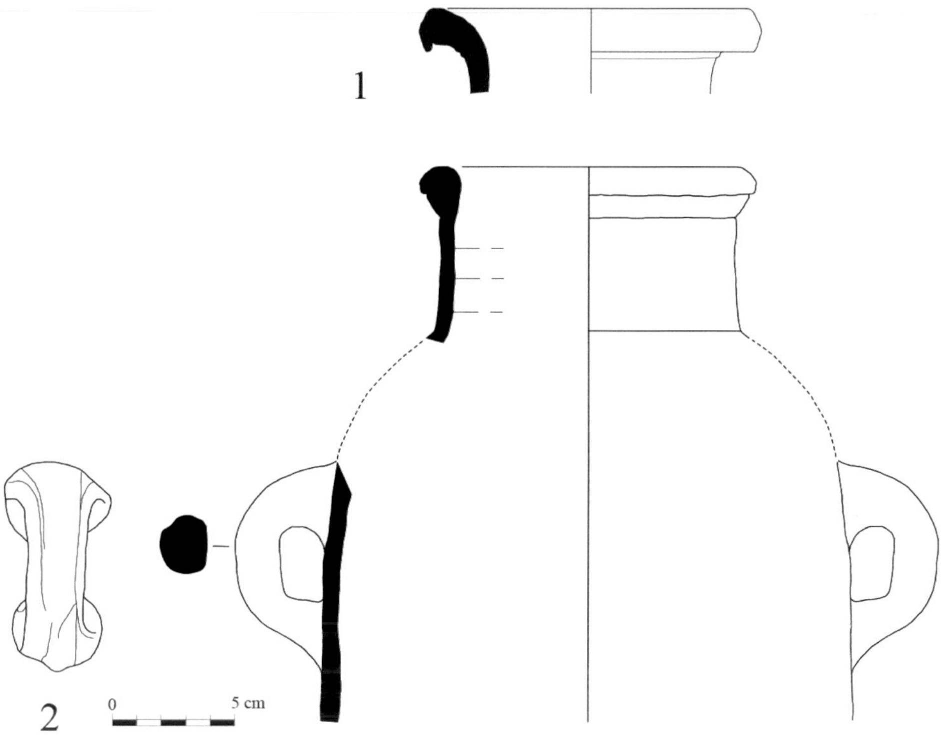

Fig. 5. A fragment of a possible Dressel 18 from Augustan Heerlen (top) and fragments of a Vindonissa 592 from Flavian Nijmegen, both from Tunisia.

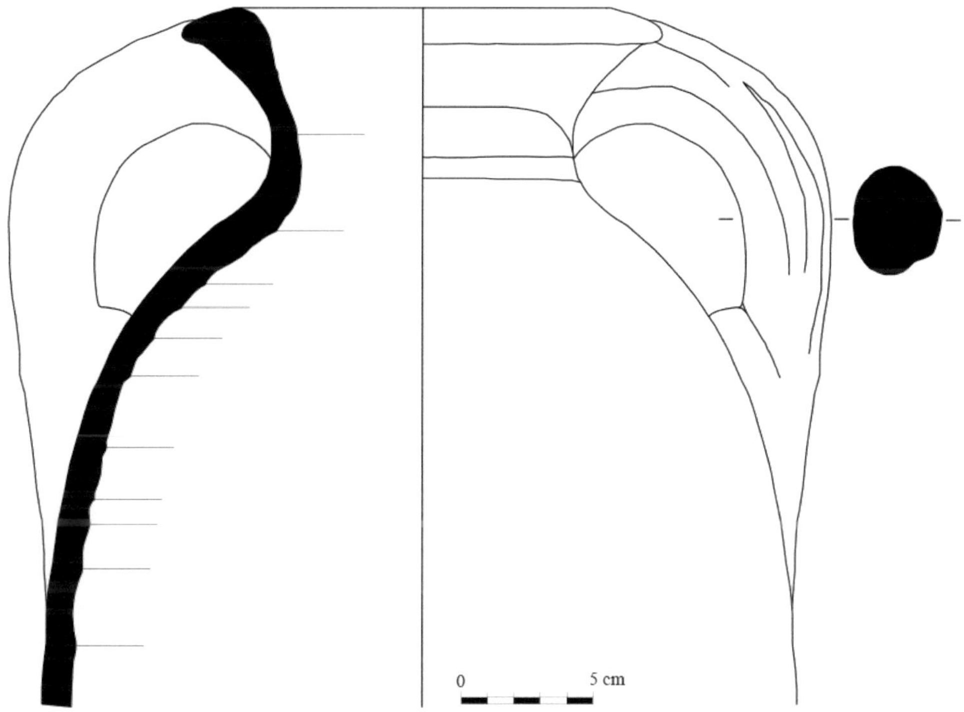

Fig. 6. A Keay XVI from Cádiz found at Vechten.

Fig. 7. Photograph of the dolium rim from Aardenburg mentioning ALIIC (© Erfgoed Zeeland).

as the early 3rd century variants of Almagro 50 (classified as Keay XVI), in one case likely produced in southern Spain (fig. 6), another from Lusitania (Van den Berg 2014, 690-691; Kloosterman 2017, 80). These later variants, however, are very uncommon.

Evidence for the production of fish-based products is primarily epigraphical. It concerns inscriptions on a number of altars found in the Scheldt estuary that were dedicated to a local deity called Nehalennia. They refer to *negotiatores allecarii*, or traders in fish-based products, who were active in the period *c.* 150-250. Van Neer *et al.* (2010, 175-185) further argue based on archaeozoological evidence that fish-based products were made on the Flemish coast. Evidence from Zeeland, for example at Koudekerke, shows production sites for salt in combination with many seashell deposits, perhaps suggesting an industry that involved salt, shell lime and potentially some kinds of fish sauce production (Van den Berg 2021, 9).

Van den Berg *et al.* (2017) have suggested fish sauce as a possible content for Scheldt valley amphorae but ended up proposing beer. Recent evidence from Nijmegen, however, shows that the rapid decline of imported Spanish fish sauce amphorae around *c.* 100 was followed by a stark rise in Group 1 Scheldt valley amphorae, suggesting that the import of fish-based products was at least partly replaced by import from the coast (Van den Berg in prep., BLAN-project Wd6).

There are a number of dolia from the Netherlands with inscriptions that refer to fish sauce. One such example comes from Aardenburg, a city located near the North Sea coast, and reads ALIIC XI S(EMIS) (fig. 7), interpreted by Bogaers as 11.5 amphorae of *allec* (nearly 300 litres) (Bogaers 1971, 40). Another such inscription on a small dolium found in Nederweert reads GARVM XXVII, interpreted by Hupperetz as 27 sextarii of garum (*c.* 14.4 litres) (Hupperetz 1990, 16-17). A find from Valkenburg could also suggest that dolia were used in the production and transport of fish-based products. This particular example was buried in manure, intended to help in warming up and fermenting the content which consisted of various species of fish (Bult and Hallewas 1987, 14; Van Enckevort 2012, 58-59).

The Import of Wine

The most varied group, both in terms of fabric (*i.e.* origin) and typology, are the wine amphorae. Before the reigns of Nero and Vespasian, wine came from many different parts of the Empire, ranging from the Aegean, Italy, Gaul, Tarraconensis and to a lesser degree southern Spain and maybe north Africa.

The largest group of wine amphorae in the earlier part of the 1st century came from the Aegean. These are primarily Camulodunum 184 and Dressel 2-5 and to a lesser degree Cretan and Knidian amphorae. The largest group, the Rhodian amphorae, can be found in most 1st-century sites on the limes. Later castella and even the civil settlements yielded comparatively few of these Aegean amphorae. The presence of Aegean Dressel 2-5 on Dutch sites is more difficult to establish, as it relies on fabric analyses. It is likely that these amphorae followed a similar pattern, in terms of distribution and chronology, as the Rhodian amphorae. Cretan amphorae replaced Rhodian amphorae and tend to appear at sites that date after the Neronian period (in particular Flavian), such as the Flavian canabae at Nijmegen, Valkenburg-Marktveld (*c.* 70-110) and from the mid-Roman civil town of Forum Hadriani (*c.* 85-270) (fig. 8).

Fig. 8. Photograph of a Dressel 43 with an intact wooden stopper, from Forum Hadriani (after: Van Kerckhove 2014, fig. II-1.195).

Italian wine was imported in types Dressel 1, Dressel 6A, Dressel 2-4 and Camulodunum 176. The earliest Republican types on Dutch sites so far only appeared with the arrival of Roman troops. In fact, Nijmegen appears to be the only site that yielded a large number of Dressel 1s. There does appear to be a later, smaller variant of Etrurian origin that is identified at sites like Vechten (Van den Berg *et al.* 2012, 62-63) and Velsen 1 (Goudswaard 1990, fig. 101). Dressel 2-4s from Italy appear at more sites, and the Campanian fabric in particular is fairly easy to recognise. There are numerous examples from Nijmegen-Kops Plateau, in fabrics from Campania, Etruria, Calabria and in many more fabrics from unknown production sites. The same is true for the castella at Vechten and Velsen 1.

Most Catalan amphorae arrived in the Netherlands during the first decades of Roman occupation. In particular, Pascual 1 is represented in the early Augustan camp on the Hunerberg (fig. 9), on the Kops Plateau, at the late Augustan castellum at Vechten and possibly Tiberian-period Velsen 1. The same is true for type Oberaden 74 which, for example, was also documented at Neuss and Vechten. The Kops Plateau yielded only a few fragments of the Catalan Dressel 2-4 and so did Vechten. However, this is the type to turn up on post-Augustan sites

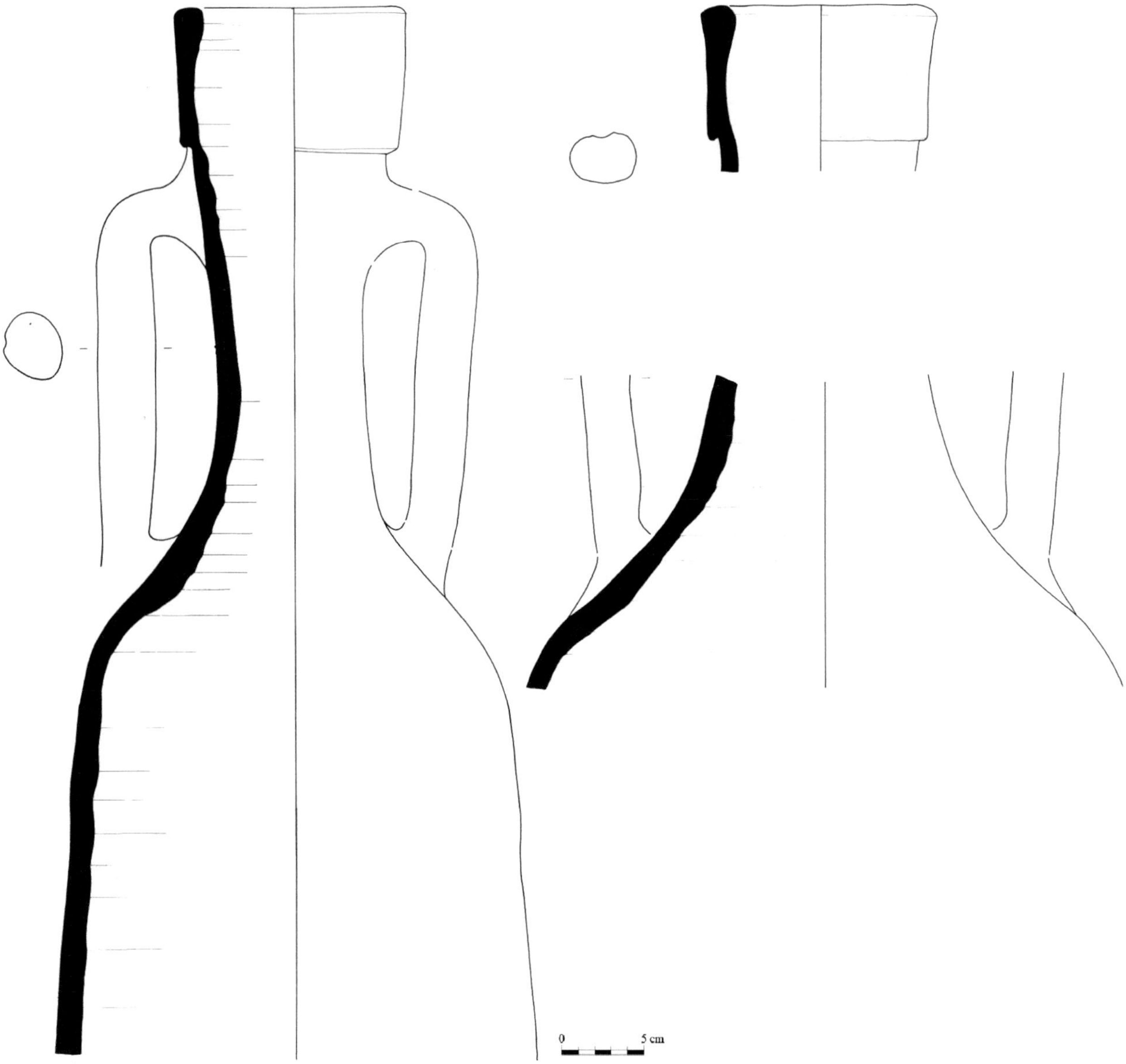

Fig. 9. Two examples of Pascual 1 found at Nijmegen-Hunerberg, likely from the early Augustan period, 19 to 16-12 BC (drawing: R. Reijnen © Radboud Universiteit).

such as Valkenburg, the settlement at Kesteren and the rural site at Wijk bij Duurstede.

The diffusion of Gaulish Dressel 2-4 is just as difficult to analyse as the Aegean and Italian versions. At Vechten, these amphorae do occur in small numbers, in particular examples from Marseille and Lyon, and some were found at Velsen. However, without diagnostic fragments, these Gaulish Dressel 2-4 are difficult to differentiate from the bulk of Gauloise flat-based amphorae or even south Gaulish fish sauce amphorae. It is perhaps not surprising that most Gaulish amphorae found at sites in the Netherlands are flat-based specimens, most of which can be classified within Laubenheimer's typology (Laubenheimer 1985). The earliest types, like Gauloise 1 and 2, are a minority, and even Gauloise 3, the transitional Gauloise 3/4 and Gauloise 5 are present, but most examples do belong to the mid-1st century (and later) Gauloise 4. Gaulish flat-based amphorae occur on virtually every Roman site in the Netherlands. It is clear that the Gaulish wine-industry, at least when it comes to amphora-borne trade, conquered the northern wine market around the Neronian-Vespasianic period and is virtually always represented by examples of Gauloise 4. After this period, until the 3rd century, almost no other Mediterranean wine amphora reached the north and Gauloise 4 seemingly held a monopoly. The difficulty with

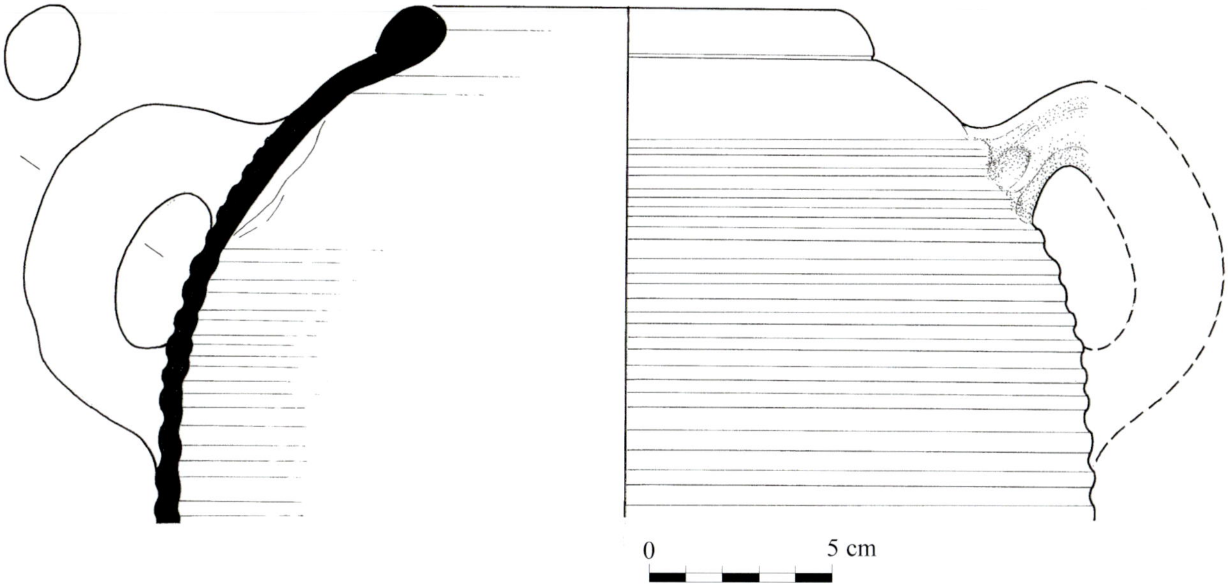

Fig. 10. Fragments of the Kingsholm 117 from Nijmegen-Kops Plateau (12/10 BC-69/70).

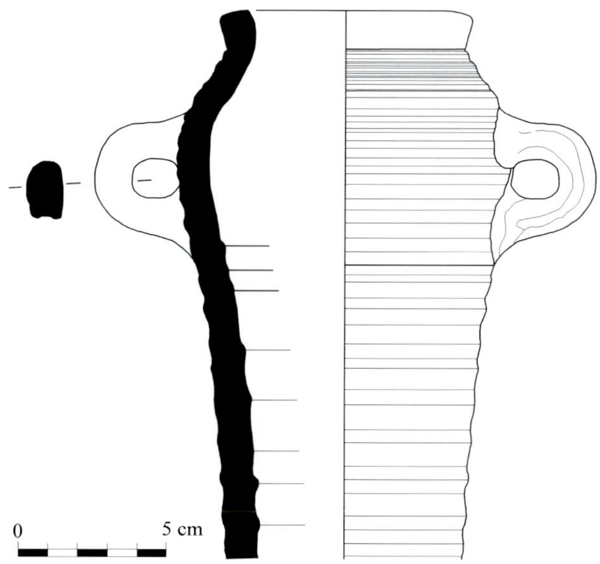

Fig. 11. a: photograph of a Stuart 24 in colour coated ware from Nijmegen (© Museum Het Valkhof, Nijmegen); b: drawing of the fragment shown under a (drawing: J. van den Berg).

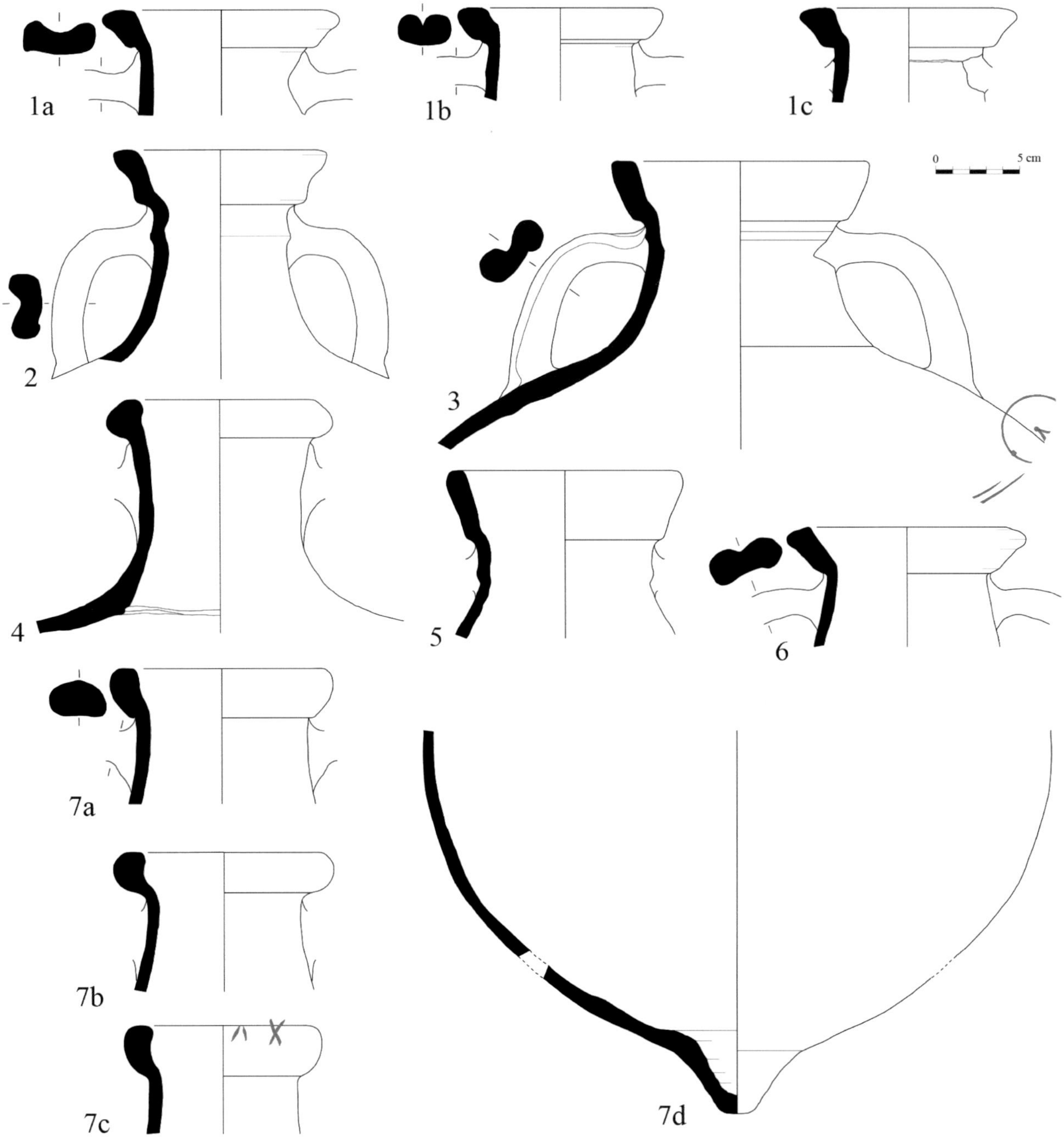

Fig. 12. Fragments of early Roman Rhineland amphorae found at Nijmegen-Kops Plateau. 1: Gauloise 1 similis (Kops Plateau type 1A); 2: Gauloise 3 similis (Kops Plateau type 2B); 3: Gauloise 2 similis (Kops Plateau type 2A); 4: Gauloise 4 similis (Kops Plateau type 4); 5: Gauloise 9 similis (Kops Plateau type 2C); 6: Rhineland amphora/Vermeulen 84A precursor (Kops Plateau type 6B); 7: Dressel 20 similis (Kops Plateau type 3).

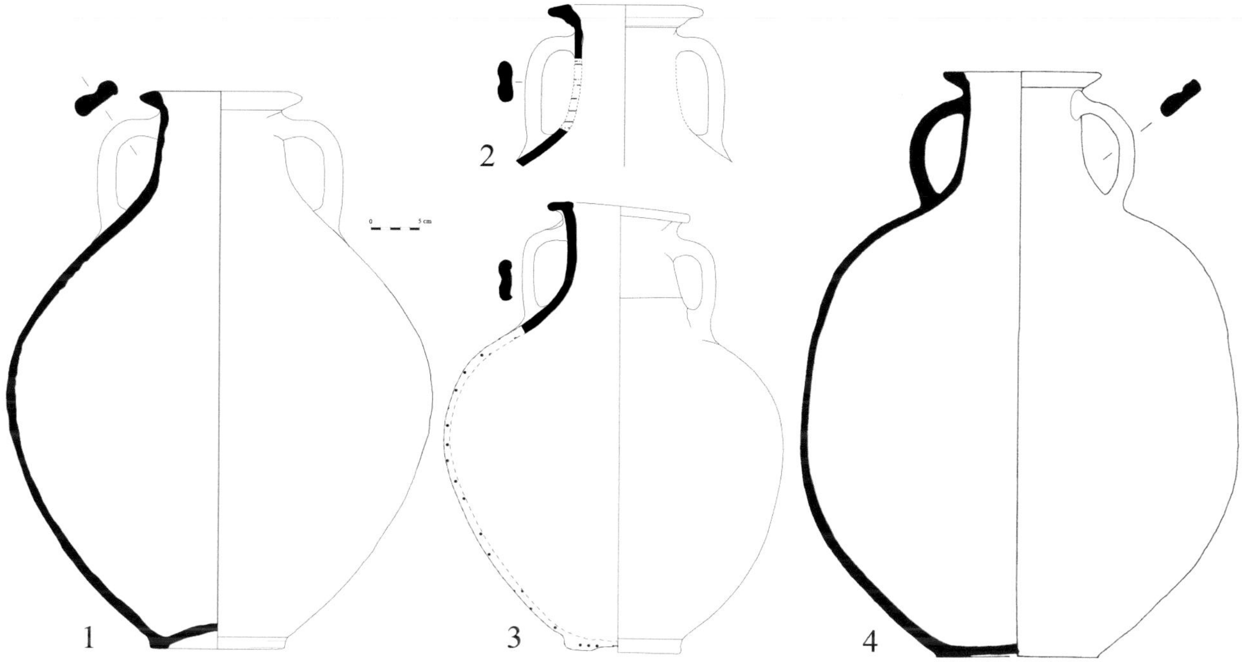

Fig. 13. Examples of Vermeulen 84A. 1: from Nijmegen-Canisius, Flavian (after: Van den Berg 2017c); 2: Nijmegen-Flavian, canabae (after: Van den Berg 2019, fig. 7.3); 3: Nijmegen- Koudekerke-Meinersweg, Flavian (after: Van den Berg 2021, 9); 4: Xanten, early 2nd century (after: Weiß-König 2003, 258, fig 11)

analysing the trade in Gallic wine is that Gauloise 4 is not the only indicator for this trade: wooden barrels and locally produced amphorae potentially also contained (transhipped) Gallic wine.

The Import of Exotic Fruit

The only amphorae that are distinctly associated with the import of exotic fruit came from the Levant. Types like Kingsholm 117 and Camulodunum 189 ('carrot' amphorae) were imported to the north in small numbers. There is an ongoing debate as to what these amphorae contained, but dates and figs are good candidates, but a liquid content (perhaps made from these exotic fruits) cannot be excluded as an option (Van den Berg 2012, 220-222; 2017d). At Nijmegen both types were found on the pre-Flavian Kops Plateau (fig. 10) and *Oppidum Batavorum*. Carrot amphorae are furthermore known from Flavian Nijmegen (the Flavian castellum on the Hunerberg and adjacent canabae), from sites in and around Vechten, and from rural sites like Nistelrode.

These types are not common but are relevant for this discussion due to the appearance of copies of carrot amphorae made in the Rhineland (classified as Stuart 24). These examples were made in various fabrics ranging from a white/beige clay with orange-brown paint to greyish coarse ware. Kloosterman has argued that Nijmegen may have been a production centre for at least a small percentage of these copies, although most seem to have come from Xanten or Cologne (Kloosterman 2014a, 125; Liesen 2018). For now, most Stuart 24s seem to date to the Flavian period, with most coming from the camp of the Tenth Legion at Nijmegen and its canabae (fig. 11).

The Import of Regional Amphorae

A lesser studied subject of the amphora trade to the Rhineland are the regional amphorae. Some of these vessels are atypical compared to their Mediterranean counterparts, either because they are smaller or due to characteristics in form or fabric. However, regardless of form or categorisation of these amphorae, they were a part of the economy of the northern provinces and cannot be ignored when telling the story of amphora-borne trade and transport. For the Dutch part of the limes, local amphorae seem to have come from three directions: the German Rhineland and later also the Moselle valley; the Meuse valley in present-day Belgium and northern France; and the Scheldt valley in western Gallia Belgica.

Amphorae from Germania Inferior

By the end of the Tiberian period amphorae from Germania Inferior started to appear and quickly became fairly dominant, at least until the Batavian Revolt of 69-70. Produced in the nearby Rhineland, most likely in Xanten, the first examples of these resembled early Gauloise

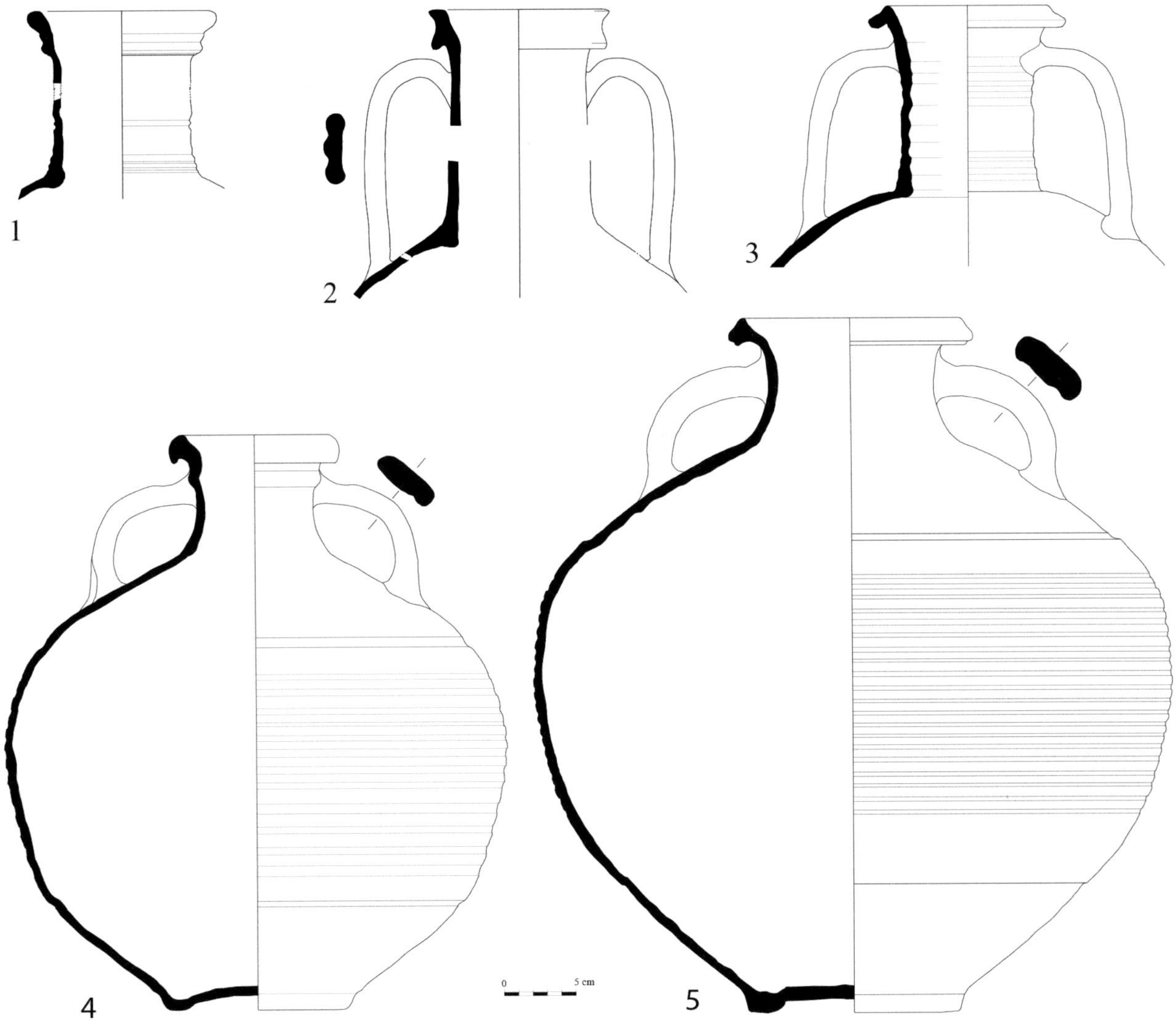

Fig. 14. Fragments of early Roman Gallo-Belgic amphorae. 1: cf. Friedberg 30; 2: Camulodunum 162 from the Meuse valley in northern Gaul (possibly Bavay) found at Nijmegen-Kops Plateau; 3: a later 1st-century Meuse valley amphora from Tongeren (possibly produced at Braives); 4-5: Mosan I amphorae of the mid-2nd and 3rd century.

amphorae (fig. 12), although some already show the characteristics of later Germanic amphorae. These early Roman Rhineland amphorae appear to have been a major component at Roman military sites and civil settlements, but also at rural sites. The relationship between these early Roman Rhineland amphorae and their Gauloise counterparts suggests (transhipped) wine as the primary content (Van den Berg 2017c; Liesen 2019).

After the Batavian Revolt, regional amphorae became less common for a period. The types that do appear are the larger Vermeulen 84A (Vermeulen 1932, 100-101) (fig. 13) and various sizes of Stuart 132B. Both were likely still produced in the same kilns as the early Roman Rhineland amphorae, although there were also other production sites. A small variant of Stuart 132B, for example, was produced at Nijmegen (Hendriks 2014, 219) and Cologne (Höpken 2005, type T41). There may also have been a production of a Rhineland variant of the Gauloise 4 in this period and this form was certainly produced during the 2nd century, for example at Cologne (Höpken 2005, 145, nos 40-019, 40-020, 41-023).

Regional amphorae became more common during the 2nd century. One trend in this period was the production of so-called mid-sized amphorae as defined by Haalebos (1990). For the Rhineland these tend to be small vessels, such as Haalebos 8020, 8220 and 8040 (Haalebos 1990, 174-175) and Brunsting 22 (Brunsting 1937). Due to the low number of complete examples found it is difficult to determine what the exact size-range of these types was, but types like Haalebos 8220 or Brunsting type 22 seem to have contained no more than 5 to 10 litres, suggesting a volume that ranged from a semimodius (4.36 litres) to a modius (8.73 litres). That said, the complete examples that have been published, mostly from cemeteries, likely only represent the smallest amphorae that were also used as large jugs. A complete regional amphora from Soller near Cologne (Höpken 2014, fig. 2d), which resembles Brunsting 22/Haalebos 8220, shows that larger amphorae were produced, suggesting that this form also occurred as a ½ to 1 amphora variant.

Larger vessels were also produced in Germania Inferior. Niederbieber 74/75 may be a continuation of Vermeulen 84A and is generally dated from the middle of the 2nd century onwards. The same is true for Niederbieber 68, which appears to be closely related to Niederbieber 74/75, at least within the production of amphorae in the lower Rhineland. For sites in the Netherlands the large regional amphorae from the lower Rhineland mostly comprise these two types (Hiddink 2014, 181), although other types are found, such as Niederbieber 64 and Soller-amphorae (*i.e.* variants of Brunsting 22). The mid-Roman regional amphorae present a non-standardised group, with a lot of variation in rim forms and sizes that ranged from ½ amphora to enormous containers with a volume of 4, 5 or 6 modii. This is in part likely due to a large amount of production sites within Germania Inferior and the long production-span of these forms, which ranged from the mid-2nd (if not earlier) to well into the 3rd century (if not later). A second issue is that the mid-Roman regional amphorae are generally classified according to Oelmann's categorisation of finds from Niederbieber (1914), which of course applies to their production in Germania Superior. The amphorae from the lower Rhine have their own typology and are similar, though not necessarily the same, as the amphorae produced around Mainz. The same difficulty is true of the regional amphorae produced in the Moselle region, the Meuse valley, and the Scheldt valley. Here too variants of Niederbieber 74/75 and 68 can be found, again with their own typological characterisations.

The earlier Rhineland amphorae were quite close derivatives of south Gaulish wine amphorae, thus suggesting the same content, albeit transhipped. However, later examples likely (also) contained different types of fermented liquids (Van den Berg 2017c). Beer is an obvious contender for this region, with intriguing evidence in the form of a graffito on a Niederbieber 68 referring to beer (Bridger 2017, 202, note 46; 2018, 216). Another example from Bonn shows possible evidence for fermented milk (Höpken 2014, 181-182). The fermentation of honey (*i.e.* mead) and fruits seems perfectly plausible as a workable substitute for wine. Therefore, the diverse set of different types of local amphorae, particularly in the 2nd and 3rd centuries, from different regions, may very well represent a complex network of diverse types for shipping (alcoholic) products which competed with wine. As stated before, figuring out which amphorae or which specific characteristic or fabric signifies a specific product, version of said product or quality, is going to be an interesting challenge for future research.

Meuse Valley Amphorae

The material from the Kops Plateau at Nijmegen shows the first amphorae from the Meuse valley in the form of Camulodunum 162 and 165 (Hawkes and Hull 1947). These types of vessels are uncommon and were not a stable import. The Meuse valley became an important trading partner for people in the Roman Netherlands from the reign of Hadrian onwards, in particular after the middle of the 2nd century until well into the 3rd century. Meuse valley amphorae are most common in the southern parts of the Netherlands such as Noord-Brabant and Limburg but were exported to sites along the limes as well (fig. 14). The most common type of Meuse valley amphora is Haalebos 8052 or Mosanes I (Haalebos 1990; Hanut 2001; Hiddink 2010, 181). Haalebos describes this form as a mid-sized amphora, with the smaller variant containing *c.* 15-20 litres or *c.* ½ amphora to 2 modii. However, these types too display a wide size range with the larger examples containing around 30-35 litres. Other types from the Meuse valley have been described by Hanut (2001) and show a variety of sizes and rim forms (usually flanged or triangular/rounded and undercut). The body of Meuse valley amphorae is usually decorated with ridges and grooves, giving this group a common and recognisable identity. For the moment it is not known whether the varied typological repertoire represents chronological changes, different production sites or even multiple contents.

Scheldt Valley Amphorae

Scheldt valley amphorae are associated with pottery production in western Belgium and the southwestern Netherlands (De Clercq and Degryse 2008, 454-456). In the pre-Flavian period, Nijmegen showed limited trading contacts with western Gallia Belgica, with only a small number of Camulodunum 163s being imported. Pre-Flavian Nijmegen also provides little evidence for a trade route that connected the site with the North Sea, with Scheldt valley amphorae or other forms of Low Lands ware being almost entirely absent. The first Scheldt valley amphorae only arrived by the late Flavian period (Van der Werff *et al.* 1997). During the 2nd and 3rd centuries they formed an important part of the amphora-borne trade, with its main area of export ranging from western Gallia Belgica and the Dutch coast up to Xanten, Cologne and Tongeren (Van der Werff *et al.* 1997; Hanut 2001, fig. 7).

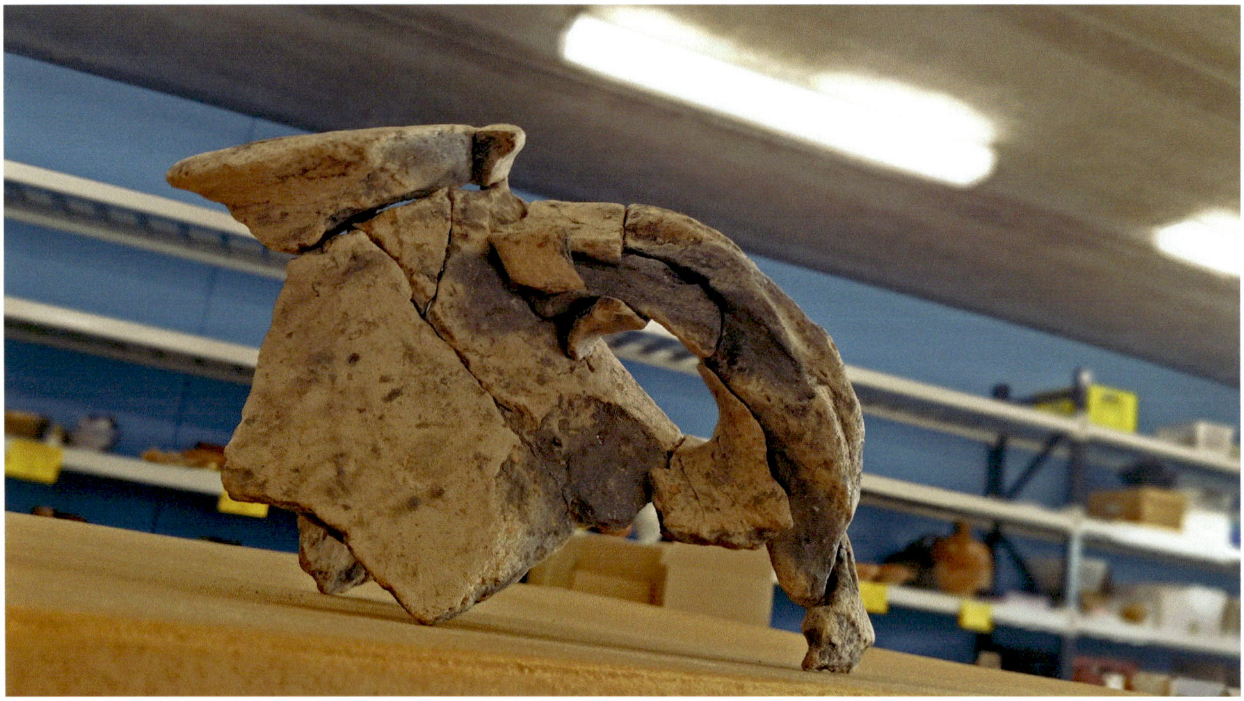

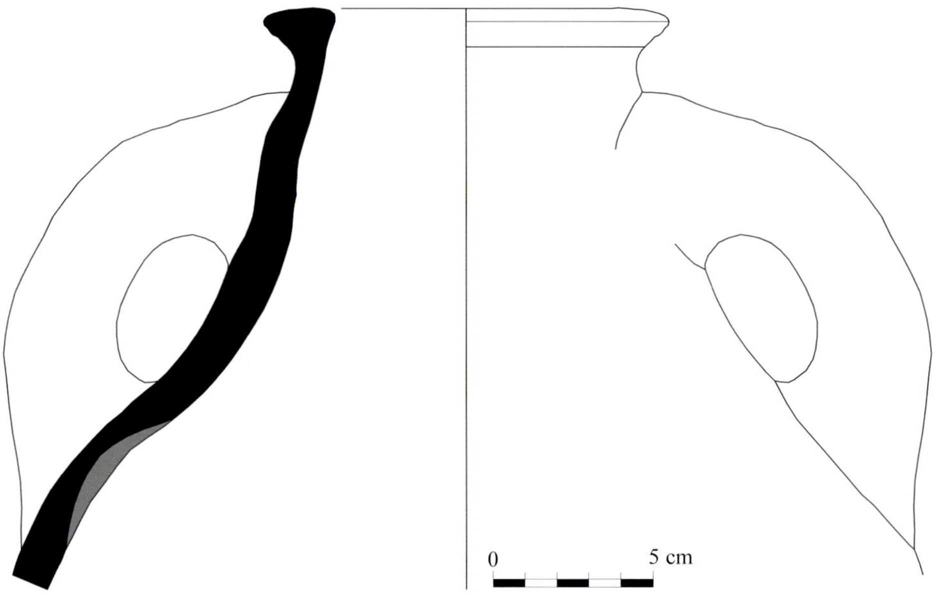

Fig. 15. a: fragments of a Gauloise 13 found at Kapelle-Smokkelhoek (after: Van den Berg and Kerckhaert 2018, 37-40); b: drawing of the fragments shown under a (drawing: J. van den Berg).

Scheldt valley amphorae are easy to distinguish from their Meuse or Rhine valley counterparts due to the red fabric. Many examples are covered in a beige-white slip and the use of grooves in ridges on the body is also not uncommon. The Scheldt valley seems to have focused on the production of ½ amphora vessels, with a volume of *c.* 15-20 litres, although some were likely bigger. As hypothesised above, Group 1 Scheldt valley amphorae may have been intended for some kind of local fish-based product. Group 2 and 3 variants seem more closely related to shapes associated with wine or perhaps some other locally produced alcoholic product, with beer being a plausible option (Van der Werff *et al.* 1997). However frustrating, this question too remains open for future research.

By the 3rd century a new amphora type was produced in the lower Scheldt valley: Gauloise 13 (fig. 15). This comparatively large amphora shows some similarities with Dressel 20 but may also (in part) have been a continuation of Scheldt valley Group 2 amphorae. This type was made in Cambrai and Bourlon, which started around the middle of the 3rd century, and continued well into the 5th century (Bocquet *et al.* 1995, 489; Baudoux *et al.* 1998, 26-36; Marlière 1998, 58-61). Its diffusion primarily encompassed Gallia Belgica, particularly along the *Via Belgica* (Baudoux *et al.* 1998, 26-36), but it can also be found in the Dutch coastal area, and an example is known from the castellum at Vechten (Van den Berg *et al.* 2012, 65).

Conclusion

When the Romans first arrived at the Dutch part of the Rhine, they found an area that did not produce the foodstuffs that were usually shipped in amphorae. Essentially, all wine, olive oil and fish sauce had to be imported.

Perhaps the most difficult to understand is the interaction between wine imports and locally produced contents because here we are not just looking at differences in the type of transport (direct or transshipment), but also competition between various types of alcoholic drinks, *e.g.* wine *vs* beer or mead. In the first decades of Roman occupation wine had to be sourced from many parts of the Empire, with a large focus on Greece/Asia Minor, Italy, and Spain. Southern Gaul only slowly started to take its place as the logical source for wine, initially with the import of Gaulish Dressel 2-4s, which was gradually taken over by flat-based Gauloise containers. Before these Gauloise amphorae fully took over the spectrum around the Flavian period, there was a large-scale production of flat-based containers in the Rhineland. Probably at Xanten, many forms of Gauloise amphorae were either copied or attest to the presence of southern Gallic potters. The Rhineland was not producing its own wine in bulk, but likely imported it in wooden vessels and then redistributed it in these early Rhineland amphorae. This system seems to have collapsed in large part around 70 and was replaced by direct import of Gauloise 4 amphorae. The local production, however, did not disappear, and evolved into distinct Rhineland amphora types, initially Vermeulen 84A and later forms related to Niederbieber 68 and 74/75. At this point, however, it is likely that the contents of these amphorae had also shifted from imported wines to locally produced alcoholic products based on the fermentation of local fruits, honey (*i.e.* mead) and wheat (*i.e.* beer), perhaps also combined products, like preserved fruit in drinkable liquids. Despite this, Gauloise 4 amphorae remained fairly dominant during the 2nd century, and gradually competed more with products from the Rhineland and amphorae from the Meuse and Scheldt valleys. Gauloise 4 did occur in the 3rd century, but by then were likely more a luxury import, with most locally consumed products being produced and exported regionally.

On the surface, the import of fish sauce seems to be a story of typically Mediterranean products that just never caught on in the far north. However, with new data about productions along the North Sea coast, this story may be more complicated. Fish sauce was imported in large quantities during the Augustan period and remained an important foodstuff during the 1st century. Southern Spain was the largest supplier of fish sauce, although southern Gaul also played a role. As the 1st century progressed, Mediterranean fish sauce became less important. An important shift regarding fish sauce seems to have happened around *c.* 100, with Beltràn II amphorae still being an important component at Flavian sites but being absent from 2nd-century contexts. A reason for this may lie in the rise of fish sauce (or fish-based products) produced on the North Sea coast in Belgium and Zeeland (southwest Netherlands). How this local fish sauce was produced, distributed, and transported remains a question, however, it seems that some of the Scheldt valley amphorae may have played a role in this, as their rise tends to mirror the decline of Spanish fish sauce amphorae. Alternatively, other types of containers, like Low Lands ware pots, may also have played a role. Despite these trends, it seems fair to hypothesise that fish sauce simply never became as popular in the Rhineland as it was in the Mediterranean.

Olive oil was imported almost exclusively from Baetica from the Augustan period onwards until well into the 3rd century. Practically all Roman sites in the Netherlands, from castella and cities, to rural sites and villae, tend to yield fragments of Dressel 20 amphorae. The trend of this import very much tends to mirror the importance of the sites where they are found, though it may be postulated that Dressel 20 were more numerous during the 2nd century than they were during the 3rd. It is noteworthy that oil amphorae were copied in the north. There already were Dressel 20 copies among the early Roman Rhineland amphorae of the Claudian-Neronian period and the production of Gauloise 14 amphorae in Germania Superior is equally noteworthy. For the Rhineland, however, perhaps the rise of Gauloise 13 amphorae is more significant. The earlier examples of these finds seem to have been inspired by the very late version of Dressel 20. This suggests that when Baetican oil imports started to wane, a new production arose in the southern Scheldt valley of Gauloise 13 amphorae, which likely contained some local type of oil (perhaps nut oil).

As indicated above, and in very general terms, the study of amphorae in the Rhineland shows an intriguing interaction between amphora imports from the Mediterranean and the rise of local industries which also involved local amphorae. This study is far from done and much work in fact remains to be done, in particular with regard to furthering our understanding of the various types of regional amphorae and their chronology, typology, distribution, and general role within the Roman economy. There is, however, much potential in studying these patterns in order to better understand how these regions developed and to further explore how the tensions between a reliance on Mediterranean products and some degree of self-sufficiency shaped the Roman Rhineland.

Conclusion and Outlook

Roderick C.A. Geerts and Philip Bes

Welcoming the 33rd Congress of the Rei Cretariæ Romanæ Fautores to Leiden in September 2024 provided the occasion for this volume to see the light of day. In their efforts, for which we are most grateful, all contributors to this volume draw attention to many facets of Roman pottery that are being studied in the Low Countries and beyond. As a whole, these papers provide an overview of the present state of research and show what potential there still is in our field of study. Following the introduction's historical overview and the first paper, what the various contributions as a whole make clear is that an increase in the number of excavations, to a significant extent because of the Valletta Treaty and subsequent development-led archaeology, also led to an increase in research and publication of Roman-period pottery. Many of the authors present a synthesis of their ceramic research, and all chapters make clear that the state of our knowledge has advanced greatly. However, the authors also underline that, as always, many research questions remain and many facets of Roman-period pottery deserve further study. In various ways in fact, they ponder how future research directions can be shaped to enhance our understanding of Roman pottery, and thus contribute to our reconstruction and understanding of the Roman period in the Low Countries more generally. It is hoped that this volume will contribute to that future direction.

Many museums have been collecting Roman pottery, and Jasper de Bruin offers his view regarding collections housed at the National Museum of Antiquities. Despite the fact that contextual data is lacking, or is less secure, for a number of such collections, it is clear that artefacts in these collections are a valuable source for research purposes. For instance, this material can complement a site's dataset, can be used to tentatively date sites, or in fact be all there is that is accessible for now. The same is of course true concerning pottery from older, pre-Valletta Treaty excavations and which is stored in municipal or provincial depots. There clearly is a wealth of sherds waiting to be studied or restudied using new methods and techniques, or benefit from the latest state of knowledge.

Change is intrinsic to the fabric of society and is easier to recognise afterwards than when it is actually happening, which seems to place archaeologists in a fortunate position. In the Low Countries, in particular in those parts that were part of the Empire, the most significant changes took place at the start and end of Roman occupation. The three papers in this section, by Peter van den Broeke, Ernst Taayke and Annet Nieuwhof, show when, where and why changes took place, both in- and outside imperial borders. The papers discussing handmade pottery show that changes indeed took place – for instance concerning the kind of temper that was added, which changed during the Roman

in: R.C.A. Geerts and Ph. Bes (eds) 2024, *Roman Pottery in the Low Countries: Past Research, Current State, Future Directions*. Leiden: Sidestone Press (= *Papers on Archaeology of the Leiden Museum of Antiquities Leiden* 32), pp. 149-152.

period – and whilst what happened in- and outside the Empire in fact followed different trajectories, there were nonetheless mutual influences. The early Roman conquest clearly impacted the tradition of handmade pottery; inside the Roman Empire, wheelthrown pottery set in motion a gradual decline in the production and usage of handmade pottery. During these formative years of imperial control, handmade wares show a greater diversity in origins than a few decades later when the limes was established. Beyond the limes handmade pottery remained in use and developed under influences from products made in present-day Germany. Nieuwhof draws attention to the occurrence of terra sigillata in the northern Netherlands. Whilst this region was located outside the Empire, this terra sigillata nevertheless represents a connection between the Empire and the inhabitants further north. After all, the limes was not impermeable, and pottery – as much as people, ideas, other goods, *etc.* – could cross and evidently end up at considerable distances from its place(s) of production. Terra sigillata vessels and fragments did not arrive in the north in large quantities, yet their long usage, reuse and modification emphasises these were valued possessions, and often embodied ceramic change quite literally. Nieuwhof's contribution furthermore shows that terra sigillata vessels and fragments were kept over extended periods of time, and thus treasured, to some extent presumably as heirlooms. Comparative research on the composition of ceramic assemblages (in terms of functionality, provenance, and otherwise) from sites inside and outside the Roman Empire would be an interesting research avenue to pursue further, especially since most studies remain regionally embedded.

Pottery is common on all sites in the northwest part of the Roman Empire. However, Bernd Liesen, Harry van Enckevort, Roderick Geerts and Frederique Reigersman-van Lidth de Jeude all draw attention to the fact that ceramic patterns are not or need not be uniform, based on pottery from different regions, different types of sites, as well as from different cultural and functional contexts. Frederique Reigersman-van Lidth de Jeude discerns patterns in grave assemblages, seeing the pottery representing a communal meal by its very composition. Trends are observed within individual cemeteries as well as within and between regions. Here, an analysis of broader geographical and chronological scope that would include multiple cemeteries would be one way forward in our understanding of burial practices and variations therein. Bernd Liesen shows that the current state of publication of urban assemblages does not allow comparative research, simply because too few assemblages have been published. As one might or should expect such differences to have existed, clearly there is room for future research here too if we wish to compare and interpret assemblages within and between urban sites in Germania Inferior. For now, only aspects can be studied, and this situation is further exacerbated by the scarcity of quantified data which prevents comparisons to be expressed in more measured ways. Roderick Geerts points out that the situation is comparatively better regarding rural settlements, many of which have been excavated. More specifically, the increase in our knowledge and improvements in ceramic dating allows for a more refined reconstruction of the period of habitation of settlements (rural and other) in the research area. To determine the starting date of many settlements during the early Roman period, handmade pottery (see above) remain imperative. Similarly, the attestation of certain ceramic types allows to observe a change at the end of occupation of settlements during the later part of the middle Roman period. Last, Harry van Enckevort shows that the role and presence of the Roman military in Nijmegen, in particular during its earliest stages, was crucial in tying together local and regional products with Roman-Mediterranean pottery. Such convergences – in terms of style, provenance, *etc.* – during formative periods remain interesting aspects.

In the fourth and last section, two papers deal with regional and long-distance exchange. Xavier Deru and Joost van den Berg approach this topic from a fine ware and amphora perspective, respectively. Deru focuses on *terra rubra* and *terra nigra*, fine wares with a strong regional production and distribution, and which were among the first wheelthrown wares that were produced in Germania Inferior. The strong typological approach nonetheless hampers to obtain clear notions about the distribution of vessels from individual production sites. In order to achieve progress here, fabric descriptions, beyond sherds being classified as *terra rubra* or *terra nigra*, as well as selected laboratory analyses are necessary. In his paper on amphorae, Joost van den Berg observes a change in the provenance of amphorae during the Roman period. This concerns a shift from imperial to regional supply systems for certain liquids, such as wine and beer, and possibly also fish-based products. Olive oil, however, continued to be imported from southern Spain during the entire Roman period; the contemporary climate simply did not allow olives to grow in northwest continental Europe. The importance of regional amphorae was long overlooked, and further detailed attention to these vessels and their distribution and production mechanisms would increase the understanding of the role of regional exchange and supply systems.

Some facets of Roman pottery studies are conspicuously absent in this volume. Two of those are archaeometric research and residue analysis. Both types of laboratory research are conducted in the Netherlands (*e.g.* Van Kerckhove and Boreel 2014; Oudemans 2014), yet not on any regular basis, and certainly are not part of the standard 'toolkit' of development-led archaeology. In the eastern Mediterranean and Aegean, for instance, archaeometry seems to be much more part of the 'fabric' of Roman-period ceramic research, though it is certainly not ubiquitous. Future research can employ both techniques (as well as others) to more fully investigate the origins, technological properties, and usage of pottery. Experimental archaeological research (*e.g.* Geerts 2024d) and detailed studies on kilns, the *chaîne opératoire* and the final products are also not included in this publication, though an important volume of these aspects has been published recently at the 29th Fautores Congress (Liesen 2014). A third lacuna is the late Roman period. An overview was recently published (Van Enckevort *et al.* 2017) that discusses pottery on a site level, yet a synthetic study of this period including its pottery assemblages is a *desideratum* for the future. In summary, the discipline would greatly benefit from more detailed fabric descriptions, the quantification and subsequent publication of ceramic data, as well as comparing and interpreting regional and supraregional patterns.

The advent of development-led archaeology caused a strong increase in archaeological research in the Netherlands: between 1998 and 2022, the number of archaeological investigations increased from 500 to over 5700[1]. The sheer quantity of the research output published each year concerns site reports – a site-based focus is in fact a requirement within development-led archaeology – which makes it a challenge obtaining an overview of the entire field. These site-based reports nevertheless include a wealth of data, including on Roman-period pottery. Each excavation is guided by a *Document of Requirements* (Dutch: *Programma van Eisen*, or PvE), which describes the motivation for the fieldwork as well as the accompanying research questions. It is herein that an opportunity lies for furthering the field of Roman pottery studies, namely, when research questions become more geared towards tackling (some of) the aforementioned opportunities and lacunae in our knowledge.

Indeed, much knowledge is to be gained when individual reports and datasets can be brought together and studied from broader geographical and thematic perspectives. One of our aims with this volume was to bring together a number of aspects into a regional ceramic overview, and we feel this has been largely achieved. We nevertheless anticipate and would welcome a next synthesis which would include some of the topics addressed above that merit further attention.

1 For this and other information see https://erfgoedmonitor.cultureelerfgoed.nl/mosaic/dashboard/archeologisch-onderzoek, viewed 29 January 2024.

Bibliography

The abbreviation of journals, series, *etc.*, is based on the list provided by the German Archaeological Institute (https://www.dainst.org/forschung/publikationen/publizieren/zitierstil-abkuerzungen).

Primary (Ancient) Sources

Caesar. *Oorlog in Galliё-De bello Gallico*. Translated by V. Hunink (2003). Amsterdam: Athenaeum – Polak & Van Gennep.

Dio Cassius. *Roman History-Historiae Romanae-Ρωμαική Ιστορία*. Translated by E. Cary (1914-1927). Cambridge (MA): Harvard University Press.

Pliny the Elder. *Natural History-Naturalis Historia*. Translated by H. Rackham (1962-1971). Cambridge (MA): Harvard University Press.

Suetonius. *Keizers van Rome-De vita Caesarum*. Translated by D. den Hengst (1996). Amsterdam: Athenaeum – Polak & Van Gennep.

Tacitus. *The Agricola and the Germania-De vita Iulii Agricolae* and *De origine et situ Germanorum (Germania)*. Translated by H. Mattingly and S.A. Handford (1975). Harmondsworth: Penguin.

Tacitus. *The Annals of Imperial Rome-Ab excessu divi Augusti (Annales)*. Translated by M. Grant (1971). Harmondsworth: Penguin.

Tacitus. *The Histories-Historiae*. Translated by K. Wellesley (1975). Harmondsworth: Penguin.

Secondary Sources

Aarts, J. and S. Heeren (eds) 2011. *Opgravingen bij Tiel Passewaaij 2. Het grafveld aan de Passewaaijse Hogeweg*. Zuidnederlandse Archeologische Rapporten 41. Amsterdam: Archeologisch Centrum van de Vrije Universiteit.

Aeissen, M. and C.C.C. Höpken 2010. Eine frühe römische Töpferei im Kölner Hinterland. *Archäologie im Rheinland* 2009, 71-73.

Albrecht, Chr. 1942. *Das Römerlager in Oberaden und das Uferkastell in Beckinghausen an der Lippe. Die römische und die belgische Keramik. Die Gegenstände aus Metall.* Veröffentlichungen aus dem Städtischen Museum für Vor- und Frühgeschichte Dortmund II, no. 2. Dortmund: Rehfus.

Anderson, A.S. 1981. Some unusual coarse ware vessels from London and their continental background, in: A.C. Anderson and A.S. Anderson (eds), *Roman pottery research in Britain and north-west Europe. Papers presented to Graham Webster*. BARIntSer 123, no. i, 93-106. Oxford: BAR Publishing.

Andrikopoulou, J.-N. and S. Jenter 2018. Straßen und Verkehr in der *Germania Inferior*, in: C. Eger (ed.), *Warenwege – Warenflüsse. Handel, Logistik und Transport am römischen Niederrhein.* Xantener Berichte 32, 201-219. Mainz: Verlag Philipp von Zabern.

Audin, A. and W. Binsfeld 1964. Médaillons d'applique rhodaniens du Musée de Cologne. *KölnJb* 7, 14-18.

Bakker, L. 2015. Spätrömische Rädchen-Terra-Sigillata in Köln II: Die Grabungen südlich und westlich des Kölner Doms IV. *KölnJb* 48, 363-395.

Bakx, J.P.L. (ed.) 2013. *Mens en landschap in de Delftse regio deel 7: met rituelen omsloten. Opgraving van een inheems-Romeinse nederzetting langs de Woudselaan in de Harnaschpolder, gemeente Midden-Delfland.* Delftse Archeologische Rapporten 107. Delft: Archeologie Delft.

Bakx, J.P.L. (ed.) in prep. *Mens en landschap in de Delftse regio: opgraving van een inheems-Romeinse nederzetting in de Harnaschpolder, gemeente Midden-Delfland.* Delftse Archeologische Rapporten. Delft: Archeologie Delft.

Barbier, S. and T. Luginbühl 2021. *La vaiselle céramique de Bibracte. De l'identification à l'analyse.* Collection Bibracte 31. Glux-en-Glenne: Bibracte, Centre Archéologique Européen.

Barclay, A., D. Knight, P. Booth, J. Evans, D.H. Brown and I. Wood 2016. *A standard for pottery studies in archaeology.* London: Historic England.

Bats, M. 1993. Céramique commune italique. *Lattara* 6, 357-362.

Baudoux, J., A. Bocquet, R. Brulet, F. Laubenheimer, E. Marlière and F. Vilvorder 1998. La production des amphores dans l'est et le nord des Gaules. Typologie et caractérisation physico-chimique, in: F. Laubenheimer (ed.), *Les amphores en Gaule – 2. Production et circulation,* 11-48. Paris: Presses Universitaires Franc-Comtoises.

Ben Redjeb, T. 1992. Une agglomération secondaire des Viromanduens: Noyon (Oise). *Revue Archéologique de Picardie* 1-2, 37-74.

Berthold, J., D. Hupka, F. Kempken and R. Nehren 2017. Ausgrabungen am Kurt-Hackenberg-Platz und am Domhof in Köln. Archäologische Untersuchungen im Rahmen des Nord-Süd-Stadtbahnbaus. *KölnJb* 50, 133-540.

Biegert, S., X. Deru, G. Fronteau and J.-C. Paicheler 2004/2005. Les productions du "groupe de pâtes champenois": caractérisations archéologiques, pétrographiques et chimiques. *Revue du Nord* 86, no. 358, 135-161.

Bloemers, J.H.F. 1973. "Fries" aardewerk uit de Romeinse legerplaatsen te Haltern (Duitsland), in: *Archeologie en historie. Opgedragen aan H. Brunsting bij zijn zeventigste verjaardag,* 225-231. Bussum: Fibula-Van Dishoeck.

Bloemers, J.H.F. 1978. *Rijswijk (Z.H.), "De Bult". Eine Siedlung der Cananefaten.* Nederlandse Oudheden 8. Amersfoort: Rijksdienst voor het Oudheidkundig Bodemonderzoek.

Bloemers, J.H.F. 1979a. Das große Lager auf dem Hunerberg, in: J.H.F. Bloemers, J.E.A.Th. Bogaers, J.K. Haalebos and S.L. Wynia, *Noviomagus. Auf den Spuren der Römer in Nijmegen,* 24-27. Nijmegen: Rijksmuseum G.M. Kam.

Bloemers, J.H.F. 1979b. Die kleine Befestigung am Trajanusplein, in: J.H.F. Bloemers, J.E.A.Th. Bogaers, J.K. Haalebos and S.L. Wynia, *Noviomagus. Auf den Spuren der Römer in Nijmegen,* 28-29. Nijmegen: Rijksmuseum G.M. Kam.

Bloemers, J.H.F. 1983. Acculturation in the Rhine/Meuse basin in the Roman period: a preliminary survey, in: R. Brandt and J. Slofstra (eds), *Roman and native in the Low Countries. Spheres of interaction.* BARIntSer 184, 159-209. Oxford: BAR Publishing.

Bloemers, J.H.F. 2016. The pre-Flavian occupation. An aspect of acculturation, in: J.H.F. Bloemers (ed.), *Four approaches to the analysis of (pre-)Roman Nijmegen. Aspects of cultural evolution, acculturation, contextual function and continuity.* Nederlandse Oudheden 19, 35-100. Amersfoort: Rijksdienst voor het Cultureel Erfgoed.

Bloemers, J.H.F. and J.K. Haalebos 1973. Roman pottery finds in Heerlen, province of Limburg. *BerOudhBod* 23, 259-272.

Blom, E. and H.M. van de Velde (eds) 2015. *De archeologie van Boxmeer Sterckwijck. 4500 jaar wonen, werken en begaven langs de Maas.* ADC Monografie 18. Amersfoort: ADC ArcheoProjecten.

Blomsma, S. and M. Brouwer 1989. *Syllabus voor het determineren van Romeins aardewerk (gevonden in Zuid-Holland).* Leiden: Rijksmuseum van Oudheden.

Bocquet, A., F. Laubenheimer, F. Vilvorder, D. Laduron and J. Baudoux 1995. Roman amphoras in north Gaul and upper Germany, in: P. Vincenzini (ed.), *The ceramics cultural heritage: proceedings of the international symposium "The Ceramics Heritage" of the 8th CIMTEC-World Ceramics Congress and Forum on New Materials, Florence, Italy, June 28-July 2, 1994,* 483-492. Faenza: Techna.

Boeleke, U. 1995. Abfall einer neu entdeckten römischen Töpferei, in: M. Zelle (ed.), *Tatort CUT. Colonia Ulpia Traiana. Die Spur führt nach Xanten. Ausstellung der Abt. Bodendenkmalpflege, Archäologischer Park, Regionalmuseum Xanten im Regionalmuseum Xanten vom 20. August bis zum 29. Oktober 1995.* Führer und Schriften des Archäologischen Parks Xanten 17, 51-54. Cologne: Rheinland-Verlag.

Boeles, P.C.J.A. 1911. Friesische Keramik und Terra Sigillata aus den niederländischen Terpen. *Römisch-Germanisches Korrespondenzblatt* IV, 60-64.

Boeles, P.C.J.A. 1917. Friesland in den Romeinschen tijd. II. De vondsten uit de terp "Groot Tolsum". De invoer van terra sigillata in Friesland. *De Vrije Fries* 25, 102-125.

Boeles, P.C.J.A. 1951[2]. *Friesland tot de elfde eeuw. Zijn vóór- en vroege geschiedenis.* 's-Gravenhage: M. Nijhoff.

Bogaers, J.E.A.Th. 1971. Nehalennia en de epigrafische gegevens, in: J.E.A.Th. Bogaers and P. Stuart (eds), *Deae Nehalenniae. Gids bij de tentoonstelling Nehalennia, de Zeeuwse godin, Zeeland in de Romeinse tijd, Romeinse monumenten uit de Oosterschelde in het stadhuis Middelburg,* 32-43. Middelburg: Koninklijk Zeeuwsch Genootschap der Wetenschappen.

Bogaers, J.E.A.Th. and J.K. Haalebos 1975. Problemen rond het Kops Plateau. *OudhMeded* 56, 127-178.

Bogaers, J.E.A.Th. and J.K. Haalebos 1977. Opgravingen in de Romeinse legioensvestingen te Nijmegen II (ten oosten en noorden van de Praetoriumstraat, 1974-1975). *OudhMeded* 58, 73-157.

Bogaers, J.E.A.Th. and J.K. Haalebos 1980. Opgravingen in de Romeinse legioensvestingen te Nijmegen III (Canisiuscollege, Hoge Veld, 1975-1977). *OudhMeded* 61, 39-111.

Bonifay, M. 2004. *Études sur la céramique romaine tardive d'Afrique*. BARIntSer 1301. Oxford: Archaeopress.

Bonifay, M. 2020. Ceramics and Atlantic connections AD 250-700: the African perspective, in: M. Duggan, M. Jackson and S. Turner (eds), *Ceramics and Atlantic connections: late Roman and early medieval imported pottery on the Atlantic seaboard. Proceedings of an international symposium at Newcastle University, March 2014*. Roman and Late Antique Mediterranean Pottery 15, 1-6. Oxford: Archaeopress.

Bonifay, M. and D. Pieri 2020. Merovingian Gaul and the Mediterranean: ceramics and trade, in: B. Effros and I. Moreira (eds), *The Oxford handbook of the Merovingian world*, 860-882. Oxford: Oxford University Press.

Borgers, B. 2023. The life-history of a dolium from the Roman site at Sittard, the Netherlands, in: B. Liesen (ed.), *Zwischen Töpfer und Verbraucher/Between potter and consumer. Internationales Kolloquium im LVR-RömerMuseum 27.-29. März 2019*. Xantener Berichte 41, 621-635. Oppenheim am Rhein: Nünnerich-Asmus Verlag.

Borgers, B., R. Wijnen-Jackson and M. Bink 2017. The Roman pottery kiln at Halder, North Brabant (the Netherlands) revisited, in: M. Müller (ed.), *Grabung – Forschung – Präsentation*. Xantener Berichte 30, 169-184. Darmstadt: Verlag Philipp von Zabern.

Borgers, B., C. Ionescu, S. Willems, L. Barbu-Tudoran, M. Bernroider and R. Clotuche 2020. Continuity and diversity of Roman pottery production at Famars (northern France) in the 2nd-4th centuries AD: insights from the pottery waste. *Archaeological and Anthropological Sciences* 12.

Bosman, A.V.A.J. 1997. *Het culturele vondsmateriaal van de vroeg-Romeinse versterking Velsen 1*. Unpublished PhD thesis, Amsterdam: Universiteit van Amsterdam.

Bosman, A.V.A.J. 2022. Velsen 2. *Het onderzoek naar de vroeg Romeinse basis in de periode 1945-2005*. Military Legacy Rapport 38. Dordrecht: Military Legacy.

Bridger, C. 2017. Befand sich Deutschlands älteste kommerzielle Brauerei in Xanten? Ein Beitrag zur Bierproduktion im römischen Germanien und Nordgallien, in: M. Müller (ed.), *Grabung – Forschung – Präsentation*. Xantener Berichte 30, 197-219. Darmstadt: Verlag Philipp von Zabern.

Bridger, C. 2018. Last (b)orders please! The beer necessities of Roman military life on the German limes, in: C.S. Sommer and S. Matešić (eds), *Limes XXIII. Proceedings of the 23rd international congress of Roman frontier studies Ingolstadt 2015. Akten des 23. internationalen Limeskongresses in Ingolstadt 2015*. Beiträge zum Welterbe Limes 4, no. 1, 215-222. Mainz: Nünnerich-Asmus Verlag.

Brongers, J.A. 2002. *Een vroeg begin van de moderne archeologie. Leven en werken van Cas Reuvens (1793-1835). Documentatie van een geleerden-leven*. Nederlandse Archeologische Rapporten 23. Amersfoort: Rijksdienst voor het Oudheidkundig Bodemonderzoek.

Brouwer, M. 1986. Het "Romeinse" aardewerk in het Maasmondgebied, in: M.C. van Trierum and H.E. Henkes (eds), *A contribution to prehistoric, Roman and medieval archaeology*. Rotterdam Papers 5, 77-90. Rotterdam: Bureau Oudheidkundig Onderzoek van Gemeentewerken Rotterdam.

Brüggler, M. 2018. Landwirtschaft und Güterversorgung im Hinterland der Colonia Ulpia Traiana bei Xanten, in: C. Eger (ed.), *Warenwege – Warenflüsse. Handel, Logistik und Transport am römischen Niederrhein*. Xantener Berichte 32, 289-303. Mainz: Verlag Philipp von Zabern.

Brulet, R. (ed.) 1983. *Braives gallo-romain. II. Le quartier des potiers*. Publications d'histoire de l'art et d'archéologie de l'Université Catholique de Louvain 37. Louvain-la-Neuve: Département d'Archéologie et d'Histoire de l'Art.

Brulet, R., R.P. Symonds and F. Vilvorder (eds) 1999. *Céramiques engobées et métallescentes gallo-romaines. Actes du colloque organisé à Louvain-la-Neuve le 18 mars 1995*. ReiCretActa Supplementum 8. Oxford: Rei Cretariæ Romanæ Fautores.

Brulet, R., F. Vilvorder and R. Delage 2010. *La céramique romaine en Gaule du nord. Dictionnaire des céramiques. La vaisselle à large diffusion*. Turnhout: Brepols.

Brunsting, H. 1937. *Het grafveld onder Hees, bij Nijmegen, een bijdrage tot de kennis van "Ulpia Noviomagus"*. Allard Pierson Stichting Archæologisch-Historische Bydragen IV. Amsterdam: N.V. Noord-Hollandsche Uitgevers-Mij.

Brunsting, H. 1969[2]. *400 jaar Romeinse bezetting van Nijmegen*. Nijmegen: gemeente Nijmegen.

Bryant, G.F. 1973. Experimental Romano-British kiln firings, in: A. Detsicas (ed.), *Current research in Romano-British coarse pottery: papers given at a CBA conference held at New College, Oxford, March 24 to 26, 1972*. Council for British Archaeology Research Report 10, 149-160. London: Council for British Archaeology.

Bult, E.J. and D.P. Hallewas 1987. De opgravingscampagne op het Marktveld in 1986, in: E.J. Bult and D.P. Hallewas (eds), *Graven bij Valkenburg 2. Het archeologische onderzoek in 1986*, 1-17. Delft: Eburon.

Cahn, E.-M. 2009. Die römischen Bildlampen aus Köln. *KölnJb* 42, 7-391.

Campbell, L. 2011. *A study in culture contact: the distribution, function and social meanings of Roman pottery from non-Roman contexts in southern Scotland*. Unpublished PhD thesis, University of Glasgow.

Campbell, L. 2012. Modifying material: social biographies of Roman material culture, in: B. Jervis and A. Kyle (eds), *Make-do and mend: archaeologies of compromise, repair and reuse.* BARIntSer 2408, 13-26. Oxford: Archaeopress.

Carre, M.B., P. Monsieur and S. Pesavento Mattioli 2014. Transport amphorae Lamboglia 2 and Dressel 6A. Italy and/or Dalmatia? Some clarifications. *JRA* 27, 417-428.

Carreras, C. and J.J.H. van den Berg (eds) 2017a. *Amphorae from the Kops Plateau (Nijmegen). Trade and supply to the lower-Rhineland from the Augustan period to AD 69/70.* Archaeopress Roman Archaeology 20. Oxford: Archaeopress.

Carreras, C. and J.J.H. van den Berg 2017b. Kops Plateau in context, in: Carreras and Van den Berg 2017a, 355-380.

Carreras Monfort, C., A. Gutiérrez, A. Alvarez and A. Doménch 2018. Producción local: las ánforas germanas, in: J. Remesal Rodríguez (ed.), *Colonia Ulpia Traiana (Xanten) y el Mediterráneo. El comercio de alimentos.* Col·lecció Instrumenta 63. Union académique internationale. Corpus international des timbres amphoriques 26, 143-169. Barcelona: Universitat de Barcelona.

Chapman, J. 2000. *Fragmentation in archaeology. People, places and broken objects in the prehistory of south eastern Europe.* London: Routledge.

Chenet, G. 1941. *La céramique gallo-romaine d'Argonne du IVe siècle et la terre sigillée décorée à la molette.* Macon: Protat.

Chevalier, N. 1709. *Recherche curieuse d'antiquités, venuës d'Italie, de la Grece, d'Egypte, & trouvées à Nimegue, a Santen, au Château de Wiltenburg proche d'Utrecht, dans le Château Britten proche de Leyde, & à Tongres.* Utrecht: Chès Nicolas Chevalier.

Collins, A., H. van Enckevort and J. Hendriks 2009. A grey area between the Batavians and the Romans. Wheel-thrown domestic pottery in the civitas Batavorum, in: H. van Enckevort (ed.), *Roman material culture. Studies in honour of Jan Thijssen,* 171-199. Zwolle: SPA Uitgevers.

Cordfunke, E.H.P., M. Eickhoff, R.B. Halbertsma, P.H.D. Leupen and H. Sarfatij (eds) 2007. *'Loffelijke verdiensten van de archeologie'. C.J.C. Reuvens als grondlegger van de moderne Nederlandse archeologie.* Stichting Centrum Archeologie en Historie Reeks 5. Hilversum: Uitgeverij Verloren.

Corsiez, A. 2019. *La céramique romaine de cinq pagi du nord de la Gaule (P. Laudunensis, Suessionensis, Tardunensis, Norviomensis et Vermandensis): caractérisation, chronologie, fonctions et économie.* Archéologie et Histoire Romaine 41. Drémil-Lafage: Éditions Mergoil.

Curle, J. 1911. *A Roman frontier post and its people. The fort of Newstead in the Parish of Melrose.* Glasgow: James Maclehose and Sons for the Society of Antiquaries of Scotland.

Dananai, A. 2019. *Entre cendres et offrandes: les pratiques funéraires en territoire atrébate de la fin du Ier s. av. J.-C. au début du IIIe s. ap. J.-C.* Revue du Nord Hors-Série Archéologie 28. Villeneuve d'Ascq: Librairie Archéologique.

Daniël, A.A.W.J. 2005. *Bewoningscontinuïteit of -discontinuïteit? Een studie naar een Bataafse nederzetting te Nijmegen-Oosterhout.* Internal Report Faculty of Archaeology. Leiden: Universiteit Leiden.

Daniël, A.A.W.J. 2018. Handgevormd aardewerk uit de Romeinse tijd, in: A.A.W.J. Daniël, *Een inheems-Romeinse nederzetting in plangebied Park Waaijenstein te Nijmegen-noord. Proefsleuvenonderzoek project Npw2.* Archeologische Berichten Nijmegen – Rapport 83, 36-37. Nijmegen: gemeente Nijmegen, Bureau Archeologie en Monumenten.

Daszkiewicz, M., B. Liesen and G. Schneider 2024. *Marbled ware of the 3rd and 4th centuries from Xanten, Germany.* Xantener Berichte 46. Oppenheim am Rhein: Nünnerich-Asmus Verlag.

De Bruin, J. 2008. Romeins aardewerk in rurale context. Verspreiding van de verschillende typen aardewerk uit de Romeinse tijd in de omgeving van het AHR-project, in: J.P. Flamman and E.A. Besselsen (eds), *Het verleden boven water. Archeologische monumentenzorg in het AHR-project.* Rapportage Archeologische Monumentenzorg 148, 217-242. Amersfoort: Rijksdienst voor Archeologie, Cultuurlandschap en Monumenten/Delft: Hoogheemraadschap van Delfland.

De Bruin, J. 2017. *Rurale gemeenschappen in de civitas Cananefatium 50-300 na Christus.* Unpublished PhD thesis, Universiteit Leiden.

De Bruin, J. 2019. *Border communities at the edge of the Roman Empire. Processes of change in the civitas Cananefatium.* Amsterdam Archaeological Studies 28. Amsterdam: Amsterdam University Press.

De Bruin, J. (ed.) in prep. *Roman villae in the Dutch province of Limburg.* Papers on Archaeology of the Leiden Museum of Antiquities. Leiden: National Museum of Antiquities.

De Bruin, J., W. Hessing and J. Noordervliet 2022. Hazerswoude. Een ontbrekende schakel in de limes? *Archeologie in Nederland* 6, no. 1, 16-21.

De Clercq, W. and P. Degryse 2008. The mineralogy and petrography of Low Lands ware I. (Roman lower Rhine – Meuse – Scheldt basin; the Netherlands, Belgium, Germany). *JASc* 35, 448-458.

De Clercq, W. and H. van Enckevort 2004. Cruches à anses torsadées augusto-tibériennes. Première approche, in: *SFECAG. Actes du congrès de Vallauris, 20-23 mai 2004,* 435-438. Marseille: SFECAG.

De Haas, M. 2023. Work in progress. Archeologisch onderzoek op de Grote Markt. *Stad & Lande* 32, no. 3, 23-25.

De Koning, J. 2023. Het vroegmiddeleeuwse aardewerk van Den Burg-Beatrixlaan, in: P.J. Woltering,

Bewoningsgeschiedenis van Texel. De opgravingen aan de Beatrixlaan in Den Burg (vroege middeleeuwen 475-900 n. Chr.). Noord-Hollandse Publicaties 13, 305-376. Castricum: Archeologiecentrum Noord-Holland Huis van Hilde.

Déchelette, J. 1904. *Les vases céramiques ornés de la Gaule romaine (Narbonnaise, Aquitaine et Lyonnaise)*. Paris: Picard.

Dekoninck, M. 2023. *Salt of the north. An interdisciplinary study into the technical and social organisation of Roman salt production in the civitas Menapiorum (Gallia-Belgica)*. Unpublished PhD thesis, Universiteit Gent.

Den Hartog, C.W.M. 2017. *Sportpark Terweide 5. LR84: Definitief archeologisch onderzoek aan de Hogeweide in Leidsche Rijn Centrum*. Basisrapportage Archeologie 106. Utrecht: Team Erfgoed gemeente Utrecht.

Deru, X. 1996. *La céramique belge dans le nord de la Gaule. Caractérisation, chronologie, phénomènes culturels et économiques*. Publications d'histoire de l'art et d'archéologie de l'Université Catholique de Louvain 89. Louvain-la-Neuve: Département d'Archéologie et d'Histoire de l'Art.

Deru, X. 2014. *Durocortorum. La céramique de César à Clovis*. Archéologie urbaine Reims 11. Bulletin de la Société Archéologique Champenoise 107, no. 2. Reims: Société Archéologique Champenoise.

Deru, X. 2021. Les transports, leur coût et le choix des consommateurs dans le nord de la Gaule romaine, in: C. Raynaud (ed.), *Voies, réseaux, paysages en Gaule. Colloque en hommage à Jean-Luc Fiches (Pont du Gard, juin 2016)*. Revue Archéologique de Narbonnaise Supplément 49, 413-427. Montpellier: Éditions de l'Association de la Revue Archéologique de Narbonnaise.

Deru, X. 2022. *L'atelier de potiers de la période romaine des "Quatre Bornes" aux Rues-des-Vignes*. Revue du Nord Hors Série Collection Art et Archéologie 31. Lille: Université de Lille.

Deru, X. and G. Fronteau 2010. Les ateliers de potiers romains entre Seine et Rhin. *ReiCretActa* 41, 539-547. Bonn: Dr. Rudolf Habelt GmbH.

Deru, X. and D. Vachard 2002. Le groupe de pâtes "savonneuses" des céramiques gallo-romaines du nord de la Gaule Belgique, in: *SFECAG. Actes du congrès de Bayeux, 9-12 mai 2002*, 477-485. Marseille: SFECAG.

Deru, X., F. Vilvorder and A.-C. Van Overbeke 1997. La céramique, méthodologie, in: R. Brulet and J.-C. Demanet (eds), *Liberchies 3. Vicus gallo-romain. Les thermes. Fouilles du CRAN (1973 et 1989-90) et zone d'habitat au nord de la voie antique: fouilles de Pro Geminiaco (1979-80 et 1987-94)*. Publications d'Histoire de l'Art et d'Archéologie de l'Université Catholique de Louvain 94, 152-155. Louvain-la-Neuve: Département d'Archéologie et d'Histoire de l'Art.

Dhaeze, W. 2011. *De Romeinse kustverdediging langs de Noordzee en het Kanaal van 120 tot 410 na Chr. Een onderzoek naar de rol van de militaire sites in de kustverdediging en drie casestudies over de militaire versterkingen van Maldegem-Vake, Aardenburg en Boulogne-sur-Mer*. Unpublished PhD thesis, Universiteit Gent.

Dhaeze, W. 2019. *The Roman North Sea Channel coastal defence. Germanic seaborne raids and the Roman response*. Wetteren: Universa Press.

Donnadieu, J. and S. Willems 2015. Facies céramique en contexte d'ateliers de sauniers. Comparaison du mobilier des sites ménapiens de Steene, Pitgam et Looberghe (nord), in: *SFECAG. Actes du congrès de Nyon 14-17 mai 2015*, 315-342. Marseille: SFECAG.

Dragendorff, H. 1894. *De vasculis romanorum rubris. Capita selecta*. PhD thesis, Rheinische Friedrich-Wilhelms-Universität. Bonn: Typis Caroli Georgi.

Dragendorff, H. 1895. Terra sigillata. Ein Beitrag zur Geschichte der griechischen und römischen Keramik. *BJb* XCVI-XCVII, 18-155.

Dressel, H. 1879. *Di un grande deposito di anfore rinvenuto nel nuovo quartiere del Castro Pretorio (Tav. VII-XVIII)*. BCom Anno VII – Serie Seconda, 36-64, 65-112, 143-196. Rome: Commissione Archeologica Comunale di Roma.

Dressel, H. 1899. *Inscriptiones urbis romae latinae. Instrumentum domesticum*. Corpus Inscriptionum Latinarum Voluminis Decimiquinti Pars Posterior Fasciculus 1. Berlin: Apud Georgium Reimerum.

Duggan, M. 2020. Britain in the Atlantic: late Antique ceramics and connections, in: M. Duggan, M. Jackson and S. Turner (eds), *Ceramics and Atlantic connections: late Roman and early medieval imported pottery on the Atlantic seaboard. Proceedings of an international symposium at Newcastle University, March 2014*. Roman and Late Antique Mediterranean Pottery 15, 13-24. Oxford: Archaeopress.

Eggenstein, G. 2003. *Das Siedlungswesen der jüngeren vorrömischen Eisenzeit und der frühen römischen Kaiserzeit im Lippebereich*. Bodenaltertümer Westfalens 40. Mainz: Verlag Philipp von Zabern.

Ehmig, U. 2007. Tituli picti auf Amphoren in Köln. *KölnJb* 40, 215-322.

Ehmig, U. 2009. Tituli picti auf Amphoren in Köln II. *KölnJb* 42, 393-445.

Erdrich, M. 2001a. *Rom und die Barbaren. Das Verhältnis zwischen dem Imperium Romanum und den germanischen Stämmen vor seiner Nordwestgrenze von der späten römischen Republik bis zum Gallischen Sonderreich*. RGF 58. Mainz: Verlag Philipp von Zabern.

Erdrich, M. 2001b. Wirtschaftsbeziehungen zwischen der Germania Inferior und dem germanischen Vorland – ein Wunschbild, in: T. Grünewald (ed.), *Germania Inferior. Besiedlung, Gesellschaft und Wirtschaft an der Grenze der römisch-germanische Welt*. Ergänzungsbände zum Reallexicon der Germanische Altertumskunde 28, 306-335. Berlin: De Gruyter.

Ettlinger, E., B. Hedinger, B. Hoffmann, P.M. Kenrick, G. Pucci, K. Roth-Rubi, G. Schneider, S. von Schnurbein, C.M. Wells and S. Zabehlicky-Scheffenegger 1990. *Conspectus formarum terrae sigillatae italico modo confectae*. Materialien zur Römisch-Germanischen Keramik 10. Bonn: Dr. Rudolf Habelt GmbH.

Frank, K. 2023. Zu den „germanischen" Fußschalen im Rheinland, in: B. Liesen (ed.), *Zwischen Töpfer und Verbraucher/ Between potter and consumer. Internationales Kolloquium im LVR-RömerMuseum 27.-29. März 2019*. Xantener Berichte 41, 303-326. Oppenheim am Rhein: Nünnerich-Asmus Verlag.

Franke, R. 2022. *Der Hafen der Colonia Ulpia Traiana, Xanten. Ausgrabungen im Vorfeld der nordöstlichen Stadtmauer 1934-1993. Die Feinkeramik*. Xantener Berichte 39. Oppenheim am Rhein: Nünnerich-Asmus Verlag.

Friedrich, S. 2012. Die römischen Töpfereien von Weißenthurm am Rhein (Lkr. Mayen-Koblenz) und ihr Umland, in: M. Grünewald and S. Wenzel (eds), *Römische Landnutzung in der Eifel. Neue Ausgrabungen und Forschungen. Tagung in Mayen, vom 3. bis zum 6. November 2011*. Römisch-Germanisches Zentralmuseum Tagungen 16, 263-277. Mainz: Verlag des Römisch-Germanischen Zentralmuseums.

Friedrich, S. 2023. Neue Untersuchungen zu Produktionsorten und Chronologie der „Urmitzer Ware", in: B. Liesen (ed.), *Zwischen Töpfer und Verbraucher/Between potter and consumer. Internationales Kolloquium im LVR-RömerMuseum 27.-29. März 2019*. Xantener Berichte 41, 537-556. Oppenheim am Rhein: Nünnerich-Asmus Verlag.

Fulford, M. 1977. Pottery and Britain's foreign trade in the later Roman period, in: D.P.S. Peacock (ed.), *Pottery and early commerce. Characterization and trade in Roman and later ceramics*, 35-84. London: Academic Press.

Galestin, M.C. 2001/2002. Winsum-Bruggeburen, second report on the excavation. The Roman pottery. *Palaeohistoria* 43/44, 435-468.

Galestin, M.C. 2009. Frisian soldiers in the Roman army, in: Á. Morille, N. Hanel and E. Martín (eds), *Limes XX. XXth international congress of Roman frontier studies*. Anejos de Gladius 13, 833-846. Madrid: Consejo Superior de Investigaciones Científicas.

Geerts, R.C.A. 2012. Aardewerk, in: L.M.B. van der Feijst (ed.), *Vechten tegen het wassende water in de Romeinse tijd. Een archeologische opgraving in het plangebied Hoogeland-Oost, 't Zand Heultje te Naaldwijk*. ADC Rapport 3186, 69-92. Amersfoort: ADC ArcheoProjecten.

Geerts, R.C.A. 2013. Aardewerken imitaties van glazen ribkommen in Zuid-Holland. *Archeologische Kroniek Zuid-Holland* 2012, 30-31.

Geerts, R.C.A. 2014. Creativity or statussymbol? Roman ceramic imitations in the Netherlands, in: S. Biegert (ed.), *ReiCretActa* 43, 771-778. Bonn: Dr. Rudolf Habelt GmbH.

Geerts, R.C.A. 2019a. Aardewerk uit de Romeinse tijd, in: Van der Feijst 2019, 57-107.

Geerts, R.C.A. 2019b. Self-made Roman. Handmade pottery as a marker of identity, in: S. Arnoldussen, E.A.G. Ball, J. van Dijk, E.H.L.D. Norde and N. de Vries (eds), *Metaaltijden 6. Bijdragen in de studie van de Metaaltijden*, 283-290. Leiden: Sidestone Press.

Geerts, R.C.A. 2020. *In de voetsporen van Braat. Een inventariserend veldonderzoek in de vorm van proefsleuven op het Raadhuisplein te Heerlen*. ADC Rapport 4747. Amersfoort: ADC ArcheoProjecten.

Geerts, R.C.A. 2021a. Het aardewerk, in: Loopik and Vos 2021, 231-378.

Geerts, R.C.A. 2021b. De vindplaats in scherven. Een eerste aanzet voor een analyse van de fragmentatie van aardewerk in de Romeinse tijd, in: P.W. van den Broeke, R.C.A. Geerts, S. Hoss and R.A. Houkes (eds), *Nieuwe inzichten in archeologisch materiaal*. ArtefActueel 1, 19-29. Zwolle: SPA Uitgevers.

Geerts, R.C.A. 2021c. Pottery on Mars. A 3rd century settlement at Trade Parc Westland, the Netherlands. *JRomPotSt* 18, 81-94.

Geerts, R.C.A. 2022. Aardewerk, in: Vossen and Geerts 2022, 82-118.

Geerts, R.C.A. 2023. Supplied with Severan sigillata. A late 2nd-3rd century assemblage from Trade Parc Westland (province of South-Holland, the Netherlands), in: B. Liesen (ed.), *Zwischen Töpfer und Verbraucher/Between potter and consumer. Internationales Kolloquium im LVR-RömerMuseum 27.-29. März 2019*. Xantener Berichte 41, 153-176. Oppenheim am Rhein: Nünnerich-Asmus Verlag.

Geerts, R.C.A. 2024a. *Ceramics creating changing culture. Ceramics and their creators in Germania Inferior and cultural change (A.D. 50-300)*. PhD thesis, Universiteit Leiden. Oxford: Archaeopress.

Geerts, R.C.A. 2024b. Romeins aardewerk, in: E. Blom, J. Loopik and W.K. Vos (eds), *Legionairs op vliegveld Valkenburg (ZH). De opgraving van een onverwachte legerplaats uit de vroeg-Romeinse tijd*. ADC Rapport 6061. Archol Rapport 725, 185-251, 395-430. Amersfoort: ADC ArcheoProjecten/Leiden: Archol.

Geerts, R.C.A. (ed.) 2024c. *Wonen aan het water. Een archeologische opgraving van een vroeg-Romeinse nederzetting aan het Valkenburgse Meer, gemeente Katwijk*. ADC Rapport 6255. Amersfoort: ADC ArcheoProjecten.

Geerts, R.C.A. 2024d. Cultuur gevormd door klei. Efficiëntere pottenbakkers aan de basis van culturele veranderingen, in: R.C.A. Geerts, P.W. van den Broeke, S. Hoss and R.A. Houkes (eds), *Nieuwe inzichten in archeologisch materiaal*. ArtefActueel 2. Zwolle: SPA Uitgevers.

Geerts, R.C.A. in prep. a. From printed paper to PowerPoint. 65 years of the Rei Cretariæ Romanæ Fautores, in: *Wo wissen entsteht. Orte der Forschung, des Austauschs und des Lernens in den Altertumswissenschaften*. Frankfurt.

Geerts, R.C.A. in prep. b. Aardewerk, in: Bakx (ed.) in prep.

Geerts, R.C.A. and W.F. Reigersman-van Lidth de Jeude 2019. Het einde van een era. Romeins aardewerk uit de late 3e eeuw in Zuid-Holland, in: R.J. van Zoolingen (ed.), *Ab harenis incultis. Artikelen voor Ab Waasdorp*, 192-203. 's-Gravenhage: gemeente Den Haag, Afdeling Archeologie.

Geerts, R.C.A., J. Hendriks, J. Van Kerckhove and S. Heeren 2020. *KNA-Leidraden Anorganisch materiaal. Leidraad 4: aardewerk uit de Romeinse tijd (ca. 20 voor Chr.-450 na Chr.).* Gouda: Stichting Infrastructuur Kwaliteitsborging Bodembeheer.

Gerrets, D.A. and R. de Leeuwe (eds) 2011. *Rituelen aan de Maas. Een archeologische opgraving te Lomm, Hoogwatergeul fase II*. ADC Rapport 2333. Amersfoort: ADC ArcheoProjecten.

Gerrets, D.A. and G.L. Williams (eds) 2011. *Water en vuur. Archeologische proefsleuvenonderzoek en opgraving te Lomm Hoogwatergeul fase III*. ADC Rapport 2703. Amersfoort: ADC ArcheoProjecten.

Glasbergen, W. 1944a [1948]. Terra sigillata uit de provincie Groningen. Bijdrage tot de geschiedenis van den handel in den Romeinschen tijd. *Jaarverslagen van de Vereniging voor Terpenonderzoek* 25-28, 317-368.

Glasbergen, W. 1944b [1948]. Versierde Claudisch-Neronische terra sigillata van Valkenburg Z.H. *Jaarverslagen van de Vereniging voor Terpenonderzoek* 25-28, 206-217.

Glasbergen, W. 1944c [1948]. Pottenbakkersstempels op terra sigillata van Valkenburg Z.H. *Jaarverslagen van de Vereniging voor Terpenonderzoek* 25-28, 218-236.

González Cesteros, H. 2014. Ánforas hispanas en la Germania Inferior antes de la formación de la provincia (20 a.*C.-69 d.C.).* Unpublished PhD thesis, Universitat Rovira i Virgili.

Goudswaard, B. 1990. *Amforen van Velsen 1. Inhoud aan de verpakking: een materiaalstudie naar bevoorrading*. Unpublished PhD thesis, Universiteit van Amsterdam.

Grunwald, L. 2023. *Die römischen und frühmittelalterlichen Töpfereien von Mayen. Ein Produktionszentrum von europäischer Bedeutung*. Monographien des RGZM 161. Vulkanpark-Forschungen 14. Heidelberg: Propylaeum.

Günther, K. 1990. *Siedlung und Werkstätten von Feinschmieden der älteren römischen Kaiserzeit bei Warburg-Daseburg*. Bodenaltertümer Westfalens 24. Münster: Verlag Aschendorff.

Haalebos, J.K. 1977. *Zwammerdam-Nigrum Pullum. Ein Auxilliarlager am niedergermanischen Limes*. Cingula 3. Amsterdam: Universiteit van Amsterdam.

Haalebos, J.K. 1990. *Het grafveld van Nijmegen-Hatert. Een begraafplaats uit de eerste drie eeuwen na Chr. op het platteland bij Noviomagus Batavorum*. Beschrijving van de Verzamelingen in het Provinciaal Museum G.M. Kam te Nijmegen 11. Nijmegen: Provinciaal Museum G.M. Kam.

Haalebos, J.K. 1991. Das große augusteische Lager auf dem Hunerberg in Nijmegen, in: R. Aßkamp and S. Berke (eds), *Die römische Okkupation nördlich der Alpen zur zeit des Augustus. Kolloquim Bergkamen 1989*. Bodenaltertümer Westfalens 26, 97-107. Münster: Verlag Aschendorff.

Haalebos, J.K. 1995. *Castra und canabae. Ausgrabungen auf dem Hunerberg in Nijmegen 1987-1994*. Libelli Noviomagenses 3. Nijmegen: Katholieke Universiteit Nijmegen.

Haalebos, J.K. 1998. *Centuriae onder Centuriae Hof. Opgravingen achter het hoofdgebouw van het voormalige Canisiuscollege te Nijmegen 1995-1997*. Libelli Noviomagenses 5. Nijmegen: Katholieke Universiteit Nijmegen, Afdeling Provinciaal-Romeinse Archeologie.

Haalebos, J.K. 2000. Mosterd na de maaltijd. Een vergeten jubileum. Traianus en het jaar 98 na Chr. in Nijmegen. *Numaga Jaarboek* 47, 5-41.

Haalebos, J.K. 2002. Die früheste Belegung des Hunerberges in Nijmegen, in: P. Freeman, J. Bennett, Z.T. Fiema and B. Hoffmann (eds), *Limes XVIII, Proceedings of the XVIIIth international congress of Roman frontier studies held in Amman, Jordan (September 2000): a conference held under the auspices of the Department of Antiquities of the Hashemite Kingdom of Jordan, the Council for British Research in the Levant and the Department of Archaeology at the University of Liverpool*. BARIntSer 1084, 403-414. Oxford: BAR Publishing.

Haalebos, J.K. 2006. Nimègue-Noviomagus, in: M. Reddé, R. Brulet, R. Fellmann, J.K. Haalebos and S. von Schnurbein (eds), *L'architecture de la Gaule romaine. Les fortifications militaires*. Documents d'Archéologie Française 100, 349-358. Bordeaux: Éditions de la Maison des Sciences de l'Homme.

Haalebos, J.K. and W.J.H. Willems 1999a. Der niedergermanische Limes in den Niederlanden, 1995-1997, in: N. Gudea (ed.), *Roman frontier studies. Proceedings of the XVIIth international congress of Roman frontier studies*, 77-87. Zălau: County Council of Sălaj, the County Museum of History and Art.

Haalebos, J.K. and W.J.H. Willems 1999b. Recent research on the limes in the Netherlands. *JRA* 12, 247-262.

Habermehl, D.S. 2019. Het aardewerk uit de late IJzertijd, in: Habermehl *et al.* 2019, 228-245.

Habermehl, D.S., J. van Kampen and J. van Renswoude (eds) 2019. *Opgravingen te Tiel-Medel-Hazenkamp en -De Reth. Twee grafvelden uit de Romeinse tijd en nederzettingssporen uit de late IJzertijd, vroeg-Romeinse tijd en laat-Romeinse tijd*. Zuidnederlandse Archeologische Rapporten 80. Amsterdam: VUhbs archeologie.

Habermehl, D.S., J. Van Kerckhove, N.G.A.M. Roymans, L. Kootker, G.L. Boreel, D. Braekmans and S. Heeren 2023. Investigating migration and mobility in the early Roman frontier. The case of the Batavi in the Dutch Rhine delta (c. 50/30 BC-AD 40). *Germania* 100, no. 2, 65-108.

Halbertsma, H. 1944. *Inventaris van terpen en wierden in de provinciën Friesland en Groningen*. Groningen: Biologisch Archeologisch Instituut (unpublished report).

Halbertsma, R.B. 2003. *Scholars, travellers and trade. The pioneer years of the National Museum of Antiquities in Leiden, 1818-1840*. London: Routledge.

Halpaap, R. 1994. *Der Siedlungsplatz Soest-Ardey*. Bodenaltertümer Westfalens 30. Mainz: Verlag Philipp von Zabern.

Hanut, F. 2001. Amphores et cruches-amphores régionales de Gaule belgique et de Germanie inférieure, in: M. Tuffreau-Libre and A. Jacques (eds), *La céramique en Gaule et Bretagne romaines. Commerce, contacts et romanisation*. Nord-Ouest Archéologie 12, 19-38. Berck-sur-Mer: Centre de Recherches Archéologiques et de Diffusion Culturelle.

Hanut, F. and D. Henrotay (eds) 2014. *«Du bûcher à la tombe»: les nécropoles gallo-romaines à incinération en Wallonie*. Namur: Institut du Patrimoine Wallon.

Harsema, O.H. 1976. Noordbarge. *Bulletin Koninklijke Nederlandse Oudheidkundige Bond* 75, no. 1, 52-55.

Hartley, B.R. and B.M. Dickinson 2008-2012. *Names on terra sigillata. An index of makers' stamps & signatures on Gallo-Roman terra sigillata* (Samian ware). Bulletin of the Institute of Classical Studies Supplement 102.1-9. London: University of London Press.

Haupt, D. 1984. Römischer Töpfereibezirk bei Soller, Kreis Düren. Bericht über eine alte Ausgrabung, in: *Beiträge zur Archäologie des römischen Rheinlands* 4. Rheinische Ausgrabungen 23, 391-476. Bonn: Rheinland-Verlag.

Hawkes, C.F.C. and M.R. Hull 1947. *Camulodunum. First report on the excavations at Colchester 1930-1939*. Reports of the Research Committee of the Society of Antiquaries of London 14. Oxford: The Society of Antiquaries.

Hayes, J.W. 1972. *Late Roman pottery. A catalogue of Roman fine wares*. London: The British School at Rome.

Hayes, J.W. 1980. *A supplement to Late Roman pottery*. London: The British School at Rome.

Heeren, S. 2009. *Romanisering van rurale gemeenschappen in de civitas Batavorum. De casus Tiel-Passewaaij*. Nederlandse Archeologische Rapporten 36. PhD thesis, Vrije Universiteit Amsterdam. Amersfoort: Rijksdienst voor het Cultureel Erfgoed.

Heeren, S. 2016. The theory of 'Limesfall' and the material culture of the late 3rd century. *Germania* 94, 185-209.

Heeren, S. and T. Hazenberg (eds) 2010. *Voorname dames, stoere soldaten en eenvoudige lieden. Begravingen en nederzettingssporen uit het Neolithicum, de laat-Romeinse tijd en middeleeuwen te Wijchen-Centrum*. Hazenberg Archeologische Serie 1. Leiden: Hazenberg Archeologie.

Heeren, S. and L.M.B. van der Feijst 2017. *Prehistorische, Romeinse en middeleeuwse fibulae uit de Lage Landen. Beschrijving, analyse en interpretatie van een archeologische vondstcategorie*. Amersfoort: s.n.

Heimberg, U. and C.B. Rüger 1972. Eine Töpferei im Vicus vor der Colonia Ulpia Traiana, in: *Beiträge zur Archäologie des römischen Rheinlands* III. Rheinische Ausgrabungen 12, 84-118. Bonn: Rheinland-Verlag.

Heimerl, F. 2016. African Red Slip Ware from *Augusta Vindelicum*/ Augsburg *(Raetia)*: range of forms and chemical analyses, in: S. Biegert (ed.), *ReiCretActa* 44, 487-495. Bonn: Dr. Rudolf Habelt GmbH.

Heirbaut, E.N.A. and H. van Enckevort 2009. *De verdedigingswerken van de Romeinse legerplaatsen op de Hunerberg. Archeologisch onderzoek in Nijmegen-Oost*. Archeologische Berichten Nijmegen – Rapport 11. Nijmegen: gemeente Nijmegen Bureau Archeologie en Monumenten.

Heirbaut, E.N.A., H. van Enckevort and A. Loonen 2009. De datering van de augusteïsche grachten, in: Heirbaut and Van Enckevort 2009, 97-98.

Hendriks, J. 2010. Handgevormd en gedraaid aardewerk uit de vroeg-Romeinse tijd, in: P.W. van den Broeke, J.A. den Braven and E.A.G. Ball, *Midden-Neolithicum tot en met vroeg-Romeinse tijd in het Zuiderveld. Onderzoek van nederzettingssporen en graven te Nijmegen-Ressen*. Archeologische Berichten Nijmegen – Rapport 15, 147-165. Nijmegen: gemeente Nijmegen, Bureau Archeologie en Monumenten.

Hendriks, J. 2014. Pottery from *Ulpia Noviomagus* – Nijmegen. First report on the Maasplein production site: kilns 1-2, in: Liesen (ed.) 2014, 175-240.

Hendriks, J. 2017. Romeins aardewerk uit geselecteerde contexten, in: C. Harmsen and H. van Enckevort (eds), *Op de grens van Oppidum Batavorum. Archeologisch onderzoek aan het Nijmeegse Hertogplein*. Archeologische Berichten Nijmegen – Rapport 70, 65-82. Nijmegen: gemeente Nijmegen, Bureau Leefomgevingskwaliteit | Archeologie.

Hendriks, J. 2018. Gedraaid aardewerk uit de Romeinse tijd, in: A.A.W.J. Daniël, *Een inheems-Romeinse nederzetting in plangebied Park Waaijenstein te Nijmegen-noord. Proefsleuvenonderzoek project Npw2*. Archeologische Berichten Nijmegen – Rapport 83, 37-46. Nijmegen: gemeente Nijmegen, Bureau Leefomgevingskwaliteit | Archeologie.

Hendriks, J. and H. van Enckevort in prep. *Het aardewerk uit enkele laat-Augusteïsche/vroeg-Tiberische kuilen in de berm van de via pricipalis*.

Hendriks, J., E. van der Linden and K. Zee 2023. Aardewerk, in: P. van de Geer, *Nieuwe kennis uit een onbekende hoek: kortstondige bewoning in noordoostelijk Ulpia Noviomagus. Een opgraving in het Waalkwartier (Waalfront), gemeente Nijmegen*. Archeologische Berichten Nijmegen – Rapport 112, 71-101. Nijmegen: Bureau Archeologie en Bodemkwaliteit gemeente Nijmegen.

Henrich, P. 2023. Die Produktion spätantiker Keramik Urmitzer Machart (UMA) in Koblenz, in: B. Liesen (ed.), *Zwischen Töpfer und Verbraucher/Between potter and consumer. Internationales Kolloquium im LVR-RömerMuseum 27.-29. März 2019*. Xantener Berichte 41, 571-581. Oppenheim am Rhein: Nünnerich-Asmus Verlag.

Herbin, P., V. Pilard and F. Ledauphin 2019. Cambrai, route de Crèvecoeur (nord): concomitance d'une activité potière et d'un espace sépulcral, in: *SFECAG. Actes du congrès de Maubeuge-Bavay 2019*, 273-289. Marseille: SFECAG.

Hessing, W.A.M., W.K. Vos and E.J. van Ginkel (eds) 2021. *Romans on the waterfront. Evaluation of archaeological interventions (1997-2020) along the Dutch part of the lower Rhine and coastal limes*. Nederlandse Archeologische Rapporten 71. Amersfoort: Rijksdienst voor het Cultureel Erfgoed.

Hiddink, H.A. 1999. *Germaanse samenlevingen tussen Rijn en Weser: 1e eeuw voor -4e eeuw na Chr.* Unpublished PhD thesis, Vrije Universiteit Amsterdam.

Hiddink, H.A. 2010. *Romeins aardewerk van de zuid-Nederlandse zandgronden*. Materiaal en Methoden 2. Amsterdam: Archeologisch Centrum van de Vrije Universiteit.

Hiddink, H.A. 2013. *VU-opgravingen in de Kempen 2. Een nederzetting en grafveld uit de Romeinse tijd op de Heesmortel bij Riethoven*. Zuidnederlandse Archeologische Rapporten 51. Amsterdam: VUhbs Archeologie.

Hiddink, H.A. 2014. *De Romeinse villa-nederzetting op de Kerkakkers bij Hoogeloon (Noord-Brabant)*. Zuidnederlandse Archeologische Rapporten 53. Amsterdam: VUhbs Archeologie.

Hinz, H. 1963. 2. Bericht über die Ausgrabungen in der Colonia Traiana nördlich von Xanten. *BJb* 163, 398-415.

Hodder, I. 1981. Pottery production and use; a theoretical discussion, in: H. Howard and E.L. Morris (eds), *Production and distribution: a ceramic viewpoint*. BARIntSer 120, 215-220. Oxford: BAR Publishing.

Holwerda, J.H. 1917. De stad der Bataven en de Romeinsche vesting te Nijmegen. *Bijblad der Nederlandsche Anthropologische Vereeniging* 1917, 4-17.

Holwerda, J.H. 1923. *Arentsburg. Een Romeinsch militair vlootstation bij Voorburg*. Leiden: E.J. Brill.

Holwerda, J.H. 1936. *Het laat-Grieksche en Romeinsche gebruiksaardewerk uit het Middellandsche-Zee-gebied in het Rijksmuseum van Oudheden te Leiden*. 's-Gravenhage: Algemeene Landsdrukkerij.

Holwerda, J.H. 1941. *De Belgische waar in Nijmegen*. Beschrijving van de verzameling van het Museum G.M. Kam te Nijmegen 2. 's-Gravenhage: Departement van Opvoeding, Wetenschap en Cultuurbescherming.

Holwerda, J.H. 1944. *Het in de pottenbakkerij van de Holdeurn gefabriceerde aardewerk uit de Nijmeegsche grafvelden*. Beschrijving van de verzameling van het Museum G.M. Kam te Nijmegen 3. Oudheidkundige Mededeelingen uit het Rijksmuseum van Oudheden te Leiden Nieuwe Reeks 24 Supplement. Internationales Archiv für Ethnographie Supplement 44. Leiden: E.J. Brill.

Holwerda, J.H. and W.C. Braat 1946. *De Holdeurn bij Berg en Dal. Centrum van pannenbakkerij en aardewerkindustrie in den Romeinschen tijd*. OMROL Supplement op Nieuwe Reeks 26. Leiden: E.J. Brill.

Höpken, C.C.C. 2005. *Die römische Keramikproduktion in Köln*. Kölner Forschungen 8. Mainz: Verlag Philipp von Zabern.

Höpken, C.C.C. 2014. Olivenöl aus Spanien, Wein aus Gallien, Bier und Milchprodukte aus der Region – Amphorenfunde aus dem Bonner vicus, in: H. Kennecke (ed.), *Der Rhein als europäische Verkehrsachse die Römerzeit*. Bonner Beiträge zur Vor-und Frühgeschichtlichen Archäologie 16, 175-190. Bonn: Universität Bonn.

Höpken, C.C.C. 2019. Amphoren als Informationsquelle für die Wirtschaft Kölns – eine Bilanz, in: M. Mirschenz, R. Gerlach and J. Bemmann (eds), *Der Rhein als europäische Verkehrsachse III*. Bonner Beiträge zur Vor- und Frühgeschichtlichen Archäologie 22, 311-328. Bonn: Universität Bonn.

Höpken, C.C.C. 2021. Von Afrika bis Köln – zur Funktion afrikanischer Teller in spätantiken Gräbern. *KölnJb* 54, 391-413.

Höpken, C.C.C. and B. Liesen 2005. Töpfereiabfall des 3. Jahrhunderts aus Köln. *KölnJb* 38, 755-771.

Höpken, C.C.C. and B. Liesen 2009. Römische Gräber im Kölner Süden. I. Von der Stadtmauer bis zur Nekropole um St. Severin. *KölnJb* 42, 447-544.

Hosdez, Chr., J. Flahaut and F. Bostyn 2019. L'officine de potiers de la rue Charles-de-Gaulle à Vermand (Aisne). De l'argile à la céramique, in: *SFECAG. Actes du congrès de Maubeuge-Bavay 30 mai-2 juin 2019*, 39-63. Marseille: SFECAG.

Huart, L. and P. Mathelart 2018. Les productions de vaisselle en terre cuite en Champagne, in: *SFECAG. Actes du congrès de Reims 2018*, 51-72. Marseille: SFECAG.

Hulst, R.S. 1981. Einheimische Keramik des 1. Jahrhunderts n.Chr. aus Aalten (Gelderland). *BerOudhBod* 31, 365-367.

Hupperetz, W. 1990. *Romeinen rond Roermond*. Roermond: Gemeentemuseum Roermond.

Ihde, C. 2018. Ausgrabungen am Chlodwigplatz in Köln. Archäologische Untersuchungen im Rahmen des Nord-Süd-Stadtbahnbaus. *KölnJb* 51, 99-367.

Jaschke, K. and D. Schmitz 2018. Das römische Köln als Handelszentrum im 1.-3. Jahrhundert, in: C. Eger (ed.), *Warenwege – Warenflüsse. Handel, Logistik und Transport am römischen Niederrhein*. Xantener Berichte 32, 317-336. Mainz: Verlag Philipp von Zabern.

Jung, P. 2014. Freigeformte Keramik aus Nordgallien im Gebiet der *Colonia Ulpia Traiana*, in: Liesen (ed.) 2014, 287-316.

Kalee, C.A. 1972/1973. Trierer Bilderschüsseln im Museum Kam, Nimwegen. *ReiCretActa* 14-15, 61-105. Tongeren: George Michiels s.a.

Kalee, C.A. 2001. *Terra sigillata langs de limes*. Leusden: BV Drukkerij Patria.

Keay, S.J. 1984. *Late Roman amphorae in the western Mediterranean. A typology and economic study: the Catalan evidence*. BARIntSer 196. Oxford: BAR.

Kemmers, F. 2005a (=Kemmers 2006). *Coins for a legion. An analysis of the coin finds from the Augustan legionary fortress and Flavian canabae legionis at Nijmegen*. Unpublished PhD thesis, Radboud Universiteit Nijmegen.

Kemmers, F. 2005b. The coin finds from the Augustan legionary fortress at Nijmegen (the Netherlands). Coin circulation in the lower Rhine area before Drusus' campaigns, in: C. Alfaro, C. Marco and P. Otero (eds), *XIII congreso internacional de numismática Madrid 2003, Actas-Proceedings-Actes*, 987-990. Madrid: Ministerio de Cultura.

Kemmers, F. 2006 (=Kemmers 2005a). *Coins for a legion. An analysis of the coin finds from the Augustan legionary fortress and Flavian canabae legionis at Nijmegen*. Studien zu Fundmünzen der Antike 21. Mainz: Verlag Philipp von Zabern.

Kemmers, F. 2007. A military presence on the lower Rhine before Drusus' campaigns. The coin finds of the Augustan legionary fortress at Nijmegen, in: G.A. Lehmann and R. Wiegels (eds), *Römische Präsenz und Herrschaft im Germanien der augusteischen Zeit. Der Fundplatz von Kalkriese im Kontext neuerer Forschungen und Ausgrabungsbefunde*. AbhGöttingen Dritte Folge 279, 183-199. Göttingen: Vandenhoeck & Ruprecht.

Kemmers, F. 2008. Marcus Agrippa and the earliest Roman fortress at Nijmegen. The coin finds from the Hunerberg, in: M.P. García-Bellido, A. Mostalac and A. Jiménez (eds), *Del imperivm de Pompeyo a la avctoritas de Augusto. Homenaje a Michael Grant*. Anejos de Español de Argueología 47, 166-172. Madrid: Consejo Superior de Investigaciones Cientificas.

Kenemans, M.C. and I. Vossen (eds) 2023. *Archeologie op diepte. Erven uit de late Steen- en vroege Bronstijd en een nederzetting en grafveld uit de Romeinse tijd aan de Panovenweg in Tiel*. ADC Monografie 32, 235-265. Amersfoort: ADC ArcheoProjecten.

Kiessel, M. 2010. The Roman pottery centres of Urmitz and Mayen (district Mayen-Koblenz, Germany). New archaeological and typological evidence for dating their production and the usage of their products, in: S. Biegert (ed.), *ReiCretActa* 41, 559-566. Bonn: Dr. Rudolf Habelt GmbH.

Klok, R.H.J. 1979. Terps: who cares? *BerOudhBod* 29, 459-489.

Kloosterman, R.P.J. 2014a. Geverfd en beschilderd aardewerk, in: R.P.J. Kloosterman, M. Polak and M.J.M. Zandstra, *Opgravingen op het terrein van het voormalige Canisiuscollege in Nijmegen, 1987-1997. Vondsten uit castra en canabae* 1, 65-135. Auxiliaria 14. Nijmegen: Auxilia.

Kloosterman, R.P.J. 2014b. Wrijfschalen, in: R.P.J. Kloosterman, M. Polak and M.J.M. Zandstra, *Opgravingen op het terrein van het voormalige Canisiuscollege in Nijmegen, 1987-1997. Vondsten uit castra en canabae* 1, 197-218. Auxiliaria 14. Nijmegen: Auxilia.

Kloosterman, R.P.J. 2017. Aardewerk, in: P. Weterings (ed.), *Vicusresten onder de wal. Archeologische opgraving op Fort Vechten. Grondwalcoupe fase 2*. BAAC Rapport A-12.0133, 67-104. 's-Hertogenbosch: BAAC Archeologie en Bouwhistorie.

Knol, E. 1993. *De Noordnederlandse kustlanden in de vroege middeleeuwen*. Unpublished PhD thesis, Vrije Universiteit Amsterdam.

Knol, E. 2014. Ezinge: metaal uit een opgraving zonder detector, in: Nieuwhof (ed.) 2014, 187-206.

Komnick, H. 2015. *Die Fundmünzen der römischen Zeit aus dem Bereich der Colonia Ulpia Traiana, Xanten*. Xantener Berichte 29. Darmstadt: Verlag Philipp von Zabern.

Krekovič, E. 2016. Mortaria in graves in the northern provinces, in: S. Biegert (ed.), *ReiCretActa* 44, 513-518. Bonn: Dr. Rudolf Habelt GmbH.

Kyritz, D.M. 2014. *Haffen-Mehr – Die Kontaktzone am niederrheinischen Limesgebiet*. Unpublished PhD thesis, Rheinischen Friedrich-Wilhelms-Universität Bonn.

Lange, H. 1994. Die Koroplastik der Colonia Claudia Ara Agrippinensium. Untersuchungen zu Typologie, Technik, Werkstattfunden, Betrieben, Signaturen und Produktionszeit. *KölnJb* 27, 117-309.

Laubenheimer, F. 1985. *La production des amphores en Gaule Narbonnaise sous le Haut-Empire*. Centre de Recherches d'Histoire Ancienne 66. Paris: Centre National de la Recherche Scientifique.

Lauinger, S. 2014. Ein Töpferofen am Xantener Hafen, in: Liesen (ed.) 2014, 113-121.

Lauwerier, R. 1993. Twenty-eight bird briskets in a pot. Roman preserved food from Nijmegen. *Archaeofauna* 2, 15-19.

Le Bomin, J. 2020. Mediterranean pottery imports in western Gaul during the late Roman period (mid 3rd-early 7th c. AD). State of knowledge, in: M. Duggan, M. Jackson and S. Turner (eds), *Ceramics and Atlantic connections: late Roman and early medieval imported pottery on the Atlantic seaboard. Proceedings of an international symposium at Newcastle University, March 2014*. Roman and Late Antique Mediterranean Pottery 15, 39-54. Oxford: Archaeopress.

Lepot, A. and F. Vilvorder 2015. La céramique à dégraissant calcite sur le territoire des Tongres, in: M. Joly and J.-M. Séguier (eds), *Les céramiques non tournées en Gaule romaine dans leur contexte social, économique et culturel. Entre tradition et innovation*. Revue Archéologique du Centre de la France Supplément 55, 231-243. Tours: Fédération pour l'Édition de la Revue Archéologique du Centre de la France.

Liesen, B. 1994. *Töpfereischutt des 1. Jahrhunderts n. Chr. aus dem Bereich der Colonia Ulpia Traiana (Schnitt 76/20) (Xanten)*. Xantener Berichte 4. Cologne: Rheinland Verlag.

Liesen, B. 1999a. Spätantike bemalte Keramik aus Köln. *KölnJb* 32, 787-806.

Liesen, B. 1999b. Ausgewählte Fundgruppen aus dem Bereich des „Hauses am kleinen Hafentor“ auf der Insula 38 der Colonia Ulpia Traiana. Xantener Berichte 8, 9-54. Cologne: Rheinland Verlag.

Liesen, B. 2001. Kölner Kopien afrikanischer Amphoren. *KölnJb* 34, 481-484.

Liesen, B. 2002. Die Grabungen südlich und westlich des Kölner Doms III. Reliefverzierte Terra Sigillata. *KölnJb* 35, 409-435.

Liesen, B. 2004a. Römische Importkeramik in Köln – eine Bestandsaufnahme. *KölnJb* 37, 463-487.

Liesen, B. 2004b. Die römischen Funde aus den Ausgrabungen an der Breite Straße in Köln. *KölnJb* 37, 699-772.

Liesen, B. 2007. Ein Komplex römischer Keramik von der Leonhard-Tietz-Straße in Köln. *KölnJb* 40, 371-427.

Liesen, B. 2008. Soziale und wirtschaftliche Entwicklungstendenzen der Colonia Ulpia Traiana im Spiegel des Fundmaterials. Von den Anfängen bis zum Beginn der Spätantike, in: M. Müller, H.-J. Schalles and N. Zieling (eds), *Colonia Ulpia Traiana. Xanten und sein Umland in römischer Zeit*, 211-226. Mainz: Verlag Philipp von Zabern.

Liesen, B. (ed.) 2014. *Römische Keramik in Niedergermanien. Produktion – Handel – Gebrauch. Beiträge zur Tagung der Rei Cretariae Romanae Fautores 21.-26. September 2014, LVR-RömerMuseum im Archäologischen Park Xanten.* Xantener Berichte 27. Xanten: LVR-Archäologischer Park Xanten/LVR-RömerMuseum.

Liesen, B. 2016. Lowlands Ware 1 containers from Xanten/Colonia Ulpia Traiana, in: S. Biegert (ed.), *ReiCretActa* 44, 389-396. Bonn: Dr. Rudolf Habelt GmbH.

Liesen, B. 2018. Carrot amphorae production in Germania Inferior, in: S. Biegert (ed.) *ReiCretActa* 45, 219-227. Bonn: Dr. Rudolf Habelt GmbH.

Liesen, B. 2019. Fernhandel und regionaler Markt. Zu den römischen Amphoren aus Xanten, in: M. Mirschenz, R. Gerlach and J. Bemmann (eds), *Der Rhein als europäische Verkehrsachse III*. Bonner Beiträge zur Vor- und Frühgeschichtlichen Archäologie 22, 329-341. Bonn: Universität Bonn.

Liesen, B. 2023. Late Roman coarse ware from Xanten, in: B. Liesen (ed.), *Zwischen Töpfer und Verbraucher/Between potter and consumer. Internationales Kolloquium im LVR-RömerMuseum 27.-29. März 2019*. Xantener Berichte 41, 583-601. Oppenheim am Rhein: Nünnerich-Asmus Verlag.

Lindhagen. A. 2009. The transport amphoras Lamboglia 2 and Dressel 6A. A central Dalmatian origin? *JRA* 22, 83-108.

Loeschcke, S. 1909. Keramische Funde in Haltern. Ein Beitrag zur Geschichte der augusteischen Kultur in Deutschland. *Mitteilungen der Altertumskommission für Westfalen* 5, 101-322.

Loeschcke, S. 1942. Die römische und belgische Keramik aus Oberaden nach den Funden der Ausgrabungen von Albert Baum, in: Albrecht (ed.) 1942, 7-148.

Loopik, J. and W.K. Vos (eds) 2021. *Weerdkampen. Graven bij Valkenburg Z.H.* ADC Monografie 29. Amersfoort: ADC ArcheoProjecten.

Loridant, F. and X. Deru 2009. *Bavay: la nécropole gallo-romaine de «La Fache des Près Aulnoys»*. Revue du Nord Hors-Série Archéologie 13. Villeneuve d'Ascq: Librairie Archéologique.

Ludowici, W. 1927. *Katalog V. Stempel-Namen und Bilder römischer Töpfer, Legions-Ziegel-Stempel, Formen von Sigillata und anderen Gefässen aus meinen Ausgrabungen in Rheinzabern 1901-1914*. Jockgrim: Eigenverlag.

Mackensen, M. 2013. Terra sigillata aus Nord- und Zentraltunesien, in: M. Mackensen and F. Schimmer (eds), *Der römische Militärplatz Submuntorium/Burghöfe an der oberen Donau. Archäologische Untersuchungen im spätrömischen Kastell und Vicus 2001-2007*. Münchner Beiträge zur provinzialrömischen Archäologie 4, 347-359. Wiesbaden: Reichert Verlag.

Maniez, J. and E. Afonso-Lopes 2019. *Avesnes-lès-Bapaume (Pas-de-Calais). Route d'Albert. Rapport final d'opération*. SRA Hauts-de-France (unpublished). Arras: s.n.

Marimon Ribas, P. and S. Calzada Banos 2018. Las ánforas de vino galas en Xanten, in: J. Remesal Rodríguez (ed.), *Colonia Ulpia Traiana (Xanten) y el Mediterráneo. El comercio de alimentos*. Col·lecció Instrumenta 63. Union académique internationale. Corpus international des timbres amphoriques 26, 99-115. Barcelona: Universitat de Barcelona.

Marlière, E. 1998. Les amphores de Bavay, in: Baudoux *et al.* (eds) 1998, 49-90.

Martin-Arroyo Sánchez, D.J. 2018. Las ánforas orientales de Xanten, in: J. Remesal Rodríguez (ed.), *Colonia Ulpia Traiana (Xanten) y el Mediterráneo. El comercio de alimentos*. Col·lecció Instrumenta 63. Union académique internationale. Corpus international des timbres amphoriques 26, 59-78. Barcelona: Universitat de Barcelona.

Mathelart, P., A. Bocquet-Liénard and G. Fronteau 2018. L'artisanat de la céramique en Champagne du cadre géographique et géologique à l'implantation des zones de production, in: *SFECAG. Actes du congrès de Reims 2018*, 13-29. Marseille: SFECAG.

Mayer, D. 2016. Stempel auf Amphoren aus Köln. *KölnJb* 49, 309-366.

Mees, A.W. and M. Schönfelder 2014. *Joseph Déchelette (1862-1914) und die Entstehung einer deutsch-französischen Forschungstradition in der Archäologie*. Mainz: Verlag des Römisch-Germanischen Zentralmuseums.

Metzler, J. 1995. *Das treverische Oppidum auf dem Titelberg. Zur Kontinuität zwischen der spätkeltischen und der frührömischen Zeit in Nord-Gallien.* Dossiers d'Archeologie du Musee National d'Historie et d'Art 3. Luxembourg: Musée National d'Histoire et d'Art, Luxembourg.

Mittag, E. 1999. Untersuchungen zu sogenannten Halterner Kochtöpfen aus dem Bereich der Colonia Ulpia Traiana (Xanten). Xantener Berichte 8, 201-311. Cologne: Rheinland Verlag.

Morris, F.M. 2010. *North Sea and Channel connectivity during the late Iron Age and Roman period.* BARIntSer 2157. Oxford: Archaeopress.

Morris, F.M. 2015. Cross-North Sea contacts in the Roman period. *OxfJA* 34, 415-438.

Nicolay, J.A.W. 2014. *The splendour of power. Early medieval kingship and the use of gold and silver in the southern North Sea area (5th to 7th century AD).* Groningen Archaeological Studies 28. Groningen: Barkhuis.

Niemeijer, R.A.J. 2013. Die westlichen Wehranlagen des augusteischen Lagers auf dem Hunerberg in Nijmegen. Die Ausgrabungen der Radboud Universiteit 1987-1997. *KölnJb* 46, 35-74.

Niemeijer, R.A.J. 2014. Das Tafelgeschirr aus dem grossen augusteischen Lager auf dem Hunerberg in Nijmegen. Die Ausgrabungen der Radboud Universiteit 1987-1997. *KölnJb* 47, 7-40.

Niemeijer, R.A.J. 2015. Die Strassen des grossen augusteischen Lagers auf dem Hunerberg in Nijmegen. Die Ausgrabungen der Radboud Universiteit 1987-1997. *KölnJb* 48, 7-18.

Niemeijer, R.A.J. 2016. Die Innenbauten des grossen augusteischen Lagers auf dem Hunerberg in Nijmegen. Die Ausgrabungen der Radboud Universiteit 1987-1997. *KölnJb* 49, 7-39.

Niemeijer, R.A.J. 2017. Keramik aus den Befunden des grossen augusteischen Lagers auf dem Hunerberg in Nijmegen. *KölnJb* 50, 7-22.

Niemeijer, R.A.J. 2018. Buildings and building materials from the large Augustan camp on the Hunerberg in Nijmegen, in: C.S. Sommer and S. Matešić (eds), *Limes XXIII. Proceedings of the 23rd international congress of Roman frontier studies Ingolstadt 2015. Akten des 23. internationalen Limeskongresses in Ingolstadt 2015.* Beiträge zum Welterbe Limes 4, no. 1, 497-504. Mainz: Nünnerich-Asmus Verlag.

Niemeijer, R.A.J. and J. Thijssen 2014. The pottery kilns at Cuijk (North Brabant, the Netherlands), in: Liesen (ed.) 2014, 93-111.

Nieuwhof, A. 2011. Discontinuity in the northern-Netherlands coastal area at the end of the Roman period, in: T.A.S.M. Panhuysen (ed.), *Transformations in north-western Europe (AD 300-1000). Proceedings of the 60th Sachsensymposion 19.-23. September 2009 Maastricht.* Neue Studien zur Sachsenforschung 3, 55-66. Hannover: Niedersachsisches Landesmuseum.

Nieuwhof, A. 2013. Anglo-Saxon immigration or continuity? Ezinge and the coastal area of the northern Netherlands in the Migration period. *Journal of Archaeology in the Low Countries* 5, no. 1, 53-83.

Nieuwhof, A. (ed.) 2014. *En dan in hun geheel. De vondsten uit de opgravingen in de wierde Ezinge.* Jaarverslagen van de Vereniging voor Terpenonderzoek 96. Groningen: Vereniging voor Terpenonderzoek.

Nieuwhof, A. 2015. *Eight human skulls in a dung heap and more. Ritual practice in the terp region of the northern Netherlands, 600 BC-AD 300.* Groningen: Barkhuis.

Nieuwhof, A. 2020a. Luxury tableware? Terra sigillata in the coastal region of the northern Netherlands, in: A. Rubel and H.-U. Voß (eds), *Experiencing the frontier and the frontier of experience. Barbarian perspectives and Roman strategies to deal with new threats.* Roman Archaeology 76, 94-110. Oxford: Archaeopress.

Nieuwhof, A. 2020b. *Ezinge revisited. The ancient roots of a terp settlement. Volume I: Excavation – Environment and economy – Catalogue of plans and finds.* Groningen Archaeological Studies 37. Groningen: Barkhuis.

Nieuwhof, A. 2021. The Frisians and their pottery: social relations before and after the fourth century AD, in: J. Hines and N. IJssennagger-van der Pluijm (eds), *Frisians of the early Middle Ages.* Studies in Historical Archaeoethnology 10, 45-77. Woodbridge: Boydell & Brewer.

Nieuwhof, A. and F. Diederik 2023. Handgemaakt aardewerk in een veranderende wereld (2[e]-4[e] eeuw), in: J.A.W. Nicolay and R. van Eerden (eds), *Noord-Holland in het 1e millennium,* 332-442. Castricum: provincie Noord-Holland.

Nieuwhof, A. and T.B. Volkers 2015. Luxe servies? Terra sigillata ten noorden van de limes. *Archeobrief* 19, 26-32.

Nieuwhof, A., M. Bakker, E. Knol, G. de Langen, J.A.W. Nicolay, D. Postma, M. Schepers, T.W. Varwijk and P.C. Vos 2019. Adapting to the sea: human habitation in the coastal area of the northern Netherlands before medieval dike building. *Ocean & Coastal Management* 173, 77-89.

Nissen, H. 1895. Zur Geschichte des römischen Köln, in: *Colonia Agrippinensis. Festschrift der XLIII. Versammlung deutscher Philologen und Schulmänner in Köln am 25. September 1895 gewidmet vom Verein von Alterthumsfreunden im Rheinlande.* BJb XCVIII, 145-171. Bonn: Universitäts-Buchdruckerei von Carl Georgi.

Nösler, D. 2013. Rhein-Weser-germanische Keramik als Import im Elbe-Weser-Dreieck?, in: G. Rasbach (ed.), *Westgermanische Bodenfunde. Akten des Kolloquiums anlässlich des 100. Geburtstages von Rafael von Uslar am 5. und 6. Dezember 2008.* Kolloquien zur Vor- und Frühgeschichte 18, 171-190. Bonn: Dr. Rudolf Habelt GmbH.

Oelmann, F. 1914. *Die Keramik des Kastells Niederbieber.* Materialien zur Römisch-Germanischen Keramik 1. Frankfurt: Joseph Baer & Co.

Oenbrink, W. 1998. *Die Kölner Jagdbecher im römischen Rheinland. Form und Dekor. Funktion und Handelsgeschichte einer Kölner Geschirrproduktion im 2. Jahrhundert n. Chr. KölnJb* 31, 71-252.

Orton, C.R., P.A. Tyers and A. Vince 1993. *Pottery in archaeology*. Cambridge: Cambridge University Press.

Oswald, F. and T.D. Pryce 1920. *An introduction to the study of terra sigillata treated from a chronological standpoint*. London: Longmans, Green and Co.

Otte, R. 2023. Die Feinkeramik der Legionsziegelei in Xanten, in: B. Liesen (ed.), *Zwischen Töpfer und Verbraucher/Between potter and consumer. Internationales Kolloquium im LVR-RömerMuseum 27.-29. März 2019*. Xantener Berichte 41, 387-482. Oppenheim am Rhein: Nünnerich-Asmus Verlag.

Otten, T. and S. Ristow 2008. Xanten in der spätantike, in: M. Müller, H.-J. Schalles and N. Zieling (eds), *Colonia Ulpia Traiana. Xanten und sein Umland in römischer Zeit*, 549-582. Mainz: Verlag Philipp von Zabern.

Oudemans, T.F.M. 2014. Melk en pap uit Maassluis. Chemische karakterisering van organische residuen uit aardewerk uit Maassluis Weverskade, in: A. van Benthem and M. van Dinter (eds), *Weverskade 60, gemeente Maassluis. Een inventariserend veldonderzoek in de vorm van proefsleuven gevolgd door een archeologische opgraving*. ADC Rapport 2742, 89-102. Amersfoort: ADC ArcheoProjecten.

Päffgen, B. 1992. *Die Ausgrabungen in St. Severin zu Köln. Teil 3. Katalog der Befunde und Funde, Tafeln, Beilagen*. Kölner Forschungen 5, no. 3. Mainz: Verlag Philipp von Zabern.

Panella, C. 1976. Per uno studio delle anfore di Pompei. *Studi Miscellanei* 22, 151-165.

Pascual Guasch, R. 1977. Las ánforas de la Layetania, in: *Méthodes classiques et méthodes formelles dans l'étude des amphores. Actes du colloque de Rome, 27-29 mai 1974*, 47-96. Publications de l'École Française de Rome 32. Rome: École Française de Rome.

Péré-Noguès, S. (ed.) 2014. *Joseph Déchelette un précurseur de l'archéologie européenne*. Arles: Actes Sud.

Perrin, R. 2011. *A research strategy and updated agenda for the study of Roman pottery in Britain*. Study Group for Roman Pottery Occasional Paper 1. s.l.: The Study Group for Roman Pottery.

Peters, J. 2003. *Housesteads ware on Hadrian's Wall*. Unpublished MA thesis, Universiteit van Amsterdam.

Pfahl, S.F. 2018. *Namenstempel auf römischen Reibschüsseln (*mortaria*) aus Deutschland*. Augsburger Beiträge zur Archäologie 8. Augsburg: Wißner-Verlag.

Pirling, R. 1974. *Das römisch-fränkische Gräberfeld von Krefeld-Gellep 1960-63*. Germanische Denkmäler der Völkerwanderungszeit Serie B, die fränkischen Altertümer des Rheinlandes 2. Berlin: Verlag Gebr. Mann.

Pirling, R. and M. Siepen 2006. *Die Funde aus den römischen Gräbern von Krefeld-Gellep*. Germanische Denkmäler der Völkerwanderungszeit Serie B, die fränkischen Altertümer des Rheinlandes 20. Stuttgart: Franz Steiner Verlag.

Polak, M. 1995. *De gestempelde Zuidgallische terra sigillata uit Vechten*. Unpublished PhD thesis, Katholieke Universiteit Nijmegen.

Polak, M. 2000. *South Gaulish terra sigillata with potters' stamps from Vechten*. ReiCretActa Supplementum 9. Nijmegen: Katholieke Universiteit Nijmegen, Afdeling Provinciaal-Romeinse Archeologie.

Polak, M. 2009. Aarden vaatwerk, in: M. Polak and T. de Groot (eds), *Vondsten langs de limes*. Rapportage Archeologische Monumentenzorg 167, 8-18. Amersfoort: Rijksdienst voor Archeologie, Cultuurlandschap en Monumenten.

Polak, M. 2014. Inleiding, in: R.P.J. Kloosterman, M. Polak and M.J.M. Zandstra, *Opgravingen op het terrein van het voormalige Canisiuscollege in Nijmegen, 1987-1997. Vondsten uit castra en canabae* I, 13-38. Auxiliaria 14. Nijmegen: Auxilia.

Polak, M. and L. Kooistra 2013. A sustainable frontier? The establishment of the Roman frontier in the Rhine delta. Part 1: from the end of the Iron Age to the death of Tiberius (c. 50 BC-AD 37). *JbRGZM* 60, 355-457.

Polak, M., R.P.J. Kloosterman and R.A.J. Niemeijer 2004. *Alphen aan den Rijn – Albaniana 2001-2002. Opgravingen tussen de Castellumstraat het Omloopkanaal en de Oude Rijn*. Libelli Noviomagenses 7. Nijmegen: Katholieke Universiteit Nijmegen, Afdeling Provinciaal-Romeinse Archeologie.

Pyl, M. 1993. Céramique non tournée protohistorique du Languedoc oriental. *Lattara* 6, 292-306.

Reigersman-van Lidth de Jeude, W.F. 2016. Pots for past people. Nine Roman cemeteries in the Dutch eastern river area, in: S. Biegert (ed.), *ReiCretActa* 44, 407-416. Bonn: Dr. Rudolf Habelt GmbH.

Reigersman-van Lidth de Jeude, W.F. 2017. Aardewerk, in: Van der Feijst *et al.* 2017, 41-45, 89, 94-96, 100-104.

Reigersman-van Lidth de Jeude, W.F. 2023. Aardewerk en keramische objecten, in: Kenemans and Vossen (eds) 2023, 235-265.

Reigersman-van Lidth de Jeude, W.F. in press. Buried with the dead. Grave goods from twelve Roman cemeteries in the Dutch eastern river area, in: H. van Enckevort, M. Driessen, E. Graafstal, T. Hazenberg, T. Ivleva and C. van Driel-Murray (eds), *Strategy and structures along the Roman frontier. Proceedings of the 25th Limescongress in Nijmegen*. Archeologische Berichten Nijmegen 10. Leiden: Sidestone Press.

Reigersman-van Lidth de Jeude, W.F. and T. Vanderhoeven 2010. Aardewerk, in: Veldman and Blom (eds) 2010, 101-147.

Reigersman-van Lidth de Jeude, W.F. and T. Vanderhoeven 2011. Aardewerk uit de nederzetting en het grafveld, in: Veldman (ed.) 2011, 97-131.

Remesal Rodríguez, J. 2018. Las ánforas olearias béticas Dressel 20, in: J. Remesal Rodríguez (ed.), *Colonia Ulpia Traiana (Xanten) y el Mediterráneo. El comercio de alimentos*. Col·lecció Instrumenta 63. Union académique internationale. Corpus international des timbres amphoriques 26, 275-419. Barcelona: Universitat de Barcelona.

Reuter, M. 2008. Wirtschaftsstandort Colonia Ulpia Traiana – Handel und Handwerk in der CUT, in: M. Müller, H.-J. Schalles and N. Zieling (eds), *Colonia Ulpia Traiana. Xanten und sein Umland in römischer Zeit*, 471-493. Mainz: Verlag Philipp von Zabern.

Reuvens, C.J.C., C. Leemans and L.J.F. Janssen 1845. *Romeinsche, Germaansche of Gallische oudheden. Gevonden in Nederland, België en een gedeelte der aangrenzende landen*. Leiden: H.W. Hazenberg & Co.

Revilla Calvo, V. 2018. Las ánforas norteafricanas de Xanten, in: J. Remesal Rodríguez (ed.), *Colonia Ulpia Traiana (Xanten) y el Mediterráneo. El comercio de alimentos*. Col·lecció Instrumenta 63. Union académique internationale. Corpus international des timbres amphoriques 26, 171-179. Barcelona: Universitat de Barcelona.

Rigby, V. and I. Freestone 1986. The petrology of the earliest identified Central-Gaulish imports. *JRS* 1, 6-21.

Rind, M. 2015. *Die römische Villa als Indikator provinzialer Wirtschafts- und Gesellschaftsstrukturen*. Archaeopress Roman Archaeology 10. Oxford: Archaeopress.

Ritterling, E. 1913. *Das frührömische Lager bei Hofheim im Taunus*. Annalen des Vereins für Nassauische Altertumskunde und Geschichtsforschung 40. Wiesbaden: Verein für Nassauische Altertumskunde und Geschichtsforschung.

Rose, H. 2006. *Die römischen Terrakottamasken in den Nordwestprovinzen. Herkunft – Herstellung – Verbreitung – Funktion*. Monumenta Artis Romanae 37. Wiesbaden: Reichert Verlag.

Rose, H. 2023. Terrakottamasken aus der Colonia Ulpia Traiana – eine Gattung mit vielen Gesichtern, in: B. Liesen (ed.), *Zwischen Töpfer und Verbraucher/Between potter and consumer. Internationales Kolloquium im LVR-RömerMuseum 27.-29. März 2019*. Xantener Berichte 41, 93-135. Oppenheim am Rhein: Nünnerich-Asmus Verlag.

Rosenplänter, P. 2010. *Der Siedlungs- und Bestattungsplatz Nortmoorer Hammrich. Untersuchungen zur Besiedlungsgeschichte des Landkreises Leer (Ostfriesland). Römische Kaiserzeit bis Frühmittelalter*. Unpublished PhD thesis, Georg-August-Universität Göttingen.

Roth-Rubi, K. 1979. *Untersuchungen an den Krügen von Avenches*. ReiCretActa Supplementum 3. Augst/Kaiseraugst: Rei Cretariæ Romanæ Fautores.

Roth-Rubi, K. 2006. *Dangstetten III. Das Tafelgeschirr aus dem Militärlager von Dangstetten*. FuBerBadWürt 103. Stuttgart: Konrad Theiss Verlag.

Roymans, N.G.A.M. 1996. The sword or the plough. Regional dynamics in the Romanisation of Belgic Gaul and the Rhineland area, in: N.G.A.M. Roymans (ed.), *From the sword to the plough. Three studies on the earliest Romanisation of northern Gaul*. Amsterdam Archaeological Studies 1, 9-126. Amsterdam: Amsterdam University Press.

Roymans, N.G.A.M. 2004. *Ethnic identity and imperial power. The Batavians in the early Roman Empire*. Amsterdam Archaeological Studies 10. Amsterdam: Amsterdam University Press.

Roymans, N.G.A.M. 2017. Gold, Germanic *foederati* and the end of imperial power in the late Roman north, in: N.G.A.M. Roymans, S. Heeren and W. de Clercq (eds), *Social dynamics in the northwest frontiers of the late Roman Empire. Beyond decline or transformation*. Amsterdam Archaeological Studies 26, 57-80, Amsterdam: Amsterdam University Press.

Roymans, N.G.A.M. 2019. Conquest, mass violence and ethnic stereotyping. Investigating Caesar's actions in the Germanic frontier zone. *JRA* 32, 439-458.

Roymans, N.G.A.M. 2020. Muntslag in crisistijd. De goudstaters van de Eburonen en Caesars verovering van de Nederrijn/Maasregio, in: V.T. van Vilsteren, J.R. Beuker, P.W. van den Broeke and E.M. Theunissen (eds), *Overpeinzingen op een vuilnisbelt. Liber amicorum aangeboden aan Wijnand van der Sanden ter gelegenheid van zijn afscheid als conservator bij het Drents Museum*, 110-121. Groningen: Barkhuis.

Roymans, N.G.A.M. and L.P. Verniers 2010. Glass Latène bracelets in the lower Rhine region. Typology, chronology and social interpretation. *Germania* 88, 195-219.

Rudnick, B. 2023. Die figürlichen Terrakotten aus Schnitt 2017/15 vor dem „Molen-Tor" der Colonia Ulpia Traiana, Xanten, in: B. Liesen (ed.), *Zwischen Töpfer und Verbraucher/Between potter and consumer. Internationales Kolloquium im LVR-RömerMuseum 27.-29. März 2019*. Xantener Berichte 41, 1-78. Oppenheim am Rhein: Nünnerich-Asmus Verlag.

Rudnick, B. 2024. Tricensimae, Xanten: die spätantike Stadtbefestigung auf den Insulae 10-12, 17-19 und 24-26 der Colonia Ulpia Traiana. Eine Bestandsaufnahme. Xantener Berichte 46. Oppenheim am Rhein: Nünnerich-Asmus Verlag.

Schäfer, A., M. Dodt and R. Schwarz 2023. Ein spätantiker Töpferofen in der südlichen römischen Vorstadt von Köln, in: B. Liesen (ed.), *Zwischen Töpfer und Verbraucher/Between potter and consumer. Internationales Kolloquium im LVR-RömerMuseum 27.-29. März 2019*. Xantener Berichte 41, 519-536. Oppenheim am Rhein: Nünnerich-Asmus Verlag.

Schmid, P. 1958. Ein Gefäßtyp der frühen Kaiserzeit von der Feddersen Wierde bei Bremerhaven. *Die Kunde* N.F. 9, 67-71.

Schmid, P. 1965. Die Keramik des 1. bis 3. Jahrhunderts nach Chr. im Küstengebiet der südlichen Nordsee. *Probleme der Küstenforschung* 8, 9-46.

Schmid, P. 1981. Chauken, in: H. Beck, D. Geuenich and H. Steuer (eds), *Reallexikon der germanischen Altertumskunde*, 398-413. Berlin: De Gruyter.

Schmid, P. 2006: *Die Keramikfunde der Grabung Feddersen Wierde (1. Jh. v. bis bis 5. Jh. n. Chr.)*. Feddersen Wierde 5. Probleme der Küstenforschung 29. Oldenburg: Isensee.

Schmitz, D. 2006. Ein Keramikkomplex der Mitte des 2. Jahrhunderts n. Chr. aus der Colonia Ulpia Traiana (Insula 20). Xantener Berichte 14, 131-188. Mainz: Verlag Philipp von Zabern.

Schmitz, S.D. 2014. Scheldt-Valley Amphoren aus der *Colonia Ulpia Traiana*, in: Liesen (ed.) 2014, 317-363.

Schotten, J. 1991. *Germanen in Gennep. 5de-eeuws handgevormd aardewerk uit een Germaanse immigrantennederzetting*. Unpublished MA thesis, Universiteit van Amsterdam.

Selke, V. 2022. *Der Hafen der Colonia Ulpia Traiana. Die Befunde*. Xantener Berichte 38. Oppenheim am Rhein: Nünnerich-Asmus Verlag.

Sieler, M. 2014. Engobierte Backplatten aus Xanten, in: Liesen (ed.) 2014, 123-135.

Sier, M.M. and C.W. Koot (eds) 2001. *Archeologie in de Betuweroute: Kesteren-De Woerd. Bewoningssporen uit de IJzertijd en de Romeinse tijd*. Rapportage Archeologische Monumentenzorg 82. Amersfoort: Rijksdienst voor het Oudheidkundig Bodemonderzoek.

Smetius, J. and J. Smetius 1678. *Antiquitates Neomagenses. Sive notitia rarissimarum rerum antiquarum, quas in veteri Batavorum Oppido studiose compavit. In qua annuli, gemmæ, amuleta, claves, styli, tintinnabula, fibulæ, lampades, aræ, marmora, mensuræ, pondera, statuæ, sigilla, lagenæ, vasa, atque alia antiquorum monumenta explicantur: & varia Romanorum numismata hactenus non visa illustrantur*. Nijmegen: Ex Typographeio Regneri Smetii.

Spickermann, W. 2018. Merkur und Nehalennia – Götter der Kaufleute und Händler, in: C. Eger (ed.), *Warenwege – Warenflüsse. Handel, Logistik und Transport am römischen Niederrhein*. Xantener Berichte 32, 599-614. Mainz: Verlag Philipp von Zabern.

Stead, I.M. and V. Rigby 1989. *Verulamium. The King Harry Lane site*. English Heritage Archaeological Report 12. London: English Heritage.

Steiner, P. 1911. *Xanten. Sammlung des niederrheinischen Altertums-Vereins*. Kataloge West- und Süddeutscher Altertumssammlungen 1. Frankfurt am Main: Baer.

Stoffels, E. 2006. *Handgevormd aardewerk uit de Augusteïsche castra op de Hunerberg in Nijmegen*. Unpublished MA thesis, Universiteit van Amsterdam.

Stoffels, E. 2009. Native service: 'Batavian' pottery in 'Roman' military context, in: M. Driessen, S. Heeren, J. Hendriks, F. Kemmers and R. Visser (eds), *TRAC 2008. Proceedings of the eighteenth annual Theoretical Roman Archaeology Conference (University of Amsterdam 4-6 March 2008)*, 143-155. Oxford: Oxbow Books.

Stoffels, E. 2014. Two pottery kilns at the Kops Plateau, in: Liesen (ed.) 2014, 15-35.

Stoop-Greijer, S.H. 2012. Handgevormd aardewerk, in: Zandstra and Polak, 127-138.

Stuart, P.J.J. 1963. *Gewoon aardewerk uit de Romeinse legerplaats en de bijbehorende grafvelden te Nijmegen*. OudhMeded Jaargang XLIII Supplement 1962. PhD thesis, Universiteit Leiden. Leiden: Brill.

Stuart, P.J.J. 1977a. *Gewoon aardewerk uit de Romeinse legerplaats en de bijbehorende grafvelden te Nijmegen*. Beschrijving van de Verzamelingen in het Rijksmuseum G.M. Kam te Nijmegen 6. 's-Gravenhage: Ministerie van Cultuur, Recreatie en Maatschappelijk Werk.

Stuart, P.J.J. 1977b. *Een Romeins grafveld uit de eerste eeuw te Nijmegen. Onversierde terra sigillata en gewoon aardewerk*. Beschrijvingen van de Verzamelingen in het Rijksmuseum G.M. Kam te Nijmegen 8. Nijmegen: Ministerie van Cultuur.

Stuart, P.J.J. and J.E.A.Th. Bogaers 2001. *Nehalennia, römische Steindenkmaler aus der Oosterschelde bei Colijnsplaat*. Collections of the National Museum of Antiquities at Leiden 11. Leiden: Rijksmuseum van Oudheden.

Symonds, M.F.A. and D.J.P. Mason (eds) 2009. *Frontiers of knowledge: a research framework for Hadrian's Wall, part of the frontiers of the Roman Empire, World Heritage Site I. Resource Assessment*. Durham: Durham County Council.

Taayke, E. 1996. *Die einheimische Keramik der nördlichen Niederlande, 600 v.Chr. bis 300 n.Chr*. Unpublished PhD thesis, Rijksuniversiteit Groningen.

Taayke, E. 2002. Handmade pottery from a Roman period settlement at Wijk bij Duurstede-De Horden. *BerOudhBod* 45, 189-218.

Taayke, E. 2009a. Handgemaakt aardewerk, in: C.M.W. den Hartog, *Sportpark Terweide 2. LR41-42: archeologisch onderzoek Sportpark Terweide*. Basisrapportage Archeologie 18, 53-59. Utrecht: Team Erfgoed gemeente Utrecht.

Taayke, E. 2009b. Handgevormd aardewerk, in: A. Luksen-IJtsma, *Oudenrijnseweg. Archeologisch onderzoek van een inheems-Romeinse nederzetting uit de eerste eeuw na Chr. en een vlasrootcomplex uit de twaalfde eeuw na Chr. in De Meern, gemeente Utrecht*. Basisrapportage Archeologie 25, 47-51. Utrecht: Team Erfgoed gemeente Utrecht.

Taayke, E. 2010a. Het handgevormd aardewerk uit de inheemse nederzetting en uit de vicus, in: M. Langeveld, A. Luksen-IJtsma and P. Weterings, *Een goede buur? LR46 en LR49: definitief archeologisch onderzoek naar de vicus, grafvelden, infrastructuur en een inheemse nederzetting in de omgeving van het Romeinse castellum in De Meern, deelgebied "De Woerd" (gemeente Utrecht)*.

Basisrapportage Archeologie 19, 227-235. Utrecht: Team Erfgoed gemeente Utrecht.

Taayke, E. 2010b. Aardewerk, in: J. Loopik (ed.), *Een Aa-typische begeleiding in Gieten.* ADC Rapport 2300, 25-27. Amersfoort: ADC ArcheoProjecten.

Taayke, E. 2013. Rhein-Weser-germanische Keramik in den Niederlanden im 1. bis 5. Jahrhundert, in: G. Rasbach (ed.), *Westgermanische Bodenfunde. Akten des Kolloquiums anlässlich des 100. Geburtstages von Rafael von Uslar am 5. und 6. Dezember 2008.* Kolloquien zur Vor- und Frühgeschichte 18, 191-198. Bonn: Dr. Rudolf Habelt GmbH.

Taayke, E. 2016. Het handgemaakt aardewerk, in: C.W.M. den Hartog, *Sportpark Terweide 3. Definitief Archeologisch Onderzoek LR75. Hogeweide/Verlengde Vleutenseweg in Utrecht.* Basisrapportage Archeologie 84, 57-67. Utrecht: Erfgoed gemeente Utrecht.

Taayke, E. 2017. Handgemaakt aardewerk, in: Den Hartog 2017, 61-67.

Taayke, E. 2020a. Handmade pottery from the Roman period, in: A. Nieuwhof (ed.), *The excavations at Wijnaldum. Volume 2: handmade and wheel-thrown pottery of the first millennium AD.* Groningen Archaeological Studies 38, 47-68. Groningen: Barkhuis.

Taayke, E. 2020b. Handmade pottery from the Migration period and the Merovingian period, in: A. Nieuwhof (ed.), *The excavations at Wijnaldum. Volume 2: handmade and wheel-thrown pottery of the first millennium AD.* Groningen Archaeological Studies 38, 69-98. Groningen: Barkhuis.

Taayke, E. 2023. Vreemd én vertrouwd: de Tritsum-variant van Hessens-Schortens aardewerk, in: A. Nieuwhof and A. Buursma (eds), *Van Drenthe tot aan 't Wad. Over landschap, archeologie en geschiedenis van noord-Nederland. Essays ter ere van Egge Knol.* Jaarverslagen van de Vereniging voor Terpenonderzoek 104, 115-123. Groningen: Vereniging voor Terpenonderzoek.

Taayke E. in prep. *Handgemaakt aardewerk in noord-Nederland, 800 v.C.-600 AD.*

Taayke, E., J.H. Looijenga, O.H. Harsema and H.R. Reinders (eds) 2003. *Essays on the early Franks.* Groningen Archaeological Studies 1. Groningen: Barkhuis.

Taayke, E., C. Peen, M. van der Harst-van Domburg and W.K. Vos 2012. *Ede vol erven. Germaanse bewoning op de rand van een wereldrijk (500 voor Chr. tot 500 na Chr.).* Leiden: Hazenberg Archeologie.

Thüry, G.E. 2017. Ein Fund von Rhônekeramik aus Xanten, in: M. Müller (ed.), *Grabung – Forschung – Präsentation.* Xantener Berichte 30, 155-167. Darmstadt: Verlag Philipp von Zabern.

Timby, J.R. 1985. Amphorae, in: H.R. Hurst, *Kingsholm. Excavations at Kingsholm Close and other sites with a discussion of the archaeology of the area.* Gloucester Archaeological Reports 1, 72-76. Gloucester: Gloucester Archaeological Publications.

Tuijn, W. 1998. Het geheim van de kurkurn. *Westerheem* 47, 236-237.

Tyers, P.A. 2001. Camulodunum type 262. Central Gaulish coarse wares in Iron Age Britain, in: M. Tuffreau-Libre and A. Jacques (eds), *La céramique en Gaule et Bretagne romaines. Commerce, contacts et romanisation.* Nord-Ouest Archéologie 12, 87-106. Berck-sur-Mer: Centre de Recherches Archéologiques et de Diffusion Culturelle.

Ulbert, G. 1977. Die römischen Funde von Bentumersiel. *Probleme der Küstenforschung im südlichen Nordseegebiet* 12, 33-65.

Unverzagt, W. 1916. *Die Keramik des Kastells Alzei.* Materialien zur Römisch-Germanischen Keramik 2. Frankfurt am Main: Joseph Baer & Co.

Van Benthem, A. (ed.) 2020. *Terug in de tijd. Een opgraving in het historische centrum van Zaltbommel.* ADC Rapport 4999. Amersfoort: ADC ArcheoProjecten.

Van Bergen, A., A. Janssen and W. Tuijn 2008. *Verslag van de verzamelde gegevens en vondsten van de Romeinse vindplaats nabij de boerderij "De Uiversnest" te Deest, gemeente Druten (Gld.).* Nijmegen: AWN Afdeling Nijmegen en Omstreken.

Van de Zande, D. 2023. Nodes and networks. Military and civilian trade and transport in the Roman Dutch southwest delta, in: A. Tibbs and P.B. Campbell (eds), *Rivers and waterways in the Roman world. Empire of water,* 146-161. London: Routledge.

Van den Berg, J.J.H. 2012. Rare and exotic amphorae in north-west Europe: finds from the Roman fort on the Kops Plateau, Nijmegen. *JRomPotSt* 15, 215-235.

Van den Berg, J.J.H. 2014. Amphora stamps from Fectio (Vechten, NL), in: J.M. Blázquez Martínez and J. Remesal Rodríguez (eds), *Estudios sobre el Monte Testaccio (Roma) 6.* Col·lecció Instrumenta 47, 683-724. Barcelona: Universitat de Barcelona.

Van den Berg, J.J.H. 2015. An amphora on a river barge: a revised dating of Druten 1, Netherlands. *IntJNautA* 44, no. 2, 446-450.

Van den Berg, J.J.H. 2017a. A few north-African amphorae from 1st century Nijmegen, in: Carreras and Van den Berg 2017a, 355-380.

Van den Berg, J.J.H. 2017b. The early Roman Gallo-Belgic regional 'amphorae', in: Carreras and Van den Berg 2017a, 151-160.

Van den Berg, J.J.H. 2017c. Early Roman Rhineland amphorae on the Kops Plateau, in: Carreras and Van den Berg 2017a, 161-184.

Van den Berg, J.J.H. 2019. De amforen, in: C.W. Koot (ed.), *Een blik in de canabae. Een opgraving aan de Kopseweg (tussen 2-7) te Nijmegen.* Archeologische Berichten Nijmegen – Rapport 291, 68-72. Nijmegen: gemeente Nijmegen, Bureau Leefomgevingskwaliteit, Archeologie.

Van den Berg, J.J.H. 2021. Romeinse wijnamfoor. De eerste wijndrinkers van Zeeland, in: G. van Keken and V. Frenks (eds), *Van Oxhoofd tot Kattekop. Geschiedenis van de Zeeuwse wijnhandel*, 8-13. Middelburg: Paard van Troje.

Van den Berg, J.J.H. and K.-J. Kerckhaert 2018. *Romeinse bewoning in Smokkelhoek. Een archeologische veldkartering door de AWN te Biezelinge (gem. Kapelle) in 2006-2008*. Middelburg: Stichting Cultureel Erfgoed Zeeland.

Van den Berg, J.J.H., M. Polak and P.G. Alders 2012. *Oppervlaktevondsten van Vechten-Fectio. De veldkartering van 2009-2010*. Auxiliaria 12. Nijmegen: Auxilia.

Van den Berg, J.J.H., H. González Cesteros and R.A.J. Niemeijer 2017. Early Augustan amphorae from Nijmegen-Hunerberg (19-16/12 BC). New evidence from selected contexts, in: Carreras and Van den Berg 2017a, 345-354.

Van den Broeke, P.W. 1986. Zeezout: een schakel tussen west- en zuid-Nederland in de IJzertijd en de Romeinse tijd, in: M.C. van Trierum and H.E. Henkes (eds), *A contribution to prehistoric, Roman and medieval archaeology*. Rotterdam Papers 5, 91-114. Rotterdam: Bureau Oudheidkundig Onderzoek van Gemeentewerken Rotterdam.

Van den Broeke, P.W. 1987. Oss-Ussen: het handgemaakte aardewerk, in: W.A.B. van der Sanden and P.W. van den Broeke (eds), *Getekend zand. Tien jaar archeologisch onderzoek in Oss-Ussen*. Bijdragen tot de Studie van het Brabantse Heem 31, 101-119. Waalre: Stichting Brabants Heem.

Van den Broeke, P.W. 1996. Southern sea salt in the Low Countries; a reconnaissance into the land of the Morini, in: M. Lodewijckx (ed.), *Archaeological and historical aspects of west-European societies. Album amicorum André Van Doorselaer*. ActaALovMono 8, 193-205. Leuven: Leuven University Press.

Van den Broeke, P.W. 2012. *Het handgevormde aardewerk uit de IJzertijd en de Romeinse tijd van Oss-Ussen. Studies naar typochronologie, technologie en herkomst*. PhD thesis, Universiteit Leiden, Leiden: Sidestone Press.

Van den Broeke, P.W. 2014. Het handgevormde aardewerk uit de prehistorie en de Romeinse tijd: een verkenning, in: H. van Enckevort (ed.), *Odyssee op het Kops Plateau 2. Aardewerk en fibulae uit Nijmegen-Oost*. Archeologische Berichten Nijmegen – Rapport 47, 11-79. Nijmegen: Bureau Archeologie Monumenten gemeente Nijmegen.

Van den Broeke, P.W. 2018. Pierenpaté? Fries aardewerk ten zuiden van de Nederrijn; in: A. Nieuwhof, E. Knol and J. Schokker (eds), *Fragmenten uit de rijke wereld van de archeologie. Opgedragen aan Ernst Taayke bij zijn afscheid als beheerder van het Noordelijk Archeologisch Depot in Nuis*. Jaarverslagen van de Vereniging voor Terpenonderzoek 99, 77-87. Groningen: Vereniging voor Terpenonderzoek.

Van den Broeke, P.W. 2020. Handgevormd aardewerk uit de IJzertijd en de Romeinse tijd van de cultusplaats te Empel, in: M.T.C. Hendriksen, E.H.L.D. Norde and N. de Vries (eds), *Metaaltijden 7. Bijdragen in de studie van de Metaaltijden*, 135-160. Leiden: Sidestone Press.

Van den Broeke, P.W., L. Kubiak-Martens, I. Joosten, L. Megens and O. Brinkkemper 2021, Giftige schoonheid. Een cosmetica-attribuut met loodwit uit een inheems-Romeins grafveld in Nijmegen-Noord, in: P.W. van den Broeke, R.C.A. Geerts, S. Hoss and R.A. Houkes (eds), *Nieuwe inzichten in archeologisch materiaal*. ArtefActueel 1, 7-18. Zwolle: SPA Uitgevers.

Van der Feijst, L.M.B. (ed.) 2019. *Op opgeworpen gronden. Van terpen, turfwinning en een bruinvis uit de Romeinse tijd. Archeologische onderzoek Trade Parc Westland Mars, zone 2*. ADC Rapport 4885. Amersfoort: ADC ArcheoProjecten.

Van der Feijst, L.M.B. and R.C.A. Geerts 2021. Roman cemeteries in the Dutch eastern river area, in: C. Agricola and E. Deschler-Erb (eds), *Memento mori. Aktuelle Forschungen zu Bestattungssitten im Rheinland*. Kölner Studien zur Archäologie der Römischen Provinzen – Digital Band 1, 10-23. Cologne: Universität zu Köln.

Van der Feijst, L.M.B. and J. Loopik (eds) 2020. *Odijk, Vinkenburgweg, gemeente Bunnik. Sporen van een langdurig gebruikt grafveld uit de Romeinse tijd en vroege middeleeuwen en hofstede Vinkenburg uit de late middeleeuwen*. ADC Rapport 5055. Amersfoort: ADC ArcheoProjecten.

Van der Feijst, L.M.B. and H.A.P. Veldman (eds) 2018. *Graven in het verleden van Valburg. Een midden-Romeins grafveld en bewoningssporen uit de laat-Romeinse tijd te Molenzicht*. ADC Rapport 2519. Amersfoort: ADC ArcheoProjecten.

Van der Feijst, L.M.B., E. Blom and J. van der Leije (eds) in press. *Een ongekend rijke dood. Het Romeinse grafveld aan de Baalsestraat te Bemmel*. ADC Rapport. Amersfoort: ADC ArcheoProjecten/Leiden: Archol.

Van der Feijst, L.M.B., L.P. Verniers and E. Blom (eds) 2017. *De grafkamer van Huissen. Opgravingen in het kader van nieuwbouwlocatie Loovelden*. ADC Monografie 23. Amersfoort: ADC ArcheoProjecten.

Van der Linden, E. 2023. South, Central and East Gaulish terra sigillata, in: H.A. Hiddink, *The Roman villa at Voerendaal/Ten Hove. Excavations of a late Iron Age enclosure, a Roman villa complex, a late Roman/early medieval settlement and burials. Part III/A specialist analyses*. Nederlandse Oudheden 20, 489-507. Amersfoort: Rijksdienst voor het Cultureel Erfgoed.

Van der Velde, H.M. (ed.) 2007. *Germanen, Franken en Saksen in Salland. Archeologisch en landschappelijk onderzoek naar de geschiedenis van het landschap en nederzettingsresten uit de Romeinse tijd en vroege middeleeuwen in centraal Salland*. ADC Monografie 1. ADC-Rapport 675. Amersfoort: ADC ArcheoProjecten.

Van der Velde, H.M. (ed.) 2008. *Cananefaten en Friezen aan de monding van de Rijn. Tien jaar archeologisch onderzoek op de Zanderij-Westerbaan te Katwijk (1996-2006).* ADC Monografie 5. Amersfoort: ADC ArcheoProjecten.

Van der Velde, H.M., S. Ostkamp, H.A.P. Veldman and S. Wyns (eds) 2009. *Venlo aan de Maas, van vicus tot stad. Sporen van een Romeinse nederzetting en stadsontwikkeling uit de middeleeuwen en Nieuwe Tijd in het plangebied Maasboulevard.* ADC Monografie 7. Amersfoort: ADC ArcheoProjecten.

Van der Werff, J.H. 1984. Roman amphoras at Nijmegen – a preliminary report. *BerOudhBod* 34, 347-387.

Van der Werff, J.H., H. Thoen and R. van Dierendonck 1997. Amphorae production in the lower Scheldt valley (Belgium)? The Valkenburg-Marktveld evidence. *ReiCretActa 35*, 63-71.

Van Diepen, L. and R.A.J. Niemeijer 2011. Die Terra Sigillata aus *Forum Hadriani* – Arentsburg. Die Funde der Grabung 2005, in: B. Liesen (ed.), *Terra Sigillata in den germanischen Provinzen. Kolloquium Xanten, 13.-14. November 2008.* Xantener Berichte 20, 163-219. Mainz: Verlag Philipp von Zabern.

Van Dinter, M. 2017. *Living along the limes. Landscape and settlement in the lower Rhine delta during Roman and early medieval times.* Utrecht Studies in Earth Sciences 135. Utrecht: Universiteit Utrecht.

Van Dongen, A.G.A. 1995. *One man's trash is another man's treasure. The metamorphosis of the European utensil in the New World.* Rotterdam: Museum Boymans-van Beuningen.

Van Enckevort, H. 2000. Catalogus van de vondsten uit de Romeinse tijd van Venray-Hoogriebroek, in: H. Stoepker (ed.), *Venray-Hoogriebroek en Venray-Loobeek. Nederzettingen uit de prehistorie, Romeinse tijd en late middeleeuwen.* Archeologisch Onderzoek in het tracé van de Rijksweg 73. Rapportage Archeologische Monumentenzorg 46, 89-166. Amersfoort: Rijksdienst voor het Oudheidkundig Bodemonderzoek.

Van Enckevort, H. (ed.) 2009. *Roman material culture. Studies in honour of Jan Thijssen.* Zwolle: SPA Uitgevers.

Van Enckevort, H. 2011. *Romeinse graven en verbrand geld op de Nijmeegse Hunerberg. Archeologisch onderzoek aan de Hugo de Grootstraat.* Archeologische Berichten Nijmegen – Rapport 27. Nijmegen: gemeente Nijmegen, Bureau Archeologie en Monumenten.

Van Enckevort, H. 2012. *Gebundelde sporen: enkele kanttekeningen bij aardewerk en nederzettingen uit Romeins Nederland.* PhD thesis, Universiteit Leiden. Archeologische Berichten Nijmegen – Rapport 7. Nijmegen: gemeente Nijmegen, Bureau Archeologie en Monumenten.

Van Enckevort, H. 2021. The Roman military complex at Nijmegen (19 BC-475 AD), in: W.A.M. Hessing, W.K. Vos and E.J. van Ginkel (eds), *Romans on the waterfront. Evaluation of archaeological interventions (1997-2020) along the Dutch part of the lower Rhine and coastal limes.* Nederlandse Archeologische Rapporten 71, 185-202. Amersfoort: Rijksdienst voor het Cultureel Erfgoed.

Van Enckevort, H. and K. Zee 1996. *Het Kops Plateau. Prehistorische grafheuvels en een Romeinse legerplaats in Nijmegen.* Abcoude: Uitgeverij Uniepers.

Van Enckevort, H., J. Hendriks and M. Nicasie 2017. *Nieuw licht op donkere eeuwen. De overgang van de laat-Romeinse tijd naar de vroege middeleeuwen in zuid-Nederland.* Nederlandse Archeologische Rapporten 58. Amersfoort: Rijksdienst voor het Cultureel Erfgoed.

Van Es, W.A. 1967. Wijster, a native village beyond the imperial frontier, 150-425 AD. *Palaeohistoria* 11. Groningen: Wolters

Van Es, W.A. 1968 [1970]. Paddepoel, excavations of frustrated terps, 200 BC-250 AD. *Palaeohistoria* 14, 187-352.

Van Es, W.A. 1981[3]. *De Romeinen in Nederland.* Haarlem: Fibula-Van Dishoeck.

Van Es, W.A. in prep. *Wijster opnieuw bekeken.*

Van Es, W.A., M. Miedema and S.L. Wynia 1985. Eine Siedlung der römischen Kaiserzeit in Bennekom, Provinz Gelderland. *BerOudhBod* 35, 533-652.

Van Giffen, A.E. 1913. *Die Fauna der Wurten. Erster Teil.* Onderzoekingen verricht in het Zoölogisch Laboratorium der Rijksuniversiteit Groningen III. Groningen: Rijksuniversiteit te Groningen.

Van Heeringen, R.M. 1988. De bewoning van Zeeland in de IJzertijd. *Archief, Mededelingen van het Koninklijk Zeeuwsch Genootschap der Wetenschappen* 1988, 1-43.

Van Heeringen, R.M. 1992. *The Iron Age in the western Netherlands.* PhD thesis, Vrije Universiteit Amsterdam. Amersfoort: Rijksdienst voor het Oudheidkundig Bodemonderzoek.

Van Kerckhove, J. 2009. Aardewerk, in: Van Renswoude and Van Kerckhove (eds), 115-192.

Van Kerckhove, J. 2013. Les faciès céramiques de la fin de l'âge du Fer au Ier s. de n.è. Comparaison entre Betuwe (province de la Gueldre) et région sud des Pays-Bas (provinces du Brabant et du Limbourg), in: *SFECAG. Actes du congrès d'Amiens 9-12 mai 2013: dynamique d'évolution de la vaisselle de la conquète de la Gaule Belgique à celle de la Bretagne. Actualité des recherches céramiques,* 179-196. Marseille: SFECAG.

Van Kerckhove, J. 2014. Het Romeinse aardewerk, in: M. Driessen and E. Besselsen (eds), *Voorburg-Arentsburg. Een Romeinse havenstad tussen Rijn en Maas.* Themata 7, 321-472. Amsterdam: Universiteit van Amsterdam.

Van Kerckhove, J. 2017. Conclusies, in: J. van Renswoude and D.S. Habermehl (eds), *Opgravingen te Houten-Castellum. Bewoning langs een restgeul in de IJzertijd, Romeinse tijd en vroege middeleeuwen.* Zuidnederlandse Archeologische Rapporten 65, 409-414. Amsterdam: VUhbs archeologie.

Van Kerckhove, J. 2018. *Standaardwerkwijze voor het uitwerken van aardewerk uit de late IJzertijd en de Romeinse tijd*. Zuidnederlandse Archeologische Notities 527. Amsterdam: VUhbs archeologie.

Van Kerckhove, J. 2019. Het aardewerk uit de Romeinse tijd, in: Habermehl *et al.* 2019, 245-344.

Van Kerckhove, J. and G.L. Boreel 2014. A characterization of the pottery production in Heerlen (Limburg, the Netherlands): fabric analysis and typo-chronology, in: Liesen (ed.) 2014, 241-285.

Van Kerckhove, J. and G.L. Boreel in press. Evidence for immigration in the Batavian region in the pre-Claudian era. The study of large handmade pottery assemblages using a combination of traditional and science-based techniques, in: H. van Enckevort, M. Driessen, E. Graafstal, T. Hazenberg, T. Ivleva and C. van Driel-Murray (eds), *Strategy and structures along the Roman frontier. Proceedings of the 25th Limescongress in Nijmegen 2*. Archeologische Berichten Nijmegen 10. Leiden: Sidestone Press.

Van Kerckhove, J., A. Lepot, B. Borgers and S. Willems 2014. Understanding consumption patterns in the civitas Tungrorum through the identification of the 'NOOR1' ware, in: S. Biegert (ed.), *RelCretActa* 43, 783-792. Bonn: Dr. Rudolf Habelt GmbH.

Van Londen, H. 2006. *Midden-Delfland. The Roman native landscape past and present*. Unpublished PhD thesis. Amsterdam: Universiteit van Amsterdam.

Van Neer, W., A. Ervynck and P. Monsieur 2010. Fish bones and amphorae. Evidence for the production and consumption of salted fish products outside the Mediterranean. *JRA* 23, 161-195.

Van Renswoude, J. and J. Van Kerckhove (eds) 2009. *Opgravingen in Geldermalsen-Hondsgemet. Een inheemse nederzetting uit de late IJzertijd en Romeinse tijd*. Zuidnederlandse Archeologische Rapporten 35. Amsterdam: Archeologisch Centrum Vrije Universiteit, Hendrik Brunsting Stichting.

Van Trierum, M.C., A.B. Döbken and A.J. Guiran 1988. Archeologisch onderzoek in het Maasmondgebied 1976-1986, in: *Bijdragen aan de bewoningsgeschiedenis van de Maasmond*, 11-105. BOORbalans 1. Rotterdam: Bureau Oudheidkundig Onderzoek van Gemeentewerken.

Vanvinckenroye, W. 1991. *Gallo-Romeins aardewerk van Tongeren*. Publikaties van het Provinciaal Gallo-Romeins Museum 44. Tongeren: Provinciaal Gallo-Romeins Museum.

Veen, C.W.A. 2018. *New artefacts, old traditions. Roman period statuettes in the Netherlands: representation and ritual use in context*. Unpublished PhD thesis, Radboud Universiteit Nijmegen.

Veenstra, J.B. and T.B. Volkers 2020. Gedraaid Romeins aardewerk, in: R. Rap and J.B. Veenstra (eds), *Bemmel, Plakse Wei, gemeente Lingewaard (Gld.). Definitief archeologisch onderzoek. Steekproefproject 2018-04/11*, 70-81. Zuidhorn: De Steekproef.

Veldman, H.A.P. (ed.) 2011. *Graven in Zoelen. De opgraving van een Romeinse nederzetting en grafveld*. ADC Rapport 2391. Amersfoort: ADC ArcheoProjecten.

Veldman, H.A.P. (ed.) 2012. *Graven te Maurik Buitenweg (gemeente Buren)*. ADC Rapport 3148. Amersfoort: ADC ArcheoProjecten.

Veldman, H.A.P. and E. Blom (eds) 2010. *Onder de zoden van Zaltbommel, een rurale nederzetting en een grafveld uit de Romeinse tijd in het plangebied De Wildeman*. ADC Monografie 8. Amersfoort: ADC ArcheoProjecten.

Veldman, H.A.P. and R.C.A. Geerts 2014. Een Flavisch pottenbakkersatelier, in: H.A.P. Veldman, R.C.A. Geerts, P.L.M. Hazen and H.M. van der Velde (eds), *Aan de rand van de Romeinse stad Atuatuca Tungrorum. Een archeologische opgraving aan de Beukenbergweg in Tongeren*. ADC Monografie 16, 78-146. Amersfoort: ADC ArcheoProjecten.

Venant, N. 2016. Apports de l'étude des chaînes opératoires de la céramique non tournée galloromaine. Le cas de la céramique à dégraissant carbonaté (sud de la civitas Tungrorum), in: L. Rivet (ed.), *SFECAG. Actes du Congrès d'Autun, 5-8 mai 2016*, 431-442. Marseille: SFECAG.

Verhart, L. 2020. Bijvangst: nogmaals Hans Dragendorff. *RMO Magazine* 49, 33-35.

Verhoeven, A. 2003. Bemerkungen zur völkerwanderungszeitlichen Keramik aus Gennep (Niederlande), in: Taayke *et al.* (eds) 2003, 115-127.

Vermeulen, W.G.J.R. 1932. *Een Romeinsch grafveld op den Hunnerberg te Nijmegen (uit den tijd van Tiberius-Nero)*. Bouwsteenen voor een geschiedenis van Nijmegen 2. Amsterdam: H.J. Paris.

Verniers, L.P. 2011. De materiële cultuur van de Germaanse nederzetting, in: H.M. van der Velde (ed.), *Germanen op De Borchert. Een oude opgraving in Denekamp opnieuw belicht*, 87-128. Amersfoort: ADC RoelBrandt Stichting.

Verniers, L.P. (ed.) 2012. *Grafheuvels in IJsselstein. Een archeologische opgraving van een Romeins grafveld uit de 2e eeuw*. ADC Rapport 3012. Amersfoort: ADC ArcheoProjecten.

Verniers, L.P., E. Blom and L.M.B van der Feijst (eds) 2018. *Park Lingezegen-De Linten, Archeologisch onderzoek tijdens de inrichting van Park Lingezegen*. ADC Rapport 4683. Amersfoort: ADC ArcheoProjecten.

Volkers, T.B. 1991a. Terra sigillata aus den friesischen Wurten in den Niederlanden. *Germania* 69, 176-186.

Volkers, T.B. 1991b. Romeinse import van 12 v. Chr. tot 70 n. Chr. in het Friese terpengebied. *Jaarverslagen van de Vereniging voor Terpenonderzoek* 75, 94-103.

Volkers, T.B. 1999. The terra sigillata from Wijnaldum-Tjitsma in regional perspective, in: J.C. Besteman, J.M. Bos, D.A. Gerrets, H.A. Heidinga and J. de Koning (eds), *The excavations at Wijnaldum. Reports on Frisia in Roman and medieval times. Volume 1*, 151-156. Rotterdam: Balkema.

Volkers, T.B. 2002. De terra sigillata uit de terp Bruggeburen bij Winsum (Fr.). *Paleo-aktueel* 13, 78-83.

Volkers, T.B. 2014. Ezinge – het Romeins aardewerk, in: Nieuwhof (ed.) 2014, 147-162.

Volkers, T.B. 2015. Buitenbeentjes, bloempotten en verloren schapen. North African Red Slip Ware (ARS) ten noorden van de limes. *Paleo-aktueel* 26, 47-54.

Volkers, T.B. 2015/2016. Die Terra Sigillata aus friesischen Terpen. *Palaeohistoria* 57/58, 235-312.

Volkers, T.B. 2017. *Die glatte Terra Sigillata aus Friesischen Terpen.* Grondsporen 25. Groningen: Rijksuniversiteit Groningen.

Von Uslar, R. 1938. *Westgermanische Bodenfunde des ersten bis dritten Jahrhunderts nach Christus aus Mittel- und Westdeutschland.* Germanische Denkmäler der Frühzeit 3. Berlin: W. de Gruyter.

Von Uslar, R. 1977. Zu einer Fundkarte der jüngsten Kaiserzeit in der westlichen Germania libera. *PZ* 52, 121-147.

Vos, P., M. van der Meulen, H. Weerts and J. Bazelmans 2011. *Atlas van Nederland in het Holoceen. Landschap en bewoning vanaf de laatste ijstijd tot nu.* Amsterdam: Bert Bakker.

Vos, W.K. 2009. *Bataafs platteland. Het Romeinse nederzettingslandschap in het Nederlandse Kromme-Rijngebied.* Nederlandse Archeologische Rapporten 35. PhD thesis, Vrije Universiteit Amsterdam. Amersfoort: Rijksdienst voor het Cultureel Erfgoed.

Vossen, I. and R.C.A. Geerts (eds) 2022. *Klei, zand en veen door de eeuwen heen. Archeologische opgravingen aan de Madepolderweg in Den Haag.* ADC Rapport 5800. Amersfoort: ADC ArcheoProjecten.

Wagner, A. and J. Ypey 2011 (A. Willemsen ed.). *Das Gräberfeld auf dem Donderberg bei Rhenen. Katalog.* Leiden: Sidestone Press.

Walters, H.B. 1908. *Catalogue of the Roman pottery in the Departments of Antiquities, British Museum.* London: Longman and Co.

Waterbolk, H.T. 1977. Walled enclosures of the Iron Age in the north of the Netherlands. *Palaeohistoria* 19, 97-172.

Waterbolk, H.T. 2009. *Getimmerd verleden: sporen van voor- en vroeghistorische houtbouw op de zand- en kleigronden tussen Eems en IJssel.* Groningen Archaeological Studies 10. Eelde: Barkhuis.

Weekers-Hendrikx, B.A.T.M. (ed.) 2018. *Heerlen Trilandis. Voormalig Domeinen Terrein.* ADC Rapport 4693. Amersfoort: ADC ArcheoProjecten.

Weiß, S. 2003. Das Fundmaterial aus einem dendrodatierten Brunnen der Colonia Ulpia Traiana, in: B. Liesen and U. Brandl (eds), *Römische Keramik. Herstellung und Handel. Kolloquium Xanten, 15.-17.6.2000.* Xantener Berichte 13. Mainz: Verlag Philipp von Zabern.

Weiß-König, S. 2008. Bevölkerungsstruktur von Xanten, in: M. Müller, H.-J. Schalles and N. Zieling (eds), *Colonia Ulpia Traiana. Xanten und sein Umland in römischer Zeit,* 525-535. Mainz: Verlag Philipp von Zabern.

Weiß-König, S. 2023. Töpfereiabfall von der Waalkade in Nijmegen, in: B. Liesen (ed.), *Zwischen Töpfer und Verbraucher/Between potter and consumer. Internationales Kolloquium im LVR-RömerMuseum 27.-29. März 2019.* Xantener Berichte 41, 483-497. Oppenheim am Rhein: Nünnerich-Asmus Verlag.

Weisshaar, H.-J. 1984. Ausgrabungen auf der Amöneburg, in: O.-H. Frey and H. Roth (eds), *Studien zu Siedlungsfragen der Latènezeit: Wolfgang Dehn zum 75. Geburtstag.* Veröffentlichung des vorgeschichtlichen Seminars Marburg, Sonderband 3, 65-88. Marburg: Marie Leidorf.

Wesselingh, D.A. 2000. *Native neighbours. Local settlement system and social structure in the Roman period at Oss (the Netherlands).* Analecta Praehistorica Leidensia 32. Leiden: Faculteit der Archeologie.

Willems, S. 2005. *Roman pottery in the Tongeren reference collection: mortaria and coarse ware/Romeins aardewerk in de Tongerse referentiecollectie: wrijfschalen en gewoon aardewerk.* VIOE-Rapporten 1. Brussels: Vlaams Instituut voor het Ontroerend Erfgoed.

Willems, S. 2014. Étude céramique, in: G. Teysseire, *Nord – Pas-de-Calais, Looberghe, Rue de Cassel. Élements d'un atelier de saunier,* 184-204. Amiens: INRAP.

Willems, S., B. Borgers, F. Thuillier and A. Ledauphin (eds) 2023. *Atlas des productions céramiques en territoire des Ménapiens, Atrébates et Nerviens.* Archéologie et Histoire Romaine 49. Drémil-Lafage: Éditions Mergoil.

Willems, W.J.H. 1977. A Roman kiln at Halder, gemeente St. Michielsgestel N.B., in: B.L. van Beek, R.W. Brandt and W. Groenman van Wateringe (eds), *Ex Horreo.* Cingula 4, 114-129. Amsterdam: Universiteit van Amsterdam.

Willems, W.J.H. 1986. *Romans and Batavians. A regional study in the Dutch eastern river area.* PhD thesis, Universiteit van Amsterdam.

Willems, W.J.H. 1990. *Romeins Nijmegen. Vier eeuwen stad en centrum aan de Waal.* Historische Reeks Nijmegen 2. Utrecht: Matrijs.

Willems, W.J.H. and H. van Enckevort (eds) 2009. *Vlpia Noviomagvs. Roman Nijmegen. The Batavian capital at the imperial frontier.* JRA Supplementary Series 73. Portsmouth (RI): Journal of Roman Archaeology.

Willmitzer, A. 2023. *Die Insula 6 der Colonia Ulpia Traiana, Xanten. Der nordwestliche Bereich der Grabungen der Jahre 2009-2014 und die Grabungen von 1982. Die Funde.* Xantener Berichte 44. Oppenheim am Rhein: Nünnerich-Asmus Verlag.

Young, C.J. 1977. *The Roman pottery industry of the Oxford region.* BAR 43. Oxford: BAR.

Zabehlicky-Scheffenegger, S. 2013. RCRF – Fifty-five years of Roman pottery studies, in: D. Bernal Casasola, L.C. Juan Tovar, M. Bustamante Álvarez, J.J. Díaz Rodríguez and A.M. Sáez Romero (eds), *Hornos, talleres y focos de producción alfarera en Hispania. 1 Congreso Internacional de la SECAH. Ex officina hispana (Cádiz) 3-4 de marzo de 2011*. Monografías ex Officina Hispana 1, 115-137. Cádiz: Universidad de Cádiz.

Zandstra, M.J.M. and M. Moust 2014. Lampen van aardewerk, in: R.P.J. Kloosterman, M. Polak and M.J.M. Zandstra, *Opgravingen op het terrein van het voormalige Canisiuscollege in Nijmegen, 1987-1997. Vondsten uit castra en canabae* 1, 137-195. Auxiliaria 14. Nijmegen: Auxilia.

Zandstra, M.J.M. and M. Polak 2012. *De Romeinse versterkingen in Vechten-Fectio. Het archeologisch onderzoek in 1946-47*. Auxiliaria 11. Nijmegen: Auxilia.